M000081344

Barley, Gold, or Fiat

Barley, Gold, or Fiat

Toward a Pure Theory of Money

Thomas Quint and Martin Shubik

Yale UNIVERSITY PRESS

NEW HAVEN AND LONDON

Published with assistance from the foundation established in memory of Calvin
Chapin of the Class of 1788, Yale College.

Yale University Press books may be purchased in quantity for
educational, business, or promotional use. For information, please e-mail
sales.press@yale.edu (U.S. office) or sales@yaleup.co.uk (U.K. office).

Set in Adobe Garamond and Stone Sans types by Newgen North America.
Printed in the United States of America.

ISBN: 978-0-300-18815-8

Library of Congress Control Number: 2013936411

A catalogue record for this book is available from the British Library.

This paper meets the requirements of ANSI/NISO Z39.48-1992
(Permanence of Paper).

10 9 8 7 6 5 4 3 2 1

To my brothers Andrew and Douglas, my kids Ted and Daphne, and in remembrance of my parents, George Quint (1919–2009) and Barbara Quint (1928–2013)

T.Q.

To my wife, Julie, and daughter Claire and her family, Seth and Elliott.

M.S.

Contents

Preface

This book is about a game-theoretic approach to the theory of money and financial institutions. In this preface, we give the reader a quick idea of what our method is, and how we use it to model many aspects of finance. But we also note what is not covered, and why.

A LITTLE BACKGROUND

History and anthropology teach us that there have been thousands of variations in money and financial institutions over the past 4,000 years. Coinage has existed for only about 2,500 years, central banks for 300 years. Thus any theory is built on fast-shifting institutional sands.

The concept of "what is money?" turns out to involve many dimensions as well as qualitative factors; hence taxonomies of "near-monies" appear. Underlying the instruments and the institutions is a mechanism of judgment, evaluation, and control. Under the welter of institutional artifacts lie control mechanisms of varying strength.

There was a golden historical age from about 1945 to 1965, when the powers of the central bank and government economic laws reached their zenith. Since then, the growth of computation and communication has changed the world of finance. Currently, in a world with roughly 200 currencies and global communication nets, an intermix of corporate and public credit systems dominates the world economies.

OUR APPROACH

Our approach is to use game-theoretic modeling to add minimal financial institutions to a simple closed economy. The resulting models differ, depending upon whether barley, gold, or fiat is the money, and upon what sort of credit system is in place. They include different sorts of agents, such as consumers, traders, moneylenders, corporate banks, and/or a central bank. But all the models are defined for all positions, in and out of equilibrium.

To erect a sound basis for a theory of money and financial institutions, we believe, it is worth starting simply, with primitive concepts aimed at understanding an already monetized economy with markets. This approach omits the fascinating works in search and binary encounter in the mathematics and anthropology of the development of markets. We take broad anonymous markets for real goods as a given, and are solely concerned with function and form. We model our agents and institutions as simply as possible, to the extent that any attempt to further simplify the model would destroy the ability of the institution to perform the function specified. Even at this level of simplicity, the mathematical description and analysis of economic processes is highly complex—especially if the reality is that the dynamics of an economy with a financial control system involves a loosely coupled system where boundary conditions play a significant role.

By ruthlessly limiting the creation, dispensing, and destruction of money and credit, we produce models simple enough that cash flow, asset levels, and the creation and destruction of all instruments are completely defined. The rules concerning conservation or its violation are made explicit, and the potential mysteries of finance are reduced to boundary conditions. The cost paid is the highly simplistic character of the models, but they will serve as the basic building blocks in any broader and more complex portrayal.

NONCOOPERATIVE EQUILIBRIUM

Our models are solved using the solution concept of noncooperative equilibrium (aka Nash or Cournot-Nash equilibrium), or, more precisely, perfect noncooperative equilibrium. Although we have equations of motion, and have a complete theory of static noncooperative equilibrium, we think the static one-period use of Nash equilibrium offers no more than the ability to provide some interesting benchmarks.

We use the (perfect) noncooperative equilibrium solution not because it provides a satisfactory behavioral solution, but because it offers a consistent connection between macroeconomics and general equilibrium theory that enables us to describe precisely the money and credit flows through minimal institutions. It offers precision at the cost of reality. This is consistent with our belief in Mathematical Institutional Economics as an approach to dynamics. We can fully specify the formal institutions that serve as the carriers of process. These provide minimal mechanisms to perform such financial and economic functions as price formation, borrowing, or bankruptcy.

We freely admit that it is inordinately difficult to verify that this approach provides a good model of economic behavior and motivation. Implicit are assumptions of common knowledge of both the physical structure of the economy and of the knowledge and motivation of the agents. Also, while one can see and gather information on economic institutions with reasonable ease, it is difficult to observe preferences and deduce intent, and it is clear that common knowledge about the rules of the game in a complex economy is counterfactual. Untrained individuals appear to behave with, at best, local knowledge.

In summary, utilizing a noncooperative equilibrium solution is an act of faith combined with an implicit acceptance by the economics fraternity that it is the best we can do now. This is being challenged by the behavioral economics and finance practitioners, but the jury is still out on whether any general behavioral models offer a better viable alternative.

Because of these concerns, we were tempted to substitute the phrase "Pre-Theory" for "Pure Theory" in the subtitle of the book—to remind all that there are deep difficulties with the application of sub-game perfect non-cooperative equilibrium players, or their cousins the rational expectations representative agents.

A SEQUENCE OF MODELS

The underlying strategy for our development of a theory of money and financial institutions is to construct a progressively more complex sequence of closed, complete exchange, production, and control models of the economy. We start as simply as possible, providing a reasonably full analysis and sensitivity analysis for a base model. Then we increase the complexity of the model to capture relevant phenomena that fall beyond the domain of the prior models.

Thus throughout this book we solve a set of simple models, each one completely, utilizing what we have called half seriously, half ironically, "death by the cuts of 10,000 Lagrangian multipliers." Unfortunately, they show that money or credit shortages at different levels can cause considerable complexity in the performance of even simple financially involved economic models. For many of our models, we provide a sensitivity analysis as we change the money supply.

DEFINING ECONOMIC IDEAS

In many problems, the meaning (for example) of a term such as "liquidity" is loosely portrayed as "an asset is liquid if it can be sold with little expense within a short time near its market price." When one attempts to deconstruct this definition, many difficulties appear. Is a more precise definition feasible, can we find it, and is it worth finding? We believe that the answer to all three of these questions is yes.

Some of the usual less-than-adequate, often-used definitions in economics include: the goals of the central bank; the goals of the firm; the nature of economic fiduciary behavior; the concept of efficiency in a world with incomplete markets; liquidity; efficiency and the concept of second best in a world without complete markets; the dividend payment policy of firms; the role of bankruptcy and default in a monetary economy; the appropriate discount rate for the investments of the firm; the appropriate discount rate for public good construction by a government; the various definitions of money and credit; the meaning of "enough money" and credit in an economy; the definition of reserves and optimal reserves for all financial institutions; and the full understanding of the breaking of the circular flow of capital required for innovation.

The various terms used by macroeconomists, such as the growth rate of the economy and the cost of living index, are obviously aggregates and approximations and belong to the domain of economic engineering. But new sets of problems appear whenever one attempts to reconcile macroeconomic practice and microeconomic theory.

The study of each of the items noted above calls for many special cases. If an economic science is to emerge (not unlike in zoology and biology), there will be vast catalogues of special cases together with taxonomic developments that have not yet taken place in economics.

Above, we gave a list of terms such as "enough money" that are in general hard to define. But we can define them more easily in the context of the simple economies presented. This enables us not only to obtain a precise definition, but to ask what is left out when we go to a more complex model. Thus the simplicity of the models serves as a preliminary exploration device for greater complexity.

WHAT HAS BEEN LEFT OUT, AND WHY

In our search for minimal models, we omit modeling various aspects of the economy that are obviously important to the understanding of the financial system. In fact, we do not model exogenous uncertainty, production, asymmetric information, conventional transactions costs, international trade, the role of expertise, or the division of labor in finance. This is because there is plenty to be done with the "basics" before one adds these features.

Almost all of the writings in finance involve uncertainty, as do many of the complexities. Furthermore, relative uncertainties reflect the critical role of expertise in the financial structure; a topic that has hardly been touched by economic theory. We do not consider it here because there is still much to be said before we reach this complication.

The addition of production immediately opens up the analysis to the critical role of long-term assets. Combining production with uncertainty calls for analyzing the role of the term rate of interest.

The role of asymmetric information gives rise to agency and contract problems. It enables one to study the important aspects of moral hazard and adverse selection. Furthermore, it makes it easy to produce plausible models where strategic bankruptcy may be an attractive act.

Conventional transactions costs are omitted because they are implicitly preset in the extreme assumption that all transactions require money or credit. In particular, setup costs are of considerable practical importance and have been addressed in operations research literature.

International trade introduces few new conceptual problems to basic financial theory. However, the subject offers a finesse to the theorist who is uncomfortable with completely closed systems that have to obey conservation laws or at least explain how they are violated. When there is a large international sector, conservation and full feedback problems can be avoided.

The full feedbacks need to be accounted for only in a closed-world model. In application, there is little question that in this world with increasingly linked international markets the political economy of international trade and finance is increasingly important—however, it is not a basis for a fundamental theory of finance.

The last and possibly most important topics missed are the roles of expertise and control over the economy. Are there individual financiers, entrepreneurs, and politicians who know considerably more than others, who are able to understand and bring about "doable deals" and workable innovations in a society? This question takes us beyond mere economics. But the financial system is the interfacing device between the economy, the polity, and society. The growth of expertise in finance is part of the increasing division of labor in a progressively complex evolving economy and will undoubtedly become more important as the role of the financial system as a perception, evaluation, and control device is recognized.

A theory of money and financial institutions calls for a rich mix of understanding abstract economic theory and institutions. The interface of the economy with the polity, the law, and the society indicates that a mathematical institutional economics must be considered. Unlike the timeless, moneyless, elegant abstraction of a static general equilibrium theory, the dynamics cannot avoid the need to clothe the carriers of process. Furthermore, when application is a goal, the identification and estimation of many parameters and functional forms are needed to further clothe the underlying model.

A Russian doll analogy is apt. In this book we offer a sequence of basic models which are consistent and complete. We can use them as experimental games to see if the predictions of noncooperative equilibrium behavior are borne out. They are testable. But they are far from institutional reality. We offer a theoretical structure based on strategic market games that plays the role of the small central Russian doll. All of the omissions noted above call for successive sequences of more complex models to be added. Function can be studied abstractly, but its manifestation in institutional form opens up a multitude of alternatives and new functions that appear with more complex forms.

Acknowledgments

The authors wish to acknowledge the many colleagues with whom we have discussed this topic, who have provided insight, and who have helped us over the years. In particular, we wish to thank Rabah Amir, Brian Arthur, Leilani Bailey, Michel Balinski, Pradeep Dubey, Charles Goodhart, Juergen Huber, Ioannis Karatzas, Jeff Mortensen, Richard Nelson, Mark Pingle, Michael Powers, Siddharta Sahi, Lloyd Shapley, Eric Smith, Matt Sobel, William Sudderth, Dimitri Tsomocas, and Jingan Zhao. We also wish to acknowledge the *ICFAI Journal of Monetary Economics*, in which earlier versions of several models here appeared (Quint and Shubik, 2005a, 2005b, 2007, 2009).

Finally, we are deeply indebted to Glena Ames, whose skills as a mathematical typist, book organizer, style editor, and all around fix-it person are second to none.

Chapter 1 Money and Context

1.1 FORMAL AND INFORMAL GAMES

This book is about a fundamental phenomenon in economic life. This is the use of money and credit in transactions, and their roles as substitutes for trust.

Money is the catalyst that enables the flow of goods and services to the body economic. The financial system is the neural network and control system, directing the money and credit flows of the economy.

A good model of the financial system should take into account the physical aspects of money, the role of government within a society, and dynamics. The general equilibrium paradigm, devoted to the study of statics, ignores these three elements. Instead, we suggest here that much of the financial system can be viewed as a formal dynamic game, where government supplies the rules and the pressures of politics and society help modify many of these rules in the fullness of time. Money flows must be tracked throughout the system. Formally, the simplest game to do so has a continuum of agents together with one atomic player, the government. The latter accounts for the control of anywhere between 15 and 50 percent of the resources and income of the society.

The conventional textbook definitions give three roles for money. They are: (1) as a means of payment; (2) as a numeraire; and (3) as a store of value. Our approach has implications regarding money's function as numeraire, the processes supporting it as a store of value, and for the trading technology aspects of the means of payment. We note a fourth feature: (4) the strategic financial actions that differentiate among individual natural persons, banks, central banks, and other financial institutions—thereby reflecting money's role in the financial control of the economy.

We believe that there is no general financial dynamics. It may be possible to make some short-term predictions of motion by utilizing detailed ad hoc models of specific institutions. Equilibrium analysis, however, can be utilized to cast light on the role of money, credit, and collateral in economizing on the needs for trust and information in an economy.

In this book, we present a series of elementary strategic market game models, all within the context of a simple two-good economy, which bring out the distinction between different types of money and financial institutions. The models emphasize the physical properties of the economic goods, trading systems, and government control. Even though we solve for equilibrium, they are *process models*; that is, they are explicit models of processes in which the moves can be laid out as an extensive form game. In fact, any model in this book could serve as the basis for an experimental game.[1]

1.2 MATHEMATICAL INSTITUTIONAL ECONOMICS

In separate publications (Shubik, 1959, 1999a) one of us argues that economic dynamics requires a deep appreciation of institutions and the context of the polity and society within which the economy is embedded. The appropriate term for an economic theory which deals explicitly with dynamics and control is "mathematical institutional economics." Here we minimize the discussion of specific institutions and concentrate on equilibrium conditions, arguing that many of the important aspects of a monetary economy are revealed in mathematical constraints imposed by cash-flow conditions.

---

1 The criterion of "playable game" insures that a fully defined process model has been specified.

The emphasis is on money—how it enters, exits, and is utilized in an economy—not on institutional form. In fact, this book is subtitled *Toward a Pure Theory of Money* to signal that, as much as possible, institutional detail (much of which is transient) has been stripped away.

Even if the emphasis is on equilibrium conditions, one cannot avoid modeling *minimal institutions*[2] in a process model. The rules of the game serve as the carriers of process and are, in essence, institutions. The board, pieces, and instructions provide the means to play chess. Similarly, the existence of markets, the rules and customs concerning the operation of those markets, the commercial code, the accounting conventions, plus contract, taxation, and bankruptcy laws, provide the means to carry out economic exchange.

In most of this work, by making use of several radical simplifications (such as assuming a finite number of types of financial agents but a continuum of "powerless" or price-taking agents of each nonfinancial type) and by considering equilibrium conditions, we minimize our concern for dynamics and the influence of institutions on both timing and the spread of information.

Any major economy is highly influenced by evolutionary forces. Products, processes, and organizations come and go. The socio-biological processes are of extreme complexity. Even the great leaps of progress in mathematical, statistical, and simulation methods hardly suffice to provide rich enough models to discover the existence of invariant properties of economics dynamics.

Such items as the Phillips Curve or the Taylor Rule become darlings of macroeconomic analysis at one point in time, but have a half life of at most five to ten years when the evolutionary circumstances of the political economy move on.

1.3 THEOREMS OR EXAMPLES?

Over the past five decades there has been a proliferation in theorem proving in mathematical economics. Possibly this was triggered by Samuelson's *Foundations* (1947) and Debreu's *Theory of Value* (1959), as well as the growth of the axiomatic method in economics aided by the deep and precise work of

---

2 A full discussion of minimal institutions is given elsewhere (Shubik 1999a) and considered in Chapters 2 and 3. In essence, "minimal institutions" refers to a mechanism where any simplification of its rules would destroy its ability to function for the purpose designed. An example in economics is the design of the simplest market mechanism capable of producing a price.

von Neumann and Morgenstern (1944) on game theory; Nash on bargaining (1950); Shapley on the value (1953); and others.

The growth of axiomatic methods in the development of economic theory is to be welcomed. Ricardo (1821) would have appreciated the clarity and ruthlessness in seeking appropriate abstractions and simplifying assumptions. But abstraction must stay in touch with purpose and insight.

The search for existence proofs avoids a fruitless search for the Philosophers' Stone. The work of Debreu, for example, was of great value in settling the validity of Walras's insight on the existence of an efficient price system. An existence proof bolsters but does not replace an insightful observation.

In keeping with the remarks above, no general existence theorems are provided in this work—we conjecture that constrained competitive prices exist for our systems with cash-flow constraints, at the level of generality for which general competitive equilibrium existence has been proved.[3] Rather, our concern is primarily with the nature, manifestation, and meaning of these constraints.

1.4 EXAMPLES AND INTUITION

In this work we consider a series of specific models, in order to investigate and compare the influence of cash-flow constraints and to be able to interpret these constraints in terms of the rules of the monetary system of a society. These models help to differentiate among commodity monies, fiat, credit, and trust.

Specific models have their virtues and dangers. In particular they are chosen to be relatively easy to calculate and explore, in comparison with the general case. However, it is important to keep in mind where the dangers lie in using them. Special forms may obliterate the phenomena being studied. For example, linear or logarithmic utility functions are often highly tractable, but have undesirable properties. Low-dimensional examples may throw the baby away with the bathwater. The selection of continuous time in contrast with a finite time grid depends upon the nature of the problem at hand (as well as ease

---

3 It is well known that features such as setup costs and indivisibilities can cause a loss of convexity in many economic models. And when one wants to carry out an investigation of a specific institution such as a money-changer, the assumption of the convexity of the outcome sets may not be reasonable. However, for many investigations the assumption that as a good first-order approximation one can convexify the payoff set is usually sound.

of mathematical analysis), as does the selection of a continuum or a finite number of individual agents.

Obviously, our models would be more realistic if we added the exogenous uncertainty that is omnipresent in the real world. For now we ignore this in our calculations, exposing the complexity that already exists in a monetary economy without exogenous uncertainty. And we do make some qualitative comments on uncertainty later.

1.5 ON THE VELOCITY OF MONEY AND BOUNDS ON TRADE

The examples presented here all have a velocity of money of one or less. In actuality the variation in velocity is an important feature of any economy. This is especially true when attributed to a monetary control variable such as a change in the bank rate. As we try to stay as noninstitutional as possible, we concentrate on simultaneous buy-sell or sell-all models of exchange.[4] The latter (where all goods are put up for sale) provides an extreme upper bound to trade and the need for money. Using the former, the lower bound on trade is clearly zero, which can happen either if: (a) initial conditions are already Pareto optimal (and hence there is no need for trade), or if (b) there is a Utopia where all completely trust each other, with memory and record keeping free.

In a world with imperfect memory, costly bookkeeping, and different laws and customs, as well as many market mechanisms tailored to the special properties of the goods for sale and the geography of the market areas, the monetary needs can vary anywhere from zero to the upper bound. Institutional detail is called for to provide estimates for individual countries. For at least three hundred years various estimates of the needs for money have been considered (see Shubik, 1999a, ch. 15).

1.6 A DISCLAIMER ON PRODUCTION

Among the radical simplifications made here, the omission of production stands high. The stress is on the transactions and control role of various forms of money and credit, so the addition of production is a needless complication for most of the questions at hand. The addition of production to a strategic market game requires a far higher level of complexity than is required to

---

4 These are defined in detail in subsequent chapters.

add production to a general equilibrium model of the economy. The former is required to deal explicitly with the underlying extensive form of the game in order to assure that a full-process model has been defined. The latter can sidestep these difficulties. A strategic market game approach to an economy with production and exchange has been dealt with elsewhere (Dubey and Shubik, 1977; Karatzas, Shubik, and Sudderth, 2006). In practice, production can hardly be considered without an operations research approach. Important time lags and indivisibilities abound, and technical and institutional detail determine the processes.

1.7 APPLICATIONS, THEORY, AND EXPERIMENTAL GAMING

The tradition in formal economic dynamics, from Domar through Solow and Lucas, has been to utilize extremely low-dimensional models to provide insight and analogy and to bolster policy suggestions. We believe that there are two other somewhat different purposes to these low-dimensional models. They can serve as a basis for experimental games, and they can suggest ways to influence (but not necessarily predict) the economy. We stress that there is a considerable difference between prediction and control. The emphasis on prediction calls for the ability to estimate trajectories; in contrast, adequate control may be achieved by changing the set of strategies available to independent agents without knowing their behavior in any detail.

1.8 A SURVEY OF CONTENTS

In Chapter 2 the properties of markets and the three simplest strategic market game structures (buy-sell, sell-all, and double-auction) are discussed.

In Chapter 3 we present our "basic model," a one-period, buy-sell exchange economy utilizing consumer perishable goods and a storable consumable money. This model is the one on which all of our others are based.

In Chapter 4 we enlarge the basic model to cover trade with a money market.

Chapter 5 is an investigation of monetary trade when there is a rich monied agent who wishes to live off his money. This agent is modeled as both a lender and a consumer. A connection is made between the role of monopolistic moneylender within the economy and a governmental central bank.

Chapter 6 is devoted to trade with a durable money such as gold. It develops the implications of the loss of consumption services of a durable utilized in transactions. The difference between a consumer storable and a durable as money is essentially the point consumption of a consumable in contrast with the interval consumption of the services of a durable.

Chapter 7 is on markets with fiat, where the money has no consumption value at all. We discuss the many ways to cope with the Hahn paradox, which arises when fiat is valueless at the end of economic activity. We also consider models with loan markets. In models with a private lender or an outside bank, the loan markets may be controlled either by an interest rate or by the quantity of loanable funds—each leads to somewhat different mathematical models.

In Chapter 8 we consider bankruptcy conditions, required as soon as borrowing is possible. In our simple model, we are able to precisely define mathematical conditions under which it will be optimal for traders to default on their loans. Incidentally, this in turn leads to a consideration of what is meant by a secured loan.

Chapter 9 introduces the sell-all model of exchange, which is the tax collector's delight, as all wealth is monetized. Thus, the relationship between assets and trade is transparent. Another reason for switching to the sell-all model (in contrast with buy-sell) is that it permits one to build the simplest multistage dynamic closed macroeconomic models. In our simple one-period game, the switch to sell-all leads to efficient consumption in all cases.

In Chapter 10 we comment first on trading structures, then on the classical equation of exchange, and then on the critical role of clearinghouses in exchange. In a simple variation on our loan-market model, we show that perfect clearing in a one-period economy is economically equivalent to complete trust.

A brief Chapter 11 offers a few statistics on the number of financial institutions and their size relationship to the individual in the United States. Its purpose is to suggest that the appropriate strategic model of a closed economy is as a game, with government as the large player, a finite number of financial and other institutional players, and only the traders treated as a continuum.

In Chapter 12 we consider oligopolistic competition with cash and a money market. A distinction dating back at least to Bagehot is between the capitalist/rich individual merely lending his own resources, and the banker/financier lending other peoples' money (possibly along with his own). This distinction lays operational stress on communication, information, expertise, and fiduciary responsibilities.

Chapter 13 is devoted to monopolistic lending, where the contrast between a monopolistic private lender and a central bank is considered. Each could have a monopoly position in the economy, but the motivation is different, as is the spending of resources to buy real goods. At the end of the chapter, we lay down a model with oligopolistic lending.

In Chapters 14 and 15 we continue our study of lending and banks, for the competitive case. In Chapter 14 we solve a model of competitive corporate bankers in an economy with a central bank, and then show how to extend this model to cover reserve banking. In Chapter 15 we tell the story of a demonetization, beginning with an economy having a gold money and private lenders. Then the demonetization occurs, resulting in a model with demonetized gold which backs trade in gold certificates. Another possibility is that a central bank is created that assumes control of the certificates.

In Chapter 16, we extend some of our previous models to multiperiod trade. Welfare considerations are discussed, and we make brief comments on overlapping generations, on varying the money supply, and on uncertainty.

Finally, Chapter 17 is a summary devoted to putting these mathematical models into a broader theoretical and institutional context. It raises considerations of experimental gaming and behavioral economics, argues why there is no general economic dynamics, and stresses the concept of "the game within the game" and the importance of recognizing the intertwining of politics, bureaucracy, finance, and economics in the functioning of a dynamic economy in its political and social environment.

In most chapters (actually, all except Chapters 2, 11, and 17), we present one or more new models in the text, in an attempt to model the various monies and financial institutions. The actual detailed mathematical analysis (some of which is quite tedious but unfortunately needed when boundary conditions must be examined) is presented in the appendixes at the end of each chapter.

Chapter 2 The Properties of Markets

Modern economies use organized markets. *Markets* are any structures that allow buyers and sellers to exchange goods, services, and/or information. Nowadays they are essentially aggregation, disaggregation devices which facilitate organized, fast, more or less anonymous efficient trade. Their emergence from barter, random encounters, or trade at festivals poses many interesting problems in economic anthropology, but those problems are not immediately relevant to the formal analysis here.

In this chapter, we discuss several aspects of markets which our process model approach allows us to study in detail. In particular, the inclusion of a market mechanism together with the specification of price formation lays stress on the importance of the trading technology. This enables us to consider the critical relationship between the real economy and the volume of trade.

2.1 TYPES OF MONEY AND CREDIT

In a modern economy there are four "physical" types of goods. They are:
(1) *perishables*, whose economic lives terminate within a single time period,
and are (to a reasonable approximation) consumed at a point in time;
(2) *storable consumables* (such as a can of beans), which are also consumed
at a point in time, but can, at the option of the individual, be carried over
and consumed several periods later; (3) *services,* which are consumed over an
interval or are otherwise lost; and (4) *durables,* which last for several periods
and give off a stream of services.[1] In addition, there is *fiat money,* which is
a fictitious durable with no consumption properties and an imputed value
derived from its acceptance and use in transactions (see Kiyotaki and Wright,
1989; Bak, Norrelykke, and Shubik, 1999).

Any of the above types of good may be used as money in an economy.
Storable consumables such as cigarettes functioned as a medium of exchange
in twentieth-century prison camps. The use of durable monies (such as gold)
and fiat monies (such as our current U.S. dollar) has been much more common. Fiat needs no more of a physical existence than a record of its existence.
It is essentially information concerning ownership rights in exchange.

A difference between a durable good money and a fiat money is that the
former may provide either transaction services or a stream of consumption
services, while the latter provides only transaction services. In either case, loan
markets provide a means for borrowers to obtain these services earlier in time
than exchange without credit would permit.

Loan markets can be set up through a variety of financial institutions. Both
private and public (central) banks play a large role here. Two other trade
arrangements are the bilateral exchange of IOU notes or a clearinghouse for
such notes, with credit or netting. These arrangements involve high levels of
communication and credit evaluation.

As mentioned in Chapter 1, we will be presenting a series of models,
all within the context of a simple two-good economy, which bring out the
distinctions among the different types of money and financial institutions
mentioned above. In Chapters 3, 4, and 5 we cover models in which the
money is a consumable storable; the economies in subsequent chapters use
durable money, fiat money, or credit. The models emphasize the physical

---

1 At this time, we abstract away from the important practical aspects of depreciation and
  decay which apply to both storable consumables and durables.

properties[2] of the economic goods, moneys, and trading systems. Their solutions provide insight into many of the financial systems that have been used throughout history.

2.2 THREE BASIC TRADING STRUCTURES

There are three basic trading structures of increasing complexity that form price in a single-period simultaneous move strategic market game. They are: (1) The sell-all model; (2) the buy-sell model; and (3) the double-auction model.

In a *sell-all model* (Shapley and Shubik, 1977), during each trading period players must sell *all* of their endowment in the marketplace, and then buy back anything they wish to consume; in a *buy-sell model* (Shubik, 1973), they may sell *any amount* before buying. Hence, in a strategic market game with m commodities, the players' strategies will be m-dimensional in a sell-all model (a strategy for player i will have the form $(b_1^i, \ldots, b_m^i)$, where b_j^i is the amount bid for commodity j by player i). In contrast, in a buy-sell model such strategies would be $2m$-dimensional, because the players also must now designate a vector $(q_1^i, \ldots, q_m^i)$ of commodities to sell.[3] Finally, in a *double-auction model*, player i must in addition specify personal selling prices p_j^i for commodity i, as well as buying prices $\tilde{p}_j^i$—hence the strategies are $4m$-dimensional.

The last two models are regarded as more general than the first; but when dealing with dynamics the sell-all model (with just a single consumer good and a money) is mathematically the easiest. The double-auction model is more complex than the buy-sell model, and a sequential version of the double-auction offers a good approximation of the functioning of a stock market, but it is not necessary for our purposes here. For many questions involving multistage models, the sell-all model is the easiest and is sufficient. However, for understanding the gains to trade financing aspects of transactions, a buy-sell model is required (see Dubey and Geanakoplos, 2003; Shubik, 1999b). All three models have been utilized for experimental games, to illustrate their

---

2 Jevons (1875) was possibly one of the earliest economists concerned with the physical properties of money.

3 However, in our upcoming models, with $m = 2$, this "$2m$" is reduced to "m," essentially because players of type i are endowed with zero of good type $3 - i$ $(i = 1, 2)$. This removes the decisions of how much of good type i to buy and also how much of good $3 - i$ to sell.

differences in price formation with ten to twenty traders (see Huber, Shubik, and Sunder, 2007).

In this book, most of our models are buy-sell; but we do consider some sell-all models in Chapters 9, 14, 15, and 16.

2.3 MICROMODELING AND GENERALIZATION

The approach adopted here is to be painstakingly explicit in the formulation of process details. After one specifies a fully defined playable game, one then attempts to establish generalizations over classes of mechanisms. Some time ago Hurwicz (1980) lamented that there is too much micromodeling in the specification of a detailed game form, but Dubey, Mas-Colell, and Shubik (1980) showed that the assumption of a continuum of agents removes much of the fine structure of many transactions mechanisms. For truly mass markets, many distinctions in structure and information do not matter. But when numbers are few they do matter. This is why the phrase "mathematical institutional economics" appears to be appropriate when examining markets with a finite number of agents.

THE TRADING DAY

Many economic models chop time into discrete intervals.[4] When a durable (such as gold) is traded or used as a money, we must specify when each of the parties obtains its consumption services. If transactions take less than a single time period, an approximation is to split the period into three ranges $(0, k_2)$, (k_2, k_3), and $(k_3, 1)$, where k_2 is the proportion of consumption use obtained by the original owner, $k_3 - k_2$ is the proportion of consumption lost in transactions use, and $1 - k_3$ is the proportion of consumption use received by the final owner of the asset. We use a variant of this structure in order to be explicit about market meetings. See Chapter 6 for details.

$MV = PQ$ AND TRANSACTIONS

In monetary models involving one or more discrete time periods, it is reasonable to ask about the exact sequence of moves. Small details, such as how many times a market meets in a single period, are critical to determining the velocity

---

4 There are three different ways to treat time, each methodologically reasonable in context. They are: (1) fixed interval discrete time; (2) continuous time; and (3) event time. For our purposes here, (1) and some considerations of (2) appear to be adequate.

of money. In most of our exchange models, we can lay out such a sequence. For example: (1) in the morning there is settlement and new financing, followed by (2) bidding and offering in the market at around noon; followed by (3) delivery and consumption of perishables and storables in the evening. In the one-period, one-market models the implicit or explicit construction of the single market meeting often imposes not only the Fisher equation $MV = PQ$ but also $PQ \leq M \cdot 1$, in the case where there is hoarding.[5] See Chapter 10 for details.

If we have the market meet many times a day, we may increase the turnover of money (see Dubey, Sahi, and Shubik, 1993). Although one can investigate the behavior of the system as the time Δt between market meetings approaches zero, in physical fact there is a finite lower bound for the time required to carry out an exchange.

The selection of trading technology makes a difference to the volume of trade. The sell-all model monetizes all assets and thus (although it is a tax collector's delight) it badly overestimates the volume of trade, setting it equal to National Wealth. This is probably not too bad when considering consumers who sell their services and buy almost everything else, but it is not a good model to capture the investment decisions of an economy with independent producers with nonliquid capital goods and time lags in production. When we separate production from consumption, we approach a formal understanding of the deep insights of Keynes on the importance of coordination. A decent formal macro-micro-modeling approach requires both a trading model such as the buy-sell model of Dubey and Shubik (1978) together with an explicit treatment of independent production. This more realistically illustrates the concerns of the macroeconomists for such items as the failure of efficient trade. Here only some of the central preliminaries are covered and the remarks are constrained to trade.

AN ASIDE ON ENOUGH MONEY

Given initial ownership claims and preferences, the upper bound on transactions requirements is given by a sell-all model where the market meets once. The lower bound is somewhat difficult to calculate as it depends on the physical properties of the maximal speed of the markets, the divisibility of the goods

---

5 The symbols stand for the following: $M =$ the amount of money in the system; $V =$ the number of transactions a unit of money performs in a period; $P =$ the average price level; and $Q =$ the quantity of goods for sale.

and monetary units, and the cost of delivery. It also depends on the thickness of the market. Thus, a game with 200 traders meeting once in a period might be deemed to have a thick enough market for competition, but if it met forty times during the period with an average of only 5 traders, it follows from small size sampling that the market would not necessarily be thick enough to avoid price fluctuations, especially if there were any transactions costs.

AN ASIDE ON TIME AND MONEY

A discussion of leisure is omitted from our models, but implicit in all of these market structures is that markets take time and an important property of any money is that it cuts down on the time involved in carrying out an exchange.

A CAVEAT ON MODELING

Over the years, there has been much insightful work on the theory of money. The volume of important contributions from Jevons onward has been considerable.[6] The approach offered here, using process models, is consistent with much of the other work and also complementary in several basic ways. In particular, we stress playable games utilizing the methods of game theory.

General equilibrium theorizing tends to abstract from any institutional structure. As Koopmans (1977) described it, it is preinstitutional. Our approach is to seek minimal institutional forms of market, banks, and other financial institutions which serve as the carriers of process, thereby producing fully defined process models which can be simulated for experimental gaming. In economic terms, the formulation of a strategic market game requires that some transactions technology be specified—thus, it is necessary to incorporate cash-flow or trading conditions. This was abstracted away in the general equilibrium analysis.

These models, with a certain amount of labor (if sufficiently symmetric and of low dimension)[7] can be solved for their noncooperative equilibria. If we assume a continuum of agents, we may prove that the noncooperative

---

6 We have made no attempt here to provide detailed coverage of the many authors whose work has influenced then our thoughts. However, we have been influenced in particular by Allais (1947), Bewley (1980), Friedman (1969), Grandmont and Younes (1972), Gurley and Shaw (1960), Hahn (1965), Lucas (1980), Magill and Quinzii (1992), Samuelson (1958), Tobin (1982b), many others, and Shubik's many collaborations with Shapley, Dubey, and Geanakoplos.

7 The advantage of closed-form solutions is that they make it easier to carry out an extensive sensitivity analysis. As the models discussed here are always fully defined, they are

equilibria of some strategic market games will coincide with the competitive equilibria of related general equilibrium models. Hence many of the mathematical techniques developed for general equilibrium can be utilized for the study of equilibria of strategic market games. Nevertheless, the methodology and the stress is different. This is shown when we contemplate a finite number of moneylenders and note the importance of the relative size of individuals and institutions.

Perhaps it is best to consider the test for our models to be whether they are plausible as playable experimental games. The test of trying to nail down all the rules, including the statement of initial and terminal conditions, provides a useful exercise in exploring the essential functions of institutions. As noted above, the sell-all, buy-sell, and double-auction setups have each been utilized in experimental games (Huber, Shubik, and Sunder, 2007).

In most actual economies, technology, custom, and law are constantly in flux, changing the nature of the transactions structure. Thus any formal game with dictated rules for transactions must be interpreted in the context that if the trading structure appears to be too costly, individuals will invent alternative payment systems.

The system appears to tend toward more and more efficient and faster trading technologies, with the ideal limit being a moneyless economy with perfect credit supplied with costless credit evaluation. But the ideal economy at the limit can obscure the structure of a system which never attains the limit. The timeless, process-free structure of general equilibrium is never attained, encouraging a schizophrenia in those who treat equilibrium as an ideal, lavish a formal mathematical structure on it, and then talk about an unverified dynamics.

---

amenable to simulation and gaming methods as well as to computational methods such as those suggested by the work of Scarf and Hansen (1973).

Chapter 3 The Basic Model

Our goal in this and subsequent chapters is to present several variations of one simple "basic model" and to perform a reasonably comprehensive analysis that shows the differences among various money and market arrangements. The mathematics is elementary (if one has the stomach for Lagrangian multipliers and boundary conditions). We consider only two types of traders with two commodities and different types of money and credit arrangements. We use a simple utility function and are explicit in our treatments of both initial and terminal conditions. Because we believe that monetary economics is intrinsically institutional, we present many different models. However, from a game-theoretic point of view it is reasonable to consider only a small set of models as providing minimal institutions, that is, mechanisms that cannot be further simplified if the ability to exhibit stated properties is to be retained.

3.1 MODELS OF MARKETS WITH A STORABLE CONSUMABLE MONEY

We commence with an examination of an economy that utilizes a storable consumable money. Tea, salt, and cocoa beans, among others, are examples of storable consumables that have been utilized as a money. Another classical example occurred in Babylon, where barley was used as one of two means of payment.[1] This type of money has the property that one can use it in transactions and consume it in the same period.

In one-period models (without a salvage value for money), the distinction between a perishable and a storable consumable is obliterated. Both would be consumed before the end of the period. Hence the analyses below, presented for the case of a storable consumable money, would also hold if the money were a perishable. However, the distinction between these and a consumer durable still remains for the one period. The durable always would be left over after the end of trade.

Those interested in macroeconomics and in applications of monetary theory may easily argue that considering commodity money is a waste of time. Those interested in search and pairwise matching of traders may argue that our models are not primitive enough. In reply to the first we argue that not only is the role of gold not fully dead, but that a careful examination of the store of value properties together with the distinction between stocks of assets and flows of services is still worthwhile. In reply to the second we suggest that the intersection between search theory and economic anthropology is fascinating and worth studying for its own merit, but for the study of a viable theory of money it may be desirable to accept as a primitive concept some form of market as an aggregating disaggregating device. Conceptually our models start hardly earlier than 1650 AD, although Rome and Babylon appear to have had some aspects of a market economy.

Finally, we remark that although storable consumables and fiat are very different monies with different physical properties, their mathematical models are close. Any time we solve a model using a consumable storable money, with little more work we can solve a corresponding model using fiat money. See Chapter 7 for details.

---

1 The other means of payment was silver, a durable with little depreciation; but unlike gold it tarnishes.

3.1.1 The Markets

Four types of agent are considered: (1) and (2) two types of traders, trading in two goods; (3) a class of monied individuals who may act as consumers, private bankers, and/or lenders; and (4) a government central bank. We consider various combinations of these agents with different types of money.

Table 3.1 shows five different treatments for trade with a storable consumable money. The columns represent the models we cover (over this and the next two chapters), while the rows represent types of agents. A cell with a "no" means that the corresponding type of agent is not present in the corresponding economy. The triples show the initial endowments of the two types of goods and the commodity money.

3.1.2 The Basic Model: Two Trader Types Using a Storable Consumable Money

THE MODEL

We consider a single-period model, with two types of symmetrically placed traders. The traders trade in two perishable goods, in a buy-sell market. They use a storable consumable commodity money which enters as a linear separable term in their utility functions. This is a special case with special properties. The more complex situation where the monetary commodity enters in a non-linear manner has been considered elsewhere (see Shapley and Shubik, 1977; Dubey and Shapley 1994) where the preference structure may influence the selection of an appropriate means of payment.[2] Here, however, the selection

Table 3.1. Models with a storable consumable money

	Cash only	Monied buyer	Money market	Monopoly banker	Altruist banker
Type 1 traders	$(a, 0, m)$	$(a, 0, m)$	$(a, 0, m_1)$	$(a, 0, m)$	$(a, 0, m)$
Type 2 traders	$(0, a, m)$	$(0, a, m)$	$(0, a, m_2)$	$(0, a, m)$	$(0, a, m)$
Monied buyer	No	$(0, 0, M - 2m)$	No	No	No
Moneylender	No	No	No	$(0, 0, M - 2m)$	No
Central bank	No	No	No	No	$(0, 0, M - 2m)$

2 In particular in a multistage economy with a discount factor $\beta \in (0, 1)$ and a stationary supply of perishables, a storable with a linearly separable utility cannot serve as an efficient money, as it would be fully consumed in the first period (Dubey, Geanakoplos, and Shubik, 2003).

of a linear separable term helps to clarify the relationship among monies which are storable consumables, durables, and fiat.

Each trader (of either type) has the same utility function $\varphi(x,y) + z$. Here x is the amount of the first good consumed, y is the amount of the second good consumed, and z is the amount of commodity money consumed at the end of the game. Function φ is assumed to be concave and increasing in both variables. Note that the nature of the "z" term implies that consuming each unit of commodity money is worth one unit of utility for the traders — we say the (marginal) *consumption value of money* is one per unit.

There is a continuum of traders of each type. Type 1 traders have a total initial endowment of $(a, 0, m)$, while Type 2 traders have $(0, a, m)$. Hence one would expect that in this model Type 1 traders would want to exchange some of their "good 1" for Type 2 traders' "good 2." The symmetric efficient level of consumption is for both trader types to end up consuming $\frac{a}{2}$ of each good.[3] As is shown below, even this simple explicit structure is adequate to illustrate many monetary properties.

We work with strategic variables. A strategy for a trader α of Type 1 is denoted by (b^α, q^α), where b^α is the amount he bids for good 2 and q^α is the amount of good 1 he offers for sale. In what follows, we assume that all of the traders of Type 1 are identical, facing the same utility maximization problems and so acting identically; hence we may also indicate a strategy for the Type 1 traders by (b, q), where $b = \int_\alpha b^\alpha =$ the total amount of money bid for good 2, summed across all Type 1 agents, and $q = \int_\alpha q^\alpha =$ the total amount of good 1 offered for sale, also summed across all Type 1 agents. For now on, we will use this "aggregate" convention for strategies—if one wishes to recover an individual trader's strategy from (b, q), all one needs to do is to divide through by the measure of the set of Type 1 traders. We believe this convention for strategies will help make the overall presentation easier to follow.[4]

---

3 Here the adjective "symmetric" means that the Type 1 traders' consumption of good 1 and good 2 matches the Type 2 traders' consumption of good 2 and good 1, respectively. Also, note that given the symmetric endowments, that $\left(\frac{a}{2}, \frac{a}{2}\right)$ and $\left(\frac{a}{2}, \frac{a}{2}\right)$ would also be the competitive outcome for the two types in an equivalent classical exchange economy. For this reason, we refer to this outcome as the "competitive outcome," as well as the "(symmetric) efficient outcome."

4 The reader will also note that the quantity m defined before is really a total amount of money initially owned by the continuum of traders; i.e., $m = \int m^\alpha$, where m^α represents the amount of money initially held by Trader α. Similarly, a denotes the aggregate endowment of good across the continuum of individuals.

Similarly, the strategies for Type 2 traders will be denoted as $(\bar{b}, \bar{q})$, where $\bar{b}$ is the total amount of money bid for good 1, summed across all Type 2 agents, and $\bar{q}$ is the total amount of good 2 offered for sale, also summed across all Type 2 agents.

We remark here that we are implicitly assuming all traders choose their strategies at the same time — game-theoretically, they are playing a "simultaneous move game."

Suppose p and $\bar{p}$ stand for the prices of good 1 and good 2, respectively. Trader Type 1's utility maximization problem is then as follows:

$$\max_{b,q} \varphi\left(a - q, \frac{b}{\bar{p}}\right) + m + pq - b$$
$$\text{s.t. } m - b \geq 0 \qquad\qquad (\lambda) \qquad\qquad\qquad (3.1)$$
$$0 \leq q \leq a \text{ and } b \geq 0.$$

The objective function here is the Type 1 players' aggregate utility, from both consumption (of the two perishable goods) and from money left over at the end of the period (which is presumably consumed). The constraint (λ) is the *cash-flow constraint*. A cash-flow constraint models the idea that traders are constrained in their spending by the amount of cash they have on hand. This type of constraint occurs in many of the models throughout this book, and will always be denoted with (λ). The corresponding Lagrangian multipliers will be denoted by λ.

Another term we use throughout the book is "hoarding." *Hoarding* is when the traders do not spend all money available to them.[5] Mathematically speaking, in these models the amount hoarded is just the value of the slack variable in the cash-flow constraint.

For the Type 2 agents, we write a similar utility maximization problem:

$$\max_{\bar{b},\bar{q}} \varphi\left(a - \bar{q}, \frac{\bar{b}}{p}\right) + m + \bar{p}\bar{q} - \bar{b}$$
$$\text{s.t. } m - \bar{b} \geq 0 \qquad\qquad (\lambda) \qquad\qquad\qquad (3.2)$$
$$0 \leq \bar{q} \leq a \text{ and } \bar{b} \geq 0.$$

---

5 In models where traders are able to make deposits into a bank, amend "do not spend" to "do not spend or deposit." When the rate of interest is zero one cannot distinguish, at this level of abstraction, the difference between hoarding and saving.

The prices are formed by the market balance conditions

$$p = \frac{\bar{b}}{q} \text{ and } \bar{p} = \frac{b}{\bar{q}}.$$

A remark: At first glance, it would seem as if the apparent trader decision variables b, $\bar{b}$, q, and $\bar{q}$ influence the prices via the above equations. However, we remind the reader that the actual trader decision variables are the infinitesimals b^α, $\bar{b}^\alpha$, q^α, and $\bar{q}^\alpha$—and so we should treat p and $\bar{p}$ as constants in the traders' decision problems.

The reader will guess that the solution to this model (in terms of the values of the multipliers λ and $\bar{\lambda}$ of constraints (λ) and ($\bar{\lambda}$), respectively) will depend upon the value of m. If m is high—that is, the traders have "enough money"—the constraints (λ) and ($\bar{\lambda}$) will be loose and the multipliers $\lambda = \bar{\lambda} = 0$. Alternatively, if the traders have "not enough money," (λ) and ($\bar{\lambda}$) will be tight and $\lambda, \bar{\lambda} > 0$.

In general, the concept of "enough money, well distributed in a competitive market" (hereafter abbreviated to "enough money w.d.") means that the initial distribution of money is sufficient to cover the volume of trade at competitive equilibrium, without borrowing or lending.[6] Mathematically this means that the competitive[7] perishable consumptions of $\left(\frac{a}{2}, \frac{a}{2}\right)$ and $\left(\frac{a}{2}, \frac{a}{2}\right)$ for the trader types are attained, yet all cash-flow constraints are nonbinding. In other words, the price of the money is precisely its consumption worth and it carries no extra valuation to account for its shadow price as a binding constraint on transactions.

In contrast, "enough money, badly distributed" means that there is sufficient money in the economy to finance efficient trade, *but only if those with surplus money will lend it to those who have cash-flow constraints at zero interest.* We discuss this further in Sections 4.1 and 5.3. For now, we note that in models without loan markets (like this one), the "enough money b.d." case cannot occur—hence we may use the phrase "enough money" in lieu of "enough money w.d."

Finally, we have the case of "not enough money," meaning that there is no way to finance the competitive equilibrium outcomes, even if zero interest loans were permitted.

---

6 The phrase "in a competitive market" refers to the assumption that all agents act as price-takers.

7 See footnote 3 of this chapter.

The precise mathematical manifestation of "enough money w.d." varies from model to model, depending upon such factors as the type of money used, its salvage value, the nature of the markets for the perishables (buy-sell versus sell-all), the presence or absence of loan markets, and the objectives of bankers. In the simple example here, it turns out that "enough money, well distributed" is the condition $m \geq \frac{a}{2}$.

In the case of "not enough money," any money in the economy is a scarce good, which has extra value because it is needed to facilitate trade. This extra value we call the (marginal) *transactions value of money* and is in addition to its consumption value. The magnitude of the transaction value is simply the shadow price λ of the cash-flow constraint.

The full derivation of the solution to this model, for the case where $\varphi(x, y) = 2\sqrt{xy}$, is given in Section 3.2. Here we indicate the solution and present Table 3.2 to provide a sensitivity analysis.

A SENSITIVITY ANALYSIS

We consider model results as m ranges from ∞ down to 0.

Case 1: $m \geq \frac{a}{2}$. When there is enough money, the (marginal) transactions value of money is at $\lambda = 0$ and efficient trade is achieved (i.e., each type of trader consumes $\frac{a}{2}$ of each good). Each individual is able to bid using his or her "cans of beans," keeps any surplus beans, and earns back the money spent (i.e., balances the budget in the goods bought or sold in the markets). Thus the consumption of the (linearly separable utility) commodity money equals its initial endowment for each individual.

Case 2: $0 < m < \frac{a}{2}$. *Example: $m = \frac{a}{10}$.* When there is a moderate amount of money, but not enough to avoid a shortage, the (marginal) transactions value of money is positive, as is reflected by $\lambda = 3$.[8] Efficient trade is not achieved. The price level is decreasing monotonically as m decreases from $\frac{a}{2}$ to 0.

Case 3: $m \to 0$. When there is little or no money in the economy there is next to no trade in the model.[9] In reality, if this happened, other means of payment would be used and other avenues of trade would spring up.

---

8 Thus, in this case the total marginal value of the money is 4 (its consumption value plus its transactions value).

9 For an interesting fictional version of the influence of a shortage of money on economic activity see Sholem Asch (1937), *A Tale of Three Cities*.

The results from the three cases outlined above appear in Table 3.2:

Table 3.2.   A sensitivity analysis as m varies

m	p	q	b	λ
$m \geq a/2$	1	$a/2$	$a/2$	0
$m = a/10$	1/2	$a/5$	$a/10$	3
$m \to 0$	$p \to 0$	$q \to 0$	$b \to 0$	$\lambda \to \infty$

It is convenient to denote the total amount of money in an economy by M. Here $M = 2m$. When more agents are considered there will be more components which will sum to M.

Figure 3.1 shows the price level as M is varied and the value of λ as M is varied. We note that because the money is a commodity with a fixed marginal utility of consumption, this places an upper bound on the competitive equilibrium prices of the consumable goods. We further note that λ (the shadow price of the cash-flow constraint) becomes infinite as m approaches zero.

Figure 3.2 shows the volume of trade $(= pq + \bar{p}\bar{q})$ as M is varied. Because of our model's simplicity, the volume of trade has a (piecewise) linear relationship to the amount of money. Thus for small m, total trade will be $2m$ and rises until $m = \frac{a}{2}$, when there is no further incentive for trade.

Owing to the symmetry in this model, there is no need for borrowing or lending. In the next chapter, when we consider an asymmetric initial distribution of the money, the conditions for a money market appear and the rate of interest equals the marginal value of money in alleviating the trade constraint. We note that because the money is a commodity of value, there is a bound on inflation—individuals would keep the money for consumption

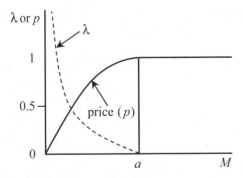

Figure 3.1.   Prices as M increases and λ as M increases

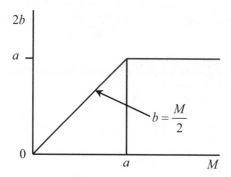

Figure 3.2. Volume of trade as M increases

if the marginal consumption utility to price did not line up with the other consumption goods.

3.2 APPENDIX: THE ANALYSIS

We present the calculations for the model in Section 3.1, with $\varphi(x,y) = 2\sqrt{xy}$. Recall that the initial endowments of Type 1 traders are a units of Type 1 good and m units of money; Type 2 traders begin with a units of Type 2 good and m units of money.

Type 1 traders face an optimization described by:

$$\max_{b,q} 2\sqrt{(a-q)\frac{b}{p}} + m + pq - b$$

s.t. $m - b \geq 0$ (cash-flow constraint)

$b \geq 0,\ 0 \leq q \leq a.$

Here the decision variables are b (the amount of money bid for the Type 2 good), and q (the amount of Type 1 good put up for sale). We may express the Lagrangian function for the optimization by

$$L = \frac{2}{\sqrt{p}}\sqrt{(a-q)b} + m + pq - b + \lambda(m - b),$$

where λ is the multiplier for the cash-flow constraint. The first-order conditions with respect to b and q yield[10]

---

10 Note that when forming the Lagrangian and the first-order conditions, we ignore non-negativity and the upper bound constraint on q. However, we note that all our solutions

$$\frac{1}{\sqrt{\bar{p}}}\sqrt{\frac{a-q}{b}}=1+\lambda \tag{3.3}$$

$$\frac{1}{\sqrt{\bar{p}}}\sqrt{\frac{b}{a-q}}=p \tag{3.4}$$

$$(m-b=0 \text{ and } \lambda \geq 0) \text{ or } (m-b\geq 0 \text{ and } \lambda =0). \tag{3.5}$$

Similarly, Type 2 traders face:

$$\max_{\bar{b},\bar{q}} 2\sqrt{(a-\bar{q})\frac{\bar{b}}{p}}+m+\bar{p}\bar{q}-\bar{b}$$

s.t. $m-\bar{b}\geq 0$ (cash-flow constraint)

$$\bar{b}\geq 0, 0\leq \bar{q}\leq a,$$

where decision variables are $\bar{b}$ and $\bar{q}$. The Lagrangian function becomes

$$\bar{L}=\frac{2}{\sqrt{p}}\sqrt{(a-\bar{q})\bar{b}}+m+\bar{p}\bar{q}-\bar{b}+\bar{\lambda}(m-\bar{b}).$$

The first-order conditions with respect to (wrt) $\bar{b}$ and $\bar{q}$ yield

$$\frac{1}{\sqrt{p}}\sqrt{\frac{a-\bar{q}}{\bar{b}}}=1+\bar{\lambda} \tag{3.6}$$

$$\frac{1}{\sqrt{p}}\sqrt{\frac{\bar{b}}{a-\bar{q}}}=p \tag{3.7}$$

$$(m-\bar{b}=0 \text{ and } \bar{\lambda} \geq 0) \text{ or } (m-\bar{b}\geq 0 \text{ and } \bar{\lambda} =0). \tag{3.8}$$

Finally, balance conditions are $p=\bar{b}/q$ and $\bar{p}=b/\bar{q}$.

Case 1: Enough money: If m is large we may assume that $\lambda =0$ and $\bar{\lambda} =0$. Equations (3.3) and (3.4) give

$$\frac{1}{\sqrt{\bar{p}}}\sqrt{\frac{a-q}{b}}=1 \Rightarrow \frac{1}{\sqrt{\bar{p}}}\frac{1}{p\sqrt{\bar{p}}}=1 \text{ or } p\bar{p}=1. \tag{3.9}$$

---

nevertheless are feasible, so our analysis is valid. We will use this same "trick" over and over again in solving the other models presented in this book.

We remark that the markets for good 1 and good 2 are isomorphic; hence we assume the existence of a *symmetric solution*, that is, one in which $b = \bar{b}$, $q = \bar{q}$, and $p = \bar{p}$. This symmetry assumption is used throughout the book in solving many of our models. Here symmetry implies $p = \bar{p} = 1$, so $a - q = b$ and $a - \bar{q} = \bar{b}$. Hence, from the balance conditions $b = \bar{q}$ and $\bar{b} = q$. This implies that $b = \bar{b} = q = \bar{q} = a/2$.

These results are valid only if the cash-flow constraints continue to hold; that is, $m \geq a/2$. Hence this is what we meant by "m large." Economically speaking, there is enough money to cover efficient trade (Shubik, 1999a).

Case 2: Not enough money: If m is small the cash-flow constraints will be tight; that is, $\lambda, \bar{\lambda} > 0$ and $b = m$, $\bar{b} = m$. This time equations (3.3) and (3.4) imply

$$\frac{1}{\sqrt{\bar{p}}} \frac{1}{(p\sqrt{\bar{p}})} = 1 + \lambda,$$

which gives (assuming symmetry)

$$p = \bar{p} = \frac{1}{\sqrt{1+\lambda}}.$$

Since $b = m = \bar{b}$, the balance constraints give $q = \bar{q} = m\sqrt{1+\lambda}$. Next, equation (3.3) implies that $(\frac{1}{p})(\frac{a-q}{b}) = (1 + \lambda)^2$, which implies $(1 + \lambda)^{1/2}(\frac{a-m\sqrt{1+\lambda}}{m}) = (1+\lambda)^2$, which in turn gives:

$$(1+\lambda)^{3/2} + (1+\lambda)^{1/2} = \frac{a}{m}. \tag{3.10}$$

Finally, since $p = \frac{1}{\sqrt{1+\lambda}}$, we have

$$\frac{1}{p^3} + \frac{1}{p} = \frac{a}{m}. \tag{3.11}$$

This shows how price varies with the money supply.

Chapter 4 Trade with a Money Market

4.1 A MODEL WITH ASYMMETRIC ENDOWMENTS

Suppose we initialize the (storable consumable) money holdings so that there is just enough money to cover efficient symmetric trade, but the money is not distributed equally. In this case we create an inefficiency, as the purchases of one type of trader are constrained by not having enough money. Trade is impeded by a cash-flow constraint. An efficient outcome can be restored by introducing a money market.

Formally, suppose the types have asymmetric endowments of $(a, 0, m_1)$ and $(0, a, m_2)$ where $m_1 > m_2$. In the money market, Type 1 traders will lend to Type 2 traders. A strategy for the Type 1 traders is denoted by (b, q, g) where b is the amount of money bid for good 2, q is the amount of good 1 offered for sale, and g is the total amount of money offered in the money market. The notation for the Type 2 agents is $(\bar{b}, \bar{q}, \bar{d})$. Here $\bar{d}$ is the total amount of personal IOU notes bid for the commodity money offered. From considerations of a dimensional analysis it must be considered as a new separate financial instrument, the personal IOU note or promise-to-pay, which is monetized by exchanging it for money. This is consistent with the observation in banking practice that a loan to an individual can be interpreted as "monetizing her personal credit." Finally, we note again that, similar to the bid and offer variables, both g and $\bar{d}$ are integral summations across the continuum of Type 1 and Type 2 players, respectively.

The players' optimization problems are

$$\max_{b,q,g} \varphi\left(a-q, \frac{b}{p}\right) + m_1 - b - g + pq + (1+\rho)g$$
$$\text{s.t. } m_1 - b - g \geq 0 \qquad (\lambda) \qquad\qquad (4.1)$$
$$m_1 - b + pq + \rho g \geq 0 \qquad (\mu)$$
$$b, g \geq 0 \text{ and } 0 \leq q \leq a$$

for the Type 1 traders (the "lenders"), and

$$\max_{\bar{b},\bar{q},\bar{d}} \varphi\left(\frac{\bar{b}}{p}, a-\bar{q}\right) + m_2 + \frac{\bar{d}}{1+\rho} - \bar{b} + \bar{p}\bar{q} - \bar{d}$$
$$\text{s.t. } m_2 - \bar{b} + \frac{\bar{d}}{1+\rho} \geq 0 \qquad (\bar{\lambda}) \qquad\qquad (4.2)$$
$$m_2 + \frac{\bar{d}}{1+\rho} - \bar{b} + \bar{p}\bar{q} - \bar{d} \geq 0 \qquad (\bar{\mu})$$
$$\bar{b}, \bar{d} \geq 0, \ 0 \leq \bar{q} \leq a$$

for the Type 2 traders (the "borrowers"). Here ρ is the interest rate on the loans.

Note that the two trader types each have an extra constraint [(μ) and $(\bar{\mu})$] in their optimization problems. These are the *budget constraints*, that is, constraints which ensure that players end up with a nonnegative amount of money when accounts are settled at the end of the game.[1] Since non-compliance of these constraints would mean that agents are not paying back their financial obligations, we sometimes also use the term "bankruptcy constraints" here.

The market balance conditions are now:

$$p = \frac{\bar{b}}{q} \text{ and } \bar{p} = \frac{b}{\bar{q}}$$

---

1 Throughout this book, budget constraints will be denoted by (μ)'s.

$$1 + \rho = \frac{\bar{d}}{g}.$$

Note that if the cash-flow constraint (λ) for the lenders is satisfied, then constraint (μ) is satisfied as well; hence (μ) can be omitted. This is not so for the borrowers. If m_2 is small relative to m_1, constraint ($\bar{\mu}$) may become binding.[2]

Finally, note that in the mechanism the loan is discounted ahead; that is, the lender gives $\frac{\bar{d}}{1+\rho}$ in return for a promise of $\bar{d}$. This assures the conservation of the commodity money in the system.

The full derivation of the solution to the model is given below in Section 4.2. Here we discuss the three important cases: (1) enough money; (2) not enough money, not too unequally distributed; and (3) not enough money, highly unequally distributed. Thereafter, we present a sensitivity analysis of our results.

ENOUGH MONEY
In the Appendix, we show that if $M = m_1 + m_2 \geq a$, equilibria exist in which the consumption is efficient and the multipliers λ and $\bar{\lambda}$ are both zero. Hence this is the case of "enough money" (see Section 3.1.2). In addition, we show the interest rate ρ is zero, and the lending from Type 1 to Type 2 traders is anywhere in the interval $[\frac{a}{2} - m_2, m_1 - \frac{a}{2}]$. Recall from Section 3.1.2 that the distinction between "enough money w.d." and "enough money b.d." is whether or not the outcome can be attained without borrowing or lending—that is, whether or not zero lies in the above interval. It is easy to see that the answer is "yes" if and only if $m_2 \geq \frac{a}{2}$; hence this is the definition of "enough money w.d." (The definition of "enough money b.d." then is $m_1 + m_2 \geq a$, with $m_2 < \frac{a}{2}$.)

If there is enough money, a lender can lend it in the morning, have it used in the market at noon, be repaid in the afternoon, and consume it in the evening.[3] In the model above this is easily seen if we suppose the initial endowments are $(a, 0, a)$ and $(0, a, 0)$. Type 1 traders lend Type 2 traders $\frac{a}{2}$ units of money at an endogenous interest rate of $\rho = 0$, and get paid back at the end of the period.

---

2 Or, we may wish to permit bankruptcy by introducing an explicit bankruptcy penalty (see Shubik and Wilson, 1977; or Chapter 8 of this book).
3 This leaves out the "fussy" but realistic details of transaction cost in terms of time and other resources.

The idea of using the beans for money and eating them in the same period appears to be fairly ridiculous, but we purposely raise it to clarify the modeling problems faced when using any commodity for both transactions and consumption purposes. We "deconstruct" this timing problem in Chapter 6.

NOT ENOUGH MONEY

If there is not enough money in the system, trade will be diminished and the price of the monetary commodity goes above its marginal value as a commodity to reflect its positive transactions value. There are two subcases. The first is where the money is not too unequally distributed between the trader types, and the second is where it is distributed in a highly skewed manner. In the first case, both trader types end up with a positive amount of commodity money. In the latter instance, the borrowers' bankruptcy constraint becomes tight. We can more fully appreciate this phenomenon by considering a monopolistic lender who owns all or nearly all of an otherwise adequate money supply, a model which is considered in Chapter 5.

A SENSITIVITY ANALYSIS

Table 4.1 shows a sensitivity analysis for our money market model:

Table 4.1.   Money market model results

$m_1 + m_2$	m_2	$\frac{m_2}{m_1+m_2}$	p	$\bar{p}$	q	$\bar{q}$	b	$\bar{b}$
$m_1 + m_2 > a$	$<m_1$	any	1	1	$\frac{a}{2}$	$\frac{a}{2}$	$\frac{a}{2}$	$\frac{a}{2}$
$m_1 + m_2 = a$	$<m_1$	any	1	1	$\frac{a}{2}$	$\frac{a}{2}$	$\frac{a}{2}$	$\frac{a}{2}$
$m_1 + m_2 = \frac{a}{5}$	$\frac{7a}{80}$	$\frac{7}{16}$	$\frac{1}{2}$	$\frac{1}{2}$	$\frac{a}{5}$	$\frac{a}{5}$	$\frac{a}{10}$	$\frac{a}{10}$
$m_1 + m_2 = \frac{a}{5}$	0	0	0.726	0.324	0.065a	0.5a	0.162a	0.047a

$m_1 + m_2$	m_2	$\frac{m_2}{m_1+m_2}$	$\bar{d}$	g	ρ	λ	$\bar{\mu}$
$m_1 + m_2 > a$	$<m_1$	any	?	?	0	0	0
$m_1 + m_2 = a$	$<m_1$	any	$\frac{m_2}{m_1+m_2}$	$\frac{m_2}{m_1+m_2}$	0	0	0
$m_1 + m_2 = \frac{a}{5}$	$\frac{7a}{80}$	$\frac{7}{16}$	$\frac{a}{20}$	$\frac{a}{80}$	3	3	3
$m_1 + m_2 = \frac{a}{5}$	0	0	0.162a	0.038a	3.251	3.251	3.251

We consider $0 \leq m_2 \leq m_1$ in the four instances where there is more than enough money, enough money, not enough—mildly skewed, and not enough—heavily skewed.

Case 1: A coordination trap: $m_1 + m_2 > a$. When there is more than enough money, the transactions value of money is $\lambda = 0$. The formal mathematics indicates that traders paying a zero interest rate could demand to borrow any amount of the storable consumable, store it, and return it. Hence there is a "coordination problem" or "liquidity trap,"[4] in that it would be difficult to get all of the infinitesimal agents to play the same strategy. The coordination aspects of a positive price for money are lost.

Case 2: $m_1 + m_2 = a$. When there is precisely enough money, and it is distributed asymmetrically, traders of one type will encounter their cash-flow constraints, but they will be able to borrow at an interest rate equal to the transactions value of money, namely, $\lambda = 0$.

Case 3: $0 < m_1 + m_2 < a$ and $m_1 \simeq m_2$. *Example:* $m_1 = \frac{9a}{80}$, $m_2 = \frac{7a}{80}$. Now we consider cases where there is a moderate amount of money, but still not enough to avoid a shortage. The transactions value of money is positive, as is reflected by $\lambda = 3$. The price level is decreasing as m_1 or m_2 decreases. The moderate asymmetry of this example avoids the extra budget constraint, and the relative prices of the two consumer goods stay the same.

Case 4: $0 < m_1 + m_2 < a$ and $m_1 \gg m_2$. *Example:* $m_1 = \frac{a}{5}$, $m_2 = 0$. When there is a moderate amount of money in the economy and it is highly asymmetrically distributed, the borrowers are limited by bankruptcy constraints in their ability to borrow. In this formal model where individuals "stick to the rules," we examine what happens. When there is enough money, credit comes free. As the money shortage becomes more and more binding, the transactions value of money increases as a function of its total supply. When the borrowers hit the extra bankruptcy constraint, the prices of the goods diverge, as shown in the last line of Table 4.1.

Figure 4.1 shows the three zones, where there is enough money (Cases 1 and 2 above); not enough money for efficient trade but enough for fully secured lending (Case 3); and not enough for efficient trade or for secured lending (Case 4).[5] We may regard the boundary zones as delineating an economic phase change.

---

4 The coordination problem is related to but not quite the same as the liquidity trap in macroeconomic writings, where coordination and control may be lost even at a small positive rate of interest.

5 "Fully secured lending" here implies that at equilibrium the borrower will have enough income to repay the lender without the lender needing to impose a lending constraint on him.

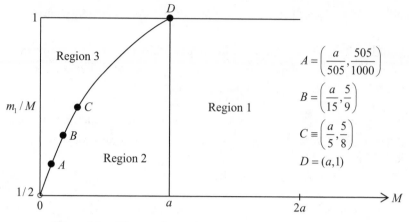

Figure 4.1. Three trading regions

Table 4.2 shows some of the points on the boundary between Regions 2 and 3:

Table 4.2.   Boundary points

M	λ	$\frac{m_1}{M}$
a	0	1
$\frac{a}{5}$	3	$\frac{5}{8}$
$\frac{a}{15}$	8	$\frac{5}{9}$
$\frac{a}{505}$	99	0.505

Table 4.3 shows some values of the variables in Region 3 where merchants of Type 2 are endowed with no money ($m_2 = 0$):

Table 4.3.   Points with $m_2 = 0$

$\frac{M^2}{a^2}$	$\frac{M}{a}$	ρ	p	$\bar{p}$
1	1	0	1	1
$\frac{9}{40}$	0.474	1	0.79	0.632
$\frac{4}{45}$	0.298	2	0.745	0.447
$\frac{25}{544}$	0.214	3	0.7276	0.3424

If in addition (to $m_2 = 0$) we assume $\frac{m_1}{a}$ is very small, a calculation at the end of the Appendix shows that

$$\rho \simeq \frac{a}{\sqrt{2m_1}} - 1. \tag{4.3}$$

In Chapter 7 we discuss the problem of the Hahn paradox, whereby in some models (with worthless fiat money) a backward induction argument implies that there will be no trade. Here the paradox is avoided because of the use of a consumable money which maintains its value at the terminal point of the game (which we can call "supper time," or "the great bean feast").

The full solution of the money market model is given in the Appendix. Even with an example as simple as this the calculations are somewhat messy.[6] For more commentary on the money market model, see Section 12.3.

4.2 APPENDIX: THE ANALYSIS

Here we present the calculations from the model of Section 4.1, where the agents take into account the existence of a money market. We have to introduce the roles of borrowing and lending. We assume initial endowments of money as m_1 and m_2 where $m_1 \geq m_2$. Hence Type 1 traders become lenders and Type 2 traders borrowers. Again we assume that $\varphi(x, y) = 2\sqrt{xy}$.

Traders of Type 1 face an optimization described by:

$$\max_{b,q,g} 2\sqrt{(a-q)\frac{b}{p}} + m_1 - g - b + pq + (1+\rho)g$$

$$\text{s.t. } m_1 - b - g \geq 0 \text{ (cash-flow constraint)}$$

$$b, g \geq 0, 0 \leq q \leq a.$$

Again, decision variables b and q represent the amounts bid for Type 2 good and the amount offered of Type 1 good, respectively. Another decision variable, g, represents the amount lent to Type 2 traders. This money is lent at an interest rate of ρ, a rate that is determined endogenously to the model.

---

6 For example, the explicit form of the rate of interest in Region 2 is given by:

$$1 + \rho = \sqrt[3]{\left(\frac{1}{27} + \frac{1}{2}K + \frac{1}{18}\sqrt{(12K + 81K^2)}\right)}$$

$$+ \frac{1}{9\sqrt[3]{\left(\frac{1}{27} + \frac{1}{2}K + \frac{1}{18}\sqrt{(12K + 81K^2)}\right)}} - \frac{2}{3}$$

where $K = (2a/(m_1 + m_2))^2$.

The Lagrangian for the above problem is

$$L = \frac{2}{\sqrt{p}}\sqrt{(a-q)b} + m_1 - g - b + pq + (1+\rho)g + \lambda(m_1 - g - b).$$

Thus the first-order conditions wrt b, q, and g are

$$\frac{1}{\sqrt{p}}\sqrt{\frac{a-q}{b}} = 1 + \lambda \qquad\qquad (4.4)$$

$$\frac{1}{\sqrt{p}}\sqrt{\frac{b}{a-q}} = p \qquad\qquad (4.5)$$

$$\lambda = \rho \qquad\qquad (4.6)$$

$(m - b - g = 0 \text{ and } \lambda \geq 0)$ or $(m - b - g \geq 0 \text{ and } \lambda = 0)$. $\qquad (4.7)$

Type 2 traders face

$$\max_{\bar{b},\bar{q},\bar{d}} 2\sqrt{(a-\bar{q})\frac{\bar{b}}{p}} + \left(m_2 + \frac{\bar{d}}{1+\rho} - \bar{b} + \bar{p}\bar{q} - \bar{d}\right)$$

s.t. $m_2 + \dfrac{\bar{d}}{1+\rho} - \bar{b} \geq 0$ (cash-flow constraint) $\qquad (\bar{\lambda})$

$\quad \bar{b}, \bar{d} \geq 0, \ 0 \leq \bar{q} \leq a.$

Here $\frac{\bar{d}}{1+\rho}$ represents the amount that the Type 2 traders borrow from the Type 1 traders (and so they must pay back $\bar{d}$). We also require a budget constraint (bankruptcy constraint) that

$$m_2 + \frac{\bar{d}}{1+\rho} - \bar{b} + \bar{p}\bar{q} - \bar{d} \geq 0 \text{ (budget constraint) } (\bar{\mu}).$$

Thus the Lagrangian expression becomes:

$$\bar{L} = \frac{2}{\sqrt{p}}\sqrt{(a-\bar{q})\bar{b}} + \left(m_2 + \frac{\bar{d}}{1+\rho} - \bar{b} + \bar{p}\bar{q} - \bar{d}\right)$$

$$+ \bar{\lambda}\left(m_2 + \frac{\bar{d}}{1+\rho} - \bar{b}\right) + \bar{\mu}\left(m_2 + \frac{\bar{d}}{1+\rho} - \bar{b} + \bar{p}\bar{q} - \bar{d}\right).$$

The first-order conditions with respect to $\bar{b}$, $\bar{q}$, and $\bar{d}$ yield

$$\frac{1}{\sqrt{\bar{p}}}\sqrt{\frac{a-\bar{q}}{\bar{b}}} = 1 + \bar{\lambda} + \bar{\mu} \tag{4.8}$$

$$\frac{1}{\sqrt{\bar{p}}}\sqrt{\frac{\bar{b}}{a-\bar{q}}} = \bar{p} + \bar{p}\bar{\mu} \tag{4.9}$$

$$\bar{\lambda} = \rho(1+\bar{\mu}) \tag{4.10}$$

$$\left(m_2 + \frac{\bar{d}}{1+\rho} - \bar{b} = 0 \text{ and } \bar{\lambda} \geq 0\right) \text{ or } \left(m_2 + \frac{\bar{d}}{1+\rho} - \bar{b} \geq 0 \text{ and } \bar{\lambda} = 0\right) \tag{4.11}$$

$$\left(m_2 + \frac{\bar{d}}{1+\rho} - \bar{b} + \bar{p}\bar{q} - \bar{d} = 0 \text{ and } \bar{\mu} \geq 0\right) \text{ or }$$
$$\left(m_2 + \frac{\bar{d}}{1+\rho} - \bar{b} + \bar{p}\bar{q} - \bar{d} \geq 0 \text{ and } \bar{\mu} = 0\right), \tag{4.12}$$

and balance conditions are $p = \frac{\bar{b}}{q}$, $\bar{p} = \frac{b}{\bar{q}}$, and $1 + \rho = \frac{\bar{d}}{g}$.

Case 1: If $m_1 + m_2 \geq a$, we may assume that $\lambda = 0$, $\bar{\lambda} = 0$, and $\bar{\mu} = 0$. Equations (4.4) and (4.5) give

$$\frac{1}{\sqrt{\bar{p}}}\sqrt{\frac{a-q}{b}} = 1 \Rightarrow \frac{1}{\sqrt{\bar{p}}}\frac{1}{p\sqrt{\bar{p}}} = 1 \text{ or } p\bar{p} = 1.$$

For the symmetric solution, $p = \bar{p} = 1$. This gives $a - q = b$, $a - \bar{q} = \bar{b}$, which together with the balance conditions $b = \bar{q}$ and $\bar{b} = q$ give one solution as $q = b = \bar{q} = \bar{b} = \frac{a}{2}$. In addition, condition (4.6) implies $\rho = 0$. The quantities $\bar{d}$ and g will be any quantities such that $\bar{d} = g$ and the cash-flow constraints hold; in particular any nonnegative value of $\bar{d} = g$ in the interval $[\frac{a}{2} - m_2, m_1 - \frac{a}{2}]$ is valid. Such a value exists by virtue of the $m_1 + m_2 \geq a$ assumption.

To summarize, the prices are 1, the interest rate is 0, and the final consumption bundles are $(\frac{a}{2}, \frac{a}{2}, m_1)$ and $(\frac{a}{2}, \frac{a}{2}, m_2)$.

Case 2: If $m_1 + m_2 < a$, we see that the cash-flow constraint will become tight; that is, $\lambda > 0$. We now have an extra case distinction to make. We must consider whether the budget constraint becomes binding, that is, whether $\bar{\mu} > 0$. This will depend on the rate of interest and the relative sizes of m_1 and m_2. The case $\bar{\mu} = 0$ is considered as Case 2, while $\bar{\mu} > 0$ is Case 3.

In Case 2, constraints (4.4) and (4.5) imply that

$$\frac{1}{\sqrt{\bar{p}}}\frac{1}{p\sqrt{\bar{p}}} = 1+\lambda.$$

Hence, assuming equal prices (we may do this in Case 2 because the Type 2 traders' extra constraint—the budget constraint—is not binding) we have $p = \bar{p} = \frac{1}{\sqrt{1+\lambda}}$. In addition, conditions (4.6), (4.10), and the assumption that $\bar{\mu} = 0$ imply that $\lambda = \bar{\lambda} = \rho$; and from $b + g = m_1$, $\bar{b} - \frac{d}{1+\rho} = m_2$, and $1 + \rho = \frac{d}{g}$, we obtain

$$b + \bar{b} = m_1 + m_2. \tag{4.13}$$

Since $\frac{\bar{b}}{\bar{q}} = \frac{b}{q} = p$, we have

$$\frac{\bar{b}+b}{\bar{q}+q} = p \Rightarrow \frac{m_1+m_2}{\bar{q}+q} = \frac{1}{\sqrt{1+\lambda}} \Rightarrow \bar{q}+q = \sqrt{1+\lambda}(m_1+m_2).$$

Now by condition (4.4) we have $\left(\frac{1}{\bar{p}}\right)\left(\frac{a-q}{b}\right) = (1+\lambda)^2$, which implies $\frac{a-q}{b} = (1+\lambda)^{3/2}$; similarly $\frac{a-\bar{q}}{\bar{b}} = (1+\bar{\lambda})^{3/2} = (1+\lambda)^{3/2}$. Hence $(1+\lambda)^{3/2} = \frac{2a-q-\bar{q}}{b+\bar{b}} = \frac{2a-\sqrt{1+\lambda}(m_1+m_2)}{m_1+m_2}$; this gives

$$(1+\lambda)^{3/2} + (1+\lambda)^{1/2} = \frac{2a}{m_1+m_2}. \tag{4.14}$$

Next, $\left(\frac{1}{\bar{p}}\right)\left(\frac{a-q}{b}\right) = (1+\lambda)^2$ implies $\frac{a-\bar{b}\sqrt{1+\lambda}}{b} = (1+\lambda)^{3/2}$, which in turn gives $a = \bar{b}(1+\lambda)^{1/2} + b(1+\lambda)^{3/2}$. Similarly, $\left(\frac{1}{p}\right)\left(\frac{a-\bar{q}}{\bar{b}}\right) = (1+\lambda)^2$ gives $a = b(1+\lambda)^{\frac{1}{2}} + \bar{b}(1+\lambda)^{3/2}$. These imply $b = \bar{b}$. But then (4.13) gives $b = \bar{b} = \frac{m_1+m_2}{2}$.

Next, starting from $\frac{a-q}{b} = (1+\lambda)^{3/2}$ gives $q = a - \frac{m_1+m_2}{2} \cdot (1+\lambda)^{3/2}$. Substituting in for m_1+m_2 using (4.14) gives

$$q = a - \frac{a(1+\lambda)^{3/2}}{(1+\lambda)^{3/2}+(1+\lambda)^{1/2}} = \frac{a}{2+\lambda}. \tag{4.15}$$

Finally,

$$g = m_1 - b = m_1 - \frac{m_1+m_2}{2} = \frac{m_1-m_2}{2} \tag{4.16}$$

$$\bar{d} = (1+\rho)(b-m_2) = (1+\lambda)\left(\frac{m_1-m_2}{2}\right). \tag{4.17}$$

We remark that computationally, given m_1, m_2, and a, one would first find λ using (4.14) and then use the value of λ to find the value of all the other variables.

We also remark that all of these results are valid only so long as the budget constraint $(\bar{\mu})$ is satisfied. This is equivalent to $\bar{p}\bar{q} \geq \bar{d}$. But

$$\bar{p}\bar{q} \geq \bar{d} \Rightarrow \frac{1}{\sqrt{1+\lambda}} \frac{a}{2+\lambda} \geq (1+\lambda)\left(\frac{m_1 - m_2}{2}\right)$$

$$\Rightarrow \frac{m_1 + m_2}{m_1 - m_2} \geq 1 + \lambda \text{ or } m_2 \geq \frac{\lambda m_1}{2+\lambda} \text{ or } \frac{m_2}{m_1 + m_2} \geq \frac{\lambda}{2(1+\lambda)}.$$

(4.18)

Case 3: We now consider the extra case where $m_1 + m_2 < a$ (so the interest rate is positive) and the ratio $\frac{m_2}{m_1 + m_2}$ is small (so that (4.18) doesn't hold). This is the case where constraint $(\bar{\mu})$ holds tightly. We then observe that borrowers could not have an optimum at a point where $(\bar{\lambda})$ holds loosely.[7] Hence we may assume that all three constraints (λ), $(\bar{\lambda})$, and $(\bar{\mu})$ hold tightly. The fact that the borrowers have an extra "meaningful" constraint here will imply that there is a basic asymmetry to the game, causing p to be different from $\bar{p}$.

We again start with constraints (4.4) and (4.5), implying that $\frac{1}{\sqrt{\bar{p}}} \cdot \frac{1}{p\sqrt{\bar{p}}} = 1 + \lambda$, which gives

$$p\bar{p} = \frac{1}{1+\lambda}.$$

(4.19)

Next, (4.9) implies that $\left(\frac{1}{p}\right)\left(\frac{\bar{b}}{a-\bar{q}}\right) = (\bar{p} + \bar{p}\bar{\mu})^2$, which gives $p\bar{p}^2 = \frac{1}{(1+\bar{\mu})^2}\left(\frac{\bar{b}}{a-\bar{q}}\right)$. Now (4.8) tells us that $\frac{\bar{b}}{a-\bar{q}} = \frac{1}{p(1+\bar{\lambda}+\bar{\mu})^2}$; hence we have $p^2\bar{p}^2 = \frac{1}{(1+\bar{\mu})^2(1+\bar{\lambda}+\bar{\mu})^2}$. This gives $p\bar{p} = \frac{1}{(1+\bar{\mu})(1+\bar{\lambda}+\bar{\mu})}$, and so

$$1 + \lambda = (1 + \bar{\mu})(1 + \bar{\lambda} + \bar{\mu}).$$

(4.20)

Now we know from (4.6) that $\rho = \lambda$, and so (4.10) gives $\bar{\lambda} = \lambda(1 + \bar{\mu})$. Hence (4.20) implies that $\bar{\mu} = 0$ and $\bar{\lambda} = \lambda$.

---

7 Proof by contradiction: Suppose in some optimum $(\bar{b}, \bar{q}, \bar{d})$ that constraint $(\bar{\mu})$ held tightly and $(\bar{\lambda})$ loosely. By inspection this would imply $\bar{d} > 0$. But then the borrowers could raise b, lower d, still satisfy all their constraints, and increase their utility.

Next, because constraints (λ) and $(\bar{\lambda})$ are tight, $b + g = m_1$ and $\bar{b} - \frac{\bar{d}}{1+\rho} = m_2$. Together with the balancing condition $1 + \rho = \frac{\bar{d}}{g}$ we obtain

$$b + \bar{b} = m_1 + m_2. \tag{4.21}$$

Next, since $(\bar{\lambda})$ and $(\bar{\mu})$ are tight, we have $\bar{p}\bar{q} = \bar{d}$. But also $\bar{p}\bar{q} = b$ because of the balancing condition. Hence $\bar{d} = b$. This implies $\bar{b} - \frac{b}{1+\rho} = m_2$. Substituting in for $\bar{b}$ using (4.21) gives

$$b = \left(\frac{1+\lambda}{2+\lambda}\right)m_1 = \bar{d} \tag{4.22}$$

$$\bar{b} = m_1 + m_2 - b = m_2 + (\frac{1}{2+\lambda})m_1 \tag{4.23}$$

$$g = m_1 - b = \left(\frac{1}{2+\lambda}\right)m_1. \tag{4.24}$$

We now are in a position to show how to calculate λ. We start with (4.5), which implies that $p^2\bar{p} = \frac{b}{a-q}$. Using (4.19), we have $p = \frac{(1+\lambda)b}{a-\frac{\bar{b}}{p}}$, which is $ap - \bar{b} = (1+\lambda)b$, or

$$p = \frac{(1+\lambda)b + \bar{b}}{a} = \frac{m_1 + m_2 + \lambda b}{a}. \tag{4.25}$$

Similarly, starting with equation (4.9) and again using (4.19), we may arrive at

$$\bar{p} = \frac{(1+\lambda)\bar{b} + b}{a} = \frac{m_1 + m_2 + \lambda\bar{b}}{a}. \tag{4.26}$$

Now we can substitute into the $p\,\bar{p} = \frac{1}{1+\lambda}$ equation, obtaining

$$\frac{m_1 + m_2 + \lambda b}{a} \cdot \frac{m_1 + m_2 + \lambda\bar{b}}{a} = \frac{1}{1+\lambda}. \tag{4.27}$$

Finally, we can use our expressions for b and $\bar{b}$, obtaining a fifth-degree equation for λ in terms of the input parameters m_1, m_2, and a. This can be solved computationally.

An interesting case is when $m_2 = 0$. Here $b = \frac{1+\lambda}{2+\lambda}m_1$ and $\bar{b} = \frac{1}{2+\lambda}m_1$. Hence the equation for λ is

$$\frac{m_1 + \lambda(\frac{1+\lambda}{2+\lambda})m_1}{a} \cdot \frac{m_1 + \lambda(\frac{1}{2+\lambda})m_1}{a} = \frac{1}{1+\lambda}, \tag{4.28}$$

which is

$$\frac{2m_1^2}{a^2}(\lambda^2 + 2\lambda + 2)\left(\frac{1+\lambda}{2+\lambda}\right)^2 = 1. \tag{4.29}$$

Table 4.4 gives λ for certain values of $\frac{m_1}{a} = \frac{M}{a}$:

Table 4.4.   Some results when $m_2 = 0$

$\frac{M^2}{a^2}$	$\frac{M}{a}$	$\lambda = \rho$	p	$\bar{p}$
1	1	0	1	1
$\frac{9}{40}$	0.474	1	$\frac{5}{3}0.474 = 0.79$	$\frac{4}{3}0.474 = 0.632$
$\frac{4}{45}$	0.298	2	$\frac{5}{2}0.298 = 0.745$	$\frac{3}{2}0.298 = 0.447$
$\frac{25}{544}$	0.214	3	$\frac{17}{5}0.214 = 0.7276$	$\frac{8}{5}0.214 = 0.3424$

Finally, suppose that $\frac{m_1}{a}$ is very small, so that $\lambda = \rho$ is very large. Then $\lambda^2 + 2\lambda + 2$ is approximated by $(1+\lambda)^2$ and $\frac{1+\lambda}{2+\lambda}$ is approximately 1. Equation (4.29) becomes $\frac{2m_1^2}{a^2}(\lambda + 1)^2 \cong 1$, which implies $\frac{\sqrt{2}m_1}{a}(\lambda + 1) \cong 1$, or $\lambda = \rho \cong \frac{a}{\sqrt{2}m_1} - 1$.

Chapter 5 Trade with a Rich
Large Agent

5.1 TRADE WITH A RICH LARGE BUYER

We introduce into the market a single agent, endowed with only a large amount of money, but with the same utility function as the others. Our object is to study how this new large player "lives off her money."[1]

---

1 It is worth noting that in accord with general equilibrium analysis, if the money is a commodity such as gold it is possible for a private individual to live off it. But also, if money is fiat (with no intrinsic value), as long as it is accepted by all, an individual could live off it as easily as he could off gold. This still leaves open how expectations are formed in a society to provide a sufficient level of trust to preserve fiat's value in trade (see Grandmont, 1983; Bak, Norrelykke, and Shubik, 1999). In spite of this, we believe that the value of paper money is supported by many different factors involving not only economic dynamics, but a mix of economics, government force, laws, customs, and taxation.

Realistically, the model is bizarre in the extreme, but it merits examination as a link to our study of the individually owned bank[2] which both lends and consumes resources. After considering the large player first just consuming, then lending and consuming, we can extend this analysis for an examination and comparison with the goals and actions of a central bank. In understanding a central bank, both its role as a monopolist and its goals are critical and need to be reflected in the formal analysis.

Formally, we have the following model. There are again two continua of traders (of Type 1 and Type 2), endowed with $(a, 0, m)$ and $(0, a, m)$, respectively. There is also a "rich large buyer," endowed with $(0, 0, M - 2m)$, where M is again the total amount of money in the game. For now, there is no loan market in the model.

As before, the optimizations are

$$\max_{b,q} \varphi\left(a - q, \frac{b}{p}\right) + m - b + pq \quad \text{(a)}$$
$$\text{s.t. } m - b \geq 0 \quad \text{(b)} \quad (5.1)$$
$$b \geq 0, 0 \leq q \leq a \quad \text{(c)}$$

and

$$\max_{\bar{b},\bar{q}} \varphi\left(\frac{\bar{b}}{p}, a - \bar{q}\right) + m - \bar{b} + \bar{p}\bar{q}$$
$$\text{s.t. } m - \bar{b} \geq 0$$
$$\bar{b} \geq 0, \ 0 \leq \bar{q} \leq a$$

for the Type 1 and Type 2 agents. For the large buyer, the optimization is

$$\max_{b_1^*, b_2^*} \varphi\left(\frac{b_1^*}{p(b_1^*)}, \frac{b_2^*}{\bar{p}(b_2^*)}\right) + M - 2m - b_1^* - b_2^* \quad \text{(a)}$$
$$\text{s.t. } M - 2m - b_1^* - b_2^* \geq 0 \quad (\lambda_P) \quad \text{(b)} \quad (5.2)$$
$$b_1^*, b_2^* \geq 0, \quad \text{(c)}$$

where b_1^*, b_2^* denote her bids for good 1 and good 2, respectively.

Note the arguments for φ in the last optimization, in contrast with the first two optimizations. In the first two problems, the infinitesimal individuals of the two agent types are in essence price-takers—but in the last problem, the large buyer takes into account the influence over prices caused by her buying.

2 For a discussion of our terminology regarding different types of banks, see Section 13.1.

Indeed, the price formation in this model must include the bids of the buyer; that is,

$$p = \frac{b_1^* + \bar{b}}{q} = \frac{b_1^* + \int_\alpha \bar{b}^\alpha}{\int_\alpha q^\alpha}. \tag{5.3}$$

A similar expression holds for $\bar{p}$. The notation here emphasizes that b_1^* is the bid of an atomic player and is not an integral, while $\bar{b}$ is the integral sum of bids over a continuum.

For a full solution to this model, in the case where $\varphi(x, y) = 2\sqrt{xy}$, see Appendix A. The results allow us to see the monopoly power of a single individual whose influence is derived from control over transactions. For example, if the initial endowments were $(a, 0, \frac{a}{12})$, $(0, a, \frac{a}{12})$, $(0, 0, \frac{a}{3})$, so the total money supply is $M = \frac{a}{2}$, our calculations show $q = \bar{q} = \frac{a}{3}$ and $\lambda = \rho = 3$, with final endowments of $(\frac{2a}{3}, \frac{a}{6}, \frac{a}{6})$, $(\frac{a}{6}, \frac{2a}{3}, \frac{a}{6})$, $(\frac{a}{6}, \frac{a}{6}, \frac{a}{6})$. The utility of the "large buyer" increases from an initial value $\frac{a}{3}$ to a final value of $\frac{a}{2}$.

However, above a certain level, as m increases, the power of the large buyer decreases. If both trader types together have at least a units of money, the near monopoly power is reduced to zero and any extra commodity money is used only for consumption.

On the other hand, if $m \to 0$, a small calculation in Case 2 of Appendix A shows that $b \to 0$, $b_1^* \to 0$, and $q \to 0$; that is, there is no trade. Indeed, one may verify that when $m = 0$, the unique equilibrium is for the traders not to offer any goods for sale, and for the large buyer not to bid anything for goods. Interestingly, if we change the model slightly (with $m = 0$) to allow bids only in integral multiples of some ε,[3] another equilibrium emerges—the traders offer all of their goods for sale, and the large buyer buys it all for ε in each market. In our vector notation, the outcome from trade is $(0, 0, \varepsilon)$, $(0, 0, \varepsilon)$, and $(a, a, M - 2\varepsilon)$. In conclusion, the placing of a "grid" on the market is of major benefit to the large buyer. In institutional reality the political pressures would change the game.

We also observe that the "no-trade" solution above (if $m = 0$) would be destroyed by the introduction of a random component to the economy. The randomness could be in the endowments or the preferences. This is noted

---

3 An interpretation for ε could be as the smallest unit of currency, e.g., a penny. Alternatively, this models highly practical situations such as when bids for shares on NASDAQ or other exchanges are allowed only in certain units, such as $\varepsilon = \frac{1}{8}$ of a dollar, $\varepsilon = \frac{1}{10}$ of a dollar, or finer amounts.

as a general warning that there is a tradeoff among mathematical precision, sensitivity analysis and contextual meaning.

5.2 TRADE WITH A STORABLE CONSUMABLE: TWO TRADER TYPES WITH A MONOPOLISTIC MONEYLENDER

In this section we model the three types of trader as in the previous section; except this time the rich large agent is a monopolistic moneylender.[4] We model the goal of this lender in two ways: (1) Her utility function is linear only in the commodity money, or (2) she has exactly the same utility function as the others. This will help us to contrast the moneylender with a central bank. Both have monopoly power, but motivations may differ.

The model is as follows. The two types have symmetric endowments of the goods $(a, 0, m)$ and $(0, a, m)$. The moneylender has resources $(0, 0, M - 2m)$. A strategy for the Type 1 traders is denoted by (b, q, d), where b is the amount of money bid for good 2, q is the amount of good 1 offered for sale, and d is the amount of personal IOU notes bid for commodity money offered by the moneylender. A strategy for the Type 2 traders is $(\bar{b}, \bar{q}, \bar{d})$, where $\bar{d}$ is the amount of personal IOU notes bid for the commodity money offered by the moneylender.[5]

Thus the Type 1 traders' problem is

$$\max_{b,q,d} \varphi\left(a - q, \frac{b}{p}\right) + m + \frac{d}{1+\rho} - b + pq - d$$

$$\text{s.t. } m + \frac{d}{1+\rho} - b \geq 0 \qquad \qquad (\lambda) \text{ (cash-flow constraint)}$$

$$m + \frac{d}{1+\rho} - b + pq - d \geq 0 \qquad (\mu) \text{ (budget constraint)}$$

$$b, d \geq 0, \, 0 \leq q \leq a.$$

(5.4)

---

4 We should emphasize here the technical difference between the terms "moneylender" and "bank": banks are multifunctional institutions, for whom lending is but one role. However, throughout this book we use the terms interchangeably. The reason is that while in most of our models the institution(s) doing the lending has only that function, these models could be embedded in models of true multifunctional banks representing their lending function.

5 We note here that b, q, d $(\bar{b}, \bar{q}, \bar{d})$ are all integral summations over the set of Type 1 (Type 2) traders. See Chapter 3 for details.

And the Type 2's traders' problem is

$$\max_{\bar{b},\bar{q},\bar{d}} \varphi\left(\frac{\bar{b}}{p}, a-\bar{q}\right) + m + \frac{\bar{d}}{1+\rho} - \bar{b} + \bar{p}\bar{q} - \bar{d}$$

$$\text{s.t. } m + \frac{\bar{d}}{1+\rho} - \bar{b} \geq 0 \qquad\qquad (\bar{\lambda}) \text{ (cash-flow constraint)}$$

$$m + \frac{\bar{d}}{1+\rho} - \bar{b} + \bar{p}\bar{q} - \bar{d} \geq 0 \qquad (\bar{\mu}) \text{ (budget constraint)}$$

$$\bar{b}, \bar{d} \geq 0, \, 0 \leq \bar{q} \leq a.$$

The endogenous rate of interest is formed as follows:

$$1+\rho = \frac{d+\bar{d}}{g} = \frac{\int_\alpha d^\alpha + \int_\gamma d^\gamma}{g}, \qquad\qquad (5.5)$$

where $0 \leq g \leq M - 2m$ is the amount of money offered for loan by the lender.

In the first model the lender's problem is simply to choose g to maximize

$$g\rho(g), \qquad\qquad (5.6)$$

that is, to maximize total monetary profit. Note that we have put ρ as a function of g. This is to emphasize the fact that since the lender is monopolistic, her actions influence the interest rate.

The second model has the moneylender also act as a consumer. Her objective function becomes:

$$\varphi\left(\frac{b_1^*}{p}, \frac{b_2^*}{\bar{p}}\right) + M - 2m - b_1^* - b_2^* + \rho g. \qquad\qquad (5.7)$$

Even if the monopolist moneylender has far more money than is needed for trade, she will not necessarily lend it. Her monetary power is maximized by making sure that the traders' cash-flow constraints are binding. In Chapter 13, on oligopolistic competition, we show how monopoly power is attenuated with many moneylenders (see also Shubik, 1976). However, as long as there is a shortage of money the interest rate will be positive, even in a one-period market.

The price formation in this model must include the bids of the moneylender, thus

$$p = \frac{b_1^* + \bar{b}}{q} \text{ and } \bar{p} = \frac{b_2^* + b}{\bar{q}}. \qquad\qquad (5.8)$$

5.2.1 Important Modeling Issues

The reader will note that our general approach in solving the models with a separate lending agent (bank) will be to first solve the traders' problems (treating either ρ or g as a given parameter), and then to solve the banker's problem once we know what the traders do as a function of ρ (or g). This includes not only the two models described above, but also all of our models with a central bank. Game-theoretically, we are considering an extensive form game in which the lender moves first, followed by the traders (all moving simultaneously). We are then finding a perfect equilibrium for the game.

CONTROLLING THE MONEY SUPPLY

This sequencing of moves suggests the following formal way of looking at the bank's problem. Suppose that the bank is using g as its decision variable. Since the bank moves first and selects a value for g, the two trader types' problems can be thought of as functions of g: let us denote them Γ_g and $\bar{\Gamma}_g$. The bank's decision problem can be written as

$$\max_{0 \leq g \leq M - 2m} \Psi(\arg\max_{b,d,q \geq 0} \Gamma_g, \arg\max_{\bar{b},\bar{d},\bar{q} \geq 0} \bar{\Gamma}_g), \tag{5.9}$$

where Ψ indicates an objective function for the bank. This function Ψ could be a measure of utility or profit (in the case of a private bank) or else some measure of social welfare (in the case of a central bank). Notice that the argument for Ψ is vector-valued, with at least a component for each type.

CONTROLLING THE RATE OF INTEREST

Instead of utilizing the quantity of money as its control variable, the bank could use the rate of interest. The traders' optimization problems are then denoted by Γ_ρ and $\bar{\Gamma}_\rho$, defined in the obvious way. The bank then solves

$$\max_{\rho \geq 0} \Psi(\arg\max_{b,d,q \geq 0} \Gamma_\rho, \arg\max_{\bar{b},\bar{d},\bar{q} \geq 0} \bar{\Gamma}_\rho). \tag{5.10}$$

The nonnegativity of ρ guarantees that the bank will not operate at a loss.

THE MONEY SUPPLY OR THE INTEREST RATE?

The choice of a lender to use the money supply or interest rate as a strategic variable will depend in practice on many details, such as the availability of money substitutes and the structure of current debt. In this highly stripped down model no outside economic, political, or social pressures are present. Thus, although there is a formal strategic difference between using g or ρ as the strategic variable, they normally lead to the same outcome.[6] For policy choice differences to matter requires a higher level of complexity.

5.2.2 The Monopolist Who Consumes Only Money

We now solve the model of the monopolist moneylender whose only concern is monetary maximization. To do this, we need to explore several cases (see Appendix B for the full solution).[7]

Case 1: If $m \geq \frac{a}{2}$ the traders' consumption is efficient and the monopolist earns zero profits. The traders can obtain all of the gains from trade without borrowing. This then is the "enough money w.d." condition defined in Section 3.1.2.

Case 2: If m is very small, the traders' cash-flow and budget constraints will both be tight. An optimal strategy for the monopolist will be to lend all of his money. His profits will be exactly the amount of money the traders start with, that is, $2m$. In particular, if the traders start with no money then the monopolist earns zero profits.

Case 3: If m is intermediate-valued, there is a third case where the traders' cash-flow constraint is tight but their budget constraint is not tight. The monopolist will lend some amount g as is calculated in Appendix B. The traders cannot obtain all of the gains from trade even if they borrow. Appendix B gives conditions under which it is optimal for the monopolist to lend all of his money, but this will not occur if M is large.

For example, suppose $m = \frac{a}{6}$ and $M = a$, so the bank has $\frac{2a}{3}$. It lends approximately $g = 0.16527a$ at a rate of interest of $\rho = 0.64$ and earns a profit of $0.10577a$. If the bank has more money than $\frac{2a}{3}$ it will still lend only $0.16527a$—it is in the monopolist's self-interest to make sure that money is short (competition could weaken this; Shubik, 1976).

A natural question to ask is: How much of a profit can the monopolist extract from the traders as a function of the amount of money they have? Is

---

6 But there could be differences at boundary solutions (e.g., solutions where the bank is altruistic). See the discussion in Section 5.3.

7 A slightly more general model is presented and solved in Chapter 13.

there an amount m such that if each trader type had that amount of money, the profits of the monopolist would be maximized?

THE PARADOX OF THE POWERLESS MONOPOLIST

Using a storable consumable money poses a paradox in monopoly power. Suppose cans of beans are money, and the monopolist has all the cans of beans in the world (so $m = 0$). If her only goal is to maximize her monetary profit, the monopolist is powerless. The simple physics of conservation indicates that in order to make a profit, she must extract money from the traders. So if the traders are endowed with no money, there is no profit to be made.

WEAK OR STRONG PARETO OPTIMALITY?

The monopolist moneylender is trapped by her own wealth. Does she wish merely to hoard all of her wealth until supper time, when she eats it, or is she willing to accept a solution showing that she will go along with weak Pareto optimality? In other words, is she willing to make interest-free loans to the traders, helping them considerably, gaining her nothing, and costing her nothing as she gets her beans back before supper time? If she elects for weak Pareto optimality she is acting as an altruistic bank.[8]

In reality, any dominant moneylender who tries to gouge too hard runs the danger of the game being changed by political action and public revolt. In fact the monetary system is highly porous, and there are many close substitutes; but a full appreciation calls for the examination of the extreme bounding levels of monetary control.

5.2.3 The Monopolist Who Consumes Everything

The second model has a monopolist with a utility function like that of the traders, hence he is active in all markets. A key difference between this model and the first is that now when the traders have no money the monopolist is no longer impotent but can extract essentially all of the gains from trade for himself.

We omit the complete analysis of this model for now, because we solve an equivalent model (which uses fiat money) in Sections 13.3.3 and 13.7.

---

8 The reader will note that in the case $m = 0$, there is a continuum of equilibria in which the monopolist lends out money at interest rate zero (see Case 2 in Appendix B).

5.3 TRADE WITH A STORABLE CONSUMABLE: TWO TRADER TYPES WITH AN ALTRUISTIC MONEYLENDER

We may replace the monopolistic moneylender with an altruistic agent that is interested only in facilitating trade rather than maximizing its own consumption or profits. This implies that this agent's payoff function involves no consumption of commodities. We may interpret this agency as a government central bank with motivations different from those of utility maximizing consumers. Giving it the same resources as the monopolistic moneylender yields some extra modeling issues when there is just enough or more than enough money.

The optimizations for the Type 1 and Type 2 traders are, as before,

$$\max_{b,q,d} \varphi\left(a - q, \frac{b}{p}\right) + m + \frac{d}{1+\rho} - b + pq - d$$

$$\text{s.t. } m + \frac{d}{1+\rho} - b \geq 0 \qquad\qquad (\lambda) \text{ (cash-flow constraint)}$$

$$m + \frac{d}{1+\rho} - b + pq - d \geq 0 \qquad (\mu) \text{ (budget constraint)}$$

$$b, d \geq 0, 0 \leq q \leq a$$

$$(5.11)$$

and

$$\max_{\bar{b},\bar{q},\bar{d}} \varphi\left(\frac{\bar{b}}{p}, a - \bar{q}\right) + m + \frac{\bar{d}}{1+\rho} - \bar{b} + \bar{p}\bar{q} - \bar{d}$$

$$\text{s.t. } m + \frac{\bar{d}}{1+\rho} - \bar{b} \geq 0 \qquad\qquad (\bar{\lambda}) \text{ (cash-flow constraint)}$$

$$m + \frac{\bar{d}}{1+\rho} - \bar{b} + \bar{p}\bar{q} - \bar{d} \geq 0 \qquad (\bar{\mu}) \text{ (budget constraint)}$$

$$\bar{b}, \bar{d} \geq 0, 0 \leq \bar{q} \leq a.$$

Also, the endogenous rate of interest is formed as before:

$$1 + \rho = \frac{d + \bar{d}}{g}. \qquad\qquad (5.12)$$

The only difference between this model and the ones from Section 5.2 is that here the bank is willing to lend all of its money at an interest rate of $\rho = 0$.

In Appendix C we show that if $M \geq a$, the bank can lend enough to the traders to finance efficient consumption. Hence $M \geq a$ is the condition for "enough money." This is to be compared with the condition $m \geq \frac{a}{2}$, which we argued in Section 5.2 was the condition for "enough money w.d." Note that the latter condition implies the former (which must be true given the definitions from Chapter 3).

An interesting comparison between the models of the altruistic central bank and the models of monopolistic private moneylenders from Section 5.2 occurs in the case of "enough money b.d.," that is, when $M \geq a$ but $m < \frac{a}{2}$. The altruistic bank would lend at least $a - 2m$ to the traders and efficient trade is accomplished; the private moneylenders might withhold some of this lending because it benefits themselves.

Suppose $B = M - 2m$ is the central bank's endowment of commodity money. If $B \geq a - 2m$, the total amount of money in the system is at least a; hence there is enough money to finance efficient trade. Like the monopolistic moneylender, the central bank has a choice of naming the interest rate or specifying the amount of loanable funds it wishes to place on the market. But whether it announces an interest rate of $\rho = 0$, or it announces $g \in [a - 2m, B]$ so that the interest rate becomes zero, there is again a coordination problem (see Chapter 4). In addition, the two trader types, each facing an interest rate of $\rho = 0$ and choosing strategies simultaneously, could each choose to borrow arbitrarily high amounts adding up to more than B.

If $B < a - 2m$, then the total amount of money is not sufficient to finance efficient trade. The bank again has the strategic choice of deciding whether to use ρ or g as its strategic variable. In this commodity money world, all it can do is to use its reserves. It cannot print cans of beans.[9] If it offers all of its reserves to the market by setting $g = M - 2m$, a positive rate of interest appears, trade is not efficient, and the central bank makes an undesired profit.[10] If it tries to be more altruistic and sets $\rho = 0$, it then faces a rationing problem and the well-known solution of taking care of "valued customers" and other sociological and informational aspects of distributing a needed rationed resource appear.

The lesson here is that (if there are no binding constraints) although the price of money ρ and the quantity of bank money g are mathematically dual variables, they have different control implications. The bank loses the decentralization and coordination features when ρ is set at zero and it makes an unwanted profit if it uses a quantity strategy.

---

9 In a world with international trade, a gold shortage would result in an importation of gold from the outside. In this simple model this is not feasible.

10 In Chapter 7 (specifically Sections 7.1.3 and 7.4), we observe this result from an equivalent model using fiat money.

Another issue: after the bank has acted and the loans have been repaid, what does the central bank do with its stock of storable consumables? Does it store them in a Fort Knox for cans of beans or bars of chocolate? Alternatively does it distribute them via subsidy to the traders who are deemed to be the owners of the government? If this is literally a one-period game, weak Pareto optimality would call for the altruistic government to liquidate the resources it no longer needs. On the other hand, if we view this as an experimental game to be played more than once, a case can be made for the referee to keep his reserves for another game.

5.4 COMPARING THE MODELS' RESULTS

The resources held by the new large agent can be regarded as central bank reserves. If the bank has no desire to make a profit from its services, it can lend the traders its commodity money in a manner that maximizes the traders' gains from trade.[11] Suppose, for example, that $B = a - 2m$. The altruistic bank will issue all of its money, $\rho = 0$, and efficient trade is achieved.

When we compare this amount of money with the amount issued by the monopolistic lender with only a utility for money, the difference between the two indicates what percent of the valuation of resources of the economy can be extracted. This in essence gives the monetary value of the transaction technology, in the sense that this is the upper bound a "currency controller" utilizing one control variable (ρ or g) could extract from a set of traders who obey the transactions rules.[12]

We now may give a strategic interpretation of the relationship between inside and outside money. If $m_1 + m_2 \geq a$ there are enough "trust-substitute pills" that the central bank has no control over transactions.[13] If the "trust pills" are badly distributed, this can be taken care of by an internal money

---

11 This can be mathematically well defined. The central bank performs a sensitivity analysis over the system as it varies its control variable, utilizing as the optimization criterion a given measure of the welfare of the agents. When the bank has enough money an easy criterion is Pareto optimality of the trade.

12 How to usefully measure the distance that a given allocation is from the Pareto-optimal surface has been a basic problem in the study of trade. See Debreu (1951), Smith and Foley (2008), Dubey and Geanakoplos (2003), Smith and Shubik (2003).

13 As in Chapter 4, m_1 denotes the initial monetary endowment for the Type 1 traders; m_2 for the Type 2 traders.

market. In fact, this requires that the lenders trust a new financial instrument, the IOU notes of the borrowers. If a control agent (a central bank or money-lender) is introduced with $B = a - 2m$, this agent supplies the "trust pills" for the facilitation of trade.

A somewhat different viewpoint emerges when we consider the money-lender who has a utility function like all the others.[14] The measure of monopolistic resource extraction is in terms of all resources, not just the commodity money.

The case where there is just enough money ($M = B + 2m = a$) provides an instructive example whereby we can compare the three models of banking. Key is the ratio of traders' monetary endowment to that of the bank ($\frac{2m}{B}$). The value of the altruistic bank is at its highest when $B = a$ (and $m = 0$), and decreases monotonically until at $B = 0$ ($m = \frac{a}{2}$) it has no power and there is no need for it.[15] In contrast, the money maximizing monopolist is impotent at both ends of the spectrum. It optimizes its profit in the interior where it can extract (via an interest rate or a restricted supply of loans) the most commodity money from the traders, in conformity with monopoly theory. Finally, the case of the general utility maximizing monopolist somewhat resembles the altruistic case. When $B = a$, the monopolist is at her most powerful, as she can extract essentially all of the gains from trade. At the other extreme when $B = 0$, the monopolist obtains nothing.

See also the discussion in Section 13.3.4.

5.5 FROM STORABLE CONSUMABLES TO FIAT

In this chapter we have been concerned with the properties of an economy utilizing a storable consumable means of payment. Although barley, salt bars, and tea bricks have all been used in exchange over the past three thousand years, the era of transactions in gold has dominated that of salt or barley or tea. In the past three hundred years gold has been superseded by fiat money, and in the past half century credit has grown considerably. We suggest that the physical properties of the means of payment, the density of population,

---

14 This is in keeping with the proposition that "The rich are different from us. They have more money."

15 These results are taken from an equivalent fiat money model. See Sections 7.1.3 and 7.4.

and the improvements in communication, information, and credit assessment together with the enforcement of contract in a mass anonymous society have made this a natural progression.

In the next chapters we lay out the path from barley to gold to fiat to credit, in a way that is naturally formalized and subject to formal mathematical modeling. Our concern is to present simple, completely well-defined mathematical models which meet the tests that they can be gamed, simulated, or have certain solutions computed. Our concern is more with the physical justification of the models and their logic than it is with explicit solution or with static equilibrium existence proofs. The vast literature in general equilibrium theory and in noncooperative game theory is such that the proof of existence may be moderately difficult but is reasonably assured. The main problem lies more in the "economic physics" of producing and justifying the appropriate models which are the carriers of process both in equilibrium and out of equilibrium. Our argument is that fiat money is society's substitute for individual trust. These words almost belong to the popular press and common knowledge, but the appropriate mathematization of these words requires some work and is the subject of Chapter 7.

5.6 APPENDIX A: THE RICH LARGE BUYER MODEL

In this Appendix we go back to the basic model of Chapter 3, except that we add a single large buyer, who is endowed with money but no goods of Type 1 or 2. This money-rich agent has a utility function identical to that of all the other traders.

To formalize an example, we put the initial endowment of the Type 1 traders at a units of good 1 and m units of money, while the Type 2 traders have a units of good 2 and m units of money. The large buyer has only $M - 2m$ units of money, where M represents the total amount of money in the game. Again we assume that all of the players' utility functions are $\varphi(x, y) = 2\sqrt{xy}$.

The Type 1 and Type 2 traders' optimization problems and Lagrangian conditions are identical to those from Chapter 3, and we reproduce them here without comment. First, for Type 1 traders

$$\max_{b,q} 2\sqrt{(a-q)\frac{b}{p}} + m + pq - b$$

$$\text{s.t. } m - b \geq 0 \qquad (\lambda) \text{ (cash-flow constraint)}$$

$$b \geq 0, \, 0 \leq q \leq a.$$

The associated first-order conditions for this problem are

$$\frac{1}{\sqrt{\bar{p}}}\sqrt{\frac{a-q}{b}} = 1+\lambda \qquad (5.13)$$

$$\frac{1}{\sqrt{\bar{p}}}\sqrt{\frac{b}{a-q}} = p \qquad (5.14)$$

$$m-b=0 \text{ or } \lambda=0.^{[16]} \qquad (5.15)$$

The Type 2 traders face the following problem:

$$\max_{\bar{b},\bar{q}} 2\sqrt{(a-\bar{q})\frac{\bar{b}}{p}} + m + \bar{p}\bar{q} - \bar{b}$$

s.t. $m - \bar{b} \geq 0$ \qquad (λ) (cash-flow constraint)

$\bar{b} \geq 0, 0 \leq \bar{q} \leq a.$

The first-order equations here are

$$\frac{1}{\sqrt{p}}\sqrt{\frac{a-\bar{q}}{\bar{b}}} = 1+\bar{\lambda} \qquad (5.16)$$

$$\frac{1}{\sqrt{p}}\sqrt{\frac{\bar{b}}{a-\bar{q}}} = p \qquad (5.17)$$

$$m-\bar{b}=0 \text{ or } \bar{\lambda}=0. \qquad (5.18)$$

The rich large buyer's problem is to decide how much of his money to bid for Type 1 goods, to bid for Type 2 goods, and to hoard.[17] Hence his decision variables will be b_1^* and b_2^*, where b_1^* is the amount he bids for Type 1 goods and b_2^* is the amount he bids for Type 2 goods. His payoff is simply the amount of utility he gets from consuming Type 1 and Type 2 goods, plus that from leftover commodity money, that is,

$$2\sqrt{\frac{b_1^* b_2^*}{p\bar{p}}} + M - 2m - b_1^* - b_2^*. \qquad (5.19)$$

---

16 This notation is shorthand for "($m-b=0$ and $\lambda \geq 0$) or ($m-b \geq 0$ and $\lambda=0$)," as in (3.5) in the Appendix to Chapter 3. We use this shorthand throughout the rest of the book (and we provide ample footnoting to remind the reader).

17 The amount of money hoarded is simply the slack variable in his cash-flow constraint ((λ_p) below).

However, the buyer's bids, unlike the traders', can influence price. This is because she is a single large trader, not a continuum of infinitesimal price-taking individuals like our Type 1 and Type 2 traders. Hence p and $\bar{p}$ must be modeled as dependent on b_1^* and b_2^*. In fact, since $p = \dfrac{b_1^* + \int_\alpha \bar{b}^\alpha}{\int_\alpha q^\alpha} = \dfrac{b_1^* + \bar{b}}{q}$ and $\bar{p} = \dfrac{b_2^* + \int_\alpha b^\alpha}{\int_\alpha \bar{q}^\alpha} = \dfrac{b_2^* + b}{\bar{q}}$, the buyer's optimization problem becomes

$$\max_{b_1^*, b_2^*} 2\sqrt{\frac{q b_1^*}{(b_1^* + \bar{b})} \frac{\bar{q} b_2^*}{(b_2^* + b)}} + M - 2m - b_1^* - b_2^*$$

$$\text{s.t. } M - 2m - b_1^* - b_2^* \geq 0 \qquad\qquad (\lambda_P)$$

$$b_1^*,\, b_2^* \geq 0.$$

(5.20)

The first-order Lagrangian conditions, with respect to the decision variables b_1^* and b_2^*, are

$$\sqrt{\frac{\bar{q} b_2^*}{(b_2^* + b)} \frac{(b_1^* + \bar{b})}{q b_1^*}} \frac{\bar{b} q}{(b_1^* + \bar{b})^2} = 1 + \lambda_P \qquad\qquad (5.21)$$

$$\sqrt{\frac{q b_1^*}{(b_1^* + \bar{b})} \frac{(b_2^* + b)}{\bar{q} b_2^*}} \frac{b \bar{q}}{(b_2^* + b)^2} = 1 + \lambda_P \qquad\qquad (5.22)$$

$$M - 2m - b_1^* - b_2^* = 0 \text{ or } \lambda_P = 0.^{[18]} \qquad\qquad (5.23)$$

Once again, using the assumption of symmetry (see Section 3.2), we have $p = \bar{p}$, $q = \bar{q}$, $b = \bar{b}$, and $b_1^* = b_2^*$. One consequence of this is that conditions (5.21) and (5.22) simplify to

$$\frac{\bar{b} q}{(b_1^* + \bar{b})^2} = 1 + \lambda_P \qquad\qquad (5.24)$$

$$\frac{b \bar{q}}{(b_2^* + b)^2} = 1 + \lambda_P \qquad\qquad (5.25)$$

Finally, the balancing constraints (see above) are as follows:

$$p = \frac{b_1^* + \bar{b}}{q} \text{ and } \bar{p} = \frac{b_2^* + b}{\bar{q}}. \qquad\qquad (5.26)$$

---

18 Once again, this notation is shorthand for "($M - 2m - b_1^* - b_2^* = 0$ and $\lambda_P \geq 0$) or ($M - 2m - b_1^* - b_2^* \geq 0$ and $\lambda_P = 0$)" (compare with footnote 16).

Case 1: We first consider the case where m is large. Here the traders' cash-flow constraints are nonbinding, so $\lambda = \bar{\lambda} = 0$. Hence (5.14) implies $\sqrt{\frac{a-q}{b}} = \frac{1}{p\sqrt{\bar{p}}}$ and so (5.13) implies $p = \bar{p} = 1$ (and so $q \neq 0$ by the balancing constraint). Recombining with (5.13) gives $\frac{a-q}{b} = 1$. But then (5.24), symmetry, and the balancing constraint (with $p = 1$) give $\bar{b}q = (b_1^* + \bar{b})^2(1 + \lambda_P) = q^2(1 + \lambda_P)$. Hence $b = q(1 + \lambda_P) = \bar{b}$. But then $1 = p = \frac{b_1^* + \bar{b}}{q} = \frac{b_1^* + q(1+\lambda_P)}{q} \Rightarrow b_1^* + q\lambda_P = 0$. But q is positive and both b_1^* and λ_P are nonnegative; hence $b_1^* = \lambda_P = 0$. So $b = q(1 + \lambda_P) = q$, and $\frac{a-q}{b} = 1$ implies $b = q = \bar{b} = \bar{q} = \frac{a}{2}$. Also, b_1^* and b_2^* are both equal to 0. Hence in this case the large buyer keeps his money and consumes nothing, while the trader types consume $(\frac{a}{2}, \frac{a}{2})$.

We remark that in order for the above results to hold, the cash-flow constraints must be satisfied. In this case this means that $m \geq \frac{a}{2}$. So this is the precise definition of "m is large."

Case 2: In this case, m is small and M is large. So the traders have little money, but the rich monopolist has a lot of money. Hence we expect the traders' cash-flow constraints to be tight and the monopolist's to be loose. In mathematical terms, this means λ and $\bar{\lambda}$ are positive, while $\lambda_P = 0$. The immediate consequence of this is that $b = \bar{b} = m$.

As in Case 1 we first use (5.14) and (5.13) to calculate an expression for price—but here we get $p = \bar{p} = \frac{1}{\sqrt{1+\lambda}}$. But then (5.13) implies $\frac{1}{p}\frac{a-q}{b} = (1 + \lambda)^2$, which gives $q = a - pb(1 + \lambda)^2 = a - m(1 + \lambda)^{3/2} = \bar{q}$.

Next, since $p = \bar{p} = \frac{1}{\sqrt{1+\lambda}}$, the balancing conditions give $b + b_2^* = \frac{q}{\sqrt{1+\lambda}}$. This implies $b + b_2^* = \frac{a}{\sqrt{1+\lambda}} - m(1 + \lambda)$. Since $b = m$, this gives $b_2^* = \frac{a}{\sqrt{1+\lambda}} - m(2 + \lambda) = b_1^*$.

We also have $bq = (b_1^* + b)^2$. This gives $m(a - m(1 + \lambda)^{3/2}) = (\frac{a}{\sqrt{1+\lambda}} - m(1 + \lambda))^2 = \frac{1}{1+\lambda}(a - m(1 + \lambda)^{3/2})^2$, which is

$$(1 + \lambda)^{3/2} + (1 + \lambda) = \frac{a}{m}. \tag{5.27}$$

We remark that since $p = \frac{1}{\sqrt{1+\lambda}}$, this can be written as (compare with (3.11) from the Chapter 3 Appendix):

$$\frac{1}{p^3} + \frac{1}{p^2} = \frac{a}{m}. \tag{5.28}$$

We also remark that in order for the above analysis to be valid, it must be that condition (λ_P) must hold; that is, $M - 2m - b_1^* - b_2^* \geq 0$. Substituting in the solutions obtained above, this condition (which is what we mean by "M is large") becomes

$$\frac{M}{2} \geq \frac{a}{\sqrt{1+\lambda}} - m(1+\lambda). \tag{5.29}$$

Next, we provide an example. Suppose $m = \frac{a}{12}$ and $M - 2m = \frac{a}{3}$ (so $M = \frac{a}{2}$). Then equation (5.27) gives $\lambda = 3$, and then we may compute $b = \bar{b} = \frac{a}{12}$, $p = \bar{p} = \frac{1}{2}$, $q = \bar{q} = \frac{a}{3}$, and $b_1^* = b_2^* = \frac{a}{12}$. Note also that condition (5.29) holds.

Finally, we observe what happens as $m \to 0$. First, since $b = \bar{b} = m$, we have $b \to 0$ (and $\bar{b} \to 0$). Next, we observe (5.27), which can be rewritten as $m = \frac{a}{(1+\lambda)^{3/2} + (1+\lambda)}$. But this implies $q = \bar{q} = a - m(1+\lambda)^{3/2} = a - \frac{a(1+\lambda)^{3/2}}{(1+\lambda)^{3/2} + (1+\lambda)}$. Now, as $m \to 0$ (5.27) implies that $\lambda \to \infty$. But this in turn implies that $q \to 0$ (and $\bar{q} \to 0$). Next, $b_1^* = b_2^* = \frac{a}{\sqrt{1+\lambda}} - m(2+\lambda) = \frac{a}{\sqrt{1+\lambda}} - \frac{a(2+\lambda)}{(1+\lambda)^{3/2} + (1+\lambda)}$. As $\lambda \to \infty$, this too approaches zero.

Case 3: The final case is where both M and m are small. This means that constraints (λ), $(\bar{\lambda})$, and (λ_P) are tight; that is, $\lambda = \bar{\lambda} > 0$ and $\lambda_P > 0$. Hence $b = \bar{b} = m$ and $b_1^* = b_2^* = \frac{M}{2} - m$. So in order to solve the model all we have to do is find p and q.

As above, we may use the Lagrangian conditions on the traders' problems to arrive at $p = \bar{p} = \frac{1}{\sqrt{1+\lambda}}$ and $q = \bar{q} = a - m(1+\lambda)^{3/2}$. To find λ, note that $p = \frac{b_1^* + \bar{b}}{q} \Rightarrow \frac{1}{\sqrt{1+\lambda}} = \frac{M}{2} \frac{1}{a - m(1+\lambda)^{3/2}}$. Cross-multiplying gives $\frac{M\sqrt{1+\lambda}}{2} = a - m(1+\lambda)^{3/2}$, or $\frac{1}{\sqrt{1+\lambda}} - \frac{m}{a}(1+\lambda) = \frac{M}{2a}$.

Summarizing, our solution is: $b = \bar{b} = m$, $b_1^* = b_2^* = \frac{M}{2} - m$, $p = \bar{p} = \frac{1}{\sqrt{1+\lambda}}$, and $q = \bar{q} = a - m(1+\lambda)^{3/2}$, where λ satisfies $\frac{1}{\sqrt{1+\lambda}} - \frac{m}{a}(1+\lambda) = \frac{M}{2a}$.

5.7 APPENDIX B: TRADE WITH A MONEY MAXIMIZING LENDER

Both trader types are endowed with m units of commodity money. The monopolistic moneylender is endowed with $M - 2m$ units of money (where $0 \leq 2m \leq M$). The lender's objective is solely to end up with the most possible money.

The Type 1 traders face an optimization described by:

$$\max_{b,q,d} 2\sqrt{(a-q)\frac{b}{\bar{p}}} + m + \frac{d}{1+\rho} - b + pq - d \qquad \text{(a)}$$

$$\text{s.t. } m + \frac{d}{1+\rho} - b \geq 0 \qquad (\lambda)\ (\text{cash-flow constraint}) \quad \text{(b)}$$

$$m + \frac{d}{1+\rho} - b + pq - d \geq 0 \qquad (\mu)\ (\text{budget constraint}) \quad \text{(c)}$$

$$b, d \geq 0, 0 \leq q \leq a. \qquad \text{(d)}$$

$$(5.30)$$

The first-order conditions wrt b, q, and d yield[19]

$$\frac{1}{\sqrt{\bar{p}}}\sqrt{\frac{a-q}{b}} = 1 + \lambda + \mu \qquad (5.31)$$

$$\frac{1}{\sqrt{\bar{p}}}\sqrt{\frac{b}{a-q}} = p + \mu p \qquad (5.32)$$

$$\frac{1}{1+\rho} - 1 + \frac{\lambda}{1+\rho} + \frac{\mu}{1+\rho} - \mu = 0 \qquad (5.33)$$

$$m + \frac{d}{1+\rho} - b = 0 \text{ or } \lambda = 0 \qquad (5.34)$$

$$m + \frac{d}{1+\rho} - b + pq - d = 0 \text{ or } \mu = 0 \qquad (5.35)$$

Similarly, the Type 2 traders face the optimization below:

$$\max_{\bar{b},\bar{q},\bar{d}} 2\sqrt{(a-\bar{q})\frac{\bar{b}}{p}} + m + \frac{\bar{d}}{1+\rho} - \bar{b} + \bar{p}\bar{q} - \bar{d} \qquad \text{(a)}$$

$$\text{s.t. } m + \frac{\bar{d}}{1+\rho} - \bar{b} \geq 0 \qquad (\bar{\lambda})\ (\text{cash-flow constraint}) \quad \text{(b)}$$

$$m + \frac{\bar{d}}{1+\rho} - \bar{b} + \bar{p}\bar{q} - \bar{d} \geq 0 \qquad (\bar{\mu})\ (\text{budget constraint}) \quad \text{(c)}$$

$$\bar{b}, \bar{d} \geq 0, 0 \leq \bar{q} \leq a. \qquad \text{(d)}$$

$$(5.36)$$

---

19 In the conditions below, the notation "$m + \frac{d}{1+\rho} - b = 0$ or $\lambda = 0$" means "($m + \frac{d}{1+\rho} - b = 0$ and $\lambda \geq 0$) or ($m + \frac{d}{1+\rho} - b \geq 0$ and $\lambda = 0$)," while the notation "$m + \frac{d}{1+\rho} - b + pq - d = 0$ or $\mu = 0$" means "($m + \frac{d}{1+\rho} - b + pq - d = 0$ and $\mu \geq 0$) or ($m + \frac{d}{1+\rho} - b + pq - d \geq 0$ and $\mu = 0$)."

The optimization conditions here are

$$\frac{1}{\sqrt{\bar{p}}}\sqrt{\frac{a-\bar{q}}{\bar{b}}} = 1 + \bar{\lambda} + \bar{\mu} \tag{5.37}$$

$$\frac{1}{\sqrt{\bar{p}}}\sqrt{\frac{\bar{b}}{a-\bar{q}}} = \bar{p} + \bar{\mu}\bar{p} \tag{5.38}$$

$$\frac{1}{1+\rho} - 1 + \frac{\bar{\lambda}}{1+\rho} + \frac{\bar{\mu}}{1+\rho} - \bar{\mu} = 0 \tag{5.39}$$

$$m + \frac{\bar{d}}{1+\rho} - \bar{b} = 0 \text{ or } \bar{\lambda} = 0 \tag{5.40}$$

$$m + \frac{\bar{d}}{1+\rho} - \bar{b} + \bar{p}\bar{q} - \bar{d} = 0 \text{ or } \bar{\mu} = 0. \tag{5.41}$$

The banker's optimization is expressed as:

$$\max_{g \text{ or } \rho} M - 2m + \rho g(\rho)$$
$$\text{s.t. } M - 2m - g(\rho) \geq 0 \quad (\lambda_B)$$
$$\text{and } g \text{ or } \rho \geq 0.$$

Finally, the balance conditions are $p = \frac{\bar{b}}{q}$, $\bar{p} = \frac{b}{\bar{q}}$ and $1 + \rho = \frac{d+\bar{d}}{g}$.

Our general approach here is to first solve the traders' problems, and then solve the banker's problem once we know what the traders do as a function of ρ. In essence we solve the trading problem parametrically for ρ, then consider $g(\rho)$ and optimize. Game-theoretically, we can imagine an extensive form game in which the lender moves first, followed by the traders. We then find the perfect equilibrium for the game.

We remark that here again the problems for Types 1 and 2 are isomorphic and so we may assume a symmetric solution where $b = \bar{b}$, $d = \bar{d}$, $p = \bar{p}$, and $q = \bar{q}$.

Case 1: First we consider the case where m is large. In this instance neither the cash-flow constraint nor the budget constraint is binding for the traders; that is, $\lambda = \mu = \bar{\lambda} = \bar{\mu} = 0$. Hence (5.31) implies $\frac{1}{\sqrt{\bar{p}}}\sqrt{\frac{a-q}{b}} = 1$, which gives $p = \bar{p} = \frac{a-q}{b}$. Also (5.32) implies $p\sqrt{\bar{p}} = \sqrt{\frac{b}{a-q}}$, which is $p^3 = \frac{b}{a-q}$. Hence $p = \frac{1}{p^3}$, which gives $p = \bar{p} = 1$.

Next, the balancing conditions give $1 = p = \frac{\bar{b}}{q} = \frac{b}{q}$, so $b = q$. Since also $1 = p = \frac{a-q}{b}$, we have $b = \bar{b} = q = \bar{q} = \frac{a}{2}$.

Next, we note that equation (5.33) (with $\lambda = \mu = 0$) implies $\rho = 0$. Hence the bank gains zero profits.

At the end of Case 3, we argue that if $0 < m < \frac{a}{2}$, the bank can earn positive profits by choosing a positive interest rate and forcing the traders' cash-flow constraints to be tight. Hence, the above results (in which the bank gains zero profits) cannot possibly be part of a perfect equilibrium. This in turn implies that the mathematical condition for Case 1 is $m \geq \frac{a}{2}$.[20]

Finally, we note that none of this analysis has placed any limits on $d = \bar{d}$. In fact, there is a degree of freedom here—d can take on any value in the interval $[0, \frac{M-2m}{2}]$, with $\bar{d} = d$ and $g = 2d$.

Case 2: The second case is where m is very small: In this instance both the cash-flow and budget constraints will hold with equality, so $m + \frac{d}{1+\rho} - b = 0$ and $pq = d$. In addition, λ, μ, $\bar{\lambda}$, and $\bar{\mu}$ can all be positive.

First, we note that $pq = d$ (see above) and $pq = \bar{b} = b$ (balancing condition plus symmetry). Hence $b = d$ $(= \bar{b} = \bar{d})$. Hence, the cash-flow constraint $m + \frac{d}{1+\rho} - b = 0$ implies

$$m + \frac{b}{1+\rho} - b = 0. \tag{5.42}$$

If $m > 0$, this in turn gives $b = \frac{1+\rho}{\rho} m = d = \bar{b} = \bar{d}$. Furthermore,

$$g = g(\rho) = \frac{d + \bar{d}}{1+\rho} = \frac{\frac{2(1+\rho)}{\rho} m}{1+\rho} = \frac{2m}{\rho}. \tag{5.43}$$

Hence the banker maximizes $\rho g(\rho) = \rho(\frac{2m}{\rho}) = 2m$. In other words, the bank's profits are $2m$ no matter what he does. Formally he can set g anywhere in $(0, M - 2m]$, with $\rho = \frac{2m}{g}$, and attain profits of $2m$. Another way to say this is that the function $g(\rho)$ has unit elasticity.

Since the bank is indifferent among its feasible strategies, it may wish to choose a policy by which it would benefit the traders most. If so, it will set g as high as possible and ρ as low as possible; that is, $g = M - 2m$ and $\rho = \frac{2m}{M-2m}$.

---

20 As we shall see, the case $m = 0$ yields a continuum of equilibria and doesn't really fit neatly into any of the three cases. Somewhat arbitrarily, we analyze it below in Case 2.

Given the values of g and ρ the bank sets, we may now calculate the optimal values of the traders' decision variables. Note that we've already calculated $b = d = \bar{b} = \bar{d} = \frac{1+\rho}{\rho} m$.

First, we have (5.32) implies $\sqrt{\frac{a-q}{b}} = \frac{1}{p\sqrt{\bar{p}(1+\mu)}}$. Together with (5.31) this implies $\frac{1}{p\bar{p}} = (1 + \lambda + \mu)(1 + \mu)$, for which symmetry implies $p = \bar{p} = \frac{1}{\sqrt{(1+\lambda+\mu)(1+\mu)}}$. Now (5.33) implies $\lambda = \rho(1 + \mu)$, so $p = \bar{p} = \frac{1}{\sqrt{1+\rho}(1+\mu)}$. Thus $p(1 + \mu) = \frac{1}{\sqrt{1+\rho}}$. But then (5.32) $\Rightarrow \sqrt{\frac{a-q}{b}} = \frac{1}{p\sqrt{\bar{p}(1+\mu)}} = \frac{\sqrt{1+\rho}}{\sqrt{\bar{p}}}$; that is, $\frac{a-q}{b} = \frac{1+\rho}{\bar{p}}$. Hence $\frac{a-q}{\bar{p}q} = \frac{1+\rho}{\bar{p}}$. Rearranging, we have $q = \frac{a}{2+\rho} = \bar{q}$. Also, $p = \frac{\bar{b}}{q} = \frac{\frac{1+\rho}{\rho} m}{\frac{a}{2+\rho}} = \frac{(1+\rho)(2+\rho)m}{\rho a} = \bar{p}$.

In the case where $m = 0$, equation (5.42) implies that either (a) $b = d = \bar{b} = \bar{d} = 0$ or (b) $\rho = 0$. In both cases (one where the traders borrow nothing, and one where the interest rate on loans is zero), the bank earns profit of zero. In (a) we obtain an equilibrium with no trade, which is of less interest to us. In (b) we have a continuum of symmetric equilibria, each with $\rho = 0$, $q = \frac{a}{2}$, $b = d = \bar{b} = \bar{d} \in (0, \frac{M}{2}]$, $g = 2d$, and $p = \frac{b}{q} = \frac{2b}{a}$. Note that the values for ρ and q represent limiting values from the $m > 0$ case, but $b = d = \bar{b} = \bar{d}$ now has a degree of freedom.

Next, for the multipliers, we have

$$1 + \mu = \frac{1}{p\sqrt{1+\rho}} = \begin{cases} \frac{\rho a}{(1+\rho)^{3/2}(2+\rho)m}, & \text{if } m > 0 \\ \frac{a}{2b}, & \text{if } m = 0 \end{cases}$$
(5.44)

$$\lambda = \rho(1 + \mu) = \begin{cases} \frac{\rho^2 a}{(1+\rho)^{3/2}(2+\rho)m}, & \text{if } m > 0 \\ 0, & \text{if } m = 0. \end{cases}$$

We remark that the quantities above are valid so long as the multiplier μ is nonnegative. This gives a condition of

$$\frac{1}{p\sqrt{1+\rho}} \geq 1 \Rightarrow \begin{cases} \frac{m}{a} \leq \frac{\rho}{(1+\rho)^{3/2}(2+\rho)}, & \text{if } m > 0 \\ b \leq \frac{a}{2}, & \text{if } m = 0. \end{cases}$$
(5.45)

Finally, note that the maximum value of $\frac{\rho}{(1+\rho)^{3/2}(2+\rho)}$ (on the interval $\rho \in [0, \infty)$) is about 0.12, which is much less than one half. Hence "Case 1" and "Case 2" do not cover all possibilities; that is, we must have at least one "intermediate value for m" case.

Case 3:   Now suppose that neither Case 1 nor Case 2 holds. Hence exactly one of the constraints (λ) and (μ) holds tightly. But just as with the borrowers' problem in the money market model, it is impossible for (μ) to hold tightly but not (λ).[21] Hence the only case to consider here is for $\lambda > 0$ (so $m + \frac{d}{1+\rho} - b = 0$) and $\mu = 0$. Also, $\bar{\lambda} = \lambda > 0$ and $\bar{\mu} = 0$.

First, note that (5.33) implies $\lambda = \rho$.

Next, we see that (5.31) is $\frac{1}{\sqrt{\bar{p}}}\sqrt{\frac{a-q}{b}} = 1 + \lambda$ and (5.32) implies $\sqrt{\frac{a-\bar{q}}{b}} = \frac{1}{p\sqrt{\bar{p}}}$, hence $\frac{1}{p\bar{p}} = 1 + \lambda$. Using symmetry, we have $p = \bar{p} = \frac{1}{\sqrt{1+\lambda}} = \frac{1}{\sqrt{1+\rho}}$.

Next, since $m - b + \frac{d}{1+\rho} = 0$ and $m - \bar{b} + \frac{\bar{d}}{1+\rho} = 0$, we have $b + \bar{b} = \frac{d+\bar{d}}{1+\rho} + 2m = g + 2m$. But now, since $\frac{\bar{b}}{q} = p = \bar{p} = \frac{b}{\bar{q}}$, we have $\frac{b+\bar{b}}{q+\bar{q}} = \frac{1}{\sqrt{1+\rho}}$, which is $q + \bar{q} = \sqrt{1+\rho}(b + \bar{b}) = \sqrt{1+\rho}(g + 2m)$.

Next, we see that (5.31) implies $\frac{1}{\bar{p}}\frac{a-q}{b} = (1+\lambda)^2 = (1+\rho)^2$, so $\frac{a-q}{b} = (1+\rho)^{3/2} = \frac{a-\bar{q}}{\bar{b}}$. This implies $(1+\rho)^{3/2} = \frac{2a-q-\bar{q}}{b+\bar{b}} = \frac{2a-\sqrt{1+\rho}(g+2m)}{g+2m} = \frac{2a}{g+2m} - \sqrt{1+\rho}$. Rearranging gives

$$g = g(\rho) = \frac{2a}{(1+\rho)^{3/2} + (1+\rho)^{1/2}} - 2m. \tag{5.46}$$

This implies

$$b = \bar{b} = \frac{g+2m}{2} = \frac{a}{(1+\rho)^{3/2} + (1+\rho)^{1/2}}. \tag{5.47}$$

Also,

$$q = \bar{q} = \frac{\sqrt{1+\rho}(g+2m)}{2} = \frac{a}{2+\rho}. \tag{5.48}$$

The banker will choose ρ so as to maximize $\rho g(\rho) = \frac{2a\rho}{(1+\rho)^{3/2}+(1+\rho)^{1/2}} - 2m\rho$. This can be done computationally. Two comments:

(1) We remark that the maximization is valid only so long as M is large enough so that the ρ so obtained does not cause $g(\rho)$ to be more than $M - 2m$. This is certainly true if $M \geq a$. Otherwise, $g(\rho)$ will stay at the bound of

---

21 To repeat the argument from the money market model: (μ) tight and (λ) loose implies $d > 0$, which in turn implies Type 1 traders could improve by simultaneously raising b and lowering d.

$M - 2m$ and ρ will satisfy $\frac{2a}{(1+\rho)^{3/2}+(1+\rho)^{1/2}} = M$. (The formulas for the other variables follow, using this "modified" value of ρ.)

(2) Suppose $m \in (0, \frac{a}{2})$. If (5.45) holds, we are in Case 2 and the bank gains positive optimal profits by choosing a positive ρ. If (5.45) does not hold, then in Case 3 there must exist a small positive ρ such that $\rho g(\rho) = \rho(\frac{2a}{(1+\rho)^{3/2}+(1+\rho)^{1/2}} - 2m) > 0$. This compares with $\rho g(\rho) = 0$ if $\rho = 0$. Hence again the bank's optimal strategy is to choose a positive ρ to gain positive profits. These conclusions are important in our analysis of Case 1.

5.8 APPENDIX C: TRADE WITH AN ALTRUISTIC BANK

In this section we replace the profit maximizing bank from Appendix B with an altruistic bank which is willing to lend money at an interest rate of zero. Our purpose here is to derive conditions under which such a bank could finance efficient trade.

Again the models for the traders are given by conditions (5.30a–d) and (5.36a–d), with first-order conditions (5.31)–(5.35) and (5.37)–(5.41). From these, we again can derive (in the case where the traders' cash-flow and budget constraints are nonbinding) that $p = \bar{p} = 1$, $b = \bar{b} = q = \bar{q} = \frac{a}{2}$, and $\rho = 0$.

We ask: How much do the traders need to borrow in order to finance efficient trade? We do have that $d = \bar{d}$ must lie in the interval $[0, \frac{M-2m}{2}]$; otherwise the two trader types together will be borrowing more than the bank has. Also, the cash-flow constraint must hold; this requires $d \geq b - m = \frac{a}{2} - m$. Putting these together gives an interval of $[\max(\frac{a}{2} - m, 0), \frac{M-2m}{2}]$ for d; this interval is nonempty so long as $M \geq a$. Thus we conclude that if $M \geq a$ the altruistic bank can finance efficient trade; that is, $M \geq a$ is the requirement for "enough money."

Chapter 6 Markets with Gold

6.1 FROM A CONSUMABLE STORABLE TO GOLD

In Chapters 3, 4, and 5 our concern was with the use of a storable consumable as a means of payment. In this chapter we repeat the analysis, in the case where the money is a durable asset which provides a stream of services. The properties of the durable together with the timing of markets provide a means to illustrate the relationship among consumable storable, durable, and fiat monies.[1]

---

1 Work on a topic as broad, basic, and diffuse as the theory of money contains large elements of synthesis as well as analysis. Thus it rarely, if ever, can be attributed to a single individual as in a theorem in pure mathematics. We cannot do justice to the work of the many authors whose work has influenced our thoughts. However, we have been influenced in particular by Allais (1947), Baumol (1952), Bewley (1980), Friedman (1969), Grandmont (1982), Grandmont and Younes (1972), Gurley and Shaw (1960), Hahn (1965), Lucas (1980), Magill and Quinzii (1992), Samuelson (1958), and Tobin (1982b), as well as by many collaborations with Dubey, Geanakoplos, and Shapley.

We stress our belief that seemingly minor institutional details such as the physical differences among storable consumables (barley), durables (gold), or fiat (base metal coin, paper banknotes, checks, or ciphers in a computer system) are vital to the understanding of money. They might be easily dismissed as too minor to be worth examination. But these details reflect the progressive complication of an exchange system starting from force, through barter, barley, gold, silver by weight, coin, bills of exchange, and banknotes, until pure electronic messages are reached. The nature of expectations and enforcement of implicit or explicit contract differs with each exchange technology. The models here provide some insights into these differences.

6.2 MODELS OF MARKETS WITH GOLD

Gold, silver, and other metals have all been utilized as a durable money. They all have the property that one can use the durable as a money in transactions or can use its services for consumption or production and at the end of the period still have the asset.

Table 6.1 shows the different treatments for trade with a durable money. Once again the columns represent the models we cover, while the rows represent types of agents. A cell with a "no" means that the corresponding type of agent is not present in the corresponding economy. Otherwise, the triples show the initial endowments of the two types of good and the durable money. As discussed below, the somewhat cumbersome notation $[m, \dot{m}]$ stands for the asset and the service it can render.

Table 6.1. Trade with gold

	Cash only	Money market	Central bank
Type 1 traders	$(a, 0, [m, \dot{m}])$	$(a, 0, [m, \dot{m}])$	$(a, 0, [m, \dot{m}])$
Type 2 traders	$(0, a, [m, \dot{m}])$	$(0, a, [m, \dot{m}])$	$(0, a, [m, \dot{m}])$
Central bank	No	No	$(0, 0, [(M - 2m), (\dot{M} - 2\dot{m})])$

A recent study of referencing in economics papers indicates that almost all of the references are to works of the past two to three years. Yet economic theory calls for a process of accretion. We cannot spend too much of our time constantly referencing the distant past, but it behooves us to remember the basic contributions of many great minds. In monetary theory, as approached here our intellectual debt to the following historical figures is considerable: Böhm-Bawerk, Cournot, Edgeworth, Fisher, Hicks, Hume, Jevons, Keynes, Menger, Ricardo, Simmel, von Mises, Wicksell, and Walras.

6.3 TWO TRADER TYPES TRADING WITH GOLD

6.3.1 Stocks and Flows

We consider two types of traders, trading in two goods, in a one-period game. As before, we assume that: (a) the Type 1 traders are endowed only with good 1; (b) the Type 2 traders are endowed only with good 2; and (c) there is a continuum of each trader type. A strategy for the Type 1 traders is denoted by (b, q), where b is the amount of gold bid for good 2 and q is the amount of good 1 offered for sale. The notation for the Type 2 traders is $(\bar{b}, \bar{q})$. We remind the reader that these strategies represent aggregations over the continuum of individual traders; for details see Chapter 3. The price p of good 1 (or price $\bar{p}$ of good 2) will then be formed in the usual strategic market game way, that is, by dividing the total amount of money bid for the good by the total amount of good put up for sale.

The Type 1 traders have total endowment $(a, 0, [m, \dot{m}])$, while the Type 2 traders have $(0, a, [m, \dot{m}])$. The reader will notice that these endowments are the same as in the basic model, except that here we distinguish between the asset gold and the stream of services it yields. The asset is a "stock variable," measured in some physical units. The services, by contrast, are a "flow variable," and so would be measured in units per unit of time. To distinguish the two types of variables, we use the "dot" notation, so m denotes the initial endowment of the asset gold, while $\dot{m}$ denotes the initial endowment of the gold's services. The dot notation is also used for other variables; hence, for example, $\dot{b}$ represents the amount of gold services the Type 1 traders bid in an effort to obtain good 2.[2] Also, "$\dot{I}$" will stand for the amount of gold services received in payment for the sale of q units of perishable sold at a price of p. Likewise, for Type 2 traders, $\bar{\dot{I}}$ is the amount of gold services received for $\bar{q}$ units of perishable at price $\bar{p}$.

We note that the asset and the service are bundled together, and unless we introduce a rental market they are sold together. In this model we do not have such a rental market; hence in what follows, necessarily always $\dot{b} = b$, $\bar{\dot{b}} = \bar{b}$, $\dot{I} = pq$, $\bar{\dot{I}} = \bar{p}\bar{q}$, and $\dot{m} = m$.[3]

---

2 It should be noted that there are strategic operational differences between (a) buying an asset, utilizing its services, and then selling it in a buy-back or in the market; and (b) renting the asset to use its services. Ownership changes in (a), but not in (b).

3 More precisely, we can select units such that one unit of the asset gold yields one unit of gold services in one unit of time, i.e., $m = \int_{t=0}^{1} \dot{m} \, dt$.

Finally, we assume that both trader types have the same utility function $\varphi(x, y) + \dot{z}$, where x and y represent the amounts of good 1 and good 2 consumed, φ is a concave function increasing in both variables, and $\dot{z}$ stands for the consumption services of (z units of) the asset. There is also the possibility that the traders will assign a salvage value to any leftover asset at the end of the game; we model this as well below.

6.3.2 Slicing up the Trading Day

In this model there are three aspects of gold to which value is attached. They are its value as an ornament, its value in transactions, and its residual value as an asset with a possible salvage value at the end of the game (Shubik, 1999b). At any particular point in time, only one of these aspects can be utilized. Hence, in order to fully define the optimization over the period we must indicate who gets to use the services of the asset, when transactions are made, and how the asset is evaluated at the end.

Type 1 traders attempt to maximize:

$$
\begin{aligned}
\max_{b,q} \varphi & \left(a - q, \frac{b}{p} \right) + k_2 \dot{m} + (k_3 - k_2)(\dot{m} - \dot{b}) \\
& + (1 - k_3)(\dot{m} - \dot{b} + \dot{I}) + \Pi(m - b + pq) \quad\quad &\text{(a)} \\
\text{s.t. } & m - b \geq 0 \quad\quad &(\lambda) \quad &\text{(b)} \\
& m - b + pq \geq 0 \quad\quad &(\mu) \quad &\text{(c)} \\
& b \geq 0, \ 0 \leq q \leq a. \quad\quad &\text{(d)}
\end{aligned}
\qquad (6.1)
$$

Here k_2 is the proportion of the time period that passes before the goods market opens; $k_3 - k_2$ is the proportion taken up by the market, when the consumption use of the gold used in transactions is lost; and $1 - k_3$ is the proportion of the period after the market, when the consumption use of gold is enjoyed by the final owner of the asset (k_1 will be defined later). The time period $[k_2, k_3]$, when goods are traded, is the zone for lawyers, brokers, and accountants. Buyers of the perishable have given up the use of the gold, but sellers have not yet obtained its use.

The parameter Π is the per-unit salvage value for the gold at the end of the game (see Section 6.3.5).

We note in the objective function above that the two arguments for φ are quantities of point consumption perishables; hence there is no need to distinguish between their stock and flow. However, the distinction must be made for the services of the gold. The numbers k_t have the dimension of time, thus $k_2 \dot{m}$ (more precisely, $\int_{t=0}^{k_2} \dot{m} dt$) stands for the consumption services of gold rendered over the interval $[0, k_2]$. The amount pq is the amount of gold earned as income from the sale of good 1, credited at time k_3. The amount $\dot{I}$ indicates the service stream available from this gold.

We point out here that our model posits no costs in switching from gold coin (the "transaction" use of gold) to jewelry (its "ornamental" use) and vice versa. Although logically feasible, this assumption is clearly counterfactual. Somewhat fancifully (but anthropologically soundly), we could imagine wearing the coins as jewelry attached to a bracelet and taking them off to make payments. In actuality, it takes time and expense to melt down jewelry into gold coins, or vice versa. So more realistically, $k_2 = 0$ and $k_3 = 1$ covers the situation where, if gold is used for money it has only transactions use in that period. See Section 6.5 for another approach to this issue.

The values $k_2 = 0$ and $k_3 \approx 0$ model the situation where the market meets for some brief time Δ at the very start of the period, all deliveries are made on the spot, and all final recipients obtain the use of all of the goods including the gold for essentially the whole of the period.

Figure 6.1 shows the general case and the two special cases just noted. These two extreme parameter settings enable us to start to bridge the gulf between a storable consumable money and a fiat money; see the discussion below.

We will also consider the case $k_2 = k_3 = 1$.[4]

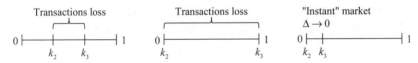

Figure 6.1. The goods market from k_2 to k_3

Finally, we note that in the optimization above, the last constraint (6.1c) is irrelevant because it is satisfied whenever (6.1b) is. Thus one may ignore

---

4 It must be noted that the division of the day into the pre-market, market, and post-market segments with the consumption and transactions uses of gold differentiated is almost a parody of physical reality in the sense that the considerable costs and time delays in minting and the manufacture of jewelry are left out. However, the explicit introduction of market mechanisms is critical to understanding the relationship among consumption value, transaction value, and asset disposal value. For this reason we concentrate on providing an explicit well-defined mechanism to produce a playable game and get the logic straight. Generalization to large classes of mechanism must come later.

it when doing the mathematical analysis. However, we leave it in the model simply because it is the "budget constraint" (see Section 4.1), and later variants of the game will have budget constraints which are not redundant.

The Type 2 traders face a similar optimization program, namely

$$\max_{\bar{b},\bar{q}} \varphi \left(\frac{\bar{b}}{p}, a-\bar{q}\right) + k_2\dot{m} + (k_3 - k_2)(\dot{m} - \bar{b})$$
$$+ (1-k_3)(\dot{m} - \bar{b} + \bar{I}) + \Pi(m - \bar{b} + \bar{p}\bar{q})$$

s.t. $m - \bar{b} \geq 0$ $\qquad\qquad (\bar{\lambda})$

$\qquad m - \bar{b} + \bar{p}\bar{q} \geq 0$ $\qquad\qquad (\bar{\mu})$

$\qquad 0 \leq \bar{q} \leq a$ and $\bar{b} \geq 0.$

Finally, as usual, price is formed by:

$$p = \frac{\bar{b}}{q} \text{ and } \bar{p} = \frac{b}{\bar{q}}. \qquad\qquad (6.2)$$

Again, we remind the reader that the quantities $b, q, \bar{b},$ and $\bar{q}$ (as well as the variables d and $\bar{d}$ defined later on) are all definite integrals taken over the continuum of Type 1 or 2 traders; the quantities p and $\bar{p}$ are just quotients of these values.

6.3.3 Model Solution

We solve the optimization for the case with $\Pi = 0$, $\varphi(x,y) = 2\sqrt{xy}$ and general values for k_2 and k_3. The full solution is given in Appendix A. A sensitivity analysis based on this solution is given in Table 6.2.

The condition of "enough money" means that m is high enough so that the cash-flow constraints (λ) and $(\bar{\lambda})$ are nonbinding. Economically, it means that the volume of the money supply at equilibrium is sufficient to cover the volume of competitive trade. In this instance, the condition turns out to be

$$m \geq \frac{a\sqrt{1-k_3}}{(2-k_2-k_3)\sqrt{1-k_2}}. \qquad\qquad (6.3)$$

In the case where (6.3) holds, price is given by $p = \bar{p} = \sqrt{\frac{1}{(1-k_2)(1-k_3)}}$ and the physical amount of trade by $q = \bar{q} = \frac{(1-k_3)a}{2-k_2-k_3}$. The bids are $b = \bar{b} = pq = \frac{a\sqrt{1-k_3}}{(2-k_2-k_3)\sqrt{1-k_2}}$. Comparing these results with those from the storable consumable money case (Chapter 3), we find that the prices of the goods have gone up to reflect the lessening of the consumption utility of gold. Somewhat surprisingly, the meeting time of the market makes a difference, even if there is no transactions loss in the market.

When $k_2 = k_3 = 0$, then $p = 1$ and the consumption services of a unit of gold are completely lost for the traders if it is used in transactions. The amount of money needed to finance trade is $m = \frac{a}{2}$.

When $k_2 = k_3 \approx 1$ price becomes infinite, and if $\Pi = 0$ an infinite amount of gold is needed. This is because as the original owner gets to enjoy almost all of its service value, the gold will have little value in consumption to the final recipient. And at the end of the game there is no salvage value for the asset—so the more its service value to the final recipient approaches zero, the more it starts to look like fiat.

When $k_2 \neq k_3$ we see from the formulas that q and $\bar{q}$ are strictly less than $\frac{a}{2}$. Hence *efficient exchange is not achieved, even though there is enough money to avoid a cash-flow constraint.* In general, the act of using a durable as money is an implicit tax or rate of interest drain on trade. This is because above a certain level the traders are motivated to use their money for consumption rather than to facilitate transactions. We note below that even the addition of a bank lending the traders extra gold will not change this.

When there is "not enough money" (i.e., (6.3) doesn't hold), we find that prices, bids, and trade all decrease, just as in the models of Chapters 3, 4, and 5.

A SENSITIVITY ANALYSIS

We consider $k_2 = \frac{1}{2}$, $k_3 = \frac{3}{4}$. These values give service losses for $\frac{1}{4}$ of the period when the market meets at mid-day. The value of $\frac{a\sqrt{1-k_3}}{(2-k_2-k_3)\sqrt{1-k_2}}$ (see condition (6.3)) is $\frac{2\sqrt{2}a}{3}$. Just as with the basic model (with storable consumable money), we examine the results as m ranges from ∞ down to 0:

Table 6.2.   Trading with a transactions loss of services

m	p	q	b	λ
$m > \frac{2\sqrt{2}a}{3}$	$2\sqrt{2}$	$\frac{a}{3}$	$\frac{2\sqrt{2}a}{3}$	0
$m = \frac{2\sqrt{2}a}{3}$	$2\sqrt{2}$	$\frac{a}{3}$	$\frac{2\sqrt{2}a}{3}$	0
$m = \frac{2a}{5}$	2	$\frac{a}{5}$	$\frac{2a}{5}$	$\frac{1}{2}$
$m \to 0$	$\to 0$	$\to 0$	$\to 0$	$\to \infty$

Case 1: $m > \frac{2\sqrt{2}a}{3}$. When there is more than enough money, the transactions value of money remains at $\lambda = 0$. However, efficient trade of the perishables

is not achieved (each type of trader consumes $\frac{2a}{3}$ of its own good and $\frac{a}{3}$ of the other). This is due to the loss of $\frac{1}{4}$ of a period of the services of gold used for transactions. Note that the price level is considerably higher than in the storable consumable money case. Surplus gold (above transactions needs) is kept for the full consumption of its services.

Case 2: $m = \frac{2\sqrt{2}a}{3}$. When there is precisely enough money for transactions, and it is distributed in a manner that each individual does not encounter his or her cash constraints, the transactions value of money is still $\lambda = 0$.

Case 3: $0 < m < \frac{2\sqrt{2}a}{3}$. *Example:* $m = \frac{2a}{5}$. When there is "not enough money," the transactions value of money is positive, as reflected by $\lambda = \frac{1}{2}$. Efficient trade of perishables is not achieved for two reasons: the transactions loss of gold, and the constraint on trade. The price level is decreasing monotonically as m decreases from $\frac{2\sqrt{2}a}{3}$ to 0.

Case 4: $m \to 0$. When there is little or no money in the economy there is next to no trade. In reality, if this happened, other means of payment would be used and other avenues of trade would spring up. The societal "trust substitutes" would be substituted by local trust substitutes if they became too expensive.

THE LINK FROM GOLD TO A STORABLE CONSUMABLE

We observe that with the special case of the values $k_2 = 0$ and $k_3 = 0$, we obtain the same results as in Chapter 3 for the storable consumable. Here we have the implausible proposition that the time taken to operate a market is so small that as a reasonable approximation it can be ignored. In this instance the strict consumption yield of a can of beans or unit of gold is the same. With a "timeless" market at the start of the period, both the consumption of the beans and the full services of the gold belong to the ultimate owner. (With fiat there is *only* transactions value.)

In this one-period game with $k_2 = 0$ and $k_3 = 0$, the markets are active regardless of the valuation attached to the salvage value of gold or beans carried over voluntarily or involuntarily to the next period.[5]

---

5 Note that there is, nevertheless, an important strategic difference between the storable consumable and the durable. The choice to not carry the asset over to the next period is available for the first but not the second.

THE LINK FROM GOLD TO FIAT

When we consider $k_2 = 0$ and $k_3 \approx 1$ we obtain an interesting but not full tran-
sition zone toward fiat.[6] These values of k_2 and k_3 imply that during the entire
period any money used for transactions will have no consumption value. In
this respect, the money is like fiat. In fact, the only difference between this
market and a corresponding one with fiat is that there *is* consumption value
attached to gold *not* used in transactions,[7] whereas there is no such value
attached to fiat.

If we further assume that the salvage value of the gold is zero, the goods
market and money market use of gold is destroyed. The Hahn paradox (see
Section 7.1.3) holds. No seller or lender is motivated to supply any item to the
markets, because she would be paid in worthless gold after it has exhausted
its stream of services. So no trade occurs. Both for gold under this scenario,
and for fiat, a way to avoid the Hahn paradox is to attach a salvage utilitar-
ian value of some sort to the surviving asset. If the asset is gold, this value
will depend upon expectations and commodity use; if fiat, it will depend
only upon expectations. We discuss this more in the next chapter, on models
with fiat.

The important case distinction between $k_2 = 0$ and $k_3 = 0$, versus $k_2 = 0$
and $k_3 = 1$, is seen in the incentives to sell. When $k_3 = 0$, the income from
goods sold is paid in gold at the start of the period and will yield almost full
service for the period. When $k_3 = 1$, the income from goods sold for gold
yields nothing.

6.3.4 Trade in Gold with a Money Market

Suppose the types have asymmetric endowments of $(a, 0, m_1)$ and $(0, a, m_2)$,
where $m_1 > m_2$. As in Chapter 4, we introduce a money market.

A strategy for Type 1 traders is denoted by (b, q, g), where b is the amount
of money bid for good 2, q is the amount of good 1 offered for sale, and g
is the amount of money offered in the money market. The notation for the

---

6 To formally make fiat money a specific case of the model, we would first need to define
   a parameter α as the per-unit-time service utility of the monetary asset. We then would
   modify the objective functions for the traders by multiplying the second, third, and
   fourth terms by α. The case of the consumable storable money would then be where
   $k_2 = 0$, $k_3 = 0$, and $\alpha = 1$ (normalized). The fiat case would be where $k_2 = 0$, $k_3 = 1$, and
   $\alpha = 0$.

7 This means any gold above what is needed for the "enough money" case.

Type 2 traders is $(\bar{b}, \bar{q}, \bar{d})$, where $\bar{d}$ is the amount of personal IOU notes bid for the gold offered. For a more detailed discussion of the variables g and $\bar{d}$, see Chapter 4.

THE INTERDAY LOAN MARKET

Before we can write down the optimizations, we must decide whether the functioning of the financial market for loans takes up any time and/or other resources. Assume (somewhat counterfactually and against "bankers' hours") that the financing takes place in a very fast market at the start of the day. Thus our single period is now broken up into four parts with two markets: a financial market and a goods market. Let the proportion of time for the financial market be $k_1 = \Delta$, where Δ is small, as shown in Figure 6.2. Thus, in the valuation of the services of gold, the interval $[0, k_1]$ is so small it makes no operational difference to the agents.

We may now write the optimization problems for our agents. The maximization for the lenders is

$$\max_{b,q,g} \varphi\left(a - q, \frac{b}{p}\right) + k_1(\dot{m}_1 - \dot{g})$$
$$+ (k_2 - k_1)(\dot{m}_1 - \dot{g}) + (k_3 - k_2)(\dot{m}_1 - \dot{g} - \dot{b})$$
$$+ (1 - k_3)(\dot{m}_1 - \dot{g} - \dot{b} + \dot{I}) + \Pi(m_1 - b + pq + \rho g)$$
$$\text{s.t. } m_1 - g - b \geq 0, \qquad (\lambda)$$
$$m_1 - b + pq + \rho g \geq 0 \qquad (\mu)$$
$$0 \leq q \leq a \text{ and } b, g \geq 0,$$

and for the borrowers it is

$$\max_{\bar{b},\bar{q},\bar{d}} \varphi\left(\frac{\bar{b}}{p}, a - \bar{q}\right) + k_1 \dot{m}_2 + (k_2 - k_1)\left(\dot{m}_2 + \frac{\bar{d}}{1+\rho}\right)$$
$$+ (k_3 - k_2)\left(\dot{m}_2 + \frac{\bar{d}}{1+\rho} - \bar{b}\right) + (1 - k_3)\left(\dot{m}_2 + \frac{\bar{d}}{1+\rho} - \bar{b} + \dot{I}\right)$$
$$+ \Pi\left(m_2 + \frac{\bar{d}}{1+\rho} - \bar{b} + \bar{p}\bar{q} - \bar{d}\right)$$
$$\text{s.t. } m_2 + \frac{\bar{d}}{1+\rho} - \bar{b} \geq 0, \qquad (\bar{\lambda})$$
$$m_2 - \frac{\bar{d}}{1+\rho} - \bar{b} + \bar{p}\bar{q} - \bar{d} \geq 0 \qquad (\bar{\mu})$$
$$0 \leq \bar{q} \leq a, \text{ and } \bar{b}, \bar{d} \geq 0.$$

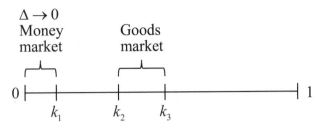

Figure 6.2. A money market and goods market

Price formation is as before

$$p = \frac{\bar{b}}{q} \text{ and } \bar{p} = \frac{b}{\bar{q}}. \tag{6.4}$$

The endogenous rate of interest is formed as follows:

$$1 + \rho = \frac{d}{g}. \tag{6.5}$$

The lack of a "dot" on top of the variables in the interest equations is to remind us that the interest rate is formed by an asset (gold) and by an IOU note denominated in this asset, and similarly the price is formed by assets.[8] Also implicit is the presence of a bankruptcy penalty that is sufficiently steep that strategic bankruptcy is not worthwhile (see the discussion of bankruptcy and default in Chapter 8).

Viewing the objective function for the lenders, a modeling problem must be faced. Do the borrowers pay the lenders back immediately at time k_3 or is their borrowing a full interday loan? We have modeled it as the latter. If it is an interday loan it will be paid back "tomorrow morning," but this apparently minor distinction means that the lender obtains no services from the gold she lent this period. Thus the next-to-last term in the objective function does not contain the term $(1 + \rho)\dot{g}$, and this in turn implies that (if $\Pi = 0$) there is no incentive for the lender to lend. Hence $g = 0$ and the money market would be inactive.

THE INTRADAY LOAN MARKET

If the loan considered above were an intraday loan which had to be paid back immediately after the goods market terminated at time $k_3 < 1$, then the lenders' problem would have the form:

---

8 Thus, the rate of interest is a dimensionless number.

$$\max_{q,b,g} \varphi\left(a-q, \frac{b}{p}\right) + k_1(\dot{m}_1 - \dot{g}) + (k_2 - k_1)(\dot{m}_1 - \dot{g})$$

$$+(k_3 - k_2)(\dot{m}_1 - \dot{g} - \dot{b}) + (1 - k_3)(\dot{m}_1 - \dot{b} + p\dot{q} + \rho\dot{g})$$

$$+\Pi(m_1 - b + pq + \rho g)$$

s.t. $m_1 - g - b \geq 0,$ $\qquad\qquad\qquad\qquad\qquad\qquad\qquad\qquad (\lambda)$

$\qquad m_1 - b + pq + \rho g \geq 0$ $\qquad\qquad\qquad\qquad\qquad\qquad (\mu)$

$\qquad 0 \leq q \leq a$ and $b, g \geq 0.$

Now it is possible that the intraday money market would go active (even if $\Pi = 0$), as some residual services may remain in this period after time k_3.

ENOUGH MONEY

As our purpose is to illustrate the basic qualitative nuances of these many structures, we are able to observe immediately (without calculation) the level of "enough money" in the money market.

Previously we found that when there is enough of a storable consumable money one can lend it at an endogenous interest rate of $\rho = 0$ in the morning, have it used in the market at noon, be repaid in the afternoon, and consume one's stock in the evening. We assumed the money entered the utility function as a linearly separable term. It was easy to see that "enough" is given by an amount which precisely equals the value of the volume of trade. In particular, we considered an example with utility functions $u = 2\sqrt{xy} + z$, and "enough money" turned out to be the condition $m_1 + m_2 \geq a$.

When we switch to a durable money, the analysis changes. The basic distinction is between point consumption for a consumable and flow consumption from a service yielded by a durable. While a unit of storable consumable money will yield both transaction value and then full consumption value when it is consumed, a unit of durable money used for transactions might lose some fraction of its consumption value. On the other hand, at the end of the period the durable money will remain an asset, which may have some salvage value.

Again consider an example with $u = 2\sqrt{xy} + z$, with a durable money having a salvage value of $\Pi = 0$. Then, instead of $m_1 + m_2 \geq a$ being enough money, the agents will require $m_1 + m_2 \geq \frac{2a\sqrt{1-k_3}}{(2-k_2-k_3)\sqrt{1-k_2}}$. If $k_1 = 0$, $k_2 = 0$, and $k_3 = 1$, the markets close. If $k_1 = k_2 = k_3$, there will never be enough money, as $k_3 \to 1$. At $k_3 = 1$ the market closes down, as there is no incentive to sell consumables for a worthless asset whose services have already been rendered. The consumption marginal utility of the services of gold is 1, but the value of gold at the end is 0.

NOT ENOUGH MONEY

If there is not enough money in the system as a whole, trade will be diminished and the price of the monetary commodity goes above its marginal value as a commodity to reflect the shadow price of the cash-flow constraint. We omit this case calculation, as it is qualitatively similar to the money market with a storable consumable.

OUTSIDE MONEY WITH NO OUTSIDE AGENT?

When we consider a money market as contrasted with a large private bank or with a central bank, three basic distinctions must be made: (1) the number and nature of the financial instruments; (2) the monopolistic power of the agents; and (3) the goals and motivation of the agents.

The Instruments: In an economy with either a money market or a central bank, there is an initial supply of commodity money or an initial injection of fiat with no offsetting debt. If we wish to let individuals obtain more money from the government, further fiat money may enter or leave the economy in exchange for government bonds, or taxes and subsidies, but not for individual IOU notes as modeled here. In general, banks monetize the IOU notes of relatively unknown individuals. But even bank drafts or clearinghouse credits are "credit," and, because the banks are better known, their IOU notes may be regarded as money substitutes.

The Monopolistic Power of the Agents: In our analysis we have purposely contrasted a monopolistic money lender with a central bank. Both are monopolists, but with different motivations and sources of power. The sources of power appear to involve a mixture of law, network, and reputation considerations (see Shubik, 2003). In the one-period games considered here, there is no need to vary the money supply from period to period. When three or more periods are considered, the banking system may be called on to both shrink and expand the money supply and a further distinction between the roles of the inside or private and the outside or central bank must be made.

The Goals and Motivation of the Agents: The institution of a central bank is around 300 years old. It is, in essence, a public good and a creature of the state. Moneylenders have been in existence for several thousand years. Some may have had a more or less monopoly position in a limited domain. But they had goals of profit maximization and consumption, and in general had less power than the whole state. One could argue that families such as the Medici came close to being moneylenders, rulers, and a central bank. But the central bank control problem is somewhat different from that of the moneylender. The moneylender wants to make sure that there is never enough money, even if he has to keep a sufficient supply in his vault, but the central bank wants to see that there is an adequate supply.

6.3.5 Expectations, or What Salvage Value Does Gold Have in This Game?

If we regard the one-period game as being a simple metaphor for an ongoing process, it is reasonable to regard durable assets as carrying over to the next stage of the game. Following dynamic programming practices, we may wish to attach a salvage value to the leftover durables. If we are concerned with being able to enlarge our model structure to encompass a multistage economy, then attaching such a salvage value may be regarded as reflecting the expectations for the value of the assets in the markets of the future.[9]

Wrapped into the expectations are all conjectures about future prices of all commodities, with no explanation as to where these conjectures came from. The expectations provide a one-dimensional measure of worth in money that must be related to a measure of utility, as indicated by a dimensional analysis of (6.1a). This point is made more clearly when bankruptcy is considered in Chapter 8, as any form of penalty denoted has the dimensions of utility/money ("utils per dollar short"), thereby establishing the link.

From the point of view of experimental gaming, it is straightforward to reward the players in proportion to their "scores" over which they have some strategic control, including the amount of money left over. An interpretation to assigning a salvage value is that the asset will have value in a future game. The existence of a positive salvage value to the remaining assets is necessary to support value, but there are many different ways in which this can be done.

We remark that the attachment of a positive salvage value to leftover gold (i.e., $\Pi > 0$) is sufficient to avoid the trade-killing backward induction

---

9 If we are concerned with a stationary economy in terms of real resources, we might wish to invoke the "rational expectations" values associated with an infinite horizon stationary state.

described for some of the models above. For example, in the case $k_2 = 0$, $k_3 = 1$ of our original model with no money market, we no longer have the Hahn paradox. And in the interday money market model from Section 6.3.4, the interday loan market will always go active for large enough Π.

What would be the value of Π in our models? One conventional approach relies on the interpretation of our one-period model as but one iteration in an infinitely repeated stationary process. Since Π represents the worth of the gold (per unit) at the end of one period, it should be equal to the service value of gold from the "end of period 1" to the "end of time." The "spot" service value of gold in our model is 1 per time period. Thus $\Pi = \beta + \beta^2 + \beta^3 + \cdots = \frac{\beta}{1-\beta}$, where β is the time discount factor for the economy. In particular, if $\beta = \frac{1}{2}$, $\Pi = 1$.

6.3.6 General Notes on Transactions Costs

Our detailed transactions model above is clearly a considerable distance from economic reality. However, it does illustrate how the problems of "who gets what, when?" depend delicately on the parameters of the model. In reality, items such as setup costs are important (see Baumol, 1952; Shubik and Yao, 1990). Furthermore, there are time lags in the payments or delivery of real goods and financial products. The payment may have been made and then three weeks later the appliance arrives. The stock is meant to be delivered, but somehow the back office failed to make the transfer.

It is on transactions details such as lags and setup costs that much of microeconomic dynamics depends. In practice, this kind of detail often calls for ad hoc (and often highly profitable) operations research modeling.

6.4 THE CENTRAL BANK CONTROL PROBLEM

We turn to the central bank control problem in an economy with gold.

With gold, it is difficult to define what we mean by an "altruistic central bank." First, to simplify things, suppose we consider a case where there is more than enough money. Then the price of gold (i.e., the interest rate on loans) should be exactly equal to its marginal consumption value, which would be positive. But a monopolist or highly powerful altruistic bank could lend at rates below this marginal value. In order to do so it would also have to place rationing restrictions on borrowing which otherwise could become unbounded. See the discussion in Section 6.4.2, entitled "A Problem in Coordination."

Second, suppose a central bank has gold reserves. If it is truly altruistic, should it lend out all of the reserves, allowing society to enjoy both its consumption and transactions services? Or should it maintain its reserves, thereby providing symbols of trust and reputation?

In the analysis below, we consider two possibilities. First, in the next section we consider a central bank which lends out all of its reserves but lets the market determine the interest rate. Then, in the following section we consider a central bank which lends out all of its reserves at an interest rate of zero.

6.4.1 Trade with Gold: Two Trader Types with an Altruistic Central Bank

In Chapter 5 we modeled an altruistic central bank, within the context of a storable consumable money. Here we do the same, except with gold as the money.

With gold, the introduction of the altruistic bank has a beneficial effect for the traders. By having the bank provide the financing for trade, the traders can keep their own endowments of gold and enjoy its service value. However, there is one thing that the altruistic bank cannot do that it could do if the money were a storable consumable or fiat—*it cannot, via the injection of money to the traders, finance trade to the efficient levels.* In Sections 7.1.3 and 7.4 (Case 1), we shall see that in a market with fiat, if the bank is endowed with a lot of money, and the money is lent to the agents at interest rate zero, the traders can use the money to finance their trade and attain the efficient consumption levels $(\frac{a}{2}, \frac{a}{2})$ and $(\frac{a}{2}, \frac{a}{2})$; the same phenomenon holds for the market with storable consumable money. However, with gold, if the altruistic bank lends a large amount of money to the traders, the traders might very well not use the gold for transactions, but instead just use its service value before paying it back. We demonstrate this below.

Of course, the above analysis depends upon our models' previously mentioned (Section 6.3.2) assumption that "monetary gold" and "gold for consumption" are costlessly interchangeable. If such costs were present in our model, the traders might not have the incentive to borrow "monetary gold" to use for consumption—and so one might not observe the altruistic bank offering "free money" to cover transactions, with the traders using the aid for other purposes.

Let us compare two models. In the first model we assume there is no lending market and no bank, and so the optimization problems for the traders are similar to those in Section 6.3.2.[10] In the second model we have a lending market with an altruistic bank. The Type 1 traders' optimization problem becomes

$$\max_{b,q,d} \varphi\left(a - q, \frac{b}{p}\right) + k_1 \dot{m} + (k_2 - k_1)\left(\dot{m} + \frac{\dot{d}}{1+\rho}\right)$$
$$+ (k_3 - k_2)\left(\dot{m} + \frac{\dot{d}}{1+\rho} - \dot{b}\right) + (1 - k_3)\left(\dot{m} + \frac{\dot{d}}{1+\rho} - \dot{b} + \dot{I}\right)$$
$$+ \Pi\left(m + \frac{d}{1+\rho} - b + pq - d\right) \tag{6.6}$$
$$\text{s.t. } m + \frac{d}{1+\rho} - b \geq 0, \tag{λ}$$
$$m + \frac{d}{1+\rho} - b + pq - d \geq 0 \tag{μ}$$
$$0 \leq q \leq a \text{ and } b, d \geq 0,$$

with a similar problem for the Type 2 traders. Prices and the interest rate are formed in the usual way:

$$1 + \rho = \frac{d + \bar{d}}{g}, \, p = \frac{\bar{b}}{q}, \text{ and } \bar{p} = \frac{b}{\bar{q}}. \tag{6.7}$$

The bank's objective is to maximize the wealth achieved by the otherwise competitive economy. Presumably it does this by lending out all of its resources.

In both models, we assume $\varphi(x, y) = 2\sqrt{xy}$, that $\Pi = 1$,[11] and that $k_1 = k_2 = 0$, $k_3 = 1$. (This is the case where the consumption value of the services of gold is completely lost when used for a transaction.) The analysis for the first model (with no bank) is in Appendix B, Section 6.7.1. For the second model, we assume the initial endowment of the bank B is large; say, $B = a$. That analysis is in Appendix B, Section 6.7.2. We note two interesting results in this model with gold and banking. First, in the "enough money" case, the equilibrium interest rate is now strictly positive ($\rho = 1$); this reflects the fact that the bank's money has a positive service value even

---

10 The only difference will be the use of a positive salvage value, i.e., $\Pi = 1$.

11 Perhaps the use of a salvage value of 1 strikes some readers as unrealistically low—indeed, we argued in the previous section that it stems from a discount rate of $\beta = 0.5$. Using β's closer to 1 would yield higher Π's.

However, using higher Π's does not change our main observation that the switch to gold money causes an inefficiency in consumption, even in the presence of "enough money." To demonstrate this, we advise the reader that we have worked out the case of "bank present, enough money" for general values of Π; the consumption levels are never efficient. See footnote 13.

when it is not used in transactions. Second, in this model it is possible in an equilibrium for the cash-flow constraint to be loose while the budget constraint is tight—this is impossible in models with a storable consumable or fiat money.[12]

6.4.2 A Problem in Coordination

A simple observation in Section 6.7.2 shows that it is impossible to have a competitively formed interest rate of $\rho = 0$. But what if the bank is truly altruistic, and lends at interest rate zero? In that case, the traders will want to borrow an infinite amount, and so the bank will have to ration the lending of its resources. This can be done by announcing an upper bound on the IOU notes that it will accept from each trader. If it imposes that $d \leq \frac{B}{2}$ and $\bar{d} \leq \frac{B}{2}$ then the bank can expect that all will borrow up to their limit. In reality, especially in a world with imperfect information, this amounts to a credit line for all borrowers.

The results for this third model (in which the bank lends all of its resources equally to all, at interest rate zero) are in Appendix B, Section 6.7.3.

6.4.3 Comparing the Results

Let us consider two examples. First, suppose the traders begin with a lot of money; say, $m = a$. With no bank, our results show that the trader types each put $\frac{a}{3}$ of their own goods up for sale and end up with the inefficient consumption levels of $(\frac{2a}{3}, \frac{a}{3})$ (for Type 1 traders) and $(\frac{a}{3}, \frac{2a}{3})$ (for Type 2 traders). We shall see that this contrasts with the efficient levels of $(\frac{a}{2}, \frac{a}{2})$ and $(\frac{a}{2}, \frac{a}{2})$ attained in an equivalent model where the money is fiat/storable consumable (see Section 7.4, Case 1).

If we now introduce a bank (with gold), the consumption levels don't change, remaining at $(\frac{2a}{3}, \frac{a}{3})$ and $(\frac{a}{3}, \frac{2a}{3})$.

Finally, if we assume that the bank lends $\frac{B}{2}$ to each player type at interest rate zero, we find that even this does not change the consumption levels. One way to see this is that at the levels $(\frac{2a}{3}, \frac{a}{3})$ and $(\frac{a}{3}, \frac{2a}{3})$, the marginal value of further gold spent on bidding for goods will be less than its service value;

---

12 The reason is that the argument from footnote 7 of Chapter 4 no longer works—the simultaneous raising of b and lowering of d no longer necessarily increases utility, because lowering d involves a loss in service use of the gold asset.

giving the traders more access to gold doesn't change this. Hence any extra gold lent to the traders is merely worn as jewelry.

Another example is where the traders have little money; say, $m = \frac{a}{10}$. With no bank, the consumption levels (Case 2, Appendix A) are $(\frac{4a}{5}, \frac{a}{5})$ and $(\frac{a}{5}, \frac{4a}{5})$. With a bank, the bank will lend at a rate of $\rho = 0.2$, leading to consumption of $(\frac{6a}{11}, \frac{5a}{11})$ and $(\frac{5a}{11}, \frac{6a}{11})$; this represents an improvement in efficiency over the "no bank" case, but it is still short of true efficiency (Case 2, Section 6.7.2). Finally, if the bank lends at the truly altruistic rate of $\rho = 0$, this has a negative effect on efficiency—the consumption levels revert back to $(\frac{2a}{3}, \frac{a}{3})$ and $(\frac{a}{3}, \frac{2a}{3})$.[13]

See the discussion in the next chapter (Section 7.1.5) for a continuation of discussion of these examples.

6.4.4 The 100 Percent Backed Credit Solution:
Fort Knox or the Bank of Amsterdam?

Historically the Bank of Amsterdam wrote paper against the gold it held. Physically the paper was easier to transport and to protect against theft. In the context of a world with exogenous uncertainty (which we do not deal with here), reserves are required to protect against fluctuations. But here they are not needed. Hence if transactions costs were low enough, from the viewpoint of an altruistic central bank (in control of its treasury), rather than keep its gold in a Fort Knox it could lend gold for consumption, thereby raising consumption levels. In reality, the ever-pervasive cost of process makes this implausible.

6.4.5 An Aside on Central Bank Reserves

One of the key reasons for first considering commodity money is that there is no mystery concerning central bank reserves. They are physically defined. The gold exists and the bank has it, or it is elsewhere. However, as it is a physical object, it is measurable. When the currency is fiat and the bank has permission to create more fiat, the problem of defining bank reserves becomes an exercise in the specification of socio-politically constructed rules of the game.

---

13 (Continuation of footnote 11.) If we assume the salvage value is a general parameter Π, all of the equilibrium consumption levels which are $(\frac{2a}{3}, \frac{a}{3})$ and $(\frac{a}{3}, \frac{2a}{3})$ become $(\frac{(1+\Pi)a}{1+2\Pi}, \frac{\Pi a}{1+2\Pi})$ and $(\frac{\Pi a}{1+2\Pi}, \frac{(1+\Pi)a}{1+2\Pi})$. These are still not efficient, but do approach efficiency as Π approaches ∞.

6.5 TWO KINDS OF GOLD

Throughout this chapter, we have considered economies in which a single good (gold) plays two roles: that of a consumption good yielding a stream of services, and that of a money which enables transactions. The essence of our models was to allow only one of these uses at a time. This makes sense in economies with continuous financial markets where one wishes to consider who holds what in time slices of less than a day.

Another possibly more realistic model is to consider that gold in the economy exists as two different commodities. They are "monetary gold" and "consumption gold." Monetary gold (or "gold coin") has transaction value but yields no stream of services. On the other hand, consumption gold ("jewelry") yields service utility but cannot be used to buy goods.

A key feature of this model is that there is now a transaction cost to convert one type of gold to the other, and vice versa. In reality it takes both time and resources for such a conversion; here we model only a monetary cost (but no time cost). About the simplest way to do this is to assume that x units of nonmonetary gold converts to $\alpha_1 x$ units of coin, while y units of coin converts to $\alpha_2 x$ units of jewelry. In reality, one would guess α_1 is no bigger than 0.97 (a 3 percent seigniorage cost), while α_2 is no smaller than 0.7 or 0.8 as a coin-melting and jewelry fabrication cost. For simplicity in the formal model we set $\alpha_1 = \alpha_2 = \alpha$.

As usual, we consider two types of traders, trading in two perishable goods, in a one-period game. As before, we assume that the Type 1 traders are endowed only with good 1; the Type 2 traders only with good 2; and there is a continuum of each type. In total, the Type 1 traders have an endowment of $(a, 0, m, [m^*, \dot{m}^*])$, where m and m^* represent the initial holdings of coin and jewelry, respectively. The quantity $\dot{m}^*$ represents the service the jewelry can provide, with $\dot{m}^* = m^*$. Type 2 traders have $(0, a, m, [m^*, \dot{m}^*])$.

Each trader (of either type) has the same utility function $\varphi(x, y) + \dot{z}^* + \Pi z + \Pi^* z^*$, where x and y represent the amounts of good 1 and good 2 consumed, $\dot{z}^*$ represents the amount of nonmonetary gold services consumed, z is the amount of coin left over at the end of the game, and z^* is the amount of jewelry left over at the end of the game. We make our usual assumption that the jewelry asset is bundled with its service; that is, $\dot{z}^* = z^*$. Thus we can write the utility as $\varphi(x, y) + \Pi z + (1 + \Pi^*) z^*$. The parameters Π and Π^* represent the salvage values for coin and jewelry, respectively.

A strategy for the Type 1 traders is denoted by (b, q, v, w), where b is the amount of gold bid for good 2, q is the amount of good 1 offered for sale, v is the amount of coin to be converted to jewelry, and w is the amount of jewelry to be converted to coin. The notation for the Type 2 traders is $(\bar{b}, \bar{q}, \bar{v}, \bar{w})$. We remind the reader that these strategies represent aggregations over the continuum of individual traders; for details see Chapter 3.

Finally, the quantities p and $\bar{p}$ are the prices of the two perishable goods, formed in the usual way.

In the simplest form of the game, without banking, the Type 1 traders attempt to maximize:

$$
\max_{b,q,v,w} \varphi\left(a - q, \frac{b}{p}\right) + \Pi(m - b + pq - v + \alpha w)
$$
$$
+ (1 + \Pi^*)(m^* - w + \alpha v)
$$
$$
\text{s.t. } m - v + \alpha w - b \geq 0 \qquad (\lambda)
$$
$$
m^* - w + \alpha v \geq 0 \qquad (\lambda^*)
$$
$$
b, v, w \geq 0, \ 0 \leq q \leq a.
$$

(6.8)

The Type 2 traders have a similar problem. Prices are formed as $p = \frac{\bar{b}}{q}$ and $\bar{p} = \frac{b}{\bar{q}}$.

A simple example shows both how the money supply is adjusted and that this formulation supplies an explicit physical valuation for the worth of liquidity. Suppose $\varphi = 2\sqrt{xy}$ and $\alpha \leq \min(\frac{\Pi}{1+\Pi^*}, \frac{1+\Pi^*}{\Pi})$. We may check that if both types have a considerable amount of coin (i.e., m is large), consumption of the perishable good will be efficient and no consumption gold will be converted to coin or vice versa. Thus $p = \bar{p} = \frac{1}{\Pi}$, $b = \bar{b} = \frac{a}{2\Pi}$, $q = \bar{q} = \frac{a}{2}$, and $v = \bar{v} = w = \bar{w} = 0.$[14]

An even better model would also have a time lag associated with conversion of one type of gold to the other. In a gold coin transaction system mining, melting, and minting are all involved in providing liquidity. These cumbersome processes contrast with the efficient (and sometimes dangerous) use of printing presses. The authors leave the full development of this model for future work.[15]

---

14 Recently, this entire model has been worked out by Leilani Bailey in her masters thesis (Bailey, 2012).

15 However, we do consider somewhat related models in Chapter 15, where we consider models in which there are both (demonetized) gold and fiat.

6.6 APPENDIX A: TRADE WITH GOLD—
NO FINANCIAL MARKETS

We present the calculations for the model in Sections 6.3.1–6.3.2, in which $\varphi(x,y) = 2\sqrt{xy}$ and the salvage value for gold is zero ($\Pi = 0$). We also assume that the gold asset and its service stream are bundled together (see the discussion in Section 6.3.1); hence $\dot{b} = b$, $\bar{b} = \bar{b}$, $\dot{I} = pq$, $\bar{I} = \bar{p}\bar{q}$, and $\dot{m} = m$. Thus the Type 1 traders' optimization is given by:

$$\max_{b,q} 2\sqrt{(a-q)\frac{b}{p} + k_2 m + (k_3 - k_2)(m - b) + (1 - k_3)(m - b + pq)}$$

s.t. $m - b \geq 0$ $\hspace{3cm}$ (λ) $\hspace{1cm}$ (6.9)

$\hspace{1cm}$ $m - b + pq \geq 0$ $\hspace{2.5cm}$ (μ)

$\hspace{1cm}$ $0 \leq q \leq a$ and $b \geq 0$.

Introducing the multiplier λ for constraint (λ) and ignoring the redundant constraint (μ), we obtain the first-order conditions[16]

$$\frac{1}{\sqrt{p}}\sqrt{\frac{a-q}{b}} = 1 - k_2 + \lambda \hspace{3cm} (6.10)$$

$$\frac{1}{\sqrt{p}}\sqrt{\frac{b}{a-q}} = p(1 - k_3) \hspace{3cm} (6.11)$$

$$m - b = 0 \text{ or } \lambda = 0. \hspace{3cm} (6.12)$$

Similarly the Type 2 traders face

$$\max_{\bar{b},\bar{q}} 2\sqrt{(a-\bar{q})\frac{\bar{b}}{p} + k_2 m + (k_3 - k_2)(\bar{m} - \bar{b})}$$
$$+ (1 - k_3)(m - \bar{b} + \bar{p}\bar{q})$$

s.t. $m - \bar{b} \geq 0$ $\hspace{2.5cm}$ ($\bar{\lambda}$) $\hspace{2.2cm}$ (6.13)

$\hspace{1cm}$ $m - \bar{b} + \bar{p}\bar{q} \geq 0$ $\hspace{2cm}$ ($\bar{\mu}$)

$\hspace{1cm}$ $0 \leq q \leq a$ and $b \geq 0$,

---

16 We remind the reader of the shorthand notation used in constraints (6.12) and (6.16) below; see footnote 19 in Chapter 5 for details.

and the first-order conditions are (ignoring redundant constraint $(\bar{\mu})$)

$$\frac{1}{\sqrt{p}}\sqrt{\frac{a-\bar{q}}{\bar{b}}} = 1 - k_2 + \bar{\lambda} \tag{6.14}$$

$$\frac{1}{\sqrt{p}}\sqrt{\frac{\bar{b}}{a-\bar{q}}} = \bar{p}(1-k_3) \tag{6.15}$$

$$m - \bar{b} = 0 \text{ or } \bar{\lambda} = 0. \tag{6.16}$$

The balance conditions are $p = \frac{\bar{b}}{q}$ and $\bar{p} = \frac{b}{\bar{q}}$.

Before continuing, we remind the reader that the problems for Type 1 and Type 2 players are isomorphic; hence we may assume that there is a symmetric solution, that is, a solution in which $p = \bar{p}$, $q = \bar{q}$, and $b = \bar{b}$.

Case 1: *m* is high. If *m* is large we may assume that $\lambda = 0$ and $\bar{\lambda} = 0$. Condition (6.11) becomes

$$\frac{1}{\sqrt{\bar{p}}}\sqrt{\frac{b}{a-q}} = (1-k_3)p \Rightarrow \sqrt{\frac{b}{a-q}} = (1-k_3)p\sqrt{\bar{p}}, \tag{6.17}$$

and so

$$\sqrt{\frac{a-q}{b}} = \frac{1}{p\sqrt{\bar{p}}(1-k_3)}. \tag{6.18}$$

Substituting this into (6.10) gives

$$\frac{1}{\sqrt{\bar{p}}}\frac{1}{(1-k_3)p\sqrt{\bar{p}}} = 1 - k_2 \Rightarrow p\bar{p} = \frac{1}{(1-k_2)(1-k_3)}, \tag{6.19}$$

hence from symmetry

$$p = \bar{p} = \sqrt{\frac{1}{(1-k_2)(1-k_3)}}. \tag{6.20}$$

Next, from (6.10) we obtain

$$\frac{1}{\bar{p}}\frac{(a-q)}{b} = (1-k_2)^2 \Rightarrow \frac{a-q}{b} = (1-k_2)^{\frac{3}{2}}(1-k_3)^{-1/2}. \tag{6.21}$$

But $b = pq$; hence we may substitute for b then p and solve for q

$$\frac{a-q}{q} = \frac{a}{q} - 1 = (1-k_2)(1-k_3)^{-1}, \tag{6.22}$$

which simplifies to

$$q = \frac{a(1-k_3)}{2-k_2-k_3} \tag{6.23}$$

and

$$b = pq = \frac{a}{2-k_2-k_3}\sqrt{\frac{1-k_3}{1-k_2}}. \tag{6.24}$$

These results hold as long as $m - b \geq 0$; that is,

$$m \geq \frac{a}{2-k_2-k_3}\sqrt{\frac{1-k_3}{1-k_2}}, \tag{6.25}$$

so this is what we mean by "m large." The economic meaning of "m large" is that there is enough money to cover efficient trade (Shubik, 1999a).

We note that if $k_2 = k_3 = 0$ we obtain the same results as with a consumable storable. In particular, the symmetric solution is $p = \bar{p} = 1$, $b = \bar{b} = q = \bar{q} = \frac{a}{2}$ (see Case 1 of Section 3.2). In this instance since $b = \frac{a}{2}$ the cash-flow constraint requires that $m \geq \frac{a}{2}$.

Case 2: m is small. If m is small then $\lambda, \bar{\lambda} > 0$ and $b = m$, $\bar{b} = m$. Equations (6.10) and (6.11) imply

$$\frac{1}{\sqrt{\bar{p}}}\frac{1}{(p\sqrt{\bar{p}})(1-k_3)} = 1 - k_2 + \lambda, \tag{6.26}$$

which gives

$$p = \bar{p} = \frac{1}{\sqrt{(1+k_2+\lambda)(1-k_3)}}.$$

Hence $q = \frac{\bar{b}}{p} = m\sqrt{(1-k_2+\lambda)(1-k_3)} = \bar{q}$.

Next, condition (6.10) gives $\frac{1}{\bar{p}}\frac{a-q}{b} = (1-k_2+\lambda)^2$. Substituting in our expressions for $\bar{p}$, q, and b gives

$$\sqrt{(1-k_2+\lambda)(1-k_3)} * \frac{a - m\sqrt{(1-k_2+\lambda)(1-k_3)}}{m} = (1-k_2+\lambda)^2, \tag{6.27}$$

from which we may obtain

$$\frac{(1-k_2+\lambda)^{3/2}}{(1-k_3)^{1/2}} + (1-k_2+\lambda)^{1/2}(1-k_3)^{1/2} = \frac{a}{m}. \tag{6.28}$$

It is not hard to see that we may rewrite (6.28) as

$$\frac{1}{p^3(1-k_3)^2} + \frac{1}{p} = \frac{a}{m}. \tag{6.29}$$

This shows how price varies with the money supply. We remark that equations (6.28) and (6.29) reduce to equations (3.10) and (3.11) from Chapter 3, in the case where $k_2 = k_3 = 0$, that is, the case where the gold is essentially a storable consumable.

Finally, if $k_3 = 1$ the Hahn paradox will hold.

6.7 APPENDIX B: TRADE WITH GOLD—
ALTRUISTIC CENTRAL BANK
6.7.1 The Case with No Bank

In order to appreciate the contribution of the central bank to the traders' welfare, we begin by considering the model with $\varphi(x,y) = 2\sqrt{xy}$, no bank, and the parameters k_1, k_2, and k_3 are set to 0, 0, and 1, respectively. Also, $\Pi = 1$. The optimization for the Type 1 traders is

$$\max_{b,q} 2\sqrt{(a-q)\frac{b}{p} + m - b} + m - b + pq \tag{a}$$

$$\text{s.t. } m - b \geq 0 \qquad\qquad (\lambda) \quad (b) \tag{6.30}$$
$$m - b + pq \geq 0 \qquad\qquad (\mu) \quad (c)$$
$$0 \leq q \leq a \text{ and } b \geq 0. \qquad\qquad (d)$$

As in Appendix A, we note that constraint (μ) is redundant—so we again ignore it. Introducing the multiplier λ for constraint (λ), we obtain the first-order conditions[17]

$$\frac{1}{\sqrt{p}}\sqrt{\frac{a-q}{b}} = 2 + \lambda \tag{6.31}$$

$$\frac{1}{\sqrt{p}}\sqrt{\frac{b}{a-q}} = p \tag{6.32}$$

$$m - b = 0 \text{ or } \lambda = 0. \tag{6.33}$$

---

17 We remind the reader of the shorthand notation used in constraints (6.33) and (6.36) below; see footnote 16 in Chapter 5 for details.

Similarly for the Type 2 traders, we obtain the first-order conditions

$$\frac{1}{\sqrt{\bar{p}}}\sqrt{\frac{a-\bar{q}}{\bar{b}}}=2+\bar{\lambda} \tag{6.34}$$

$$\frac{1}{\sqrt{\bar{p}}}\sqrt{\frac{\bar{b}}{a-\bar{q}}}=\bar{p} \tag{6.35}$$

$$m-\bar{b}=0 \text{ or } \bar{\lambda}=0. \tag{6.36}$$

We also have the balance conditions $p=\frac{\bar{b}}{q}$ and $\bar{p}=\frac{b}{\bar{q}}$.

Case 1: Enough money: Here we assume that the cash-flow constraint is loose; that is, $\lambda=0$. In this case (6.31) implies $\sqrt{\frac{a-q}{b}}=2\sqrt{p}$, while (6.32) gives $\sqrt{\frac{b}{a-q}}=p\sqrt{\bar{p}}$. This in turn implies $2\sqrt{\bar{p}}=\frac{1}{p\sqrt{\bar{p}}}$, and then symmetry gives $p=\bar{p}=\frac{\sqrt{2}}{2}$. Then (6.31), the balance conditions, and symmetry give $\sqrt{\frac{a-q}{b}}=(2+\lambda)\sqrt{\bar{p}} \Rightarrow \sqrt{\frac{a-q}{\bar{p}q}}=(2+\lambda)\sqrt{\bar{p}} \Rightarrow \sqrt{\frac{a-q}{q}}=2\bar{p}=\sqrt{2} \Rightarrow \frac{a-q}{q}=2$. This gives $q=\bar{q}=\frac{a}{3}$. The balance conditions plus symmetry then give $b=\bar{b}=\frac{\sqrt{2}a}{6}$.

In order for this case to hold, we need $b\leq m$, which is $m\geq\frac{\sqrt{2}a}{6}$. So this is the precise definition of "enough money" here.

Case 2: Not enough money: Here we assume that the cash-flow constraint is tight, so $\lambda>0$ and $b=m$. To find q, we write (6.32) as $\sqrt{\frac{b}{a-q}}=p\sqrt{\bar{p}}=\frac{b\sqrt{b}}{q\sqrt{q}}$. This is $\frac{b}{a-q}=\frac{b^3}{q^3}$, and since $b=m$, we have $q^3+m^2q-m^2a=0$. This can be solved computationally, and thereafter we can use the balance conditions to find p. As an example, suppose that $m=\frac{a}{10}$. Then $b=\bar{b}=\frac{a}{10}$, $q=\bar{q}=\frac{a}{5}$, and $p=\bar{p}=\frac{b}{q}=\frac{1}{2}$.

6.7.2 The Case with the Altruistic Bank

Again we assume that $\varphi(x,y)=2\sqrt{xy}$; the parameters k_1, k_2, and k_3 are set to 0, 0, and 1, respectively; and $\Pi=1$. But in this model we have an altruistic strategic dummy bank, which always lends out all of its cash,—that is, $g=B$— but then the interest rate is determined competitively. The Type 1 traders' optimization problem is

$$\max_{b,q} 2\sqrt{(a-q)\frac{b}{p}} + m + \frac{d}{1+\rho} - b + m + \frac{d}{1+\rho} - b + pq - d \quad \text{(a)}$$

$$\text{s.t. } m + \frac{d}{1+\rho} - b \geq 0 \qquad\qquad (\lambda) \quad \text{(b)} \qquad (6.37)$$

$$m + \frac{d}{1+\rho} - b + pq - d \geq 0 \qquad (\mu) \quad \text{(c)}$$

$$0 \leq q \leq a \text{ and } b, d \geq 0. \qquad\qquad \text{(d)}$$

The first-order conditions with respect to b, q, and d give[18]

$$\frac{1}{\sqrt{p}}\sqrt{\frac{a-q}{b}} = 2 + \lambda + \mu \qquad\qquad (6.38)$$

$$\frac{1}{\sqrt{p}}\sqrt{\frac{b}{a-q}} = p + \mu p \qquad\qquad (6.39)$$

$$\frac{1-\rho+\lambda-\rho\mu}{1+\rho} = 0 \qquad\qquad (6.40)$$

$$m + \frac{d}{1+\rho} - b = 0 \text{ or } \lambda = 0 \qquad\qquad (6.41)$$

$$m + \frac{d}{1+\rho} - b + pq - d = 0 \text{ or } \mu = 0. \qquad\qquad (6.42)$$

We have a similar problem and first-order conditions for the Type 2 traders, as well as the balancing conditions $p = \frac{\bar{b}}{q}$, $\bar{p} = \frac{b}{\bar{q}}$, and $1 + \rho = \frac{d+\bar{d}}{B}$.

Before we begin our analysis, let us note that it is impossible to have a competitively formed interest rate of $\rho = 0$. For, if so, the strictly dominant strategy for both trader types would be to demand an infinite amount of cash for loan.

Case 1: Enough money: Here we assume that both the cash-flow and budget constraints are loose; that is, $\lambda = \mu = 0$. Then (6.38) implies $\sqrt{\frac{a-q}{b}} = 2\sqrt{p}$ and (6.39) implies $\sqrt{\frac{b}{a-q}} = p\sqrt{p}$, and so $p = \bar{p} = \frac{\sqrt{2}}{2}$, just as in (Case 1 of the) the no-banking model above. Continuing as in that model's analysis,

---

18 We remind the reader of the shorthand notation used in constraints (6.41) and (6.42) below; see footnote 19 in Chapter 5 for details.

we have (6.38), the balance conditions and symmetry[19] yielding $\sqrt{\frac{a-q}{b}} =$
$(2+\lambda)\sqrt{\bar{p}} \Rightarrow q = \bar{q} = \frac{a}{3}$. Also, $b = \bar{b} = pq = \frac{\sqrt{2}a}{6}$. Next, $\lambda = \mu = 0$ and condition (6.40) together imply $\rho = 1$; the balancing condition for the formation of the interest rate then gives $d = \bar{d} = B$.

Finally, these results depend upon *both* the cash-flow and budget constraints holding. The cash-flow constraint in this case says $m + \frac{B}{2} - \frac{\sqrt{2}a}{6} \geq 0$; the budget constraint says $m + \frac{B}{2} - \frac{\sqrt{2}a}{6} - B + \frac{\sqrt{2}a}{6} \geq 0$. Hence the conditions for "enough money" are when both of these hold simultaneously, that is, when $m \geq \max(\frac{\sqrt{2}a}{6} - \frac{B}{2}, \frac{B}{2})$.

Case 2: Intermediate amount of money (I):   This is a case that cannot occur when the money is fiat or storable consumable, namely, when the cash-flow constraint is loose and the budget constraint is tight. The reason this is possible now is that raising b and lowering d in such a way as to keep the budget constraint tight (and the cash-flow constraint loose) no longer necessarily improves utility—because the lowering of d causes an extra utility loss in the service value of the gold. So let us assume that $\lambda = 0$ and $\mu > 0$.

The analysis goes as follows. First, (6.38) implies $\sqrt{\frac{a-q}{b}} = (2+\mu)\sqrt{\bar{p}}$ and (6.39) implies $\sqrt{\frac{b}{a-q}} = p\sqrt{\bar{p}}(1+\mu)$; putting these together gives $(2+\mu)\sqrt{\bar{p}} = \frac{1}{p\sqrt{\bar{p}}(1+\mu)}$. Using symmetry, we have $p = \bar{p} = \frac{1}{\sqrt{(1+\mu)(2+\mu)}}$. Since (6.40) implies $1 + \mu = \frac{1}{\rho}$, we may write this as $p = \bar{p} = \frac{1}{\sqrt{\frac{1}{\rho}(1+\frac{1}{\rho})}} = \frac{\rho}{\sqrt{1+\rho}}$.

In addition, (6.39) implies $\sqrt{\frac{\bar{p}\bar{q}}{a-q}} = p\sqrt{\bar{p}}(1+\mu)$; symmetry then gives $\frac{a-q}{q} = p^2(1+\mu)^2 = \frac{\rho^2}{1+\rho}\frac{1}{\rho^2} = \frac{1}{1+\rho}$. This in turn gives $q = \bar{q} = \frac{a}{2+\rho}$. Also, $b = \bar{b} = pq = \frac{\rho a}{\sqrt{1+\rho}(2+\rho)}$. Next, we can derive d as follows. First, $\mu > 0$ implies $m + \frac{d}{1+\rho} - b - d + pq = 0$. But the balancing condition together with symmetry implies $b = pq$; hence $m + \frac{d}{1+\rho} - d = 0$, which is $d = \bar{d} = [\frac{1+\rho}{\rho}]m$.[20]

19 By "symmetry," we of course mean the assumption that the trader types' decisions must be identical because they face essentially the same optimization problem, i.e., $b = \bar{b}$, $q = \bar{q}$, and $d = \bar{d}$. As a result, we may also assume $p = \bar{p}$.

20 If $m = 0$, one might think that another possibility is $d = \bar{d} = 0$; however, this would imply a negative interest rate via the balancing condition $1 + \rho = \frac{d+\bar{d}}{B}$. Thus we do not have an equilibrium with no trade, as in Chapter 5, Appendix B, Case 2—this is because here the amount the bank lends is a fixed positive quantity.

Finally, we determine ρ by noting that $1 + \rho = \frac{d+\bar{d}}{B} = \frac{2^{\frac{1+\rho}{\rho}}m}{B} \Rightarrow \rho = \frac{2m}{B}$.
Thus we can now go back and substitute for ρ in our formulas for p, $\bar{p}$, q, $\bar{q}$, b, $\bar{b}$, d, and $\bar{d}$.

We note that these values can hold only if the cash-flow constraints hold, that is, if $m + \frac{d}{1+\rho} - b \geq 0$. Substituting, this is $m + \frac{m}{\rho} - \frac{\rho a}{\sqrt{1+\rho}(2+\rho)} \geq 0$, where $\rho = \frac{2m}{B}$. It is straightforward to verify that this condition always holds if $B \geq a$. We also must have $m \leq \max(\frac{\sqrt{2}a}{6} - \frac{B}{2}, \frac{B}{2})$.

Finally, we demonstrate that this case can actually occur via an example. Suppose $m = \frac{a}{10}$ (and $B = a$). Then we obtain $\rho = 0.2$, $q = \bar{q} = \frac{5}{11}a$, $p = \bar{p} \approx 0.18$, $b = \bar{b} \approx 0.083a$, and $d = \bar{d} = 0.6a$. Note in particular that the introduction of the bank has raised q and $\bar{q}$ (compare with the example in Case 2 of subsection 6.7.1 above) and thereby increased efficiency, but it has not attained the maximally efficient levels of $q = \bar{q} = \frac{a}{2}$.

Case 3: Intermediate amount of money (II):   This is the case where the cash-flow constraint is tight ($\lambda > 0$) and the budget constraint is loose ($\mu = 0$). We have (6.38) implies $\sqrt{\frac{a-q}{b}} = (2 + \lambda)\sqrt{\bar{p}}$ and (6.39) implies $\sqrt{\frac{b}{a-q}} = p\sqrt{\bar{p}}$, which gives $(2+\lambda)\sqrt{\bar{p}} = \frac{1}{p}\sqrt{\bar{p}}$, or, after using symmetry, $p = \bar{p} = \frac{1}{\sqrt{2+\lambda}}$. Also, (6.39) and balance together imply $\sqrt{\frac{\bar{p}q}{a-q}} = p\sqrt{\bar{p}}$, which gives (symmetry) $\frac{q}{a-q} = p^2 = \frac{1}{2+\lambda}$. But $2 + \lambda = 1 + (1 + \lambda) = 1 + \rho$, where the last equality follows from (6.40). Hence $\frac{q}{a-q} = 1 + \rho$, which gives $q = \bar{q} = \frac{a}{2+\rho}$. Also, $b = \bar{b} = pq = \frac{1}{\sqrt{2+\lambda}} \frac{a}{2+\rho} = \frac{1}{\sqrt{1+\rho}} \frac{a}{2+\rho}$. Finally, because the cash-flow constraint is tight, $d = \bar{d} = (1 + \rho)(b - m) = (1 + \rho)(\frac{1}{\sqrt{1+\rho}} \frac{a}{2+\rho} - m)$.

We remark here that condition (6.40) together with the multiplier λ's non-negativity in this case implies $\rho \geq 1$; hence in particular here $q \leq \frac{a}{3}$. The precise value of ρ is determined in a similar fashion to the previous case, that is, via the formulas for d and $\bar{d}$ given above, plus the balancing condition $1 + \rho = \frac{d+d}{B}$.

Also, we remark here that since the cash-flow constraint is tight and the budget constraint is loose, we must have $pq \geq d$; that is, $b \geq (1 + \rho)(b - m)$. Rearranging gives $(1 + \rho)m \geq \rho b = \frac{a\rho}{\sqrt{1+\rho}(2+\rho)}$, or $m \geq \frac{a\rho}{(1+\rho)^{3/2}(2+\rho)}$. Thus the conditions for this case are $\frac{a\rho}{(1+\rho)^{3/2}(2+\rho)} \leq m \leq \frac{\sqrt{2}a}{6}$.

Finally, we remark that although this case cannot occur with our value of $B = a$, it can happen with smaller B's. An example would be where $m = \frac{a}{12}$ and $B = \frac{a}{60}$. In that case, $\rho = 3$ and $q = \bar{q} = \frac{a}{5}$.

Case 4: Smallest amount of money: Now we assume $\lambda > 0$ and $\mu > 0$. We have (6.38) implies $\sqrt{\frac{a-q}{b}} = (2+\lambda+\mu)\sqrt{\bar{p}}$ and (6.39) implies $\sqrt{\frac{b}{a-q}} = p\sqrt{\bar{p}}$ $(1+\mu)$. Therefore $(2+\lambda+\mu)\sqrt{\bar{p}} = \frac{1}{p\sqrt{\bar{p}}(1+\mu)}$. Now here (6.40) is $1+\lambda = \rho(1+\mu)$, so we have (after symmetry) $p = \bar{p} = \frac{1}{(1+\mu)\sqrt{1+\rho}}$. Also, (6.39) $\Rightarrow$ $\sqrt{\frac{\bar{p}\bar{q}}{a-q}} = p\sqrt{\bar{p}}(1+\mu) \Rightarrow \frac{q}{a-q} = p^2(1+\mu)^2 = \frac{1}{1+\rho}$. So again $q = \bar{q} = \frac{a}{2+\rho}$. In addition, the tightness of both constraints implies that: (a) $b = d$; and (b) $m + \frac{d}{1+\rho} - b = 0$. Hence $m + \frac{b}{1+\rho} - b = 0$, which gives $b = \frac{1+\rho}{\rho}m = \bar{b} = d = \bar{d}$.[21] The interest rate ρ can now be calculated. From the balance conditions, we have $1 + \rho = \frac{d+\bar{d}}{B} = \frac{2(1+\rho)m}{\rho B}$, which gives $\rho = \frac{2m}{B}$. Again, we can now go back and get expressions for the other variables in terms of m, a, and B.

The results here hold only if the multiplier μ remains nonnegative. To get an expression for μ, we set our two expressions for q equal to each other; that is,

$$\frac{a}{2+\rho} = q = \frac{b}{p} = \frac{\frac{1+\rho}{\rho}m}{\frac{1}{(1+\mu)\sqrt{1+\rho}}} = \frac{(1+\mu)(1+\rho)^{3/2}m}{\rho}.$$

This yields the following expression: $\mu = \frac{\rho a}{(1+\rho)^{3/2}(2+\rho)m} - 1$. Substituting in $\frac{2m}{B}$ for ρ, we can write the nonnegativity of μ as $B(1+\frac{2m}{B})^{3/2}(2+\frac{2m}{B}) \leq 2a$. We note that again this condition cannot hold if $B \geq a$; however, it can hold if, say, $B = \frac{a}{50}$ and $m = \frac{a}{100}$.

6.7.3 The Case with the *Really* Altruistic Bank

We noted before that in the model above, the traders would each demand infinite amounts of loan if the interest rate ρ were zero. But what if via a rationing system the trader types each were permitted to borrow $\frac{B}{2}$ at an interest rate of zero? Clearly, the trader types would both do this, and so the optimization problem for the traders would be

---

21 Again, as in Case 2, if $m = 0$ it is impossible for $b = \bar{b} = d = \bar{d} = 0$ because that would imply a negative interest rate. In fact, if $m = 0$ in this case, limiting arguments show an equilibrium with $\rho = 0$, $q = \bar{q} = \frac{a}{2}$, and $b = \bar{b} = d = \bar{d} = \frac{B}{2}$.

$$\max_{b,q} 2\sqrt{(a-q)\frac{b}{p}} + m + \frac{B}{2} - b + m + \frac{B}{2} - b + pq - \frac{B}{2}$$

$$\text{s.t. } m + \frac{B}{2} - b \geq 0 \ (\lambda) \tag{6.43}$$

$$m + \frac{B}{2} - b + pq - \frac{B}{2} \geq 0 \qquad (\mu)$$

$$0 \leq q \leq a \text{ and } b \geq 0$$

for the Type 1 traders, with a similar problem for the Type 2 traders. We still have the balance conditions for the prices; that is, $p = \frac{b}{q}$ and $\bar{p} = \frac{b}{q}$.

Immediately we note that condition (μ) has become redundant, and so we will ignore it in our analysis. Hence, there will be only two cases: that where the cash-flow constraint is loose, and that where it is tight.

The first-order conditions wrt b and q for the Type 1 traders' problem are

$$\frac{1}{\sqrt{p}}\sqrt{\frac{a-q}{b}} = 2 + \lambda \tag{6.44}$$

$$\frac{1}{\sqrt{p}}\sqrt{\frac{b}{a-q}} = p, \tag{6.45}$$

with a similar set of conditions for the Type 2 traders. *The reader will note that these are the exact same first-order conditions as in the no-bank case (Subsection 6.7.1).* Hence, we can use the solutions generated from that model. However, the extra term "$\frac{B}{2}$" in the cash-flow constraint will mean that mathematical definition of "enough money" will be different.

Case 1: Enough money: This is the case where the multiplier $\lambda = 0$. Our results from Section 6.7.1 give $p = \bar{p} = \frac{\sqrt{2}}{2}$, $q = \bar{q} = \frac{a}{3}$, and $b = \bar{b} = \frac{\sqrt{2}a}{6}$. These results are valid so long as the cash-flow constraint holds; that is, $m + \frac{B}{2} \geq \frac{\sqrt{2}a}{6}$.

Case 2: Not enough money: This is the case where the multiplier $\lambda > 0$. Our results from Section 6.7.1 give $b = \bar{b} = m$, q (and $\bar{q}$) the solution to $q^3 + m^2 q - m^2 a = 0$, and $p = \bar{p}$ determined by the balancing conditions $p = \frac{b}{q}$ and $\bar{p} = \frac{b}{q}$. Note that this case would be rare, as both m and B must be small.

Chapter 7 Markets with Fiat

WHOLESALER TO RETAILER: "Why are you complaining?"

RETAILER TO WHOLESALER: "Those sardines you sold me, customers ate them and were poisoned."

WHOLESALER TO RETAILER: "You fool, those were trading sardines, not eating sardines."

—*Old New York Story (abbreviated)*

7.1 TWO TRADER TYPES TRADING WITH FIAT

We now move to economies using fiat money, which will be the medium of exchange in all the models throughout the rest of this book (unless otherwise noted). In this chapter, the models we solve are presented in Table 7.1:

Table 7.1. Two treatments for trade with fiat money and credit

	Cash only	Altruistic central bank
Type 1 traders	$(a, 0, m)$	$(a, 0, 0)$
Type 2 traders	$(0, a, m)$	$(0, a, 0)$
Central bank	No	$(0, 0, B)$

7.1.1 The Treatment of the Service Value of Fiat

The transactions aspects of the services of fiat are different in many ways from, often superior to, and sometimes inferior to those of gold.[1] In Chapter 6 we noted three aspects of gold to which value is attached. They are its value as an ornament or in production, its value in transactions, and its residual value as an asset with a possible salvage value at the end of the economy. Fiat has only two values: its value in transactions, and its residual value as an asset with a possible salvage value at the end of the game.[2]

Let us recall the way the service value of gold money was modeled in Chapter 6. Type 1 traders attempt to solve:

$$
\begin{aligned}
\max_{q,b} \varphi &\left(a - q, \frac{b}{\bar{p}} \right) + k_2 \dot{m} + (k_3 - k_2)(\dot{m} - \dot{b}) \\
&+ (1 - k_3)(\dot{m} - \dot{b} + \dot{I}) + \Pi(m - b + pq) \\
\text{s.t. } & m - b \geq 0 \qquad\qquad (\lambda) \\
& m + pq - b \geq 0 \qquad (\mu) \\
& b \geq 0, \ 0 \leq q \leq a.
\end{aligned}
\tag{7.1}
$$

Here k_2 is the proportion of the period before the goods market opens, $k_3 - k_2$ is the proportion of time spent during the market where the consumption use of the gold used as money is lost, and $1 - k_3$ is the proportion of time after the market where the consumption use of gold held by the final owner of the asset is realized. The parameter Π is the salvage value for the asset. The distinction between fiat and gold is that whereas gold has worth in consumption or transactions but not both, fiat almost never has consumption worth.[3]

---

1 Transportability is easier and much faster; durability is extremely different; cognizability raises different questions; and divisibility is easier. In a decaying or war-ridden society, gold may be more trustworthy than the political legal and societal guarantees of its paper. (See Jevons, 1875; Shubik, 1999a.)

2 This assumes an economy without a loan market.

3 The "almost" is there to take care of its consumption uses to satisfy scriptophilia or to decorate one's walls after a hypoinflation.

Hence in our models of fiat money, all quantities with dots are equal to zero; so, for example, we can effectively remove the second, third, and fourth terms from the objective function above. The result, when $\Pi = 1$, is a model that is mathematically identical to our "basic model" from Chapter 3; in general, *given one of our models using fiat money, it is mathematically equivalent to a "corresponding" consumable storable money model in which the marginal consumption utility of money is equal to* Π. So, for example, when in Chapter 13 we solve the model with a fiat-money-lending monopolist who also consumes the two perishables, we will also be solving the model (proposed in Section 5.2.3) featuring a consumable storable money lending monopolist.

7.1.2 The Treatment of the Salvage Value of Fiat

Because fiat is an ersatz durable, it has physical properties concerning its utilization, creation, and destruction that are different from other physical assets. In particular, if the residual worth of fiat is not supported by general expectations, it might be supported by its use in debt repayment. A finite economy can be considered as "cash consuming," where an outside government agency initially finances market trade through a free issue of outside money. Then, if the central bank is willing to lend, it will extract all of the outside money from the system at the end of time. In essence, the rate of interest and borrowing serve as a backward operator through time—so that at the start of the final settlement day $T + 1$, after a T-period economy has closed down, the fiat in the system is just adequate to pay the debt owed to the central bank. If an infinite horizon is considered, the rate of interest charged by the outside bank in order to remove all outside money approaches (but does not attain) zero.

7.1.3 The Hahn Paradox Revisited: Many Feasible Fixes

THE PARADOX

The Hahn paradox deals with why there are problems with introducing fiat money[4] into the general equilibrium system. Hahn (1965) observed that if

---

4 We say "fiat" here, but in the original work of Debreu (1959) even commodity money cannot be made to fit without explicitly introducing period-by-period cash-flow conditions. The model was the right abstraction to get away from transactions problems and the host of boundary conditions and inequalities their control system structure generates. A model that is excellent for one purpose may blind one to the facts needed for other purposes.

worthless paper money were introduced into a general equilibrium model with a finite duration of T time periods, then one could work a backward induction as follows. First, at time $T + 1$ any of the money left over is worthless; hence there is no point in selling any item at time T if one is going to be paid in a durable with no future worth and no current consumption value. Hence no individual small agent will offer any item of value for sale in period T. If this happens, the markets are inactive at time T and we may repeat the argument for time $T - 1$, concluding that the markets never go active.

The mathematics and logic point out the problem, but the solution lies in formulating the appropriate models of economic activity. As a good approximation, we live embedded in time. There has been a yesterday, and with a high probability there will be a tomorrow. The finite horizon economic model is embedded in society and time. In order to make the model more plausible we must approximate the conditions posed by the existence of history and the future. It is necessary to be specific about how initial or "pre-game" conditions are specified and to provide explicit instructions for the terminal conditions of the game.

THE MANY SUFFICIENT CONDITIONS FOR A FIX

It has been suggested elsewhere (Shubik, 1999a) that there are many plausible ways to achieve a fix. We must pay attention not only to the meaning of the terminal conditions, but how they depend on the initial conditions.

Initial Conditions: Debt and Ownership: From the viewpoint of the econo- mist, the initial conditions specify property rights and ownership claims. These conditions may also include debts owed to agents outside of the game, or who preexisted but still exist in the game. Examples are the government and the first generation in an overlapping generations model.

Terminal Conditions: Salvage Values and Expectations:

> There are six and thirty ways of constructing Tribal lays and every single one of them is right!
> —Rudyard Kipling, "In the Neolithic Age" (1892)

Simplicity calls for us to seek the basic "cleanest" conditions. The whole philosophy of the approach here has been that of "minimal institutions." Yet in a complex world sometimes more than one set of conditions are both plausible and sufficient. Several different ways for taking care of terminal conditions are noted: The detailed discussions of most of them have been given elsewhere by many scholars of monetary theory. As these specifics are not germane to the main thrust of this book, they are not discussed in detail here, and no attempt is made to provide an exhaustive treatment. The list includes:

1. The existence of a randomly distributed initial amount of outside money which must, by the rules of the game, be returned at the end (passed to the next generation, or back to society in some other way) (Shubik and Wilson, 1977).
2. The existence of a private bank of such reputation that only the paper it issues is treated as a money. It is trusted to the extent that it may print its money, in the sense that it can pay for goods and services or monetize the credit of others with its notes.[5]
3. There may be oligopolistic private banks who control much of the supply of the outside money (see Shubik, 1970, 1976).[6]
4. There may be an outside central bank which, by charging a positive rate of interest in what would physically be a stationary state, will be able to "consume all of the original free issue of fiat by the end of any finite horizon" (Shubik, 1980).
5. There is an outside bank which offers loans and imposes default conditions on those who fail to cover their debts at the end of the game (Shubik and Wilson, 1977).
6. Salvage values may be attached to any leftover assets attributed to any type of expectations proposed.
7. The valuation could be based on some form of rational expectations.[7]

---

5 If a private merchant bank's paper is universally accepted, some of its previously issued paper, such as "gift certificates," could circulate as the equivalent of government outside money where, in general, they are never called. If they are called, they are redeemable as "goods at the store." In such an economy real assets back the "outside money"; the interest rate can be positive, representing the merchant banker's revenues which may be consumed, thereby balancing all books internally.

6 A completely different way of modeling the trust problem is via cooperative game theory—this was attempted (Shubik, 1970), but abandoned for the more institutional strategic form approach. The utilization of the core concept to a monetary economy to illustrate the properties of trust appears to be promising and is treated elsewhere, in other sources.

7 An excellent discussion of expectations is given by Grandmont (1982). For a treatment of rational expectations with nonsymmetric information see Dubey, Geanakoplos, and Shubik (1987).

8. One can assume that as the processes are intrinsically dynamic, the correct fix is to deal directly with the infinite horizon; thus a backward induction is not relevant (Karatzas, Shubik, and Sudderth, 1994; Lucas, 1980; Shubik, 1972).

9. Overlapping generations may be postulated as a better model than either the finite termination or the dynasty economies (Balasko and Shell, 1980).

10. One can introduce taxes, subsidies, and public goods in many different ways, providing a variety of realistic "fixes" for the terminal conditions.

11. All agents issue their own credit notes. A bankruptcy law is specified, and a credit agency evaluates each agent's credit so that she or he conforms with her or his budget constraints (see Sahi and Yao, 1989; Sorin, 1996). This imaginative but somewhat counterfactual solution stresses the ever-growing importance of credit evaluation in a mass anonymous market economy. The evaluation poses problems in coordination (for a connection with related problems in physics see Smith and Shubik, 2003).

12. A wedge between buying and selling costs intermediated by a money can be introduced in several ways (Foley, 1970; Hahn, 1971; Kurz, 1974; Ostroy and Starr, 1974).

13. Credit considerations.

14. Legal considerations (Bryant and Wallace, 1983).

15. More or less any combination of the above list can be considered. Any of them can be used to set up a playable experimental game.

All of the above are sufficient to avoid the Hahn paradox, but none are necessary, even the government bank. The government bank can use a rate of interest to remove the outside fiat money, which is the basis for an essentially costless financing of the transactions needs (Shubik, 1980). Even with an outside bank, in a finite horizon game it is unreasonable to attach zero worth to all other durables such as land and other highly durable resources which will physically be there at time $T + 1$.

The mathematical treatments linking infinite horizon and finite horizon dynamic programming appear to be appropriate. The initial conditions specify the ownership claims, including items such as goods-in-process—these are parameters of the game rather than control variables. At the end of time the conditions must be specified that appropriately reflect the possibility that the actual process continues but is being approximated by a finite horizon. A reasonably sophisticated way to handle this problem is to assign a positive salvage value to all leftover assets and money at the end of the game.[8]

In this chapter we model two ways to avoid the Hahn paradox. First, in Section 7.1.4 we designate a positive salvage value Π to leftover fiat. Then, in Section 7.1.5 we analyze a model which includes a central bank making loans; in that case even if $\Pi = 0$, there is no paradox. In both models we are able to calculate equilibria with trade in all cases.

7.1.4 Two Trader Types Trading with Fiat: The Model

Our previous model of a market with gold is now modified for trade in fiat.

We again consider two types of traders trading in two goods, with initial endowments of $(a, 0, m)$ and $(0, a, m)$.[9] The common utility function for the types is $\varphi(x, y) + \Pi z$, where the z stands for the terminal amount of fiat held by the traders of either type, and the parameter $\Pi > 0$ is the end-of-game salvage value for the fiat (which can be interpreted as an expectation of its value in future trade).

As before, there is a continuum of each trader type. A strategy of the Type 1 traders is denoted by (b, q), where b is the amount of fiat bid for good 2 and q is the amount of good 1 offered for sale. The notation for Type 2 traders is $(\bar{b}, \bar{q})$.

The Type 1 traders attempt to solve:

$$\max_{b,q} \varphi\left(a - q, \frac{b}{p}\right) + \Pi(m + pq - b)$$
$$\text{s.t. } m - b \geq 0 \qquad\qquad (\lambda) \tag{7.2}$$
$$b \geq 0, \ 0 \leq q \leq a.$$

---

8 In assigning a salvage value to the one-period model, there are few problems; but a salvage value for a multiperiod model poses new and highly practical problems. For most corporations, five years out is just about as far as any planning process goes. Furthermore, in keeping with flexibility and evolution, the process is evolutionary. Each year the plans are updated. The forming of expectations and anticipations about the future is an iterative process.

9 Note that there is no longer a breakdown of monetary endowment into an asset component and a service (consumption) component. This is due to our observation that fiat has no consumption value. See Section 7.1.1, "The Treatment of the Service Value of Fiat."

The Type 2 traders face a similar maximization problem:

$$\max_{\bar{b},\bar{q}} \varphi\left(a - \bar{q}, \frac{\bar{b}}{p}\right) + \Pi(m + \bar{p}\bar{q} - \bar{b})$$

$$\text{s.t. } m - \bar{b} \geq 0 \qquad\qquad (\bar{\lambda})$$

$$\bar{b} \geq 0, \ 0 \leq \bar{q} \leq a. \tag{7.3}$$

Price is formed by:

$$p = \frac{\bar{b}}{q} \text{ and } \bar{p} = \frac{b}{\bar{q}}. \tag{7.4}$$

If our stress is on stationarity we can consider an extra "rational expectations" condition (see below) and impose extra constraints on expectations. Thus here if we feel that predictions of future prices are absolutely precise, we require that $\Pi = \frac{1}{p} = \frac{1}{\hat{p}}$, that is, that money is expected to preserve its purchasing power. If $\hat{p} = p$, the predicted price will equal the actual price. When there is more than one durable, the rational expectations condition requires values for each durable. If we desire to reflect different levels of uncertainty for different durables, this can be done by assuming that Π_j (the expected price of the jth durable) lies within a range $p_j - \Delta \leq \Pi_j \leq p_j + \Delta$, and that a subjective probability distribution for Π_j over the range is common knowledge.[10]

We note that the combination of the rational expectations together with the implicit "no bankruptcy law" in the constraint essentially reduces this problem to the model for gold, with $k_1 = 0$, $k_2 = 0$, $k_3 = 1$, and $\Pi_i > 0$. The concept of "enough fiat money" cannot be defined without specifying the bankruptcy rules and the salvage conditions. But once both bankruptcy and salvage conditions are given, then fiat (in an appropriate range) becomes "as good as gold."

The solution to the above model, in the case where $\varphi(x, y) = 2\sqrt{xy}$, is given in Appendix A.

A CAVEAT ON RATIONAL EXPECTATIONS

Since the 1970s, economists have increasingly used the concept of "rational expectations." *Rational expectations* is the modeling assumption that agents

---

10 Refinements of the information set of the subjective probability distribution may be regarded as reflecting expertise. This way of reflecting expertise is suggested in Dubey, Geanakoplos, and Shubik (1987).

use forecasting mechanisms that are mutually consistent, given the information available to them. From the viewpoint of game theory, it appears to be nothing more than a different description of the consistency conditions for the existence of a perfect noncooperative equilibrium. From the viewpoint of parallel dynamic programming models of the economy, it provides a mathematical device to patch up needed terminal conditions in such a way as to make learning and the formation of expectations irrelevant to the equilibria being studied. A great and desirable simplification is provided at the cost of accompanying the mathematics with verbal implications that a system not in equilibrium will learn how to achieve the coordination called for by an equilibrium. We have considerable doubts that this finesse in the formulation of expectations provides an adequate description of macroeconomic reality. Yet there is a certain attraction to the simplicity of rational expectations, in that it presents a nice test for experimental gaming—to investigate if experimental subjects presented with given expectations of the terminal value of assets will approach the equilibrium predicted.[11] In the literature on experimental games, Huber, Shubik, and Sunder (2007, 2008) investigate the predictive value of rational expectations in the context of a market game.

7.1.5 Two Trader Types Trading with Fiat:
The Model with a Strategic Dummy
Central Bank

We first consider an accommodating bank which has a fixed strategy (hence it is a strategic dummy and we do not ascribe a payoff function for it, much less attribute profit maximization).[12]

A strategy for the Type 1 traders is as before, and is denoted by (b, q, d), where b is the amount of money bid for good 2, q is the amount of good 1 offered for sale, and d is the amount of personal IOU notes bid for the fiat money offered by the bank. The notation for Type 2 traders is $(\bar{b}, \bar{q}, \bar{d})$.[13]

---

11 The problem of uniqueness of an equilibrium is by no means guaranteed in models utilizing rational expectations. Koopmans (1977) provides an elegant counterexample.
12 In institutional fact, central banks have often made a profit.
13 In an economy involving several periods, we would wish to consider the central bank as both a lender and a borrower; thus the strategy sets would involve d and g on one side and a matching $\bar{d}$ and $\bar{g}$ on the other. We do not deal with this in this book.

Thus Trader Type 1's optimization problem is

$$\max_{b,q,d} \varphi \left(a - q, \frac{b}{p} \right) + \Pi \left(m + \frac{d}{1+\rho} - b + pq - d \right)$$

$$\text{s.t. } m + \frac{d}{1+\rho} - b \geq 0 \qquad\qquad (\lambda)$$

$$m + \frac{d}{1+\rho} - b + pq - d \geq 0 \qquad\qquad (\mu)$$

$$b, d \geq 0, \ 0 \leq q \leq a,$$

(7.5)

with a similar optimization for the Type 2 traders. The endogenous price formation and rate of interest are formed as before:

$$p = \frac{\bar{b}}{q}, \bar{p} = \frac{b}{\bar{q}}, \text{ and } 1 + \rho = \frac{d + \bar{d}}{g},$$

where $0 \leq g \leq B = M - 2m$ is the amount of money offered for loan by the central bank, which could face one of the two following optimization problems:

PROBLEM I: CONTROLLING THE MONEY SUPPLY

The initial endowment of the bank is $(0, 0, B)$. Here we assume it has a fixed strategy, which is to simply lend out B no matter what the other players do.

If the central bank is granted the right of issue, then there is no clear physical meaning to the upper bound B of the amount of money it has, other than as a legally or societally imposed limit. However, if $2m$ of fiat is held by the public, then the upper bound on the loans of the bank for any ρ must be $g = \frac{2m}{\rho}$ if it expects to be paid back with interest. The actual desired borrowing of the traders will be determined by their transactions needs, and thus the equating of the money supply and effective demand at any interest rate may be interior or lie on a boundary.

If the bank is a strategic dummy and if it uses the money supply as its strategic variable, it is constrained to offer B units of money to the loan market. This formalization implicitly assumes that the concept of central bank reserves of fiat has been solved by the arbitrary selection of B. This, however, requires the appropriate normalization of the value of a unit of fiat.[14]

The model outlined above is solved completely (in the case where $\varphi(x, y) = 2\sqrt{xy}$) in Appendix B. In particular, we note that if $\Pi = 1$ and $B + 2m \geq a$

---

14 Fortunately, this can be done through the specification of the default penalty for failing to repay debt. This links the fiat unit with the disutility of the penalty.

(Case 1), the infusion of cash from the bank is sufficient to finance trade to the efficient levels. This contrasts with the case where the money is gold – the reader will recall from Sections 6.4 and 6.6 that no amount of lending was able to induce efficiency in that model. To continue the examples from that section, let us consider the case where the money is fiat, $\Pi = 1$, $B = a$, and $m = a$. With or without a bank, the consumption levels are the efficient $(\frac{a}{2}, \frac{a}{2})$ and $(\frac{a}{2}, \frac{a}{2})$. If $m = \frac{a}{10}$, our calculations yield consumptions of $(\frac{4a}{5}, \frac{a}{5})$ and $(\frac{a}{5}, \frac{4a}{5})$ for the trader types if there is no bank; with a bank, the consumption levels are efficient.

Table 7.2 summarizes the results from these examples, from Chapters 6 and 7. The upper first column gives the type of money—in the case of gold, we assume the parameter values k_1, k_2, and k_3 (see Chapter 6) are equal to 0, 0, and 1, respectively. The next two columns give the initial endowments. The "No bank" column gives the equilibrium consumption levels if there is no bank in the model, and the following "Utility" column gives the utility to the trader types of their equilibrium consumption levels of good, asset, and asset service (in the case of gold). The "Bank" column gives the consumption levels if there is an altruistic bank, endowed with $(0, 0, a)$, which lends out all of its resources at an endogenously determined interest rate. We then have another "Utility" column, defined similarly to the last one. "Gain" means the gain to the trader types caused by the introduction of the central bank, which is the seventh column minus the fifth column. Finally, we

Table 7.2. Gold and fiat money: Results

	Money	Trader 1	Trader 2	No bank	Utility
1.	Gold	$(a, 0, [a, a])$	$(0, a, [a, a])$	$(\frac{2a}{3}, \frac{a}{3})$; $(\frac{a}{3}, \frac{2a}{3})$	$\left(2 + \frac{\sqrt{2}}{2}\right) a$
2.	Fiat[a]	$(a, 0, a)$	$(0, a, a)$	$(\frac{a}{2}, \frac{a}{2})$; $(\frac{a}{2}, \frac{a}{2})$	$2a$
3.	Gold	$\left(a, 0, \left[\frac{a}{10}, \frac{a}{10}\right]\right)$	$\left(0, a, \left[\frac{a}{10}, \frac{a}{10}\right]\right)$	$(\frac{4a}{5}, \frac{a}{5})$; $(\frac{a}{5}, \frac{4a}{5})$	$1.3a$
4.	Fiat	$\left(a, 0, \frac{a}{10}\right)$	$\left(0, a, \frac{a}{10}\right)$	$(\frac{4a}{5}, \frac{a}{5})$; $(\frac{a}{5}, \frac{4a}{5})$	$1.3a$

	Bank	Utility	Gain	Bank, $\rho = 0$
1.	$(\frac{2a}{3}, \frac{a}{3})$; $(\frac{a}{3}, \frac{2a}{3})$	$\left(2 + \frac{\sqrt{2}}{2}\right) a$	0	$(\frac{2a}{3}, \frac{a}{3})$; $(\frac{a}{3}, \frac{2a}{3})$
2.	$(\frac{a}{2}, \frac{a}{2})$; $(\frac{a}{2}, \frac{a}{2})$	$2a$	0	—
3.	$(\frac{6a}{11}, \frac{5a}{11})$; $(\frac{5a}{11}, \frac{6a}{11})$	$1.513a$	$0.213a$	$(\frac{4a}{5}, \frac{a}{5})$; $(\frac{a}{5}, \frac{4a}{5})$
4.	$(\frac{a}{2}, \frac{a}{2})$; $(\frac{a}{2}, \frac{a}{2})$	$1.5a$	$0.2a$	—

[a] The results are the same if the fiat is replaced by a storable consumable money.

give the results from Chapter 6 with a bank lending all of its gold at interest rate zero.

In conclusion: There tends to be a gain in efficiency (in the consumption of perishables) both when we switch from a gold to a fiat money, and when we introduce a central bank. We explore these ideas again in Chapter 15, on demonetization.

PROBLEM 2: CONTROLLING THE RATE
OF INTEREST

Instead of utilizing the quantity of money as its control variable, the bank could use the rate of interest. The bank's fixed strategy would be to hold the interest rate at some ρ that it specifies. The condition $\rho \geq 0$ guarantees that the bank will not operate at a loss. But the use of the rate of interest without the specification of a bound on bank issue produces an endogenous demand for bank funds that could be unbounded.

For the solution to this model, we refer the reader to Chapter 8, where we solve a slightly more general model in which the traders are permitted to default on their loans.

AN ASIDE ON CLEARINGHOUSES, CREDIT
EVALUATION, AND INDIVIDUAL CREDIT

In all of the games described so far, we expected the players to stick to the rules of monetary usage. In fact, for the most part anyone can trade with anyone in more or less any way that they want. Thus the ability of any rule-making is limited by custom and individual acceptance. Some years ago, one of us coined the phrase "mathematical institutional economics" (Shubik, 1959) to reflect the importance of institutional detail in economic dynamics. For example, there is and should be a vast literature on intraday credit arrangements, which we do not cover here. This is a zone where the current micro-micro detail of financial practices intersects with economic theory.

7.1.6 A Profit Maximizing Monopolistic Bank?

We now consider a variant of one of the models from Chapter 5. Suppose that most of the means of payment are given to a private individual. Thus we assume two continua of traders as before, endowed with $(a, 0, m)$ and $(0, a, m)$. There is also a single agent of a third type, the moneylender, endowed with $(0, 0, B)$. The moneylender is a profit maximizer who will consume real resources and thus provide a measure of the worth of transactions in terms of resources extracted.

A DIGRESSION ON CURRENCY, REPUTATION,
AND CREDIT

Before analyzing this model, we note that the initial conditions could contain a mix of currencies. One currency could be the free issue of government fiat in the hands of the public. Another could be the existence of outstanding paper from the merchant banker's store, redeemable at his store in some form of "value received" such as coffee, beans, or government fiat. The existence of currency at the start does not require the existence of an outside bank. All it needs is to be honored by everyone in acceptance, recognition, trust, and enforcement.

THE FORMAL MODEL RESUMED

We formulate the simplest model, where there is just the outside fiat in circulation.

A strategy for the Type 1 traders is denoted by (b, q, d), where b is the amount of money bid for good 2, q is the amount of good 1 offered for sale, and d is the amount of money offered in the money market. The notation for the Type 2 traders is $(\bar{b}, \bar{q}, \bar{d})$, where $\bar{d}$ is the amount of personal IOU notes bid for the personal money offered by the moneylender.

Thus for Type 1 we consider

$$
\max_{b,q,d} \varphi \left(a - q, \frac{b}{p} \right) + \Pi \left(m + \frac{d}{1+\rho} - b + pq - d \right)
$$
$$
\text{s.t. } m + \frac{d}{1+\rho} - b \geq 0
$$
$$
m + \frac{d}{1+\rho} - b + pq - d \geq 0 \tag{7.6}
$$
$$
b, d \geq 0, \ 0 \leq q \leq a.
$$

There is a similar optimization problem for the Type 2 traders. Price formation and the endogenous rate of interest is formed as before:

$$
p = \frac{\bar{b}}{q}, \ \bar{p} = \frac{b}{\bar{q}}, \text{ and } 1 + \rho = \frac{d + \bar{d}}{g},
$$

where $0 \leq g \leq 2m$ is the amount of money offered for loan by the monopolistic moneylender. The lender's problem is

$$\max_{b_1^*, b_2^*, g} \varphi \left(\frac{b_1^*}{p}, \frac{b_2^*}{\bar{p}} \right)$$

$$\text{s.t. } \rho g - b_1^* - b_2^* \geq 0 \qquad (\lambda_B) \tag{7.7}$$

$$b_1^*, b_2^* \geq 0.$$

This constraint (7.7) is imposed that the monopolistic banker cannot spend more than his profits. This prevents the banker from dipping into reserves for personal use.

We shall see that a bankruptcy law can be interpreted as implicitly included in the nonnegativity constraint on the final budgets of the traders (see Chapter 8). We do not need a rational expectations condition which would have us set the appropriate price for a leftover durable gold, because there is no real durable in this model. The full amount of money in the system that includes the bank is a fiction, as the bank can write its own paper, possibly up to some bound B imposed by law or custom or intrinsic in the dynamics. Fortunately, the combination of the traders' no-bankruptcy constraint and the bank not being permitted to spend more than its booked profits balances the books.[15]

Qualitatively, the details of a solution to this model are along the lines of the model of the monopolistic bank presented in Chapter 5.

7.2 TRADE WITH FIAT AND DEMONETIZED GOLD, THE ROLE OF EXPECTATIONS, AND THE ALTRUISTIC CENTRAL BANK

The models with gold and two perishable consumables have only one real durable, and that durable is the gold used as money. The models with fiat and two consumables have only one ersatz or "constructive" durable and that is the fiat money, which we may destroy at the end by the backward operation of debt if borrowing is permitted. Gold, however, is not destroyed—and if it has a positive monetary salvage value, then the surviving asset can also be utilized to extinguish debt. In Section 6.4.1, we considered an altruistic bank with gold, and we noted the paradox that (without uncertainty) the only reason for

---

15 Pro forma we could also include a salvage value for the fiat left over in the bank, but without a full institutional dynamics this becomes almost a theological problem in accounting. If the bank is in control of being able to print the money supply, how should it define and evaluate the "leftover money supply"?

bank reserves is distrust among traders. We note here that when the economy switches from gold to fiat, a problem of the altruistic bank is solved—it no longer has to store reserves of major intrinsic value, but instead can use fiat, whose creation and storage costs are relatively small.

Suppose that our simple economy was using gold as its money (as in Section 6.4.1) and now switches from gold to fiat. This economy is now trading in five items: two perishable consumables, one durable, one constructive durable, and individual IOU notes. As our purpose is to indicate qualitatively the new phenomenon introduced by the demonetization, we purposely stay with a simple, highly symmetric example with just a central bank.

Such a model is proposed as "Model 3" in Chapter 15. We find that the switch from a gold to a fiat currency can increase efficiency in the economy, again because the traders are now motivated to use their money to facilitate transactions rather than for consumption.

7.3 APPENDIX A: TRADE WITH FIAT: NO BANKING

Our first model has trade where leftover fiat has a positive salvage value Π.

Type 1 traders attempt to solve:

$$\max_{q,b} 2\sqrt{(a-q)\frac{b}{\bar{p}}} + \Pi(m+pq-b)$$
$$\text{s.t. } m - b \geq 0 \qquad\qquad (\lambda)$$
$$b \geq 0,\ 0 \leq q \leq a. \tag{7.8}$$

First-order conditions wrt b, q, and λ give[16]

$$\frac{1}{\sqrt{\bar{p}}}\sqrt{\frac{a-q}{b}} = \Pi + \lambda \tag{7.9}$$

$$\frac{1}{\sqrt{\bar{p}}}\sqrt{\frac{b}{a-q}} = \Pi p \tag{7.10}$$

$$m - b = 0 \text{ or } \lambda = 0. \tag{7.11}$$

---

16 Recall the shorthand notation in conditions (7.11) and (7.15). See footnote 16 of Chapter 5 for details.

Type 2 traders attempt to solve:

$$\max_{\bar{q},\bar{b}} 2\sqrt{(a-\bar{q})\frac{\bar{b}}{p} + \Pi(m+\bar{p}\bar{q}-\bar{b})}$$

(7.12)

s.t. $m - \bar{b} \geq 0$ $(\bar{\lambda})$

$\bar{b} \geq 0, 0 \leq \bar{q} \leq a.$

First-order conditions give

$$\frac{1}{\sqrt{p}}\sqrt{\frac{a-\bar{q}}{\bar{b}}} = \Pi + \bar{\lambda}$$

(7.13)

$$\frac{1}{\sqrt{p}}\sqrt{\frac{\bar{b}}{a-\bar{q}}} = \Pi\bar{p}$$

(7.14)

$m - \bar{b} = 0$ or $\bar{\lambda} = 0.$

(7.15)

Price is formed by:

$$p = \frac{\bar{b}}{q} \text{ and } \bar{p} = \frac{b}{\bar{q}}.$$

(7.16)

Case 1: m is large. In this case $\lambda = \bar{\lambda} = 0$. Then equation (7.9) gives $\Pi = \frac{1}{\sqrt{\bar{p}}}\sqrt{\frac{a-q}{b}}$, from which $\sqrt{\frac{b}{a-q}} = \frac{1}{\Pi\sqrt{\bar{p}}}$. Substituting into (7.10) gives $\Pi p = \frac{1}{\sqrt{\bar{p}}}\frac{1}{\Pi\sqrt{\bar{p}}}$, which is $\Pi^2 p\bar{p} = 1$. From symmetry, $p = \bar{p} = \frac{1}{\Pi}$.

We have $\frac{1}{\Pi} = p = \frac{b}{q}$ and also $\frac{b}{a-q} = (\frac{1}{\Pi\sqrt{\bar{p}}})^2 = \frac{1}{\Pi}$. Hence $\frac{b}{q} = \frac{b}{a-q}$, which implies $q = \frac{a}{2}$. Also, $b = \bar{b} = pq = \frac{a}{2\Pi}$.

The implication is that fiat is hoarded and carried forward and the allocations from trade are efficient.

Finally, we remark that the above analysis is valid so long as the cash-flow constraint $m - b \geq 0$ holds; that is, $m \geq \frac{a}{2\Pi}$. So this is formally what we mean by "m is large."

Case 2: m is small. Here the cash-flow constraints are tight; that is, $\lambda > 0$ and $\bar{\lambda} > 0$. This further implies $b = m = \bar{b}$. Then (7.9) implies $\frac{1}{\sqrt{\bar{p}}}\sqrt{\frac{a-q}{b}} = \Pi + \lambda$, which is $\sqrt{\frac{b}{a-q}} = \frac{1}{\sqrt{\bar{p}}(\Pi+\lambda)}$. Substituting into (7.10) gives $\Pi p = \frac{1}{\sqrt{\bar{p}}}\frac{1}{\sqrt{\bar{p}}(\Pi+\lambda)}$, which is $p\bar{p} = \frac{1}{\Pi(\Pi+\lambda)}$. Hence by symmetry we have

$$p = \bar{p} = \frac{1}{\sqrt{\Pi(\Pi+\lambda)}}.$$

Next, equation (7.9) gives $\frac{1}{\bar{p}}\frac{a-q}{b} = (\Pi + \lambda)^2$. Substituting in our values for $\bar{p}$ and b, we get $q = a - \bar{p}b(\Pi + \lambda)^2 = a - \frac{1}{\sqrt{\Pi(\Pi+\lambda)}}m(\Pi + \lambda)^2 = a - m\frac{(\Pi+\lambda)^{3/2}}{\sqrt{\Pi}}$. But also $b = \bar{b} = pq$, hence $m = \frac{1}{\sqrt{\Pi(\Pi+\lambda)}}\left(a - m\frac{(\Pi+\lambda)^{3/2}}{\sqrt{\Pi}}\right)$. We can solve this computationally to find λ, and use the value of λ to find p and q.

7.4 APPENDIX B: TRADE WITH FIAT:
A STRATEGIC DUMMY BANK

We consider the market with a bank that is constrained to offer B units of fiat for loan to the market. Fiat is assumed to have a salvage value $\Pi \geq 0$. The Type 1 traders face

$$\max_{b,q,d} 2\sqrt{(a-q)\frac{b}{\bar{p}}} + \Pi\left(m + \frac{d}{1+\rho} - b + pq - d\right)$$

$$\text{s.t. } m + \frac{d}{1+\rho} - b \geq 0 \qquad\qquad (\lambda)$$

$$m + \frac{d}{1+\rho} - b + pq - d \geq 0 \qquad\qquad (\mu)$$

$$b,d \geq 0, \ 0 \leq q \leq a.$$

Similarly, for the Type 2 traders we have

$$\max_{\bar{b},\bar{q},\bar{d}} 2\sqrt{(a-\bar{q})\frac{\bar{b}}{p}} + \Pi\left(m + \frac{\bar{d}}{1+\rho} - \bar{b} + \bar{p}\bar{q} - \bar{d}\right)$$

$$\text{s.t. } m + \frac{\bar{d}}{1+\rho} - \bar{b} \geq 0 \qquad\qquad (\lambda)$$

$$m + \frac{\bar{d}}{1+\rho} - \bar{b} + \bar{p}\bar{q} - \bar{d} \geq 0 \qquad\qquad (\mu)$$

$$\bar{b},\bar{d} \geq 0, \ 0 \leq \bar{q} \leq a.$$

The first-order conditions for the Type 1 players are:

$$\frac{1}{\sqrt{\bar{p}}}\sqrt{\frac{a-q}{b}} = \Pi + \lambda + \mu \qquad\qquad (7.17)$$

$$\frac{1}{\sqrt{\bar{p}}}\sqrt{\frac{b}{a-q}} = (\mu + \Pi)p \qquad\qquad (7.18)$$

$$\lambda = (\mu + \Pi)\rho \text{ or } d = 0 \qquad\qquad (7.19)$$

$$m + \frac{d}{1+\rho} - b = 0 \text{ or } \lambda = 0 \tag{7.20}$$

$$m + \frac{d}{1+\rho} - b + pq - d = 0 \text{ or } \mu = 0, \tag{7.21}$$

and similarly, for the Type 2 players we have

$$\frac{1}{\sqrt{\bar{p}}} \sqrt{\frac{a - \bar{q}}{\bar{b}}} = \Pi + \bar{\lambda} + \bar{\mu} \tag{7.22}$$

$$\frac{1}{\sqrt{\bar{p}}} \sqrt{\frac{\bar{b}}{a - \bar{q}}} = (\bar{\mu} + \Pi)\bar{p} \tag{7.23}$$

$$\bar{\lambda} = (\bar{\mu} + \Pi)\rho \text{ or } \bar{d} = 0 \tag{7.24}$$

$$m + \frac{\bar{d}}{1+\rho} - \bar{b} = 0 \text{ or } \bar{\lambda} = 0 \tag{7.25}$$

$$m + \frac{\bar{d}}{1+\rho} - \bar{b} + \bar{p}\bar{q} - \bar{d} = 0 \text{ or } \bar{\mu} = 0. \tag{7.26}$$

The strategic dummy bank offers B for loan no matter what the other players do.

The balance conditions are:

$$p = \frac{\bar{b}}{q}, \ \bar{p} = \frac{b}{\bar{q}} \text{ and } 1 + \rho = \frac{d + \bar{d}}{B}. \tag{7.27}$$

Before beginning the analysis, we comment that the two trader types' problems are isomorphic; hence we may make the assumption of "symmetry," that is, that in a solution $p = \bar{p}$, $q = \bar{q}$, $d = \bar{d}$, and $b = \bar{b}$.

Case 1: m is large. This is the case where both the cash-flow constraints ((λ) and ($\bar{\lambda}$)) and the budget constraints ((μ) and ($\bar{\mu}$)) will be loose; that is, $\lambda = \mu = \bar{\lambda} = \bar{\mu} = 0$. Our first observation is that this case could not occur if $\Pi = 0$, because then the traders could increase their utilities by raising b and d, preserving the budget constraint, until such time as the cash-flow constraint becomes tight. Hence we may assume here that $\Pi > 0$.

If $\lambda = \mu = \bar{\lambda} = \bar{\mu} = 0$, equation (7.18) is $\frac{1}{\sqrt{\bar{p}}} \sqrt{\frac{b}{a-q}} = \Pi p$, which is $\sqrt{\frac{a-q}{b}} = \frac{1}{\Pi p \sqrt{\bar{p}}}$. Substitution into (7.17) gives $\frac{1}{\sqrt{\bar{p}}} \frac{1}{\Pi p \sqrt{\bar{p}}} = \Pi$, or $p\bar{p} = \frac{1}{\Pi^2}$. Symmetry then gives $p = \bar{p} = \frac{1}{\Pi}$.

Next, condition (7.17) gives $\sqrt{\frac{a-q}{b}} = \Pi\sqrt{\bar{p}} = \sqrt{\Pi}$; hence $\frac{a-q}{b} = \Pi$. But $b = \bar{b} = pq = \frac{q}{\Pi}$, so we have $\frac{a-q}{\frac{q}{\Pi}} = \Pi$. This simplifies to $q = \frac{a}{2} = \bar{q}$. Also, $b = \bar{b} = pq = \frac{a}{2\Pi}$.

Next, we note that since $\lambda = 0$, equation (7.19) implies $\rho = 0$.[17] Hence the balance condition $1 + \rho = \frac{d+\bar{d}}{B}$ implies $d = \bar{d} = \frac{B}{2}$.

We remark that the above analysis will be valid only so long as the cash-flow constraints (λ) and ($\bar{\lambda}$) remain satisfied. Since $d = \bar{d} = \frac{B}{2}$, this is $m \geq b - \frac{B}{2}$, or $m \geq \frac{a}{2\Pi} - \frac{B}{2}$. So this is what is meant by "m is large." Finally, note that the requirements for "m is large" become less onerous the higher Π is. This makes sense — Π higher means that the fiat is worth more at the end, which means that there is more incentive for the traders to hoard their money, which in turn means they are less likely to bump up against their cash-flow constraints.

Case 2: m is very small. In this case both the cash-flow constraints ((λ) and ($\bar{\lambda}$)) and the budget constraints ((μ) and ($\bar{\mu}$)) will be tight; that is, $\lambda > 0$, $\mu > 0$, $\bar{\lambda} > 0$, and $\bar{\mu} > 0$.

Since (λ) and (μ) both hold tightly, we have $d = pq$. Also from the balance condition $pq = \bar{b} = b$, hence $b = d$. So then (7.20) is

$$m - d + \frac{d}{1+\rho} = 0. \tag{7.28}$$

If $m > 0$, this gives $d = \frac{1+\rho}{\rho} m = b = \bar{b} = \bar{d}$. But then the balance condition for the interest rate gives $1 + \rho = \frac{2\frac{1+\rho}{\rho} m}{B}$, which is $\rho = 2m/B$.

Next, (7.18) implies that $\sqrt{\frac{a-q}{b}} = \frac{1}{(\mu+\Pi)p\sqrt{\bar{p}}}$. Substituting into (7.17), we have $\frac{1}{\sqrt{\bar{p}}} \frac{1}{(\mu+\Pi)p\sqrt{\bar{p}}} = \lambda + \mu + \Pi$, which is $p\bar{p} = \frac{1}{(\mu+\Pi)(\lambda+\mu+\Pi)}$. But (7.19) means $\lambda = (\mu + \Pi)\rho$; hence $p\bar{p} = \frac{1}{(\mu+\Pi)((\mu+\Pi)\rho+\mu+\Pi)} = \frac{1}{(1+\rho)(\mu+\Pi)^2}$. So by symmetry, $p = \bar{p} = \frac{1}{(\mu+\Pi)\sqrt{1+\rho}}$.

But also (7.18) implies $\frac{a-q}{b} = \frac{1}{(\mu+\Pi)^2 p^3}$, which is $q = a - \frac{b}{(\mu+\Pi)^2 p^3}$. Substituting in our expressions for b and p gives

$$q = a - \frac{\frac{1+\rho}{\rho} m}{(\mu+\Pi)^2 \left(\frac{1}{(\mu+\Pi)\sqrt{1+\rho}}\right)^3} = a - \frac{(1+\rho)^{5/2}(\mu+\Pi)m}{\rho} = \bar{q}. \tag{7.29}$$

---

17 We cannot have $d = 0$ here, because the balance condition $1 + \rho = \frac{d+\bar{d}}{B}$ would then imply a negative interest rate.

But then the balance equation $b = \bar{b} = pq$ is just $\frac{1+\rho}{\rho} m = \frac{1}{(\mu+\Pi)\sqrt{1+\rho}} \left(a - \frac{(1+\rho)^{5/2}(\mu+\Pi)m}{\rho} \right)$, which simplifies to

$$\mu = \frac{\rho a}{m(1+\rho)^{3/2}(2+\rho)} - \Pi. \tag{7.30}$$

Substituting (7.30) into (7.29) gives

$$q = a - \frac{(1+\rho)^{5/2} \left(\frac{\rho a}{m(1+\rho)^{3/2}(2+\rho)} \right) m}{\rho} = \frac{a}{2+\rho} = \bar{q}. \tag{7.31}$$

Also $p = \bar{p} = \frac{b}{q} = \frac{(1+\rho)(2+\rho)m}{\rho a}$, where $\rho = 2m/B$.

If $m = 0$, equation (7.28) implies $\rho = 0$ (we can't have $d = \bar{d} = 0$ because $1 + \rho = \frac{d+\bar{d}}{B}$ would imply a negative interest rate). But this in turn implies $d = \bar{d} = \frac{B}{2}$, and $b = d$ means $b = \bar{b} = \frac{B}{2}$. Next, the same argument as above gives $p = \frac{1}{(\mu+\Pi)\sqrt{1+\rho}}$, which here gives $p = \frac{1}{\mu+\Pi}$. But $q = \frac{b}{p}$, so $q = (\mu + \Pi)\frac{B}{2}$. But also (7.18) implies $\frac{a-q}{b} = \frac{1}{(\mu+\Pi)^2 p^3}$, which is $q = a - \frac{b}{(\mu+\Pi)^2 p^3} = a - (\mu + \Pi)\frac{B}{2}$. Setting these two expressions for q equal to each other gives $(\mu + \Pi)\frac{B}{2} = a - (\mu + \Pi)\frac{B}{2}$, or $\mu = \frac{a}{B} - \Pi$. But then $p = \bar{p} = \frac{1}{\mu+\Pi} = \frac{B}{a}$ and $q = \bar{q} = \frac{b}{p} = \frac{a}{2}$.

We remark that the results in Case 2 are valid only so long as the expression for the multiplier μ (or $\bar{\mu}$) remains nonnegative. From (7.30), this condition is $\frac{\rho a}{m(1+\rho)^{3/2}(2+\rho)} \geq \Pi$. Substituting in $\rho = 2m/B$ and rearranging gives

$$\Pi(B + 2m)^{3/2}(B + m) \leq B^{3/2} a. \tag{7.32}$$

Hence (7.32) gives the precise mathematical definition of "m is very small."[18] In particular we note that the condition is always satisfied if $\Pi = 0$. Intuitively this makes sense, because $\Pi = 0$ means the fiat is worthless at the end of the game. So the traders will spend all they have and borrow to such a degree that any future income will just cover their debts. But this is just another way of saying that their cash-flow and budget constraints will be tight.

Case 3: m is intermediate-valued. This is the case in which neither Case 1 nor Case 2 holds. Hence it must be that precisely one of the constraints (λ)

---

18 If $m = 0$, condition (7.32) reduces to $\Pi \leq \frac{a}{B}$, which is exactly right because in the previous paragraph we derived that $\mu = \frac{a}{B} - \Pi$ in this case.

and (μ) holds tightly, while the other is loose. But it is impossible for (λ) to be loose and (μ) tight in an optimum. This is because if (λ) were loose and (μ) tight the Type 1 traders could raise b and lower d in such a way that (μ) stays tight, (λ) stays satisfied, and the objective function value is improved.

So, in Case 3 (λ) and ($\bar{\lambda}$) are tight (i.e., $\lambda > 0$ and $\bar{\lambda} > 0$) while (μ) and ($\bar{\mu}$) are loose ($\mu = \bar{\mu} = 0$). Then (7.18) is $\frac{1}{\sqrt{p}}\sqrt{\frac{b}{a-q}} = \Pi p$, which is $\sqrt{\frac{a-q}{b}} = \frac{1}{\Pi p \sqrt{p}}$. Substituting into (7.17) gives $\frac{1}{\sqrt{p}}\frac{1}{\Pi p \sqrt{p}} = \Pi + \lambda$, which gives $p\bar{p} = \frac{1}{\Pi(\Pi+\lambda)}$. Now (7.19) is $\lambda = \Pi\rho$, so we have $p\bar{p} = \frac{1}{\Pi(\Pi+\Pi\rho)} = \frac{1}{\Pi^2(1+\rho)}$. Symmetry then gives $p = \bar{p} = \frac{1}{\Pi\sqrt{1+\rho}}$.

Next, (7.18) implies $\frac{1}{p}\frac{b}{a-q} = \Pi^2 p^2$. But $\frac{b}{p} = \bar{q} = q$, so we have $\frac{q}{a-q} = \Pi^2 p^2 = \frac{1}{1+\rho}$. Solving for q gives $q = \frac{a}{2+\rho} = \bar{q}$. And then $b = \bar{b} = pq = \frac{a}{\Pi\sqrt{1+\rho}(2+\rho)}$. Also, $d = (1+\rho)(b-m) = (1+\rho)\left(\frac{a}{\Pi\sqrt{1+\rho}(2+\rho)} - m\right) = \bar{d}$.

So now all that remains is to find ρ. But by the balance equation $1 + \rho = \frac{d+\bar{d}}{B} = \frac{2}{B}(1+\rho)\left(\frac{a}{\Pi\sqrt{1+\rho}(2+\rho)} - m\right)$. This means the value of ρ will be that which satisfies $\frac{a}{\Pi\sqrt{1+\rho}(2+\rho)} = \frac{B}{2} + m$. This calculation can easily be done using computational methods.

Chapter 8 Default and Bankruptcy

8.1 A POSSIBILITY NOT YET MODELED

Some readers will have observed that in our models with lending, we have not yet modeled the possibility that the traders might choose to default on their loans, declare bankruptcy, and thereby derive the benefit of having the bank's money without full repayment. If we include this as a strategic choice for the traders, we must also specify the penalties that would apply if they do in fact default.

In institutional fact, the bankruptcy laws are not changed daily by an all-seeing government who knows how to solve a mammoth general stochastic strategic market game. We hope the law is "good enough" and, in a world with uncertainty, it should accommodate to a positive level of bankruptcy (see Dubey, Geanakoplos, and Shubik, 2005; Shubik, 1999a, chs. 11, 12). An adequate discussion of the structure of bankruptcy concerns its treatment as a public good and its relationship to society's risk propensity for innovation.[1] This is not dealt with here.

There are two ways to model bankruptcy which illustrate a difference both in economic analysis and in administrative and informational reality. If we consider a budget constraint such as:

$$m + \frac{d}{1+\rho} - b + pq - d \geq 0 \qquad (\mu) \qquad (8.1)$$

and treat μ as a Lagrangian variable,[2] in essence we are offering an immediate adjustment of the bankruptcy penalty to the actions in the economy. By doing so we avoid a host of analytical, computational, informational, and administrative difficulties. In effect this is what is going on implicitly in general equilibrium theory. The Lagrangians can be interpreted as the marginal utility of income, which is just high enough to make strategic bankruptcy not worthwhile. Thus the bankruptcy penalty is equal to the marginal utility of wealth for each individual.

Another way, which we employ in Section 8.2, is to introduce a societally legally fixed parameter μ^*, which is adjusted every few years or decades by the socio-legal processes. In such an instance we remove the constraint shown above, and add an extra term to the objective function, of the form[3]

$$\mu^* \min \left(m + \frac{d}{1+\rho} - b + pq - d, 0 \right). \qquad (8.2)$$

An economy is embedded in its polity and society. Thus, in spite of the aesthetic appeal of the general equilibrium formulation, it is fruitful to seek abstract formulations, where outside parameters connecting naturally to the polity and society fit without attempting to find a premature purely economic endogenization of these parameters. This is especially true when we observe that the dynamics of the society, polity, and economy tend to be on considerably different timescales. The first step in constructing a mathematical model

---

1 The bankruptcy laws may be viewed as controlling the mutation rate of innovations in a society.

2 By this we mean that the penalty for going bankrupt is exactly the value of the Lagrangian multiplier μ, whatever it may be.

3 Although the parameter μ^* may seem somewhat abrupt and not as nice as a smoothly adjusting Lagrangian, in institutional fact there are only a few aggregate parameters for bankruptcy; but the more or less "smoothness," be it efficient or inefficient, is taken care of by the lawyers, accountants, and courts who personalize the highly aggregated parameters.

that treated bankruptcy conditions as societally given was made in Shubik and Wilson (1977).

A natural way for the lender to try to avoid the burden of the bankruptcy process is by utilizing the secured loan. The richer in durable assets a country is, the easier it is to construct asset secured loans; but in essence the phenomenon of bankruptcy is still called for by the dynamics of the economy as a loosely coupled system.

In practical banking, the terms of a secured loan implicitly include a "haircut" given in the valuation of the assets providing the security. Thus the individual may be lent only 80 percent of the value of the secured assets, in order to account for a possible decrease in the price of the secured assets over the loan period. Or even just 20 percent, if there is a chance that those prices could fall more. If prices drop really precipitously, there may be some point where secured loans are no longer offered.

8.2 TWO TRADER TYPES TRADING WITH FIAT: THE MODEL WITH BANKING AND BANKRUPTCY

In this section we explicitly lay down the model with the central bank from Chapter 7, except this time the traders have the option to not pay back their loans. In this case they incur a penalty of μ^* times the amount of money that is in arrears.[4]

Again we have two types of trader, trading in two types of good plus fiat money. The optimization for the Type 1 traders is

$$\max_{b,d,q} 2\sqrt{(a-q)\frac{b}{p} + \mu^*\left[m+\frac{d}{1+\rho}-b+pq-d\right]^-}$$
$$+\,\Pi\left[m+\frac{d}{1+\rho}-b+pq-d\right]^+$$

s.t. $m+\frac{d}{1+\rho}-b\geq 0$ $\qquad\qquad$ (λ) (cash-flow constraint)

$\qquad b,d\geq 0,\ 0\leq q\leq a.$

Here the notation $[x]^-$ means $\min(x,0)$ and $[x]^+$ means $\max(x,0)$. Hence the nonpositive quantity $\mu^*[m+\frac{d}{1+\rho}-b+pq-d]^-$ is the penalty assessed

---

4 The μ^* should take into account the fact that the penalty occurs at the *end* of the game, i.e., *after* one period has transpired. So perhaps we should write $\mu^* =$ (discount factor) $\times$ ("the spot" default penalty).

traders for bankruptcy at the end of the period, and $\Pi[m + \frac{d}{1+\rho} - b + pq - d]^+$ is the nonnegative worth of excess cash at the end of the period. Notice that there is now no budget constraint, because there is now no requirement that the traders repay their loans at the end of the game.

For the Type 2 traders, we have

$$\max_{\bar{b}, \bar{d}, \bar{q}} 2\sqrt{(a - \bar{q})\frac{\bar{b}}{p}} + \mu^* \left[m + \frac{\bar{d}}{1+\rho} - \bar{b} + \bar{p}\bar{q} - \bar{d} \right]^-$$

$$+ \Pi \left[m + \frac{\bar{d}}{1+\rho} - \bar{b} + \bar{p}\bar{q} - \bar{d} \right]^+ \qquad (\bar{\lambda}) \text{ (cash-flow constraint)}$$

$$\text{s.t. } m + \frac{\bar{d}}{1+\rho} - \bar{b} \geq 0$$
$$\bar{b}, \bar{d} \geq 0, \ 0 \leq \bar{q} \leq a.$$

As before, prices are formed via $p = \bar{b}/q$ and $\bar{p} = b/\bar{q}$. Now all that remains is to describe the role of the bank.

8.2.1 A Strategic Dummy Bank Holding g Constant

In this model, the bank's strategy is simply to offer a constant amount $g = G$ for loan. Thus our model is precisely the model from Sections 7.1.5 and 7.4, except for the default possibility and the "G" instead of "B" for the bank's strategy.[5] The interest rate ρ varies as a function of how much the traders wish to borrow $\left[1 + \rho = \frac{d + \bar{d}}{G} \right]$.

The model solutions are as follows. Note that the only difference between these results and those obtained in Chapter 7 is a subcase of "m very small," where strategic default is optimal.

Case 1: m large ($m \geq \frac{a}{2\Pi} - \frac{G}{2}$). In this case, as usual, the traders attain the efficient trading outcome without the use of a loan market.

Case 2: m very small ($\Pi(G + 2m)^{3/2}(G + m) \leq G^{3/2}a$). In this case the traders spend all their money on bidding, and also end up with no money at the end of the game. A subcase of this (when $(\Pi + \mu^*)(G + 2m)^{3/2}(G + m) \leq G^{3/2}a$) is when strategic default is optimal.

---

5 In Chapter 7, we used a "B" because the (altruistic) bank's strategy was to always offer to lend out all of its reserves (and the amount of its reserves is denoted as "B"). Here, we generalize to a strategy in which the bank's strategy is always to offer a constant amount G for loan (but G need not necessarily be equal to B). Mathematically, this makes no difference in the analysis.

Case 3: m intermediate. In this case the traders spend all their money on bidding at the first stage, but do end up with a positive amount of cash at the end.

8.2.2 A Strategic Dummy Bank Holding ρ Constant

Now we consider the same model as above, except now the bank's strategy is to offer whatever amount is necessary to satisfy demand for loans at the interest rate ρ. (This model, without the default option, was referred to in Chapter 7, but not solved.) Our first assumption, then, is that the bank has enough money to do this; that is, $g \le B$, where $g = \frac{d+\bar{d}}{1+\rho}$. In particular, the model solutions are:

Case 1: m large $(m \ge \frac{a}{2\Pi})$. In this case, as usual, the traders attain the efficient trading outcome without the use of a loan market.

Case 2: m very small $\left(m \le \frac{\rho a}{\Pi(1+\rho)^{3/2}(2+\rho)} \right)$. In this case the traders spend all their money on bidding, and also end up with no money at the end of the game. A subcase of this $\left(\text{when } m \le \frac{\rho a}{(\mu^*+\Pi)(1+\rho)^{3/2}(2+\rho)} \right)$ is when strategic default is optimal.

Case 3: m intermediate $\left(\frac{\rho a}{\Pi(1+\rho)^{3/2}(2+\rho)} \le m \le \frac{a}{2\Pi} \right)$. In this case the traders spend all their money on bidding at the first stage, but do end up with a positive amount of cash at the end.

The reader will note how closely its analysis follows that for the case in which the bank holds g constant.

8.2.3 Bankruptcy and the Conservation of Fiat

We note some problems in accounting for fiat and credit in bankruptcy. In economic fact, when a firm or individual goes bankrupt the only instruments that are destroyed are credit instruments. All physical goods and fiat money are conserved and redistributed in the settlement. In a simple one-period game, this paradox can be seen if an individual is permitted to borrow fiat from the outside bank, spends it, and goes bankrupt. The instrument that is destroyed is his IOU note (denominated in fiat). The amount of fiat in the system after one period is larger than it was initially, and is in the hands of the other agents who, are not required to return it to the government. However, who pays for economic misallocation is spelled out only in the future dynamics. In the one-period game this is encapsulated in the salvage value for fiat, that is, its expected future worth.

8.2.4 Further Comments

We remark that we essentially get the original models (with no default allowed) if μ^* is sufficiently large.[6] Also, in Chapter 16 we discuss how to model default in the case of a multiperiod model.

8.3 FIAT AND THE PRICE LEVEL

In the analysis above, there are three parameters that control the price level p. Two are governmentally determined, and one arises from expectations. They are μ^* (the bankruptcy penalty), $G + 2m$ (the amount of fiat money available to the system),[7] and the expected future worth of fiat (Π). Given Π as fixed and μ^* legally specified, we conclude that the price level is controlled by the selection of G. The upper bound on price occurs when G takes on its maximum value, that is, $G = B$.[8] The lower bound on price, that is, the lowest prices could be without the traders' strategic default, is dependent on μ^*. If strategic bankruptcy is to be avoided, we require that the strategic bankruptcy price level is below the price established with $G = B$.

The key observation is that in the general equilibrium economy the price level is homogeneous of order zero; in an economy with gold entering in as a quasi-linear term the price level is fully determined; but with fiat money the price level is confined to a closed range determined by the bankruptcy penalty and the amount of fiat in circulation.

8.4 APPENDIX: TRADE WITH A STRATEGIC DUMMY BANK, BANKRUPTCY ALLOWED

8.4.1 Appendix A: Trade with a Strategic Dummy Bank Holding g Constant

We consider the market with a bank that is constrained to offer $g = G$ units of fiat for loan to the market. The parameter μ^* is the penalty per unit for default. Fiat is assumed to have a salvage value Π. The Type 1 traders face

---

6 This may, in some instances, require that $\mu^* \to \infty$.

7 Alternatively, if ρ is the strategic variable of the bank, then replace "$G + 2m$" by "$B + 2m$" here.

8 This is borne out in the analysis of Case 2 and Case 3 in Appendix A. In both cases, p is inversely related to ρ, and ρ is inversely related to G. (In Case 2 this is true if $G \geq \sqrt{2}m$.)

$$\max_{b,d,q} 2\sqrt{(a-q)\frac{b}{p} + \mu^*\left[m + \frac{d}{1+\rho} - b + pq - d\right]^-}$$

$$+ \Pi\left[m + \frac{d}{1+\rho} - b + pq - d\right]^+ \qquad \text{(a)} \qquad (8.3)$$

$$\text{s.t. } m + \frac{d}{1+\rho} - b \geq 0 \qquad\qquad (\lambda) \quad \text{(b)}$$

$$b,d \geq 0, \ 0 \leq q \leq a. \qquad\qquad \text{(c)}$$

For the Type 2 traders, we have

$$\max_{\bar{b},\bar{d},\bar{q}} 2\sqrt{(a-\bar{q})\frac{\bar{b}}{p} + \mu^*\left[m + \frac{\bar{d}}{1+\rho} - \bar{b} + \bar{p}\bar{q} - \bar{d}\right]^-}$$

$$+ \Pi\left[m + \frac{\bar{d}}{1+\rho} - \bar{b} + \bar{p}\bar{q} - \bar{d}\right]^+ \qquad \text{(a)} \qquad (8.4)$$

$$\text{s.t. } m + \frac{\bar{d}}{1+\rho} - \bar{b} \geq 0 \qquad\qquad (\bar{\lambda}) \quad \text{(b)}$$

$$\bar{b},\bar{d} \geq 0, \ 0 \leq \bar{q} \leq a. \qquad\qquad \text{(c)}$$

As usual, prices are formed via $p = \frac{\bar{b}}{q}$ and $\bar{p} = \frac{b}{\bar{q}}$. Since the bank always lends G, the interest rate is given by $1 + \rho = \frac{d+\bar{d}}{G}$.

To solve this model, we first solve the same model except with strategic default not allowed. Thus the Type 1 traders' optimization problem reduces to that of the model in Sections 7.1.5 and 7.4; that is,

$$\max_{b,q,d} 2\sqrt{(a-q)\frac{b}{\bar{p}} + \Pi\left(m + \frac{d}{1+\rho} - b + pq - d\right)} \qquad \text{(a)}$$

$$\text{s.t. } m + \frac{d}{1+\rho} - b \geq 0 \qquad\qquad (\lambda) \quad \text{(b)}$$

$$m + \frac{d}{1+\rho} - b + pq - d \geq 0 \qquad\qquad (\mu) \quad \text{(c)} \qquad (8.5)$$

$$b,d \geq 0, \ 0 \leq q \leq a. \qquad\qquad \text{(d)}$$

Similarly, for the Type 2 traders we have

$$\max_{\bar{b},\bar{q},\bar{d}} 2\sqrt{(a-\bar{q})\frac{\bar{b}}{p} + \Pi\left(m + \frac{\bar{d}}{1+\rho} - \bar{b} + \bar{p}\bar{q} - \bar{d}\right)} \qquad \text{(a)}$$

$$\text{s.t. } m + \frac{\bar{d}}{1+\rho} - \bar{b} \geq 0 \qquad\qquad (\lambda) \quad \text{(b)}$$

$$m + \frac{\bar{d}}{1+\rho} - \bar{b} + \bar{p}\bar{q} - \bar{d} \geq 0 \qquad\qquad (\mu) \quad \text{(c)} \qquad (8.6)$$

$$\bar{b},\bar{d} \geq 0, \ 0 \leq \bar{q} \leq a. \qquad\qquad \text{(d)}$$

The idea here is that if strategic default is not allowed, and the parameters m and G are such that an equilibrium solution has constraint (μ) loose, then the model *with* strategic default has an equilibrium with the exact same values of b, q, d, $\bar{b}$, $\bar{q}$, and $\bar{d}$. Hence we can use much of the analysis from Section 7.4 here—in particular, Cases 1 and 3 below—however, for completeness we reproduce that analysis.

As we saw in Section 7.4, the first-order conditions for the Type 1 players are:

$$\frac{1}{\sqrt{p}}\sqrt{\frac{a-q}{b}} = \Pi + \lambda + \mu \tag{8.7}$$

$$\frac{1}{\sqrt{p}}\sqrt{\frac{b}{a-q}} = (\mu + \Pi)p \tag{8.8}$$

$$\lambda = (\mu + \Pi)\rho \text{ or } d = 0 \tag{8.9}$$

$$m + \frac{d}{1+\rho} - b = 0 \text{ or } \lambda = 0 \tag{8.10}$$

$$m - \frac{d}{1+\rho} - b + pq - d = 0 \text{ or } \mu = 0, \tag{8.11}$$

and similarly, for the Type 2 players we have

$$\frac{1}{\sqrt{p}}\sqrt{\frac{a-\bar{q}}{\bar{b}}} = \Pi + \bar{\lambda} + \bar{\mu} \tag{8.12}$$

$$\frac{1}{\sqrt{p}}\sqrt{\frac{\bar{b}}{a-\bar{q}}} = (\bar{\mu} + \Pi)\bar{p} \tag{8.13}$$

$$\lambda = (\bar{\mu} + \Pi)\rho \text{ or } \bar{d} = 0 \tag{8.14}$$

$$m + \frac{\bar{d}}{1+\rho} - \bar{b} = 0 \text{ or } \bar{\lambda} = 0 \tag{8.15}$$

$$m + \frac{\bar{d}}{1+\rho} - \bar{b} + \bar{p}\bar{q} - \bar{d} = 0 \text{ or } \bar{\mu} = 0. \tag{8.16}$$

Case 1: m is large. This is the case where both the cash-flow constraints ((λ) and ($\bar{\lambda}$)) and the budget constraints ((μ) and ($\bar{\mu}$)) will be loose; that is, $\lambda = \mu = \bar{\lambda} = \bar{\mu} = 0$. Our first observation is that this case could not occur if $\Pi = 0$, because then the traders could increase their utilities by raising b

and d—preserving the budget constraint—until such time as the cash-flow constraint become tight. Hence we may assume here that $\Pi > 0$.

If $\lambda = \mu = \bar{\lambda} = \bar{\mu} = 0$, equation (8.8) is $\frac{1}{\sqrt{\bar{p}}}\sqrt{\frac{b}{a-q}} = \Pi p$, which is $\sqrt{\frac{a-q}{b}} = \frac{1}{\Pi p \sqrt{\bar{p}}}$. Substitution into (8.7) gives $\frac{1}{\sqrt{\bar{p}}}\frac{1}{\Pi p \sqrt{\bar{p}}} = \Pi$, or $p\bar{p} = \frac{1}{\Pi^2}$. Symmetry then gives $p = \bar{p} = \frac{1}{\Pi}$.

Next, condition (8.7) gives $\sqrt{\frac{a-q}{b}} = \Pi\sqrt{\bar{p}} = \sqrt{\Pi}$; hence $\frac{a-q}{b} = \Pi$. But $b = \bar{b} = pq = \frac{q}{\Pi}$, so we have $\frac{a-q}{q/\Pi} = \Pi$. This simplifies to $q = \frac{a}{2} = \bar{q}$. Also, $b = \bar{b} = pq = \frac{a}{2\Pi}$.

Next, we note that since $\lambda = 0$, equation (8.9) implies $\rho = 0$.[9] Hence the balance condition $1 + \rho = \frac{d+\bar{d}}{G}$ implies $d = \bar{d} = \frac{G}{2}$.

We remark that the above analysis will be valid only so long as the cash-flow constraints (λ) and ($\bar{\lambda}$) remain satisfied. Since $d = \bar{d} = \frac{G}{2}$, this is $m \geq b - \frac{G}{2}$, or $m \geq \frac{a}{2\Pi} - \frac{G}{2}$. So this is what is meant by "enough money." Finally, note that the requirements for "m is large" become less onerous the higher Π is. This makes sense—Π higher means that the fiat is worth more at the end, meaning that there is more incentive for the traders to hoard their money, which in turn means they are less likely to bump up against their cash-flow constraints.

Case 2: m is very small. In this case both the cash-flow constraints ((λ) and ($\bar{\lambda}$)) and the budget constraints ((μ) and ($\bar{\mu}$)) will be tight; that is, $\lambda > 0$, $\mu > 0$, $\bar{\lambda} > 0$, and $\bar{\mu} > 0$.

Since (λ) and (μ) both hold tightly, we have $d = pq$. Also from the balance condition $pq = \bar{b} = b$, hence $b = d$. So then (8.10) is

$$m - \frac{d}{1+\rho} - d = 0. \tag{8.17}$$

If $m > 0$, this gives $d = \frac{1+\rho}{\rho} m = b = \bar{b} = \bar{d}$. But then the balance condition for the interest rate gives $1 + \rho = \frac{2\frac{1+\rho}{\rho} m}{G}$, which is $\rho = 2m/G$.

Next, (8.8) implies that $\sqrt{\frac{a-q}{b}} = \frac{1}{(\mu+\Pi)p\sqrt{\bar{p}}}$. Substituting into (8.7), we have $\frac{1}{\sqrt{\bar{p}}}\frac{1}{(\mu+\Pi)p\sqrt{\bar{p}}} = \lambda + \mu + \Pi$, which is $p\bar{p} = \frac{1}{(\mu+\Pi)(\lambda+\mu+\Pi)}$. But (8.9)

---

9 We cannot have $d = 0$ here because the balance condition $1 + \rho = (d + \bar{d})/G$ would then imply a negative interest rate.

means $\lambda = (\mu + \Pi)\rho$; hence $p\bar{p} = \frac{1}{(\mu+\Pi)((\mu+\Pi)\rho+\mu+\Pi)} = \frac{1}{(1+\rho)(\mu+\Pi)^2}$. So by symmetry, $p = \bar{p} = \frac{1}{(\mu+\Pi)\sqrt{1+\rho}}$.

But also (8.8) implies $\frac{a-q}{b} = \frac{1}{(\mu+\Pi)^2 p^3}$, which is $q = a - \frac{b}{(\mu+\Pi)^2 p^3}$. Substituting in our expressions for b and p gives

$$q = a - \frac{\frac{1+\rho}{\rho}m}{(\mu+\Pi)^2 \left(\frac{1}{(\mu+\Pi)\sqrt{1+\rho}}\right)^3} = a - \frac{(1+\rho)^{5/2}(\mu+\Pi)m}{\rho} = \bar{q}. \quad (8.18)$$

But then the balance equation $b = \bar{b} = pq$ is just $\frac{1+\rho}{\rho}m = \frac{1}{(\mu+\Pi)\sqrt{1+\rho}}\left(a - \frac{(1+\rho)^{5/2}(\mu+\Pi)m}{\rho}\right)$, which simplifies to

$$\mu = \frac{\rho a}{m(1+\rho)^{3/2}(2+\rho)} - \Pi. \quad (8.19)$$

Substituting (8.19) into (8.18) gives

$$q = a - \frac{(1+\rho)^{\frac{5}{2}}\left(\frac{\rho a}{m(1+\rho)^{3/2}(2+\rho)}\right)m}{\rho} = \frac{a}{2+\rho} = \bar{q}. \quad (8.20)$$

Also $p = \bar{p} = \frac{b}{q} = \frac{(1+\rho)(2+\rho)m}{\rho a}$, where $\rho = 2m/G$.

If $m = 0$, equation (8.17) implies $\rho = 0$ (we can't have $d = \bar{d} = 0$ because $1 + \rho = \frac{d+\bar{d}}{G}$ would imply a negative interest rate). But this in turn implies $d = \bar{d} = \frac{G}{2}$, and $b = d$ means $b = \bar{b} = \frac{G}{2}$. Next, the same argument as above gives $p = \frac{1}{(\mu+\Pi)\sqrt{1+\rho}}$, which here gives $p = \frac{1}{\mu+\Pi}$. But $q = \frac{b}{p}$, so $q = (\mu + \Pi)\frac{G}{2}$. But also (8.8) implies $\frac{a-q}{b} = \frac{1}{(\mu+\Pi)^2 p^3}$, which is $q = a - \frac{b}{(\mu+\Pi)^2 p^3} = a - (\mu+\Pi)\frac{G}{2}$. Setting these two expressions for q equal to each other gives $(\mu + \Pi)\frac{G}{2} = a - (\mu+\Pi)\frac{G}{2}$, or $\mu = \frac{a}{G} - \Pi$. But then $p = \bar{p} = \frac{1}{\mu+\Pi} = \frac{G}{a}$ and $q = \bar{q} = \frac{b}{p} = \frac{a}{2}$.

We remark that the results in Case 2 are valid only so long as the expression for the multiplier μ (or $\bar{\mu}$) remains nonnegative. From (8.19), this condition is $\frac{\rho a}{m(1+\rho)^{3/2}(2+\rho)} \geq \Pi$. Substituting in $\rho = 2m/G$ and rearranging gives

$$\Pi(G + 2m)^{3/2}(G + m) \leq G^{3/2}a. \quad (8.21)$$

Hence (8.21) gives the precise mathematical definition of "m very small."[10] In particular, we note that the condition is always satisfied if $\Pi = 0$. Intuitively

---

10 If $m = 0$, condition (8.21) reduces to $\Pi \leq \frac{a}{G}$, which is exactly right because in the previous paragraph we derived that $\mu = a/G - \Pi$ in this case.

this makes sense, because $\Pi = 0$ means the fiat is worthless at the end of the game. So the traders will spend all they have and borrow to such a degree that any future income will just cover their debts. But this is just another way of saying that their cash-flow and budget constraints will be tight.

Finally, this analysis gives us the solution to the model with the bankruptcy condition present (i.e., the traders' problems are given by (8.3)–(8.4) instead of by (8.5)–(8.6)). In Case 1 above and Case 3 below, the traders' optima occur with their budget constraints loose—hence, adding the default penalty back into the model will not change the solutions.[11] For Case 2, optimization theory tells us that strategic bankruptcy will become an optimal strategy for the traders if and only if the per-dollar cost of going bankrupt is less than the per-dollar worth of money in the budget constraint; that is, $\mu^* \leq \mu$. Substituting using (8.19), this is $\mu^* \leq \frac{\rho a}{m(1+\rho)^{3/2}(2+\rho)} - \Pi$, or (using $\rho = \frac{2m}{G}$)

$$(\mu^* + \Pi)(G + 2m)^{3/2}(G + m) \leq G^{3/2}a. \qquad (8.22)$$

If (8.22) *does not* hold, then the Case 2 solutions above for p, q, b, and d (as well as $\bar{p}$, $\bar{q}$, $\bar{b}$, and $\bar{d}$) are correct. If (8.22) *does* hold (so we are in the "strategic default" case), we can rewrite our traders' problems as

$$\max_{b,d,q} 2\sqrt{(a-q)\frac{b}{\bar{p}}} + \mu^* \left(m + \frac{d}{1+\rho} - b + pq - d \right)$$

$$\text{s.t. } m + \frac{d}{1+\rho} - b \geq 0 \qquad (\lambda) \text{ (cash-flow constraint)}$$

$$m + \frac{d}{1+\rho} - b + pq - d \leq 0 \qquad (\mu) \text{ ("modified" budget constraint)}$$

$$b, d \geq 0, \ 0 \leq q \leq a$$

---

11 To make this argument more precise, let us define three models. Model 1 is the no-default-allowed model, Model 2 is the model defined by (8.3)–(8.4), except without the $\mu^*[m + \frac{d}{1+\rho} - b + pq - d]^-$ and $\mu^*[m + \frac{\bar{d}}{1+\rho} - \bar{b} + \bar{p}\bar{q} - \bar{d}]^-$ terms in the objective functions. Finally Model 3 is the full default-allowed model, i.e., that where the traders' problems are (8.3)–(8.4). Now suppose there is a solution satisfying the first-order conditions for Model 1, with $\mu = 0$. Then this solution will be an equilibrium for Model 2, because the first-order conditions for Model 2 are identical to those for Model 1 with $\mu = 0$. But then the solution will also be an equilibrium for Model 3, because they attain the maximum possible value (of zero) for the expressions $\mu^*[m + \frac{d}{1+\rho} - b + pq - d]^-$ and $\mu^*[m + \frac{\bar{d}}{1+\rho} - \bar{b} + \bar{p}\bar{q} - \bar{d}]^-$.

and

$$\max_{\bar{b},\bar{d},\bar{q}} 2\sqrt{(a-\bar{q})\frac{\bar{b}}{p}} + \mu^*(m + \tfrac{\bar{d}}{1+\rho} - \bar{b} + \bar{p}\bar{q} - \bar{d})$$

s.t. $m + \tfrac{\bar{d}}{1+\rho} - \bar{b} \geq 0$ $\qquad\qquad$ ($\bar{\lambda}$) (cash-flow constraint)

$\qquad m + \tfrac{\bar{d}}{1+\rho} - \bar{b} + \bar{p}\bar{q} - \bar{d} \leq 0$ $\qquad$ ($\bar{\mu}$) ("modified" budget constraint)

$\qquad \bar{b}, \bar{d} \geq 0,\ 0 \leq \bar{q} \leq a.$

We note the presence of the "modified" budget constraint, to account for the fact that we are now searching in the region where the traders default on their loans. We also remark that the cash-flow constraint will be tight in this case ($\bar{\lambda} > 0$) and the modified budget constraint will be loose ($\bar{\mu} = 0$). Finally, the balance conditions $p = \frac{\bar{b}}{q}$ and $\bar{p} = \frac{b}{\bar{q}}$ still hold.

The analysis turns out to be the same as that for Case 3 below, except with μ^* playing the role of Π. The solution turns out to be $p = \bar{p} = \frac{1}{\mu^*\sqrt{1+\rho}}$, $q = \bar{q} = \frac{a}{2+\rho}$, $b = \bar{b} = \frac{a}{\mu^*\sqrt{1+\rho}(2+\rho)}$, and $d = \bar{d} = (1+\rho)\left(\frac{a}{\mu^*\sqrt{1+\rho}(2+\rho)} - m\right)$, where ρ satisfies $\frac{a}{\mu^*\sqrt{1+\rho}(2+\rho)} = \frac{G}{2} + m$. This calculation of ρ can be done by computational methods. The multipliers λ and $\bar{\lambda}$ turn out to be equal to $\rho\mu^*$.

As an example, consider the case where $m = \frac{a}{8}$, $G = 2a$, and $\mu^* = \Pi = 0.01$. We end up with an interest rate ρ equal to approximately 18, with $p \cong 22.9$, $q \cong .05a$, and $d \cong 19.4a$. The traders' equilibrium strategies involve defaulting on about $18.2a$ of debt.

Case 3: m is intermediate-valued. This is the case in which neither Case 1 nor Case 2 holds. Hence it must be that precisely one of the constraints (λ) and (μ) holds tightly, while the other is loose. But it is impossible for (λ) to be loose and (μ) tight in an optimum. This is because if (λ) were loose and (μ) tight the Type 1 traders could raise b and lower d in such a way that (μ) stays tight, (λ) stays satisfied, and the objective function value is improved.

So, in Case 3 (λ) and ($\bar{\lambda}$) are tight (i.e., $\lambda > 0$ and $\bar{\lambda} > 0$) while (μ) and ($\bar{\mu}$) are loose ($\mu = \bar{\mu} = 0$). Then (8.8) is $\frac{1}{\sqrt{\bar{p}}}\sqrt{\frac{b}{a-q}} = \Pi p$, which is $\sqrt{\frac{a-q}{b}} = \frac{1}{\Pi p\sqrt{\bar{p}}}$. Substituting into (8.7) gives $\frac{1}{\sqrt{\bar{p}}}\frac{1}{\Pi p\sqrt{\bar{p}}} = \Pi + \lambda$, which gives $p\bar{p} = \frac{1}{\Pi(\Pi+\lambda)}$. Now (8.9) is $\lambda = \Pi\rho$, so we have $p\bar{p} = \frac{1}{\Pi(\Pi+\Pi\rho)} = \frac{1}{\Pi^2(1+\rho)}$. Symmetry then gives $p = \bar{p} = \frac{1}{\Pi\sqrt{1+\rho}}$.

Next, (8.8) implies $\frac{1}{\bar{p}}\frac{b}{a-q} = \Pi^2 p^2$. But $\frac{b}{\bar{p}} = \bar{q} = q$, so we have $\frac{q}{a-q} = \Pi^2 p^2 = \frac{1}{1+\rho}$. Solving for q gives $q = \frac{a}{2+\rho} = \bar{q}$. And then $b = \bar{b} = pq = \frac{a}{\Pi\sqrt{1+\rho}(2+\rho)}$. Also, $d = (1+\rho)(b-m) = (1+\rho)\left(\frac{a}{\Pi\sqrt{1+\rho}(2+\rho)} - m\right) = \bar{d}$.

So now all that remains is to find ρ. But by the balance equation $1+\rho = \frac{d+\bar{d}}{G} = \frac{2}{G}(1+\rho)\left(\frac{a}{\Pi\sqrt{1+\rho}(2+\rho)} - m\right)$. This means the value of ρ will be that which satisfies $\frac{a}{\Pi\sqrt{1+\rho}(2+\rho)} = \frac{G}{2} + m$. This calculation can easily be done using computational methods.

8.4.2 Appendix B: Trade with a Strategic Dummy

Bank Holding ρ Constant

We now consider the same market, except this time the bank's strategy is to offer for loan whatever amount of money is required to keep the interest rate at an exogenously given $\rho > 0$. The optimization problems for the two types of trader are again given by (8.3)–(8.4). As in Appendix A, we solve this by first ignoring the default possibility, obtaining (8.5)–(8.6) with first-order conditions (8.7)–(8.16).

The balance conditions are:

$$p = \frac{\bar{b}}{q}, \quad \bar{p} = \frac{b}{\bar{q}}, \text{ and } 1+\rho = \frac{d+\bar{d}}{g}. \tag{8.23}$$

We reiterate that the role of the bank is to offer the exact amount of money for loan (g) so that the interest rate is maintained at ρ. Thus $g = \frac{d+\bar{d}}{1+\rho}$. Hence, implicitly we are assuming that the bank's initial endowment of money is at least this amount; that is,

$$\frac{d+\bar{d}}{1+\rho} \leq B. \tag{8.24}$$

Finally, we comment that again we may make the assumption of "symmetry", that is, that in a solution $p = \bar{p}$, $q = \bar{q}$, $d = \bar{d}$, and $b = \bar{b}$.

Case 1: m is large ("enough money w.d."). This is the case where both the cash-flow constraints ((λ) and ($\bar{\lambda}$)) and the budget constraints ((μ) and ($\bar{\mu}$)) will be loose; that is, $\lambda = \mu = \bar{\lambda} = \bar{\mu} = 0$. As we saw in Case 1 of the previous model (from Appendix A), we must have $\Pi > 0$.

If $\lambda = \mu = \bar{\lambda} = \bar{\mu} = 0$, equation (8.8) is $\frac{1}{\sqrt{\bar{p}}}\sqrt{\frac{b}{a-q}} = \Pi p$, which is $\sqrt{\frac{a-q}{b}} = \frac{1}{\Pi p\sqrt{\bar{p}}}$. Substitution into (8.7) gives $\frac{1}{\sqrt{\bar{p}}}\frac{1}{\Pi p\sqrt{\bar{p}}} = \Pi$, or $p\bar{p} = \frac{1}{\Pi^2}$. Symmetry then gives $p = \bar{p} = \frac{1}{\Pi}$.

Next, condition (8.7) gives $\sqrt{\frac{a-q}{b}} = \Pi\sqrt{\bar{p}} = \sqrt{\Pi}$; hence $\frac{a-q}{b} = \Pi$. But $b = \bar{b} = pq = \frac{q}{\Pi}$, so we have $\frac{a-q}{\frac{q}{\Pi}} = \Pi$. This simplifies to $q = \frac{a}{2} = \bar{q}$. Also, $b = \bar{b} = pq = \frac{a}{2\Pi}$.

Finally, we note that since $\lambda = 0$ (and $\Pi > 0$), equation (8.9) implies $d = 0 = \bar{d}$.

We remark that the above analysis will be valid only so long as the cash-flow constraints (λ) and ($\bar{\lambda}$) remain satisfied. Since $d = \bar{d} = 0$, this is $m \geq b$, or $m \geq \frac{a}{2\Pi}$. So this is what is meant by "m large."

Case 2: m is very small ("very little money"). In this case both the cash-flow constraints ((λ) and ($\bar{\lambda}$)) and the budget constraints ((μ) and ($\bar{\mu}$)) will be tight; that is, $\lambda > 0$, $\mu > 0$, $\bar{\lambda} > 0$, and $\bar{\mu} > 0$.

Since (λ) and (μ) both hold tightly, we have $d = pq$. Also from the balance condition $pq = \bar{b} = b$, hence $b = d$. But then (8.10) is $m - d + \frac{d}{1+\rho} = 0$, which gives $d = \frac{1+\rho}{\rho}m = b = \bar{b} = \bar{d}$.[12] So condition (8.24) becomes $B \geq \frac{d+\bar{d}}{1+\rho} = \frac{2m}{\rho}$.

Next, (8.8) implies that $\sqrt{\frac{a-q}{b}} = \frac{1}{(\mu+\Pi)p\sqrt{\bar{p}}}$. Substituting into (8.7), we have $\frac{1}{\sqrt{\bar{p}}}\frac{1}{(\mu+\Pi)p\sqrt{\bar{p}}} = \lambda + \mu + \Pi$, which is $p\bar{p} = \frac{1}{(\mu+\Pi)(\lambda+\mu+\Pi)}$. But (8.9) means $\lambda = (\mu + \Pi)\rho$; hence $p\bar{p} = \frac{1}{(\mu+\Pi)((\mu+\Pi)\rho+\mu+\Pi)} = \frac{1}{(1+\rho)(\mu+\Pi)^2}$. So by symmetry, $p = \bar{p} = \frac{1}{(\mu+\Pi)\sqrt{1+\rho}}$.

But also (8.8) implies $\frac{a-q}{b} = \frac{1}{(\mu+\Pi)^2p^3}$, which is $q = a - \frac{b}{(\mu+\Pi)^2p^3}$. Substituting in our expressions for b and p gives

$$q = a - \frac{\frac{1+\rho}{\rho}m}{(\mu+\Pi)^2\left(\frac{1}{(\mu+\Pi)\sqrt{1+\rho}}\right)^3} = a - \frac{(1+\rho)^{5/2}(\mu+\Pi)m}{\rho} = \bar{q}. \quad (8.25)$$

But then the balance equation $b = \bar{b} = pq$ is just $\frac{1+\rho}{\rho}m = \frac{1}{(\mu+\Pi)\sqrt{1+\rho}}\left(a - \frac{(1+\rho)^{5/2}(\mu+\Pi)m}{\rho}\right)$, which simplifies to

$$\mu = \frac{\rho a}{m(1+\rho)^{3/2}(2+\rho)} - \Pi. \quad (8.26)$$

---

12 The reader will note that at this point in the analysis of Appendix A, it was necessary to split into the two cases $m > 0$ and $m = 0$. This was because in that model $m = 0$ implied $\rho = 0$, and so the expression $\frac{1+\rho}{\rho}m$ is ambiguous. However, here ρ remains positive even if $m = 0$; hence we do not need to divide into the two cases.

Substituting (8.26) into (8.25) gives

$$q = a - \frac{(1+\rho)^{5/2}\left(\frac{\rho a}{m(1+\rho)^{3/2}(2+\rho)}\right)m}{\rho} = \frac{a}{2+\rho} = \bar{q}. \tag{8.27}$$

Also $p = \bar{p} = \frac{b}{q} = \frac{(1+\rho)(2+\rho)m}{\rho a}$.

We remark that the results in Case 2 are valid only so long as the expression for the multiplier μ (or $\bar{\mu}$) remains nonnegative. From (8.26), this condition is $\frac{\rho a}{m(1+\rho)^{3/2}(2+\rho)} \geq \Pi$, or

$$m\Pi(1+\rho)^{3/2}(2+\rho) \leq \rho a. \tag{8.28}$$

Hence (8.28) gives the precise mathematical definition of "m very small." In particular, we note that the condition is always satisfied if $\Pi = 0$. Intuitively this makes sense, because $\Pi = 0$ means the fiat is worthless at the end of the game. So the traders will spend all they have and borrow to such a degree that any future income will just cover their debts. But this is just another way of saying that their cash-flow and budget constraints will be tight.

Finally, as in Appendix A, we now can solve the model with the bankruptcy condition present (i.e., the traders' problems are given by (8.3)–(8.4) instead of by (8.5)–(8.6)). In Case 1 above and Case 3 below, the traders' optima occur with their budget constraints loose—and so adding the default penalty back into the model will not change the solutions. For Case 2, we again observe that optimization theory tells us that strategic bankruptcy will become an optimal strategy for the traders if and only if $\mu^* \leq \mu$. Substituting using (8.26), this is

$$\mu^* \leq \frac{\rho a}{m(1+\rho)^{3/2}(2+\rho)} - \Pi, \text{ or}$$

$$m(\mu^* + \Pi)(1+\rho)^{3/2}(2+\rho) \leq \rho a. \tag{8.29}$$

If (8.29) *does not* hold, then the Case 2 solutions above for p, q, b, and d (as well as $\bar{p}$, $\bar{q}$, $\bar{b}$, and $\bar{d}$) are correct. If (8.29) *does* hold (so we are in the "strategic default" case), we rewrite our traders' problems as

$$\max_{b,d,q} 2\sqrt{(a-q)\frac{b}{p}} + \mu^*\left(m + \frac{d}{1+\rho} - b + pq - d\right)$$

$$\text{s.t. } m + \frac{d}{1+\rho} - b \geq 0 \qquad\qquad (\lambda) \text{ (cash-flow constraint)}$$

$$m + \frac{d}{1+\rho} - b + pq - d \leq 0 \qquad (\mu) \text{ ("modified" budget constraint)}$$

$$b,d \geq 0,\ 0 \leq q \leq a$$

and

$$\max_{\bar{b},\bar{d},\bar{q}} 2\sqrt{(a-\bar{q})\frac{\bar{b}}{p}} + \mu^* \left(m + \frac{\bar{d}}{1+\rho} - \bar{b} + \bar{p}\bar{q} - \bar{d} \right)$$

$$\text{s.t. } m + \frac{\bar{d}}{1+\rho} - b \geq 0 \qquad\qquad (\lambda) \text{ (cash-flow constraint)}$$

$$m + \frac{\bar{d}}{1+\rho} - \bar{b} + \bar{p}\bar{q} - \bar{d} \leq 0 \qquad (\mu) \text{ (``modified'' budget constraint)}$$

$$\bar{b}, \bar{d} \geq 0, \ 0 \leq \bar{q} \leq a.$$

We note the presence of the "modified" budget constraint, to account for the fact that we are now searching in the region where the traders default on their loans. We also remark that the cash-flow constraint will be tight in this case ($\lambda > 0$) and the modified budget constraint will be loose ($\mu = 0$). Finally, the balance conditions $p = \frac{\bar{b}}{q}$ and $\bar{p} = \frac{b}{\bar{q}}$ still hold.

The solution turns out to be $p = \bar{p} = \frac{1}{\mu^*\sqrt{1+\rho}}$, $q = \bar{q} = \frac{a}{2+\rho}$, $b = \bar{b} = \frac{a}{\mu^*\sqrt{1+\rho}(2+\rho)}$, and $d = \bar{d} = \left(\frac{a}{\mu^*\sqrt{1+\rho}(2+\rho)} - m \right)(1+\rho)$. The multipliers λ and $\bar{\lambda}$ turn out to be equal to $\rho\mu^*$.

Case 3: m is intermediate-valued ("a moderate amount of money, but still *not enough w.d.*"). This is the case in which neither Case 1 nor Case 2 holds. Hence it must be that precisely one of the constraints (λ) and (μ) holds tightly, while the other is loose. But it is impossible for (λ) to be loose and (μ) tight in an optimum. This is because if (λ) were loose and (μ) tight the Type 1 traders could raise b and lower d in such a way that (μ) stays tight, (λ) stays satisfied, and the objective function value is improved.

So, in Case 3 (λ) and ($\bar{\lambda}$) are tight (i.e., $\lambda > 0$ and $\bar{\lambda} > 0$), while (μ) and ($\bar{\mu}$) are loose ($\mu = \bar{\mu} = 0$). Then (8.8) is $\frac{1}{\sqrt{\bar{p}}}\sqrt{\frac{b}{a-q}} = \Pi p$, which is $\sqrt{\frac{a-q}{b}} = \frac{1}{\Pi p\sqrt{\bar{p}}}$. Substituting into (8.7) gives $\frac{1}{\sqrt{\bar{p}}}\frac{1}{\Pi p\sqrt{\bar{p}}} = \Pi + \lambda$, which gives $p\bar{p} = \frac{1}{\Pi(\Pi+\lambda)}$. Now (8.9) is $\lambda = \Pi\rho$, so we have $p\bar{p} = \frac{1}{\Pi(\Pi+\Pi\rho)} = \frac{1}{\Pi^2(1+\rho)}$. Symmetry then gives $p = \bar{p} = \frac{1}{\Pi\sqrt{1+\rho}}$.

Next, (8.8) implies $\frac{1}{p}\frac{b}{a-q} = \Pi^2 p^2$. But $\frac{b}{p} = \bar{q} = q$, so we have $\frac{q}{a-q} = \Pi^2 p^2 = \frac{1}{1+\rho}$. Solving for q gives $q = \frac{a}{2+\rho} = \bar{q}$. And then $b = \bar{b} = pq = \frac{a}{\Pi\sqrt{1+\rho}(2+\rho)}$. Also, $d = (1+\rho)(b-m) = (1+\rho)\left(\frac{a}{\Pi\sqrt{1+\rho}(2+\rho)} - m \right) = \bar{d}$. We note again that the result is valid so long as (8.24) holds; that is, $B \geq \frac{d+\bar{d}}{1+\rho} = 2\left(\frac{a}{\Pi\sqrt{1+\rho}(2+\rho)} - m \right)$.

Chapter 9 A One-Period Sell-All Model

9.1 BUY-SELL OR SELL-ALL?

A simple exchange economy can be modeled in several different ways. Among the two simplest are the buy-sell and sell-all models of exchange. So far, we have been exclusively using *buy-sell* models. Here, the traders have two strategic moves — how much of their endowments to put up for sale, and how much money to bid for goods to consume. In *sell-all* models, they no longer may decide how much endowment to sell — the rules of the game require that *all* endowments be offered for sale. This leaves only the monetary offer to buy as a strategic choice, as the amount for sale is now completely determined.

9.2 THE USES OF SELL-ALL

There are several reasons to use sell-all models. First, from an accounting point of view, valuation of the total wealth of the economy becomes obvious since all of the economy's goods are brought to market. Second, sell-all models represent the maximum opportunity for tax collection, and an extreme case for government strategic control. It is not possible to limit the strategies of the individuals further and still preserve an individually influenced price formation mechanism.

Third, since there is no longer a decision in terms of how much to sell, the agents' strategy sets in sell-all models generally have lower dimension.[1] This in turn makes them simpler and thus mathematically easier to solve. It also means that we can add complication, such as moving to multiperiod models, and still hope to be able to solve. In particular, it has enabled the formulation of tractable parallel dynamic programming models of an elementary financially controlled economy — see Lucas (1978); Lucas and Stokey (1983); Karatzas, Shubik, and Sudderth (1994); Shubik (1972); and many others. The low-dimensionality per period of these models facilitates their analysis but limits their applicability, except for experimental games and as a means of "sweetening the intuition."

9.3 TRADE WITH A SALVAGE VALUE AND NO LOAN MARKET (SELL-ALL)

We now lay down a simple one-period sell-all model with fiat money and no loan market. As usual, there are two types of agents, with a continuum of each. The Type 1 agents are endowed with a units of good 1 and m units of money, while the Type 2 agents are endowed with a units of good 2 and m units of money. These endowments are depicted in Table 9.1. The salvage value (per unit) of the fiat at the end of the game is Π.

Under the sell-all framework, both types of players will necessarily have to bid for both types of good; hence we need to introduce some extra notation. The quantities b_1 and b_2 will represent the amounts that the Type 1 players

Table 9.1.   A sell-all model

	Cash only
Type 1 traders	$(a, 0, m)$
Type 2 traders	$(0, a, m)$

---

1 However, the agents' strategy sets in our upcoming sell-all model in Section 9.3 have the same dimension as in the corresponding buy-sell model. See the discussion in Section 9.3.

bid for goods 1 and 2, respectively. The quantities $\bar{b}_1$ and $\bar{b}_2$ will represent the amounts that Type 2 players bid for goods 1 and 2. Note that the variables q and $\bar{q}$ are not in this model, because the amount of endowment put up for sale is now no longer a strategic choice. The quantities p and $\bar{p}$ still represent the prices of good 1 and good 2, respectively.

In the case where $\Pi = 0$ and there is no loan market, the switch to sell-all kills the backward induction argument that gives the Hahn paradox. However, the one-period sell-all model is highly arbitrary in the sense that individual gains depend only upon the initial distribution of the fiat money, and *not* on the distribution of initial ownership claims to the real goods![2] This dependence on initial fiat would be somewhat mitigated by introducing an outside bank.[3] See Shubik (1980). It would also be mitigated in a multiperiod game where the influence of the initial conditions is modified by the many periods.

The optimization for the Type 1 traders is given by

$$\max_{b_1, b_2} 2\sqrt{\frac{b_1}{p} \frac{b_2}{\bar{p}}} + \Pi(m - b_1 - b_2 + pa)$$
$$\text{s.t. } m - b_1 - b_2 \geq 0 \qquad (\lambda) \text{ (cash-flow constraint)}$$
$$b_1, b_2 \geq 0. \tag{9.1}$$

Note that we still have the same number of decision variables for the traders as we did in the corresponding buy-sell model. The reason for this is that while we have one *less* variable because the traders no longer decide how much to sell, we have one *more* variable because the traders are now bidding for *both* goods.

Similarly, for the Type 2 traders we have

$$\max_{\bar{b}_1, \bar{b}_2} 2\sqrt{\frac{\bar{b}_1}{p} \frac{\bar{b}_2}{\bar{p}}} + \Pi(m - \bar{b}_1 - \bar{b}_2 + \bar{p}a)$$
$$\text{s.t. } m - \bar{b}_1 - \bar{b}_2 \geq 0 \qquad (\bar{\lambda}) \text{ (cash-flow constraint)}$$
$$\bar{b}_1, \bar{b}_2 \geq 0. \tag{9.2}$$

---

2 One can see this by looking at the analysis in the Appendix. In particular, it is easy to see that the traders' first-order conditions (9.5)–(9.6) do not depend upon their initial endowments; the price formation depends only on the *total* endowment in the game. Hence, the solutions would be the same even if the Type 1 traders were endowed with a of both goods (and the Type 2 traders with nothing), or if the Type 2 traders were endowed with a of both goods, or any distribution in between.

3 Suppose ρ is the interest rate at which this outside bank lends. Then, if ρ is small, the shares of real consumption will line up with the initial ownership claims to real goods.

The prices will be given by

$$p = \frac{b_1 + \bar{b}_1}{a} \text{ and } \bar{p} = \frac{b_2 + \bar{b}_2}{a}.$$

Note that the denominators above are simply a, which is necessarily the total amount of either good put up for sale.

The analysis for this model follows in the Appendix. The results are:

Case 1: m large $\left(m \geq \frac{a}{\Pi} \right)$. We get $b_1 = b_2 = \bar{b}_1 = \bar{b}_2 = \frac{a}{2\Pi}$ and $p = \bar{p} = \frac{1}{\Pi}$. Thus both player types end up consuming $\frac{a}{2}$ of each type of good.

Case 2: m small $\left(m \leq \frac{a}{\Pi} \right)$. We get $b_1 = b_2 = \bar{b}_1 = \bar{b}_2 = \frac{m}{2}$ and $p = \bar{p} = \frac{m}{a}$. So again both player types end up consuming $\frac{a}{2}$ of each type of good.

In conclusion, for *all* values of the parameters m, a, and Π (with $\Pi > 0$), the traders consume at the efficient levels. This has not been true in any of our buy-sell models so far.

9.4 APPENDIX: THE ANALYSIS

We consider a model which is "sell-all"; that is, the players all must sell all of their endowment at the marketplace, and then buy back all they wish to consume (even of their own original good). This is contrasted with all of the previous models we have considered, where players only needed to sell that part of their endowment which they did not wish to consume.

As usual, the Type 1 agents are endowed with a units of good 1 and m units of money, while the Type 2 agents are endowed with a units of good 2 and m units of money. The salvage value of money at the end of the game is Π.

As described above, the quantities b_1 and b_2 represent the amounts that the Type 1 players bid for goods 1 and 2, respectively. The quantities $\bar{b}_1$ and $\bar{b}_2$ represent the amounts that Type 2 players bid for goods 1 and 2, respectively. Again, we remark that the variables q and $\bar{q}$ are not in this model, because the amount of endowment put up for sale is now no longer a strategic choice. The quantities p and $\bar{p}$ still represent the prices of good 1 and good 2, respectively.

The optimization problem for the Type 1 players is

$$\max_{b_1, b_2} 2 \sqrt{\frac{b_1}{p} \frac{b_2}{\bar{p}}} + \Pi(m - b_1 - b_2 + pa)$$

$$\text{s.t. } m - b_1 - b_2 \geq 0 \qquad (\lambda) \text{ (cash-flow constraint)}$$

$$b_1, b_2 \geq 0.$$

(9.3)

For the Type 2 traders, we have

$$
\max_{\bar{b}_1, \bar{b}_2} 2\sqrt{\frac{\bar{b}_1}{p}\frac{\bar{b}_2}{\bar{p}}} + \Pi(m - \bar{b}_1 - \bar{b}_2 + \bar{p}a)
$$
$$
\text{s.t. } m - \bar{b}_1 - \bar{b}_2 \geq 0 \qquad (\bar{\lambda}) \text{ (cash-flow constraint)} \tag{9.4}
$$
$$
\bar{b}_1, \bar{b}_2 \geq 0.
$$

The first-order conditions for the Type 1 traders' problem are

$$
\sqrt{\frac{b_2}{b_1 p\bar{p}}} - \Pi - \lambda = 0 \tag{9.5}
$$

and

$$
\sqrt{\frac{b_1}{b_2 p\bar{p}}} - \Pi - \lambda = 0. \tag{9.6}
$$

Similar first-order conditions hold for the Type 2 traders.

Prices are formed as:

$$
p = \frac{b_1 + \bar{b}_1}{a} \text{ and } \bar{p} = \frac{b_2 + \bar{b}_2}{a}. \tag{9.7}
$$

Finally, we aim to look for solutions to (9.5)–(9.7) which satisfy symmetry. Since upon entering the marketplace the players first sell off all of their endowments (so they essentially make their consumption decision with no good 1 or good 2 in their pocket), and because their utility functions are symmetric in the goods, one symmetry assumption is that $b_1 = \bar{b}_1 = b_2 = \bar{b}_2$. The other symmetry assumption is that $p = \bar{p}$.

Case 1: m is large. This means that the cash-flow constraints are loose; that is, the multipliers λ and $\bar{\lambda}$ are both zero. We first note that it is impossible for $\Pi = 0$ in this case, because if so the traders could always raise their bids, increasing their utility, until such time as the cash-flow constraints become tight. Hence $\Pi > 0$ here.

To solve this case, note that (9.5) implies that $\Pi = \sqrt{\frac{b_2}{b_1 p\bar{p}}}$. Substituting in for p and $\bar{p}$ using (9.7) gives $\Pi = \sqrt{\frac{b_2 a^2}{b_1(b_1 + \bar{b}_1)(b_2 + \bar{b}_2)}} = \sqrt{\frac{b_1 a^2}{b_1(2b_1)(2b_1)}} = \frac{a}{2b_1}$, where the second equality follows from symmetry. Thus $b_1 = \frac{a}{2\Pi} = \bar{b}_1 = b_2 =$

$\bar{b}_2$. Then $p = \bar{p} = \frac{b_1 + \bar{b}_1}{a} = \frac{1}{\Pi}$. The player types each end up consuming $\frac{b}{p}$ of each good,[4] which is the efficient bundle $\left(\frac{a}{2}, \frac{a}{2}\right)$.

We note that the above analysis is valid so long as the cash-flow constraint holds, which is $m - b_1 - b_2 \geq 0$ or $m \geq \frac{a}{\Pi}$.

Case 2: m is small. In this case the cash-flow constraints are tight; that is, the multipliers λ and $\bar{\lambda}$ are both positive. Here, condition (9.7), symmetry, the tight cash-flow constraints, and symmetry again imply that $p = \frac{b_1 + \bar{b}_1}{a} = \frac{b_1 + b_2}{a} = \frac{m}{a} = \bar{p}$. In addition, the tight cash-flow constraint (λ) plus symmetry implies that $b_1 = b_2 = \frac{m}{2} = \bar{b}_1 = \bar{b}_2$. So again the consumption levels $\left(\frac{b}{p}, \frac{b}{p}\right)$ turn out to be the efficient $\left(\frac{a}{2}, \frac{a}{2}\right)$. The moral of the story is that the "sell-all" assumption eliminates the need to have "enough money" on hand in order to finance efficient trade.

---

4 The expression "$\frac{b}{p}$" here means any of the quantities b_1, b_2, $\bar{b}_1$, or $\bar{b}_2$ in the numerator (they are all the same due to symmetry), and either p or $\bar{p}$ in the denominator.

Chapter 10 Clearinghouses, Credit, and Control

10.1 SOME COMMENTS ON THE TRADING STRUCTURE

In all of the models presented in this book, transactions take time and may use resources. All individuals are locked into using commodities, pieces of paper, or ciphers which are defined as means of payment in the game. But although the use of a specified means of payment in a classroom game is low-cost and is determined by a referee enforcing a small set of rules, in an actual economy when the price of the government-enforced credit arrangements becomes too high, alternative means are sought. Netting arrangements between well-known traders can easily replace cash. New markets can spring up. New instruments are invented. Legal, social, and technological change influences the costs of running a trading technology. Market meeting frequencies and hours of trade are all in flux.

Even with payment and price-formation systems as simple as the ones considered here, individual exchange relations can circumvent the standard trading relations and change both the velocity and volume of transactions. At best, a government's control over prices, the velocity, and the volume of trade is limited. Exchange relationships are a complex intermix of both law and custom.

In the modern world governments exert control over the money supply, but the monetary control over the economy depends heavily on the transactions technology—and this is in a state of constant flux. General monetary theory can at best provide upper and lower bounds on monetary use and control. The sell-all model presented in Chapter 9 presents the upper bound, and the clearinghouse considered below presents the lower bound.

10.2 VARIATIONS ON THE EQUATION OF EXCHANGE

The pristine, "physics-like" Equation of Exchange, given by Fisher (1931), says that $PQ = MV$, where P is the price level, Q is the real gross national product, M is the amount of money in the system, and V is the income velocity (turnover rate) of money. It may be regarded as the basis for a quantity theory of money suggested in the writings of Hume (1748), and formalized in the work of Newcomb (1886).

We are now in a position to revisit this equation from a somewhat more detailed microeconomic modeling perspective. The idea is to consider as our "economy" several of our previous simple strategic market games, examining the ramifications for the Equation of Exchange for each one. We readily admit that our simple one-period, one-good market structure cannot capture all of the necessary nuance — indeed, a complete treatment of this topic would require a model with several alternate markets within the same period in order to reflect velocity as a strategic choice.[1]

Let us use a shorthand notation for a strategic market game with a given transactions and financial structure. Thus $\Gamma(N, \varphi, a, m | \Theta_j)$ stands for the game where N is the set of n agent types; φ is the utility functions for the agents; $a = \{a_1^i, a_2^i, \ldots, a_k^i\}_{i=1}^n$ denotes the endowments of k goods; m is the amount of outside money endowed to each agent type; and Θ_j denotes the transactions and financial structure. Since the "M" in the equation of exchange should not include central bank reserves, it is equal to the total of all players' money endowments. This is $2m$ in the case of our basic models.

---

1 This was done in part by Dubey, Sahi, and Shubik (1993).

Let Θ_1 stand for a storable consumable cash, buy-sell economy where the market meets once.[2] In such an economy $\Gamma(N, \varphi, a, m | \Theta_1)$

$$PQ = MV \text{ is modified to } PQ \leq M \tag{10.1}$$

as in a one-market-period world without any form of banking or money market, the velocity is at most one (and could be less than one if there is hoarding or storage of the storable consumable money).

Suppose Θ_2 stands for the sell-all structure but is otherwise the same as Θ_1. In $\Gamma(N, \varphi, a, m | \Theta_2)$ the Q has been considerably enlarged to include all assets except the money.

Let Θ_3 stand for a fiat cash, buy-sell economy where the goods market meets once, but there is a preceding money market (also meeting once) in which an outside bank arranges for loans of g. These loans represent an increase in the system's money supply, and so that money supply is now $M + g$. Hence, in such an economy $\Gamma(N, \varphi, a, m | \Theta_3)$

$$PQ = MV \text{ is modified to } PQ \leq M + g.^{[3]} \tag{10.2}$$

These few examples are given merely in order to indicate that it is necessary and feasible but practically difficult to develop a scheme to classify and specify market structures to reflect their need for money or trust. The concept of "enough money" can be made meaningful and can be calculated—but it requires considerable microeconomic detail and the tradeoff between the cost and worth of extra precision must be considered.

10.3 A DIGRESSION ON PAYMENTS
AND MICROVARIABLES

"In every big transaction," [he] said, "there is a magic moment during which a man has surrendered a treasure, and during which the man who is due to receive it has not yet done so. An alert lawyer will make that moment his own, possessing the treasure for a magic microsecond, taking a little of it, passing it on. If the man who is to receive the treasure is unused to wealth, has an inferiority complex and shapeless feelings of guilt, as most people do, the lawyer can

---

2 In fact, in all of the models treated in this book, the market meets only once per period. If the markets meet many times (such as a sequential stock market), then trade velocity becomes a strategic choice for each trader.

3 We have a "$\leq$" here because if the equation is meant to reflect transactions, not necessarily optimization, then individuals could borrow but not utilize the money.

often take as much as half the bundle, and still receive the recipient's blubbering thanks."
—Kurt Vonnegut Jr., *God Bless You, Mr. Rosewater*, pp. 4–5

The size and anonymity of transactions are inversely related. Small exchanges can be consummated without notice. But large and complex transactions (such as Vonnegut's "treasure") call for contracts, lawyers, and accountants. Documents must be verified, checks certified.

Even considering only transactions taxonomies used in mass markets, there are several micro-microeconomic factors that distinguish payment systems. For instance, historically the selection of a means of payment has been molded by factors such as portability, durability, cognizability, nonmonetary value, and difficulty to forge. Starting early with coinage, and through the use of paper and symbolic money, different requirements for small, for middling, and for large transactions emerged. Copper coin was adequate for buying a glass of beer or paying bus fare, silver was more convenient to buy a suit, and gold more convenient for a house. Even when transactions switched primarily to paper and then to electronic data processing, coins were still used for small transactions, and the distinction remained between middling and large transactions. In the United States less than 1 percent of the recorded transactions account for more than 99 percent of the face value of all transactions.

Currently, considerable effort is devoted to computerizing small payment systems profitably. Custom and self-interest die hard, and the forces of anonymity and habit help to keep coins and fiat money in circulation. A million dollars in hundred-dollar bills can still be carried with comfort.

10.4 CLEARINGHOUSES, FIAT, CREDIT, AND CREDIT EVALUATION

In Utopia all greed for money was entirely removed with the use of money. What a mass of troubles were then cut away!... Who does not know that fear, anxiety, worries, toils and sleepless nights will also perish at the same time as money? What is more, poverty, which alone money seemed to make poor, forthwith would itself dwindle and disappear if money were entirely done away with everywhere.
—Thomas More, *Utopia*, Book II, p. 149

Up to now, we have progressed from a storable consumable money (such as the barley of Mesopotamia or cans of beans) to a consumer durable (such as gold) and thence to a paper money backed in many different ways (gold in Fort Knox, other national assets, convention, law, expectations, and bankruptcy penalties). A further step is required to take us back to the sublime equilibrium with no worries, no time, no constraints on the system, and no outside money whatsoever.

We consider an economy with two types of traders, a profit maximizing monopolist banker,[4] and an initial supply of outside fiat money.

As in Chapter 6, we assume that first the financial market meets to establish borrowing and lending for the period, and then the trade markets meet and clear by the end of the period. In order to be completely specific we resort to the proposition that the financial markets meet at the start of the period and engage in establishing a single interday loan which is paid back at the start of next period. The trade markets open for some hours in the middle of the period, and all settlement takes place immediately after they close.

We add a clearinghouse, a credit evaluation agency, and the courts to complete the market structure, as shown in Figure 10.1.

Before we present the formal symbolic model, we provide an interpretation of Figure 10.1. The individuals have goods and a certain amount of fiat money. We look upon them as a composite of consumers and traders. They inform the credit evaluation agency of their total holdings. The credit agency informs the bank about personal cash positions and the clearinghouse about goods for sale and its estimate of what they are worth. The bank issues one-period loans and the clearinghouse extends clearinghouse credits. The traders may go to the bank.[5] At the bank they can exchange their IOU notes for the bank's money. They are required to redeem their IOU notes at the start of the next period with whatever interest payments promised.

The clearinghouse gives each agent a credit line based on three parameters. They are the assessment of the valuation of prices supplied by the credit agency, which we call $\hat{p}$ and $\bar{p}$, and the valuation of the individuals' assets

---

4 There are at least eight reasonable models which can be mathematically specified, involving a private or a public bank.

Four cases involve the choice of (1) a public bank, (2) a profit maximizing monopolist bank individually held, (3) a profit maximizing monopolist bank owned by stockholders, and (4) an overall utility maximizing monopolist bank.

These four choices are multiplied by two. The strategic alternatives are choice of the rate of interest or quantity of money as the strategic variable.

We limit our analysis to one of the models, as the essential demonstration of the disappearance of outside money can be demonstrated with any of the models.

5 In this simple one-period model this may be the government bank or a private monopolist bank with the same powers of issue as the central bank.

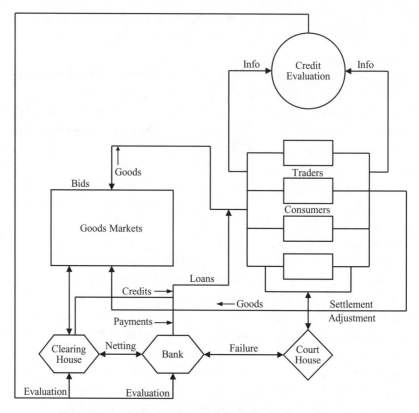

Figure 10.1. Market structure with clearinghouse, credit evaluation agency, and courts

which will act as security,[6] which we call $\hat{a}$ and $\bar{\hat{a}}$. The clearinghouse extends a credit to the traders based on a "haircut" of its credit information. This haircut or credit limit (for Type 1 traders) is given by $\theta \hat{p} q$, where $\theta \in [0, 1]$ is a measure of the trust level the clearinghouse has for the traders.[7] If the clearinghouse managers believe the security assessment is completely accurate and face no expenses or uncertainties the θ could be close to 1.

---

6 Even here another nasty institutional and technological fact enters into our modeling. If the goods for sale are an ounce of caviar which can be eaten before the bailiffs close in, the "secured loan aspects of the caviar" are somewhat less than an immoveable durable such as an acre of prime land.

7 The bound on the credit line is set by the information of the amount a (if there is truthful disclosure $\hat{a} = a$) available for sale, but the actual credit line realized would be based on realized sales and thus will be $\theta \hat{p} q$.

The Type 1 traders, with initial assets of $(a, 0, m)$, may regard their purchasing power as being $(a, 0, m + \theta \hat{p} q)$. Assuming the "usual" utility function of $\varphi(x, y) = 2\sqrt{xy}$, their optimization problem becomes

$$\max_{b,d,q} 2\sqrt{(a-q)\frac{b}{p}} + \Pi\left(m + \frac{d}{1+\rho} - b + pq - d\right)$$

$$\text{s.t. } m + \frac{d}{1+\rho} - b + \theta\hat{p}q \geq 0 \qquad (\lambda) \qquad\qquad (10.3)$$

$$m + \frac{d}{1+\rho} - b + pq - d \geq 0 \qquad (\mu)$$

$$0 \leq q \leq a, \text{ and } b, d \geq 0.$$

Let λ and μ be the Lagrangian multipliers for constraints (λ) and (μ), respectively.

The first-order conditions wrt b, q, d, λ, and μ (respectively) yield

$$\frac{1}{\sqrt{p}}\sqrt{\frac{a-q}{b}} - \Pi - \lambda - \mu = 0 \qquad\qquad (10.4)$$

$$-\frac{1}{\sqrt{p}}\sqrt{\frac{b}{a-q}} + \Pi p + \lambda\theta\hat{p} + \mu p = 0 \qquad\qquad (10.5)$$

$$\frac{-\Pi\rho}{1+\rho} + \frac{\lambda}{1+\rho} + \frac{\mu\rho}{1+\rho} = 0 \qquad\qquad (10.6)$$

$$m + \frac{d}{1+\rho} - b + \theta\hat{p}q = 0 \text{ or } \lambda = 0 \qquad\qquad (10.7)$$

$$m + \frac{d}{1+\rho} - b + pq - d = 0 \text{ or } \mu = 0. \qquad\qquad (10.8)$$

Similarly, Type 2 traders face an optimization described by:

$$\max_{\bar{b},\bar{d},\bar{q}} 2\sqrt{(a-\bar{q})\frac{\bar{b}}{p}} + \Pi\left(m + \frac{\bar{d}}{1+\rho} - \bar{b} + \bar{p}\bar{q} - \bar{d}\right)$$

$$\text{s.t. } m + \frac{\bar{d}}{1+\rho} - \bar{b} + \theta\hat{p}\bar{q} \geq 0 \qquad (\bar{\lambda}) \qquad\qquad (10.9)$$

$$m + \frac{\bar{d}}{1+\rho} - \bar{b} + \bar{p}\bar{q} - \bar{d} \geq 0 \qquad (\bar{\mu})$$

$$0 \leq \bar{q} \leq a, \text{ and } \bar{b}, \bar{d} \geq 0.$$

The first-order conditions wrt $\bar{b}$, $\bar{q}$, $\bar{d}$, $\bar{\lambda}$, and $\bar{\mu}$ yield

$$\frac{1}{\sqrt{\bar{p}}}\sqrt{\frac{a-\bar{q}}{\bar{b}}} - \Pi - \bar{\lambda} - \bar{\mu} = 0 \tag{10.10}$$

$$-\frac{1}{\sqrt{\bar{p}}}\sqrt{\frac{\bar{b}}{a-\bar{q}}} + \Pi\bar{p} + \lambda\theta\hat{p} + \bar{\mu}\bar{p} = 0 \tag{10.11}$$

$$\frac{-\Pi\rho}{1+\rho} + \frac{\bar{\lambda}}{1+\rho} + \frac{\bar{\mu}\rho}{1+\rho} = 0 \tag{10.12}$$

$$m + \frac{\bar{d}}{1+\rho} - \bar{b} + \theta\hat{p}\bar{q} = 0 \text{ or } \bar{\lambda} = 0 \tag{10.13}$$

$$m + \frac{\bar{d}}{1+\rho} - \bar{b} + \bar{p}\bar{q} - \bar{d} = 0 \text{ or } \bar{\mu} = 0. \tag{10.14}$$

The banker's optimization is given by:

$$\max_{\rho} \rho g(\rho)$$
$$M - 2m - g(\rho) \geq 0 \tag{10.15}$$
$$\rho \geq 0,$$

and balance conditions are $p = \frac{\bar{b}}{q}$, $\bar{p} = \frac{b}{q}$, and $1 + \rho = \frac{d+\bar{d}}{g}$.

A Simple Case: Suppose that $\hat{p} = p$, $\bar{p} = \bar{p}$, and $\theta = 1$. (Π can be any positive value.)

It is clear that since $\hat{p} = p$, we have $\hat{p}q = pq = \bar{b} = b$ (from symmetry). Hence the conditions (λ) and ($\bar{\lambda}$) must hold loosely; that is, $\lambda = \bar{\lambda} = 0$.

Since $b = pq$, the constraint (μ) is $m - \frac{\rho d}{1+\rho} \geq 0$. But then it is clear that there is no need for borrowing; that is, $d = 0 = \bar{d}$ (any solution with d or $\bar{d} > 0$ can be improved upon by lowering d or $\bar{d}$ to zero). In words, the amount of outside money called for is zero. But this then implies that (μ) (and ($\bar{\mu}$)) holds loosely. Hence $\mu = 0 = \bar{\mu}$.

Next, since $\lambda = \bar{\lambda} = \mu = \bar{\mu} = 0$, equation (10.6) gives $\frac{-\Pi\rho}{1+\rho} = 0 \Rightarrow \rho = 0$. Hence the bank cannot make a profit, no matter what it does.

The rest of the values can be found as follows. First, (10.5) (with $\lambda = \mu = 0$) gives $\Pi p = \frac{1}{\sqrt{p}}\sqrt{\frac{b}{a-q}}$, which is $\sqrt{\frac{b}{a-q}} = \Pi p\sqrt{p}$. Substituting into (10.4), we have $\Pi = \frac{1}{\sqrt{p}}\sqrt{\frac{a-q}{b}} = \frac{1}{\sqrt{p}}\frac{1}{\Pi p\sqrt{p}} = \frac{1}{\Pi p\bar{p}}$. Assuming symmetry ($\bar{p} = p$), this is $p = \bar{p} = \frac{1}{\Pi}$. Using the balance equation for price (plus symmetry $q = \bar{q}$), we have $b = p\bar{q} = pq = \frac{q}{\Pi}$. But then condition (10.4) is $\Pi = \frac{1}{\sqrt{p}}\sqrt{\frac{a-q}{b}} = \sqrt{\Pi}\sqrt{\frac{a-q}{\frac{q}{\Pi}}}$, which yields $q = \frac{a}{2}$. So then $b = pq = \frac{a}{2\Pi}$. To summarize, the final values for this case are: $b = \bar{b} = \frac{a}{2\Pi}, p = \bar{p} = \frac{1}{\Pi}, q = \bar{q} = \frac{a}{2}, \lambda = \mu = \rho = 0$, and $d = \bar{d} = 0$.

Note that in this case consumption is efficient no matter what the initial monetary endowment m is. So, just as in a "general equilibrium world," this Utopia does not need outside money, as it has total trust and accurate forecasting and so runs on perfect individual credit.[8]

---

8 In a world without outside money there are problems in fixing the price level, which are discussed elsewhere (see Smith and Foley, 2008; Smith and Shubik, 2003; Sorin, 1996).

Chapter 11 The Size and Role of Financial Institutions

11.1 THE ROLE OF FINANCIAL INSTITUTIONS

In preceding chapters, we have stressed the physical properties of items utilized as a means of payment. For the most part, we were able to analyze these properties using models with a continuum of agents and possibly one outside bank. But in a modern economy, the evolution of a monetary and credit system goes far beyond a simple means of payment mimicking the barter concept of a value-for-value transaction. The financial system is a perception, evaluation, and control device. It is the brain and sensory system of the body economic. It provides guidance and evaluation over production and consumption. These special functions are provided by an intricate structure involving relatively few private and central banks, insurance companies, other financial institutions, and credit evaluation agencies,[1] together

---

1 Nonbank institutions are not discussed further here, but are considered in strategic models elsewhere (Shubik, 2011).

with producers and the mass of consumers. In addition, the government is a strategic agent and plays a critical role in virtually all economies.

Over the next few chapters, we focus more on the modeling of these institutions (in particular, banking). Since numbers are small, monopoly and oligopoly theories are relevant. But first, in order to get some intuition concerning what these "numbers" actually are, we provide a few basic statistics on the relative sizes of individuals and institutions, including the government. In addition (even though our formal models do not directly concern production and retailing), we supply a few figures on corporate form and industrial structure. Again, we do this to stress that one needs to consider whether the numbers of and size of agents matter.

We use the United States as an example.

11.2 THE SIZE AND NUMBER OF FINANCIAL INSTITUTIONS

The objects which you see in Lombard Street, and in that money world which is grouped about it, are the Bank of England, the Private Banks, the Joint Stock Banks, and the bill brokers. But before describing each of these separately we must look at what all have in common, and at the relation of each to the others.
—Walter Bagehot, *Lombard Street*, p. 11

In the year 2000 the U.S. population was approximately 281,000,000 (SAUS,[2] 2001, table 1), with a density of 79.6 per square mile. Roughly 80 percent lived in a metropolitan area (CMSA, consolidated metropolitan statistical area; or PMSA, primary metropolitan statistical area).

If we assume that those younger than age fifteen are not significant direct economic agents in finance, then the number of economic agents can be estimated as around 220,000,000.

As shown in Table 11.1, these individuals were serviced at the retail level by around 1,100,000 establishments, with 14,480,000 employees in 1999, or 1 establishment per 200 of population. The size of establishments within retailing may be highly skewed, as exemplified by food retailing. Out of 247,800 food stores (SAUS, 1999, p. 1031) with sales of \$458,000,000,000, 23,800 (or 9.6 percent) were supermarkets, accounting for \$321,000,000,000 (70.1 percent) of sales.

At the wholesale level there were around 450,000 establishments with 5,972,000 employees. The ratio of retail to wholesale is 2.45 to 1.

---

2 SAUS = *Statistical Abstract of the United States.*

Table 11.1. Ratio of institutions to population

Sector	Numbers	Employees	Ratio to population
Retail	1,100,00	14,480,000	1 per 200
Wholesale	450,000	5,972,000	1 per 490
Services	3,790,000	59,000,000	1 per 83.2
Manufacturing	360,000	16,700,000	1 per 611

Services were supplied by around 3,790,000 establishments, with 59,000,000 employees and an annual payroll of $1,750,000,000,000; thus employees earned roughly $29,700 per capita (SAUS, 1999, table 1263). There was 1 establishment per 83.2 of population. Many of these establishments were one-person proprietorships.

There were around 360,000 manufacturing establishments in 1999 with 16,700,000 employees and an annual payroll of $607,000,000,000. This computes to one establishment per 611 of population.

For finance, we have Table 11.2 for 2002 (*Financial Services Fact Book*, 2004). Aggregate employment in the financial services sector in 2002 was 5,800,000, ranging from 23,100 in the monetary authority to 2,223,000 in insurance and related activities.

When we compare the size of government organizations to the single individual (for 1996), we have Table 11.3. These numbers are given to provide

Table 11.2. Ratio of financial institutions to populations

Sector	Numbers	Assets (in $trillions)	Ratio firms to individuals
Banking	9,910[a]	7.34	1 per 22,200
Life insurance	1,506	3.33	1 per 146,080
Insurance	3,163 (2001)	0.92	1 per 69,550
Mutual funds	8,256	6.39	1 per 26,650
Private pension funds	–[b]	3.36	–
Brokerage firms	6,766	1.34	1 per 32,520
Central bank	1	–[c]	1 per 220,000,000
Treasury	1	0.0096	1 per 220,000,000

[a]The 9,910 surviving banks in 2000 had around 87,500 locations and branches. The ratio of banking outlet to population was 1 per 2,526 of population.

[b]Definitional problems make a count of the number of pension funds as firms or independent decision makers, not particularly useful here.

[c]Definitional problems in accounting and in the appropriater aggregation or disaggregation of government accounts make any single number here subject to considerable leeway in interpretation.

Table 11.3. Ratio of financial size of government institutions to population by expenditure

Institution	Numbers	Expenditure	Expenditure per institution	Ratio to individual
Federal government	1	1.57×10^{12}	1.57×10^{12}	$55,387,324$
State government	50	9.67×10^{11}	1.93×10^{10}	$680,986$
Local	85,000	8.04×10^{11}	9.46×10^{6}	333
Individuals	2.70×10^{8}	7.66×10^{12}	2.84×10^{4}	1

some orders of magnitude of the institutions of the U.S. economy vis-à-vis the individual citizen. In each instance the size distribution of the institutions is highly skewed, with a few institutions accounting for a substantial part of the economic activity. For example, eighty banks held 71.5 percent of the banking assets, and fifty property insurance companies wrote 49.5 percent of the policies. Furthermore, there has been considerable growth in financial supermarkets, blurring the distinctions among categories.

11.3 INSTITUTIONS, INSTRUMENTS, AND ABSTRACTIONS

Our main goal in this book is to provide simple models which help us understand the role of money and our financial system. Our approach is for a description using minimal institutions. The utilization of a money is essentially a dynamic phenomenon, and thus requires a process description. This in turn means that there is no opportunity to avoid fully the role of institutions, as they are implicit in the rules. The influence of institutions and most of the aspects of information are simplified by modeling a continuum of agents, but, as suggested above, there is a danger because finite numbers and information play a critical role. At the very least, one needs to model the role of government as a large agent.

Other important methodological features are the selection of grid size for both time and the divisibility of money, as well as the dimensional analysis of the financial instruments being introduced and their influence on the degrees of freedom available in the economic system. In economic affairs, specific time phenomena such as the day and the tax year matter. The modeling of economic activity often requires not only the specification of the length of time covered, but also whether time is modeled as a continuum, as a sequence of equal intervals, or as a sequence of events. The specification of time length is important if the velocity of money plays a role in the model.

A useful way to consider financial instruments is to view them as poker chips of different colors. For example, as soon as a loan market is created someone has to issue IOU notes. The IOU note is a new financial instrument. If government money consists of blue chips, then the lending of government money is an activity that involves exchanging blue chips for IOU notes that can be regarded as green chips. If instead the loan is by an agent such as a bank (creating a deposit rather than exchanging government money), this physical act involves the exchange of yellow chips (the bank's IOU notes) for green chips (the individual's IOU notes).

In the understanding of the structure of the financial system, details such as the number of degrees of freedom in the system and the selection of a numeraire are not innocent, but instead have ramifications in the specification of items such as bank reserves, default conditions, and even the criminal code.[3]

11.4 EQUILIBRIUM, POLITICS, BUREAUCRACY, AND SOCIETY

In all of the models presented here, our solution concept of choice is noncooperative equilibrium. This is not because we believe in its descriptive power, but rather because it provides useful insights offering a crude first-order descriptor of individualistic (and often myopic) decentralized economic behavior. It is important to reiterate that our models, although exceedingly "stripped down," are process models. Thus, even though all of the models are examined for their equilibrium properties they all are defined for all feasible states.

Macroeconomics and policy advice deal with dynamics where equilibrium is of little concern. The dynamics of disequilibrium adjustment must account for the influence of: (a) politicians, (b) the bureaucracy, and (c) the courts, on both the direction and the timing of policy.

To get a sense of the size of these three establishments, we provide some more figures. In 2001, the United States had a population of 290.8 million and a work force of 146.5 million. The government employed 21.6 million, which works out to 7.42 percent of the population, or 14.73 percent of the work force. There was 1 senator for roughly each 3 million of the population; one U.S. representative per 690,000.

---

3 The distinction between a crime and a misdemeanor may depend on the amount of money involved.

According to the American Bar Association, there were (to the nearest 1,000) 1,143,000 lawyers by the end of 2007, or roughly 1 per 300 in population. The number of supreme court, appeals courts, and district court judges has varied over time recently, but as of 2007 the authorized judgeships were 9 for the supreme court, 179 for the courts of appeal, and 678 for the district courts.[4] There were 13 appeals court districts and 94 district court districts.

The time lag aspects of law cases on economic processes can be considerable, and the lengths of settlements in major economic cases are highly variable. It is an act of considerable faith that the macroeconomic aggregate statistics used to justify dynamic economic growth models adequately reflect the nature and the variability of the lags imposed by the political, bureaucratic, and legal processes in the society.

When wars, famines, strikes, riots, elections, and other political, social, or natural upheavals are taken into account, it is clear that at best the concept of equilibrium refers only to a tendency. Even if there is a unique equilibrium and even if convergence to equilibrium could be proved, the transient states depend on ad hoc conditions, and another shock is highly likely in the interim. This justifies the frequent reestimation of parameters by the intrepid users of large macroeconomic models. As far as innovation is concerned, we suspect that there may well be increasing returns in the stochastic processes that characterize it. This can easily lead to history-dependent trajectories. The relative sizes of the institutions noted above give us an intuitive feeling for two important features in economic dynamics: (1) the "many numbers" effect of oligopolistic behavior, as contrasted with simple price-taking behavior, and (2) the "arthritis" or "bureaucracy effect" on the speed of adjustment as organizational structures become larger.

Regarding our own parsimonious models, we suggest that fully defined low-dimensional mathematical models may well help bolster insight into some particular issue. However, if not used as experimental games, they are still sufficiently far from applied macroeconomics so as to be at best in the realm of parable or analogy.

---

4 The salary spreads are narrow. In January 2008 a district court judge was paid $169,300, an appellate court judge $179,500, an associate supreme court judge $208,100, and the Chief Justice $217,400.

Chapter 12 Oligopolistic Competition with Cash and with a Money Market

12.1 MONOPOLISTIC OR OLIGOPOLISTIC LENDING

In Chapter 13, we investigate models with monopolistic and oligopolistic banking. These models will necessarily focus on bankers modeled as large atomic players. As a preliminary to this, in this chapter we focus on a model with no banking, where the *traders* are atomic players. We first consider a model with no finance at all, then one with a money market among the traders.

An underlying theme in the study of institutions is that they are almost always larger (and often considerably larger) than natural persons. They often consist of specialized groups of natural persons. In particular, the financial sector has aggregations of special expertise, be it commercial banking, investment banking, insurance, mortgage lending, or credit evaluation; the structure of virtually all of them fits under the rubric of oligopolistic competition. Whether this is good or bad is an open question. In a dynamic society, a case can be made that an oligopolistic structure promotes

Table 12.1.   Models with a finite number of traders ($n = 2$ case)

	Cash only	Money market
Type 1 traders	$(a, 0, m)$	$(a, 0, m_1)$
Type 2 traders	$(0, a, m)$	$(0, a, m_2)$

production efficiency and innovation. Unfortunately, without considering a detailed ad hoc study of the industry, little can be said except as we have done here, where we indicate the influence of numbers on price under the simple conditions of replication.

In one of the examples below, we have oligopolistic competition among individual lenders and borrowers in a money market. The model might be more realistic for a market with a small number of large firms, because large firms have the richness of structure and expertise that enables them to borrow directly from a money market. On the other hand, small firms might require an intermediary to set this up, and so a reasonable model of the case with a large number of small firms might be more complex.

The models we consider in this chapter are shown in Table 12.1. The values in the table are for the specific case in which there are two types of trader. The three entries in each cell are the initial endowments of the two types of good and the initial endowment of (fiat) money for the individual traders of each type.

12.2 AN OLIGOPOLISTIC MARKET WITHOUT FINANCIAL INSTITUTIONS

The first formal model considered here is a finite player more general version of the initial market considered in Chapter 3. It is a game with exchange using a commodity money and no credit of any variety. In several previous papers competition in exchange with a finite number of traders has been considered (Shapley and Shubik, 1977; Shubik, 1976). Here we model one-period symmetric oligopolistic exchange where the individuals use either a storable consumable or a fiat money with a salvage value.[1]

We consider a strategic market game in which there are n types of trader and n commodities, plus an $n + 1$st commodity—a storable consumable money. Traders of type i ($i = 1, \ldots, n$) are endowed with a units of commodity

---

1 We have argued in Section 7.1.1 that they are operationally close.

i, as well as m units of money. All traders have the same utility function $\varphi(x_1, x_2, \ldots, x_n) + x_{n+1}$, where x_i is the amount of commodity i consumed $(i = 1, \ldots, n+1)$. Here φ is a symmetric, increasing, and concave function of n variables—in the calculations below, φ is specialized to $\varphi(x_1, x_2, \ldots, x_n) = n(\Pi_{i=1}^{n} x_i^{1/n})$.

So far, there is no difference between this model (with $n = 2$) and the "basic model" from Chapter 3. However, now, instead of a continuum of each type of agent, we model a "replication" form of the game, in which there are K identical individuals of each type. Hence there are nK players in the game. The kth player of the ith type is denoted "player ik." A strategy for player ik would be a vector of the form $(b_1^{ik}, b_2^{ik}, \ldots, b_{i-1}^{ik}, q^{ik}, b_{i+1}^{ik}, \ldots, b_n^{ik})$, where

$$b_j^{ik} \geq 0, \sum_{j:j \neq i} b_j^{ik} \leq m \text{ and } 0 \leq q^{ik} \leq a. \tag{12.1}$$

Here b_j^{ik} is the amount of money she bids for commodity j and q^{ik} denotes the amount of her own good (good i) that she puts up for sale. Price in the jth $(j = 1, 2, \ldots, n)$ market is formed as follows:

$$p_j = \frac{\sum_{i:i \neq j} \sum_{k=1}^{K} b_j^{ik}}{\sum_{k=1}^{K} q^{jk}}. \tag{12.2}$$

Her final consumption $x^{ik} = (x_1^{ik}, \ldots, x_{n+1}^{ik})$ is then given by

$$x_j^{ik} = \frac{b_j^{ik}}{p_j} \text{ for } j \neq i; x_i^{ik} = a - q^{ik} \tag{12.3}$$

$$x_{n+1}^{ik} = m - \sum_{j:j \neq i} b_j^{ik} + p_i q^{ik}. \tag{12.4}$$

Thus, her optimization problem can be written as

$$\max_{\{b_j^{ik}\}, q^{ik}} n \left(\frac{b_1^{ik}}{p_1} \frac{b_2^{ik}}{p_2} \cdots \frac{b_{i-1}^{ik}}{p_{i-1}} \cdot (a - q^{ik}) \cdot \frac{b_{i+1}^{ik}}{p_{i+1}} \cdots \frac{b_n^{ik}}{p_n} \right)^{1/n} + m - \sum_{j:j \neq i} b_j^{ik} + p_i q^{ik}$$

$$\tag{12.5}$$

subject to the conditions (12.1).

Since all players of a type are identical, and since all types are equivalent, it makes sense to solve for type-specific noncooperative equilibria (TSNE). Hence we have $b_j^{ik} = b$, $q^{ik} = q$, and $p_j = p$ for all i, j, k. In the Appendix, we solve the model (in the case of "enough money"), obtaining

$$q = \frac{a[K(n-1)-1](K-1)}{K^2(n-1)^{2(1-\frac{1}{n})} + [K(n-1)-1](K-1)}, \tag{12.6}$$

$$b = \frac{a[K(n-1)-1]^{(2-\frac{1}{n})}(K-1)^{(1-\frac{1}{n})}(n-1)^{(\frac{3}{n-2}-\frac{2}{n^2})}K^{(\frac{2}{n}-1)}}{K^2(n-1)^{2(1-\frac{1}{n})} + [K(n-1)-1](K-1)}, \tag{12.7}$$

and

$$p = (nK-K-1)^{1-\frac{1}{n}}(K-1)^{-\frac{1}{n}}(n-1)^{\frac{3}{n}-1-\frac{2}{n^2}}K^{\frac{2}{n}-1}. \tag{12.8}$$

When there is only one trader of each type, the influence of monopolistic competition suggests a TSNE with no trade. Indeed, setting $K=1$ in (12.6) and (12.7) gives $q=b=0$.

THE CASE WHERE $n=2$

When we specialize to the case where $n=2$ (i.e., we consider a market with two types of traders, each trading one commodity and each utilizing a third commodity as a means of payment), we obtain

$$q = \frac{a(K-1)^2}{K^2+(K-1)^2}, \tag{12.9}$$

$$b = \frac{a(K-1)^2}{K^2+(K-1)^2}, \text{ and} \tag{12.10}$$

$$p = 1. \tag{12.11}$$

Finally, if furthermore $K \to \infty$, we obtain $q \to \frac{a}{2}$, $b \to \frac{a}{2}$, and $p \to 1$, just as in the "basic model" of Chapter 3.

We observe that an influence of oligopoly is to distort trade, with the sellers underselling (as compared with the "efficient" outcome of the continuum-of-agents case); however, as $K \to \infty$ this attenuates. Indeed, the final utility attained by individuals (of either type) is $\frac{2aK(K-1)}{K^2+(K-1)^2} + m$. This is increasing in K, and approaches the efficient payoff of $a+m$ in the limit.

ENOUGH MONEY

In our model, we are in the "enough money" case if each trader i has enough money for all of his optimal bids; that is,

$$m \geq \sum_{j:j\neq i} b_j^{ik} = (n-1)b. \tag{12.12}$$

In the case where $n = 2$, the right-hand side of the equation above is always less than $\frac{a}{2}$, and only approaches $\frac{a}{2}$ as $K \to \infty$.[2] Comparing to the case where there is a continuum of agents of each type, we know that the equilibrium in the continuum case will be the competitive equilibrium of the economy. By symmetry, this will be where each player consumes $\left(\frac{a}{n}, \frac{a}{n}, \frac{a}{n}, \ldots, \frac{a}{n}, m\right)$. This in turn implies that m is "enough money" if for all i

$$m \geq \sum_{j:j \neq i} p_j \frac{a}{n}, \tag{12.13}$$

which reduces to $m \geq \frac{a}{2}$ in the case where $n = 2$.

VARYING THE SIZE OF THE AGENTS

Another effect we would like to model is the oligopolistic aspects of having some enterprises in an economy much larger than individual consumers. We can do this by making a slight change in our basic model. Suppose r is an integer parameter greater than 1. We consider a market in which there are K Type 1 traders, each with endowment $(ra, 0, rm)$. On the other hand, there are rK Type 2 agents, each with endowment $(0, a, m)$. This parametrization reflects the role of Type 1 traders as large in both physical and financial endowment relative to Type 2, but keeps the total "size" of the two sides of this market equal. We would again let $K \to \infty$ and observe what happens.

BERTRAND-EDGEWORTH CONVERGENCE

The strategic variables selected in the Cournot model above are quantities of goods and money. When there are n goods plus a monetary good there are only n markets and price is formed by quantities of goods and money being offered. When a money market or banking is introduced, at least one new market is created and a new strategic option is present. The financial strategic variable can be either the quantity of money or its price (the interest rate). When there is only one institution (such as a central bank or a monopolistic private bank), the quantity of money and the rate of interest are essentially dual variables, and unless boundary conditions interfere they give the same results. As soon as there are two or more institutions, the convergence properties to the competitive equilibrium are strikingly different.

---

2 If we had utilized a money that entered in the Cobb-Douglas utility symmetrically, there would never be enough money, because its cross-elasticity falls too fast as its amount is increased.

When there is considerably more than enough money,[3] the presence of two banks is sufficient for convergence. If the banking system has only just enough money, there is no pure strategy equilibrium and the convergence—as the number of banks increases—is of mixed strategy equilibria (Shubik, 1959). The behavior of price competition is somewhat modified by many other conditions left out of the stripped-down models. For example, spatial location, product differentiation, and increasing costs are all important for banks and are left out of these simple models. Furthermore, the nature of communication and information offers opportunities for many forms of quasi-cooperation.

12.3 THE MONEY MARKET

We may now consider adding a money market to the ($n = 2$ case of) model of Section 12.2. The comments below apply either to this new model or to the "original" money market model (with two continua of traders) from Chapter 4.

Suppose that our economy uses a point consumption commodity money, but that it is asymmetrically distributed between the two types. We consider a money market as follows. Borrowers are permitted to create IOU notes, which they offer in exchange for the monetary commodity offered by lenders. Thus the money market is an extra market where the rate of interest (i.e., the price of money) is formed by the amount of money offered against the amount of IOU notes offered. The IOU note is presumed to be a legally enforceable contract and requires that a society in which such a note exists should have a legal system which both enforces contract and specifies the conditions that prevail if the contract is not fulfilled.

When there is enough money, but it is badly distributed, the money market rectifies the situation. In the one-period economy the rate of interest that emerges is $\rho = 0$. This is easily explained for an economy utilizing a point consumption money such as a can of beans or brick of tea. A commodity money

---

3 Specifically, if the money is fiat with negligible cost of production, each bank will need to hold enough money to satisfy the demands for trade at a zero rate of interest. The banking model is equivalent to the pure Bertrand-Edgeworth game solved in Shubik (1959, ch. 6). When there are n banks, if any $n - 1$ banks can cover the capacity needed for a competitive equilibrium, that is sufficient; thus, as the number of banks increases the needed excess capacity decreases as $\frac{1}{n}$.

has two functions: its value in consumption, and its value in transacting. When there is enough money there will be no cash-flow constraint shadow price; furthermore, if the consumption value can be realized within the period there is no relevant time discount.[4] The full calculations for the "original" money market model are given in the Appendix to Chapter 4.

When there is not enough money a positive rate of interest emerges, and the monied agents are able to earn a rent or profit from the money market, reflected in the value $\lambda = \rho > 0$. If the monied agents are few in number (as here in Chapter 12), an extra profit will be available as an outcome of oligopolistic behavior.

12.4 APPENDIX: AN OLIGOPOLISTIC MODEL WITHOUT FINANCIAL INSTITUTIONS

We present the calculations for the model in Section 12.2.

The model parameters:

n commodities, plus money (the $n + 1$st commodity).

n types of player, indexed by $i = 1, \ldots, n$. Each player of type i initially owns a units of commodity i, plus m units of money.

K individuals of each type, indexed by $k = 1, \ldots, K$. The kth player of type i is called "player ik."

Utility function for each player ik is $u(x_1, \ldots, x_n, x) = n(\Pi_{i=1}^{n} x_i^{1/n}) + x$.

Strategy for player ik is $(b_1^{ik}, \ldots, b_n^{ik}, q^{ik})$, where

$b_j^{ik} = $ amount player ik bids for good j $(j \neq i)$

$q^{ik} = $ amount of own commodity i that ik puts up for sale $(0 \leq q^{ik} \leq a)$

$p_j = $ price of good j.

Player $\hat{i}\hat{k}$'s utility maximization problem is:

$$
\max_{q^{\hat{i}\hat{k}}, \{b_j^{\hat{i}\hat{k}}\}_{j:j \neq \hat{i}}} n \left(\prod_{j:j \neq \hat{i}} \frac{b_j^{\hat{i}\hat{k}}}{p_j} \right)^{1/n} (a - q^{\hat{i}\hat{k}})^{1/n} + m - \sum_{j:j \neq \hat{i}} b_j^{\hat{i}\hat{k}} + p_{\hat{i}} q^{\hat{i}\hat{k}}
$$

$$
\text{s.t.} \sum_{j:j \neq \hat{i}} b_j^{\hat{i}\hat{k}} \leq m \text{ (cash-flow constraint),} \qquad (\lambda) \qquad (12.14)
$$

$$
0 \leq q^{\hat{i}\hat{k}} \leq a, \ \{b_j^{\hat{i}\hat{k}}\}_{j:j \neq \hat{i}} \geq 0.
$$

---

4 This will depend on the selection of grid size and raises empirical questions concerning the selection of units of time in the description of economic activity.

The balance conditions are just those defining price:

$$p_j = \frac{\sum\limits_{i:i\neq j}\sum\limits_{k=1}^{K} b_j^{ik}}{\sum\limits_{k=1}^{K} q^{jk}} \quad \text{for } j=1,\ldots,n.$$ (12.15)

Substituting in this expression for p_j (and $p_{\hat{\imath}}$), we can rewrite $\hat{\imath}\hat{k}$'s problem as:

$$\max_{q^{\hat{\imath}\hat{k}},\{b_j^{\hat{\imath}\hat{k}}\}_{j:j\neq\hat{\imath}}} n\left(\prod_{j:j\neq\hat{\imath}} \frac{b_j^{\hat{\imath}\hat{k}}\sum\limits_{k=1}^{K}q^{jk}}{\sum\limits_{i:i\neq j}\sum\limits_{k=1}^{K}b_j^{ik}}\right)^{1/n} (a-q^{\hat{\imath}\hat{k}})^{1/n}$$

$$+m-\sum_{j:j\neq\hat{\imath}}b_j^{\hat{\imath}\hat{k}}+\frac{\sum\limits_{i:i\neq\hat{\imath}}\sum\limits_{k=1}^{K}b_{\hat{\imath}}^{ik}}{\sum\limits_{k=1}^{K}q^{\hat{\imath}k}}q^{\hat{\imath}\hat{k}}$$

$$\text{s.t. } \sum_{j:j\neq\hat{\imath}}b_j^{\hat{\imath}\hat{k}}\leq m \quad\quad\quad (\lambda)$$

$$0\leq q^{\hat{\imath}\hat{k}}\leq a,\ \{b_j^{\hat{\imath}\hat{k}}\}_{j:j\neq\hat{\imath}}\geq 0.$$

Next, assume that m is large (so that constraint (λ) is not binding), and also that the nonnegativity constraints and upper bounds on q are not binding. Then, all we need to do in order to find the optimal strategy for $\hat{\imath}\hat{k}$ is to set the partial derivatives of the objective function above (call it f) all equal to zero.

First, for all $\hat{\imath}$, $\hat{\jmath}$, $\hat{k}$, we have $\partial f/\partial b_{\hat{\jmath}}^{\hat{\imath}\hat{k}}=0$, which is

$$\left(\prod_{j:j\neq\hat{\imath}} \frac{b_j^{\hat{\imath}\hat{k}}\sum\limits_{k=1}^{K}q^{jk}}{\sum\limits_{i:i\neq j}\sum\limits_{k=1}^{K}b_j^{ik}}\right)^{\frac{1}{n}-1} (a-q^{\hat{\imath}\hat{k}})^{1/n}\left(\frac{T_1-T_2}{T_3}\right)-1=0,$$ (12.16)

where

$$T_1 = \prod_{j:j\neq\hat{\imath}}\left(\sum_{i:i\neq j}\sum_{k=1}^{K}b_j^{ik}\right)\left(\sum_{k=1}^{K}q^{\hat{\jmath}k}\right)\prod_{j:j\neq\hat{\imath},\hat{\jmath}}\left(b_j^{\hat{\imath}\hat{k}}\sum_{k=1}^{K}q^{jk}\right),$$

$$T_2 = \prod_{j:j \neq \hat{\imath}} \left(b_j^{\hat{\imath}\hat{k}} \sum_{k=1}^{K} q^{jk} \right) \prod_{j:j \neq \hat{\imath}, \hat{\jmath}} \left(\sum_{i:i \neq j} \sum_{k=1}^{K} b_j^{ik} \right), \text{ and}$$

$$T_3 = \left(\prod_{j:j \neq \hat{\imath}} \left(\sum_{i:i \neq j} \sum_{k=1}^{K} b_j^{ik} \right) \right)^2.$$

Similarly, for all $\hat{\imath}$ and $\hat{k}$, we have $\partial f / \partial q^{\hat{\imath}\hat{k}} = 0$, which is

$$- \left(\prod_{j:j \neq \hat{\imath}} \frac{b_j^{\hat{\imath}\hat{k}} \sum_{k=1}^{K} q^{jk}}{\sum_{i:i \neq j} \sum_{k=1}^{K} b_j^{ik}} \right)^{1/n} \left(a - q^{\hat{\imath}\hat{k}} \right)^{\frac{1}{n}-1}$$

$$+ \frac{\left(\sum_{i:i \neq \hat{\imath}} \sum_{k=1}^{K} b_{\hat{\imath}}^{ik} \right) \left(\sum_{k=1}^{K} q^{\hat{\imath}k} - q^{\hat{\imath}\hat{k}} \right)}{\left(\sum_{k=1}^{K} q^{\hat{\imath}k} \right)^2} = 0. \tag{12.17}$$

For an equilibrium, of course, all of these optimization conditions must hold simultaneously. Let us assume that their solution is symmetric, that is, there exist b and q such that $b_j^{\hat{\imath}\hat{k}} = b$ for all $\hat{\imath}$, $\hat{\jmath}$, $\hat{k}$, and $q^{\hat{\imath}\hat{k}} = q$ for all $\hat{\imath}$, $\hat{k}$. Then, we can simplify equation (12.16) to:

$$\left(\prod_{j:j \neq \hat{\imath}} \frac{bKq}{K(n-1)b} \right)^{\frac{1}{n}-1} (a-q)^{1/n}$$

$$\frac{\prod_{j:j \neq \hat{\imath}} ((n-1)Kb)Kq \prod_{j:j \neq \hat{\imath}, \hat{\jmath}} bKq - \prod_{j:j \neq \hat{\imath}} bKq \prod_{j:j \neq \hat{\imath}, \hat{\jmath}} ((n-1)bK)}{\left(\prod_{j:j \neq \hat{\imath}} ((n-1)Kb) \right)^2} = 1,$$

which is

$$\left(\frac{q}{n-1} \right)^{2-n-\frac{1}{n}} (a-q)^{1/n}$$

$$\frac{((n-1)Kb)^{n-1} Kq(bKq)^{n-2} - (bKq)^{n-1}((n-1)bK)^{n-2}}{((n-1)Kb)^{2n-2}} = 1,$$

or

$$q^{1-\frac{1}{n}}(a-q)^{\frac{1}{n}}(nK-K-1)=(n-1)^{2-\frac{1}{n}}Kb. \qquad (12.18)$$

Similarly, equation (12.17) simplifies to

$$\left(\prod_{j:j\neq\hat{\imath}}\frac{bKq}{K(n-1)b}\right)^{1/n}(a-q)^{\frac{1}{n}-1}=bK(n-1)\frac{(K-1)q}{(Kq)^2},$$

which becomes

$$q^{2-\frac{1}{n}}(a-q)^{\frac{1}{n}-1}K=b(K-1)(n-1)^{1/n}. \qquad (12.19)$$

Equations (12.18) and (12.19) represent two equations in the two unknowns b and q. We solve this by finding an expression for b from (12.19), and then substituting back into (12.18):

$$q^{1-\frac{1}{n}}(a-q)^{\frac{1}{n}}(nK-K-1)=(n-1)^{2-\frac{1}{n}}K\frac{q^{2-\frac{1}{n}}(a-q)^{\frac{1}{n}-1}K}{(K-1)(n-1)^{\frac{1}{n}}},$$

which gives

$$q=\frac{a(nK-K-1)(K-1)}{(n-1)^{2-\frac{2}{n}}K^2+(nK-K-1)(K-1)}. \qquad (12.20)$$

As the number of agents of each type (K) approaches infinity, we have

$$q^{\text{inf}}=\lim_{K\to\infty}q=\frac{a}{(n-1)^{1-\frac{2}{n}}+1}. \qquad (12.21)$$

If $n=2$, then $q^{\text{inf}}=\frac{a}{2}$.

We can also solve for b using (12.19) and (12.20); we get

$$b=\frac{q^{2-\frac{1}{n}}(a-q)^{\frac{1}{n}-1}K}{(K-1)(n-1)^{\frac{1}{n}}}$$

$$=\frac{a(nK-K-1)^{2-\frac{1}{n}}(K-1)^{1-\frac{1}{n}}(n-1)^{\frac{3}{n}-2-\frac{2}{n^2}}K^{\frac{2}{n}-1}}{(n-1)^{2-\frac{2}{n}}K^2+(nK-K-1)(K-1)}. \qquad (12.22)$$

Again, as $K\to\infty$, we get

$$b^{\text{inf}}=\lim_{K\to\infty}b=\frac{a}{(n-1)^{\frac{2}{n^2}}(1+(n-1)^{1-\frac{2}{n}})}, \qquad (12.23)$$

and, if $n=2$, then $b^{\text{inf}}=\frac{a}{2}$.

Finally, there will be a single price for all n goods, given by $p = \frac{(n-1)Kb}{Kq}$. Using (12.20) and (12.22) and simplifying, we get

$$p = (nK - K - 1)^{1-\frac{1}{n}}(K-1)^{-\frac{1}{n}}(n-1)^{\frac{3}{n}-1-\frac{2}{n^2}}K^{\frac{2}{n}-1}. \tag{12.24}$$

Again, as $K \to \infty$, we get

$$p^{\mathrm{inf}} = (n-1)^{\frac{2}{n}-\frac{2}{n^2}}, \tag{12.25}$$

and, if $n = 2$, we get $p^{\mathrm{inf}} = 1$.

Chapter 13 Monopolistic and

Oligopolistic Bankers

13.1 THE MANY MODELS OF BANKING

In this chapter and the two following, we examine several variations of banking. We begin with models of a single central bank and then consider corporate banks, stockholder-held corporate banks, and individually held private banks. In this chapter we consider monopolistic and oligopolistic market structures; Chapters 14 and 15 cover competitive banking markets.

Banks are complex institutions with many different functions. Here we model only one such function—short-term lending—and we model the lending without uncertainty. Thus our models are gross oversimplifications of institutional reality, but they are justified because they represent first steps beyond static general equilibrium models and into the realm of process models. The process models here are designed to answer only a few questions concerning competition, ownership, purpose, and structure.

TYPES OF BANKS

In our models in this chapter and Chapter 14, we consider several types of banks. A *central bank* is the government bank. As pointed out in Section 13.2, it can have many motivations, but usually it aims to maximize some measure of social welfare and/or perform some regulatory function. Any bank which is not a central bank we call a *private bank*. Private banks can be either *individually owned* or *corporate*. An *individually owned bank* (or *utility maximizing bank*) is one that is controlled by a single individual or family;[1] hence its motives are similar to those of our private traders (i.e., it derives utility directly from consumption of the goods and services of the economy and indirect utility from monetary profit). Alternatively, a *corporate bank* (or *profit maximizing bank*) is run primarily for monetary profit. A special type of corporate bank (considered in Chapters 14 and 15) is a *stockholder-held* (*100 percent dividend*) *corporate bank* or "*corporate bank with full payout to owners*"; there we assume that the bank is actually owned by the traders, and so its monetary profits are cycled back to them.

The private banks can exist in markets that are monopolistic, oligopolistic, or competitive. Also, we model cases where one or more private banks are considered in the presence of a central bank.

NINE SIMPLE MODELS

There are at least nine related simple one-period models involving trade with money and with various forms of money market, credit, and banking that merit consideration. Suppose n denotes the number of trader types (not financial institutions or government entities) in a model. Table 13.1 lays out the various cases together with some of their distinguishing properties.

The reader will note that in all of these models, the number of nonmonetary commodities (s) is equal to n.[2] The symmetry $s = n$ (together with the condition that all agent types have the same symmetric utility function) is useful because it cuts out concerns with complex problems in consumption, so we can concentrate on the financing of exchange and on the boundary

---

1 We do not deal here with the empirically important aspects of structures such as cooperatives, partnerships, or holding companies for corporate banks. These are critical for understanding the shadings in the motivations and goal structure of the institutions. In essence, we study only the simplified extremes.

2 One issue is: Mathematically, does s being $<, =, > n$ make any difference? Empirically, in the various aggregations of consumers and products there are fewer consumer types than there are products, i.e., $s > n$.

Table 13.1. Many models of trade with money and credit

Model	No. of goods	No. of goods markets	No. of fin. markets	Money	Financial instru.	Agent types
1. Cash market	$n + 1$	n	0	Tea[a]	0	n
2. Money market	$n + 1$	n	1	Tea	1	n
3. Dummy central bank	n	n	1	Fiat	1	$n + 1$
4. Profit max. central bank	n	n	1	Fiat	1	$n + 1$
5. Altruistic central bank	n	n	1	Fiat	1	$n + 1$
6. Tax & public goods central bank	$n + 1$	n	1	Fiat	1 or 2	$n + 1$
7. Corp. bank, profit max. 1	n	n	1	Fiat	3	$n + 1$ or $n + 2$
8. Corp. bank, profit max. 2	$n + 1$	n	1	Tea	3	$n + 1$
9. Private bank, utility max.	$n + 1$	n	1	Tea	1	$n + 1$

[a] The term "tea" stands for a storable consumable money such as tea, cocoa beans, barley, or rice.

conditions imposed by financial considerations. In our analyses so far, we have concentrated on the case $n = s = 2$.[3]

The following comments describe further each of the nine models listed above:

1. The cash market is characterized by there being n agent types, each with an endowment of one real good and each with a symmetric utility function, and each endowed with the same amount of a storable consumable (point consumption) commodity money which we call *tea*. There are n markets and all transactions are in terms of goods in exchange for a commodity money. No financial institutions are needed. Note that the case with $n = 2$ is just our basic model from Chapter 3.

---

3 Shubik and Smith (2007) and Smith and Shubik (2003) have investigated general models with $n > 2$.

2. The money market model is characterized by $n + 1$ markets (n goods markets and a money market between IOU notes and money). The individual IOU note[4] is a new financial instrument. The financial institution is the money market. Again, we note that we have analyzed this model before, where $n = 2$, in Chapter 4.

3. The model with a dummy central bank introduces a fiat that is worthless to all traders as a consumption good, but is required for transactions. The traders are not trapped by the Hahn paradox, as they may rid themselves of residual fiat at the end of the period by appropriate borrowing from the bank. In the one-period model, as the bank only lends (i.e., increases the money supply), the new financial instrument is still only the individual IOU note.[5] If there were more than one period, the bank might wish to borrow as well as lend, in which instance we would need to invent the government IOU note or bond. Either way, the bank must be added to the list of player types, as it may have a strategy set, even though it is not a natural person. Again we note that we have studied such a model before, this time in Chapters 7 and 8.

4. The model with a profit maximizing central bank assigns a utility function and a motivation to the bank. Here it is a "cash-consuming bank." We have examined such a model in Section 5.2.2.[6] However, there we did not consider how the bank utilizes the money it earns—and this should be a critical part of any analysis. In fact, central banks may earn a profit which might be paid to the government.

5. A different motivation for the bank might call for it to optimize some form of welfare function for the society as a whole. Whatever the goal or routine may be (such as ensuring enough money), formal modeling requires that it must be well defined. See the discussion in Section 5.2.1.

---

4 More strictly, the individual IOU note calls for n new financial instruments reflecting the differences in creditworthiness among all n agent types, but as we assume symmetry all agents are equally creditworthy and this distinction disappears.

5 We face a definitional problem in the switch from a commodity money to fiat. Is fiat a new financial instrument or is it a synthetic or artificial commodity? If we regard it as a financial instrument then it is the only financial instrument for which there is not necessarily a second financial instrument that nets the two to zero. Here we treat fiat as an artificial asset.

6 The model in Section 5.2.2 utilized a storable consumable money, not fiat. However, as discussed earlier, that model is essentially equivalent to a model with fiat.

6. A richer and more realistic model calls for the introduction of taxation and a public good. The minimal model requires at least one public good[7] and an extra financial instrument, the tax bill (Karatzas, Shubik, and Sudderth, 2008). Institutionally, the central bank and the tax authority both pertain to the government; thus they could be modeled utilizing one institutional player called "government." However, one may wish to consider them as two financial institutions, with goals and policies which may or may not be highly correlated. Economics alone does not justify a monetary policy–fiscal policy distinction, but there could be political and bureaucratic reasons that call it forth.

7. A simple corporate banking model with fiat has the corporation maximize profits,[8] which may be paid out as dividends. This model requires the specification of shares and dividends. The simplest model, as presented in Debreu (1959), has markets for neither shares nor dividends. A more complex multistage model could have both a stock market and a financial market for shares stripped of dividends. Beyond the money there are three financial instruments: IOU notes, stock, and dividends. Terminal conditions are required to specify the worth of any goods or financial assets left over after the end of the single period. Thus the bank must liquidate and a salvage value must be attached to any goods, debts, or fiat remaining. The salvage value may be interpreted as an expectation of future worth. If the corporate banks use fiat a central bank needs to be included as the bank of issue. Hence there are at least two financial institutions, the corporate banks and the central bank.

8. A second corporate banking model would be with a point consumption commodity money such as tea, beans, or chocolate bars. Here the banks' assets at the end of the game need to be liquidated and must be flowed through to the natural persons who are stockholders. Thus the one-period game may end with a tea party or chocolate fest as the money is consumed. No central bank is needed.

---

7 The minimal modeling of a public good requires a production function operated by the government or privately.

8 If there is any form of uncertainty, the corporation will maximize some risk-adjusted form of profits such as expected profits. If the stockholders have different risk profiles, then the corporation has a problem in fulfilling its fiduciary duty in selecting the most representative risk policy.

9. The individually owned bank model has a special class of monied individuals—the capitalists—who own and lend a commodity money, who
accept deposits, and whose only concern is their personal consumption.
With commodity money there need be only one financial institution: the
utility maximizing bank.

We do not cover all of these models; we solve several, but stress that all of
these distinctions make a difference and suggest that in monetary control the
devil may be in the details. The most realistic and complex of these models
has corporate bank competition in an economy with a central bank and fiat
money.

In this chapter, the models we solve are summarized in Table 13.2:

Table 13.2.   Models of monopolistic and oligopolistic banking

	Profit max. bank	Indiv. owned bank	Olig. banking
Type 1 traders	$(a, 0, m)$	$(a, 0, m)$	$(a, 0, m)$
Type 2 traders	$(0, a, m)$	$(0, a, m)$	$(0, a, m)$
Profit max. monopoly bank	$(0, 0, M - 2m)$	No	No
Individually owned monopoly bank	No	$(0, 0, M - 2m)$	No
Oligopolistic bank i $(i = 1, \ldots, n)$	No	No	$(0, 0, B_i)$

13.2 THE MONOPOLIST CENTRAL BANK

Suppose there is a single central bank. The goals of this bank are modeled
in several different ways and its strategic choices in two ways, that is, the
choice between controlling either the money supply or the interest rate. In
the following analysis the assumption is that the money is a fiat money that
is recognized as having no intrinsic value beyond being accepted in trade and
accepted in payment of debts by the central bank and the private banks. The
parameter $\widehat{\Pi}$ denotes the expected per unit salvage value of fiat.

13.2.1 The Bank as a Strategic Dummy

The first and easiest way to model the central bank, which we have done
in Chapters 7 and 8, is as a strategic dummy. For comparison purposes, we
reproduce that model here (but not its solution).

Our model of the trader sector is the usual one with two consumable goods,
and two trader types (each consisting of a continuum of agents) endowed with

$(a, 0, m)$ and $(0, a, m)$ as previously. We assume that the utility functions for all traders are $u(x, y, z) = 2\sqrt{xy} + \hat{\Pi}z$, where x and y are the amounts of goods 1 and 2 consumed, and z is the amount of fiat in hand at the end of the game. As defined above, $\hat{\Pi}$ is the expected per-unit salvage value of the fiat money.

A strategy for the Type 1 traders is denoted by (b, q, d), where b is the amount of money bid for good 2, q is the amount of good 1 offered for sale, and d is the amount of personal IOU notes bid for the fiat money offered by the central bank.[9] The notation for the Type 2 traders is $(\bar{b}, \bar{q}, \bar{d})$, with a similar interpretation.

The optimization problem for the Type 1 traders is then

$$\max_{d,q,b} 2\sqrt{(a-q)\frac{b}{\bar{p}}} + \hat{\Pi}\left(m + \frac{d}{1+\rho} - b + pq - d\right)$$

$$\text{s.t. } m + \frac{d}{1+\rho} - b \geq 0 \qquad\qquad (\lambda) \qquad\qquad (13.1)$$

$$m + \frac{d}{1+\rho} - b + pq - d \geq 0 \qquad\qquad (\mu)$$

$$b, d \geq 0, \ 0 \leq q \leq a.$$

Here p is the price at which the Type 1 traders sell their good 1, while $\bar{p}$ is the price at which they buy good 2. Also, ρ is the interest rate they pay on the IOU notes.

The Type 2 traders face a similar optimization problem.

The bank has an initial endowment of $(0, 0, M - 2m = B)$, and may issue any amount $g \in [0, B]$ for loan to the traders. The endogenous rate of interest is formed as

$$1 + \rho = \frac{d + \bar{d}}{g}.$$

The strategic dummy bank then can be modeled in two ways:

Controlling the Money Supply.   We assume the bank has a fixed strategy, which is to always offer some amount G for loan ($G \in [0, B]$). This model is solved in Sections 7.1.5 and 7.4, and then again in Sections 8.2 and 8.3.1, where we allow the traders to strategically default.

---

9 In an economy involving several periods we would wish to consider the central bank as both a lender and a borrower. We do not deal with this in this book. Furthermore, we could introduce an internal money market. We also omit this complication at this point.

Controlling the Rate of Interest.   Here the bank's fixed strategy is always to offer whatever amount for loan is necessary to maintain the interest rate at a particular ρ. This model was formulated in Section 7.1.5, but not solved until Sections 8.2 and 8.4.2.

13.2.2 The Central Bank Maximizing an Objective Function

THE "CASH CONSUMING CENTRAL BANK"

Modeling the central bank as a strategic dummy sidestepped the need to specify an objective function for it. But one of the two most important problems in understanding central banking is the specification of the goals of the bank (the other is delimiting its strategic powers). We consider several alternatives, noting that the efficacy of central banking depends on both its strategic power and its motivation. These properties are often empirically associated with government, but this is not a logical necessity. A central bank could be private or quasi-private, as was the Bank of England.

For example, we may consider the goal of the central bank as that of making a profit from its issue of fiat money. Thus we can give it a well-defined objective function, namely, to maximize

$$(1 + \rho)g - g = \rho g \geq 0.$$

The formal model, at this level of abstraction, will be equivalent to one with a profit maximizing monopolist bank. We investigate such a model in Section 13.3.1.

THE UTILITY MAXIMIZING CENTRAL BANK

Suppose that the central bank were owned by and operated for a king. He would wish to maximize his utility, derived from consuming perishables and owning cash. This is as though the central bank were a private monopolist individual banker. Again, an equivalent model (for a private bank) is treated in Section 13.3.3.

THE ALTRUISTIC CENTRAL BANK

An altruistic central bank may wish to optimize some social welfare function, possibly subject to some constraints on its costs and revenues, such as being required to break even. Such goals are more naturally considered in the context of policies concerning taxation, subsidy, and/or public goods. Examples are the control of inflation or employment goals. These are not considered further here.

Without considering public goods per se, a reasonable goal for a public bank might be to help to maximize the sum of individual welfare. This would imply an interpersonal comparison of welfare, such as a set of weights, to enable us to well define a sum. Although such a condition is strong, it is a matter of empirical investigation as to whether or not it is a reasonable approximation of the political process in evaluating social tradeoffs.

13.3 THE MONOPOLIST PRIVATE BANK

We now consider the possibility that instead of a government central bank there is a single private banker whose notes supply the transactions needs of the economy. At this level of abstraction, one can hardly tell a central bank apart from a private bank except by considering what it is trying to optimize—in the previous section, the central bank was a strategic dummy or was optimizing some social welfare function, while here the private bank will be optimizing its own utility function. In actuality, as is well known, the strategic variables under control may be different, as are the political links. Thus taxes, subsidies, and reserve ratios may be influenced strategically by a central bank, but far less by a private bank.

13.3.1 The Profit Maximizing Bank:
Interest Rate

Suppose that the goal of the private (corporate) bank is to maximize monetary profits. The model is mathematically the same for a private monopolistic bank as for a central bank, although their consumption patterns may differ.

In Chapter 5, we presented and analyzed a related model using a consumable storable money. Here we solve a slight generalization, in which the money (in this case, fiat) has a salvage value of Π. To summarize, the Type 1 traders' objective is

$$\max_{b,q,d} 2\sqrt{(a-q)\frac{b}{\bar{p}}} + \Pi\left(m + \frac{d}{1+\rho} - b + pq - d\right)$$

$$\text{s.t. } m + \frac{d}{1+\rho} - b \geq 0 \qquad\qquad (\lambda) \text{ (cash-flow constraint)} \qquad (13.2)$$

$$m + \frac{d}{1+\rho} - b + pq - d \geq 0 \qquad (\mu) \text{ (budget constraint)}$$

$$b, d \geq 0, \ 0 \leq q \leq a.$$

Type 2 traders face a similar optimization problem. Prices are formed by $p = \frac{\bar{b}}{q}$ and $\bar{p} = \frac{b}{\bar{q}}$, while the interest rate is formed by $1 + \rho = \frac{d + \bar{d}}{g}$. For the bank, the rate of interest ρ is the strategic variable and the bank attempts to maximize $\rho g(\rho)$.

The model is solved in Appendix A. If there is "enough money w.d." there is an equilibrium where the bank makes zero profit (see Case 1 of Appendix A). If the public has sufficiently small amounts of money, the bank can extract all $2m$ of it (Case 2). In this case, there is a continuum of equilibrium lending by the bank, ranging from all $M - 2m$ of their endowment down to zero.

There is also a third intermediate case (Case 3). Here we display an example from this third zone, where demand for funds is elastic. In that case, the traders' cash-flow constraints are tight (i.e., $\lambda = \bar{\lambda} > 0$) and their budget constraints are loose ($\mu = \bar{\mu} = 0$). Calculations in Appendix A yield $b = \bar{b} = \frac{a}{\Pi(1+\rho)^{3/2} + \Pi(1+\rho)^{1/2}}$, $d = \bar{d} = \left(\frac{a}{\Pi(1+\rho)^{1/2}(2+\rho)} - m \right)(1 + \rho)$, and $q = \bar{q} = \frac{a}{2+\rho}$. Thus, a nonzero rate of interest drives a wedge between buying and selling. As the interest rate increases, it cuts down trade.

The banker will choose ρ so as to maximize $\rho g(\rho) = \frac{2a\rho}{\Pi(1+\rho)^{3/2} + \Pi(1+\rho)^{1/2}} - 2m\rho$. This optimization can be done computationally. For example, if $m = \frac{a}{4}$ and $\Pi = 1$, we obtain $\rho = 0.38317$. This single solution point is selected because it illustrates something we saw with the monopolistic moneylender models of Section 5.2. In particular, for efficient trade, one needs more than just "enough" or "more than enough" commodity money in the system—it has to be well-distributed. If (as in Case 3) a monopolist has a sufficient part of the money supply, a shortage of money is created among the traders even with a loan market. Trade is inefficient. The positive rate of interest at the equilibrium may be purely due to monopolistic banking.

The final utility to the Type 1 traders in this example is 1.1961, which represents a large improvement over their valuation 0.25 for their initial endowments. However, in an "enough money w.d." equilibrium with $\rho = 0$, the traders could realize a final utility of 1.25.

13.3.2 The Profit Maximizing Bank: Money Supply

Instead of utilizing the interest rate as the control variable, we could have the bank utilize the money supply as its strategic variable. As long as the boundary conditions do not interfere, ρ and g are dual variables and the maximization of $g\rho(g)$ will be equivalent to that of $\rho g(\rho)$. Mathematically, this means we work with the inverse function $\rho(g)$ of $g(\rho)$. In Appendix B we calculate this inverse function for Case 3 of the model in Section 13.3.1. Indeed, we find that $\rho(g)$ is a lot more complicated than $g(\rho)$ in this case, making the computations much more difficult. However, in some of the cases of the next model,[10] we will find that it is easier to work with $\rho(g)$.

13.3.3 The Individually Owned Bank

A MODELING ISSUE

Now suppose we consider a monopolistic utility maximizing banker, who values money *and* consumes goods. Thus, the banker's problem changes to

$$\max_{b^*,\bar{b}^*,g} 2\sqrt{\frac{b^*}{p}\cdot\frac{\bar{b}^*}{\bar{p}}} + \Pi\left(M - 2m - b^* - \bar{b}^* + \rho(g)\cdot g\right)$$
$$\text{s.t. } M - 2m - g - b^* - \bar{b}^* \geq 0 \qquad (\lambda_B)$$
$$\bar{b}^*, b^*, g \geq 0.$$

Here the new variables b^* and $\bar{b}^*$ represent the amounts bid by the bank for good 1 and good 2, respectively. Note that these variables will also enter the objective function for a third time, since prices are dependent on b^* and $\bar{b}^*$ via the new balancing conditions $p = \frac{\bar{b}+b^*}{q}$ and $\bar{p} = \frac{b+\bar{b}^*}{q}$.

Recall that in our solution to the "profit maximizing bank" model (see Section 13.3.2 and also Appendix A), we solved the model by first solving the traders' problems parametrically in ρ, then using this to find $g(\rho)$ (which is the amount of money the traders will borrow, as a function of ρ), and then finally substituting into the bank's problem to optimize. Thus we were essentially modeling a two-stage game, in which the banks first announce a ρ, and then the traders give their strategies (or "response functions" to ρ) afterward. The equilibrium that we found was a perfect Nash equilibrium for this game.

Here we take the same approach. We assume that the bank makes its decisions (b^*, $\bar{b}^*$, and g) first, and then the traders make their decisions afterward (regarding b^*, $\bar{b}^*$, and g as given parameters). Again we will find not merely a Nash equilibrium for the game, but a perfect Nash equilibrium.

When we solve the game in Appendix C, we still can use the traders' first-order conditions as before, but we will not write down explicit first-order

---

10 Cases 2 and 3 of Appendix C (the model where the bank consumes goods as well as money).

conditions for the bank. Rather, once we find the traders' response functions, we will substitute back directly into the bank's decision problem and solve.

The analysis in Appendix C turns out to be quite complex. To save complication, we present our analysis for the specific case where $\Pi = 1$. We believe that the results for other values of Π would be qualitatively similar, in that we would still see the same four cases as we do below.

MODEL RESULTS

Our model breaks into four cases, depending on the size and distribution of money. The analysis is presented in Appendix C.

Case 1: If the trader types each have a lot of money, they have enough to achieve trading efficiency without needing to borrow from the bank.

Case 2: If the traders have very little money and the bank also has little money (but still relatively more than the traders), the bank will lend, spend on consumption, and hoard (maintain reserves).

Cases 3/4: If the traders have very little money and the bank has a lot of money, the bank will spend some of its money on bidding for consumption and hoard the rest. It will not lend anything to the traders. By not lending any money, it deprives the traders of a chance to bid much for the commodity— thereby allowing it (the bank) to consume relatively more of the commodity.

Case 5: If the traders and bank both have very little money, but this time with the traders having relatively more money in comparison with the bank, the budget constraints of the traders will be loose ($\mu, \bar{\mu} = 0$). A whole range of behaviors for the traders and bank is possible—see Appendix C.

13.3.4 A Comparison of the Profit Maximizing and Utility Maximizing Banks When *m* Is Small

It is interesting to compare the models of monopolistic banking when m is small. In the model with the profit maximizing bank, since the bank profits are simply the traders' original monetary endowments, we have that bank profits approach 0 as $m \to 0$. (We should note, though, that there is a continuum of equilibrium ρs when m is small but positive.) When $m = 0$, by the same logic, profits are zero (but now the only equilibrium interest rate is $\rho = 0$). Since it has no profit opportunity, the only motivation it has to lend is the altruism associated with lending at a zero interest rate.[11] If it does this, it will be of considerable benefit to the traders, who will able to achieve the efficient consumptions of $(\frac{a}{2}, \frac{a}{2})$ and $(\frac{a}{2}, \frac{a}{2})$.[12]

Things are different in the case of the utility maximizing bank when $m \to 0$. Since it is bidding against the traders, the bank has a definite interest in keeping money scarce for the traders. Hence $\rho \to \infty$, and again the bank makes no profit from lending. However, the bank does well in this model, because it is able to extract all of the goods from the traders for its own consumption. Interestingly, this is due to the *traders* being altruistic: with $m = 0$ and ρ unboundedly high, they get zero utility no matter what they do; yet they still choose to put all of their commodity endowment up for sale.

To make all this more precise, we compare the two monopolistic bank model solutions and the general equilibrium model solution for the case where $a = 1$, $M = 1$, $\Pi = 1$, and $m = 0$. For the profit maximizing bank, this puts us in Case 2 of Appendix A. For the utility maximizing bank, we are in Case 4 of Appendix C. By "competitive equilibrium," we mean a simple nondynamic general equilibrium model with no banking, in which all transactions are instantaneous.

Table 13.3 gives the comparisons. Of particular interest are the rows labeled "$a - q$," "$\frac{\bar{b}}{p}$," and "$\frac{b^*}{p}$." These represent the consumption of good 1 by the Type 1 agents, by the Type 2 agents, and by the bank (if applicable), respectively. One can see that in the limiting case where $m = 0$, the traders' consumption is efficient in the case of the profit maximizing bank, and zero in the case of the consuming bank.

In comparing the three situations, we note that the consumption of the bank will depend on the utility function ascribed to it. We made it the same as the traders', which can be interpreted as the bureaucrats having the same preferences as others. A discussion of the consumption of government as payment to a bureaucracy for enforcing the rules is given elsewhere (Shubik and Smith, 2005).

We remark that in cases where the traders have little money (such as here), strategic default is a real possibility. Thus one could consider modifications to these models along the lines of those presented in Chapter 8.

---

11 See the discussion in the subsection "Weak or Strong Pareto Optimality?" in Section 5.2.2.

12 Keep in mind that in cases like this, in which there is an interest rate of $\rho = 0$, we again have a "coordination problem" (see Chapter 4).

Table 13.3. Comparing model solutions

	Profit max. bank	Utility max. bank	Competitive equilibrium
ρ	0	$\to \infty$	Not defined
g	$g \in (0,1]$	0	Not defined
b^*	Not defined	$\to 0$	Not defined
b	$\frac{g}{2}$	$\to 0$	0.5
d	$\frac{g}{2}$	0	Not defined
q	0.5	$\to 1$	0.5
p	g	$\to 0$	1
$a - q$	0.5	$\to 0$	0.5
$\frac{\bar{b}}{p}$	0.5	$\to 0$	0.5
$\frac{b^*}{p}$	Not defined	$\to 1$	Not defined

13.4 A MODEL WITH OLIGOPOLISTIC BANKING

13.4.1 The Model

In this section we propose a model with oligopolistic banking, which is meant to be compared with the model of the monopolistic corporate bank from Section 13.3.1.

As in the earlier model, there are two continua of traders, endowed with $(a, 0, m)$ and $(0, a, m)$, respectively. However, now we replace the single monopolist banker with n bankers, each of which is an atomic player able to influence the interest rate via the amount it lends. Bank i ($i = 1, ..., n$) is endowed with only B_i units of fiat. Hence M (the total amount of money in the game) is equal to $2m + \sum_{i=1}^{n} B_i$.

The traders' optimization problems are the same as in 13.3.1, namely equation (13.2) for the Type 1 traders, with a similar problem for the Type 2 traders. For the banks, Bank i's decision variable is g_i, the amount of money it puts up for loan. Its objective is simply to end up with the most cash possible; hence its optimization problem is

$$\max_{g_i} B_i + \rho g_i$$
$$\text{s.t. } B_i - g_i \geq 0 \quad (\lambda_{B_i}) \tag{13.3}$$
$$g_i \geq 0.$$

The balance conditions are the same as before, save for the one determining the interest rate:

$$p = \frac{\bar{b}}{q}, \; \bar{p} = \frac{b}{\bar{q}}, \; 1 + \rho = \frac{d + \bar{d}}{g_1 + \cdots + g_n}.$$

Note that the bankers' optimization in (13.3) is more complex than it appears, because the selection of g_i directly affects ρ, which indirectly affects the amount of money the banks can lend via the traders' optimization problems.

13.4.2 Results

The model is solved in Appendix D. Not surprisingly, the results mirror the cases with the money maximizing monopolistic bank, solved in Appendix A—there is an "m large" case, an "m very small" case, and an intermediate case:

Case 1: Enough money w.d.:   If m is large, that is, $m \geq \frac{a}{2\Pi}$, there is an equilibrium in which consumption is efficient and the traders can finance their trading without having to borrow. The interest rate on loans is zero, so the banks each earn profits of zero.

Case 2: Very little money: Here we assume m is very small, so that the traders' cash-flow and budget constraints both are tight. As in the corresponding monopoly case (Case 2 from Section 13.3.1), the banks extract all of the traders' money. However, here the unique equilibrium has all the banks lending out all of their money. Comparing this to the monopoly case, we find that the addition of more banks has eliminated the equilibria with reduced lending (and thus higher interest rates). Thus we have a version of the classical result from oligopoly theory, where a move from monopoly to oligopoly causes higher output and lower prices.

Case 3: An intermediate amount of money: In between these two cases, there is a third, intermediate case, in which the traders are endowed with an intermediate amount of money. Not surprisingly, the solutions have the banks providing some (but not all) of their funds for loan. Mathematically, this is the hardest case, involving a system of equations which must be solved computationally.

13.5 APPENDIX A: TRADE WITH A MONEY MAXIMIZING BANK

The Type 1 traders are endowed with a units of good 1 and m units of fiat money. The Type 2 traders are endowed with a units of good 2 and m units of money. The monopolistic bank is endowed with $M - 2m$ units of money (where $0 \leq 2m \leq M$). The bank's objective is solely to end up with the most possible money.

The Type 1 traders face an optimization described by:

$$\max_{b,q,d} 2\sqrt{(a-q)\frac{b}{p}} + \Pi\left(m + \frac{d}{1+\rho} - b + pq - d\right)$$

$$\text{s.t. } m + \frac{d}{1+\rho} - b \geq 0 \qquad\qquad (\lambda)\text{ (cash-flow constraint)} \qquad (13.4)$$

$$m + \frac{d}{1+\rho} - b + pq - d \geq 0 \qquad (\mu)\text{ (budget constraint)}$$

$$b, d \geq 0,\ 0 \leq q \leq a.$$

The first-order conditions wrt b, q, and d yield

$$\frac{1}{\sqrt{p}}\sqrt{\frac{a-q}{b}} = \Pi + \lambda + \mu \qquad\qquad\qquad\qquad (13.5)$$

$$\frac{1}{\sqrt{p}}\sqrt{\frac{b}{a-q}} = \Pi p + \mu p \qquad\qquad\qquad\qquad (13.6)$$

$$\frac{\Pi}{1+\rho} - \Pi + \frac{\lambda}{1+\rho} + \frac{\mu}{1+\rho} - \mu = 0 \qquad\qquad (13.7)$$

$$m + \frac{d}{1+\rho} - b = 0 \text{ or } \lambda = 0 \qquad\qquad\qquad (13.8)$$

$$m + \frac{d}{1+\rho} - b + pq - d = 0 \text{ or } \mu = 0. \qquad\qquad (13.9)$$

Similarly, the Type 2 traders face the optimization below:

$$\max_{\bar{b},\bar{q},\bar{d}} 2\sqrt{(a-\bar{q})\frac{\bar{b}}{p}} + \Pi\left(m + \frac{\bar{d}}{1+\rho} - \bar{b} + \bar{p}\bar{q} - \bar{d}\right)$$

$$\text{s.t. } m + \frac{\bar{d}}{1+\rho} - \bar{b} \geq 0 \qquad\qquad (\bar{\lambda})\text{ (cash-flow constraint)} \qquad (13.10)$$

$$m + \frac{\bar{d}}{1+\rho} - \bar{b} + \bar{p}\bar{q} - \bar{d} \geq 0 \qquad (\bar{\mu})\text{ (budget constraint)}$$

$$\bar{b}, \bar{d} \geq 0,\ 0 \leq \bar{q} \leq a.$$

The optimization conditions here are

$$\frac{1}{\sqrt{p}}\sqrt{\frac{a-\bar{q}}{\bar{b}}} = \Pi + \bar{\lambda} + \bar{\mu} \qquad\qquad\qquad\qquad (13.11)$$

$$\frac{1}{\sqrt{p}}\sqrt{\frac{\bar{b}}{a-\bar{q}}} = \Pi\bar{p} + \bar{\mu}\bar{p} \qquad\qquad\qquad\qquad (13.12)$$

$$\frac{\Pi}{1+\rho} - \Pi + \frac{\bar{\lambda}}{1+\rho} + \frac{\bar{\mu}}{1+\rho} - \bar{\mu} = 0 \qquad (13.13)$$

$$m + \frac{\bar{d}}{1+\rho} - \bar{b} = 0 \text{ or } \bar{\lambda} = 0 \qquad (13.14)$$

$$m + \frac{\bar{d}}{1+\rho} - \bar{b} + \bar{p}\bar{q} - \bar{d} = 0 \text{ or } \bar{\mu} = 0. \qquad (13.15)$$

The banker's optimization is expressed as:

$$\max_{g \text{ or } \rho} M - 2m + \rho g(\rho)$$
$$\text{s.t. } M - 2m - g(\rho) \geq 0 \quad (\lambda_B) \qquad (13.16)$$
$$g \text{ or } \rho \geq 0.$$

Finally, the balance conditions are $p = \frac{\bar{b}}{q}$, $\bar{p} = \frac{b}{q}$, and $1 + \rho = \frac{d + \bar{d}}{g}$.

Our general approach here is to first solve the traders' problems, and then solve the banker's problem once we know what the traders do as a function of ρ. In essence we solve the trading problem parametrically for ρ, then consider $g(\rho)$ and optimize. Game-theoretically, we can imagine an extensive form game in which the lender moves first, followed by the traders. We then find the perfect equilibrium for the game.

We remark that here again the problems for Types 1 and 2 are isomorphic and so we may assume a symmetric solution where $b = \bar{b}$, $d = \bar{d}$, $p = \bar{p}$, and $q = \bar{q}$.

Case 1: First we consider the case where m is large. This is the case where both the cash-flow constraints ((λ) and $(\bar{\lambda})$) and the budget constraints ((μ) and $(\bar{\mu})$) will be loose; that is, $\lambda = \mu = \bar{\lambda} = \bar{\mu} = 0$. Our first observation is that this case could not occur if $\Pi = 0$, because then traders could raise b and/or lower q in such a way as to increase their utility while maintaining feasibility. Hence we may assume here that $\Pi > 0$.

Next, if $\lambda = \mu = \bar{\lambda} = \bar{\mu} = 0$, equation (13.5) implies $\sqrt{\frac{a-q}{b}} = \Pi\sqrt{\bar{p}}$. Also (13.6) implies $\sqrt{\frac{b}{a-q}} = \Pi p \sqrt{\bar{p}}$. Hence $\Pi\sqrt{\bar{p}} = \frac{1}{\Pi p \sqrt{\bar{p}}}$, which (using symmetry) gives $p = \bar{p} = \frac{1}{\Pi}$.

Next, the balancing conditions give $\frac{1}{\Pi} = p = \frac{\bar{b}}{q} = \frac{b}{q}$, so $q = \Pi b$. Since also $\sqrt{\frac{a-q}{b}} = \Pi\sqrt{\bar{p}} = \sqrt{\Pi}$, we have $\frac{a-q}{b} = \Pi$, or $q = a - \Pi b$. Hence $q = \bar{q} = \frac{a}{2}$ and $b = \bar{b} = \frac{a}{2\Pi}$.

Next, we note that equation (13.7) (with $\lambda = \mu = 0$) implies $\rho = 0$. Hence the bank gains zero profits.

At the end of Case 3, we argue that if $0 < m < \frac{a}{2\Pi}$, the bank can earn positive profits by choosing a positive interest rate and forcing the traders' cash-flow constraints to be tight. Hence, the above results (in which the bank gains zero profits) cannot possibly be part of a perfect equilibrium. This in turn implies that the mathematical condition for Case 1 is $m \geq \frac{a}{2\Pi}$.[13]

Finally, we note that none of this analysis has placed any limits on $d = \bar{d}$. In fact, there is a degree of freedom here—d can take on any value in the interval $\left[0, \frac{M-2m}{2} \right]$, with $\bar{d} = d$ and $g = 2d$.

Case 2: The second case is where m is very small: In this instance both the cash-flow and budget constraints will hold with equality, so $m + \frac{d}{1+\rho} - b = 0$ and $pq = d$. In addition, λ, μ, $\bar{\lambda}$, and $\bar{\mu}$ are all positive.

First, we note that $pq = d$ (see above) and $pq = \bar{b} = b$ (balancing condition plus symmetry). Hence $b = d$ ($= \bar{b} = \bar{d}$). Hence, $m + \frac{d}{1+\rho} - b = 0$ implies $m + \frac{b}{1+\rho} - b = 0$. If $m \neq 0$, this gives $b = \frac{1+\rho}{\rho} m = d = \bar{b} = \bar{d}$. Furthermore,

$$g = g(\rho) = \frac{d + \bar{d}}{1 + \rho} = \frac{\frac{2(1+\rho)}{\rho} m}{1 + \rho} = \frac{2m}{\rho}. \qquad (13.17)$$

Hence the banker maximizes $\rho g(\rho) = \rho(\frac{2m}{\rho}) = 2m$. In other words, the bank's profits are $2m$ no matter what he does. Formally he can set g anywhere in $(0, M - 2m]$, with $\rho = \frac{2m}{g}$, and attain profits of $2m$. Another way to say this is that the function $g(\rho)$ has unit elasticity.

Since the bank is indifferent among its feasible strategies, it may wish to choose a policy by which it would benefit the traders most. If so, it will set g as high as possible and ρ as low as possible; that is, $g = M - 2m$ and $\rho = \frac{2m}{M-2m}$.

Given the values of g and ρ the bank sets, we may now calculate the optimal values of the traders' decision variables. Note that we've already calculated $b = d = \bar{b} = \bar{d} = \frac{1+\rho}{\rho} m$.

First, we have (13.6) implies $\sqrt{\frac{a-q}{b}} = \frac{1}{p\sqrt{\bar{p}(\Pi+\mu)}}$. Together with (13.5) this implies $\frac{1}{p\bar{p}} = (\Pi + \lambda + \mu)(1 + \mu)$, for which symmetry implies $p = \bar{p} = \frac{1}{\sqrt{(1+\lambda+\mu)(1+\mu)}}$. Now (13.7) implies $\lambda = \rho(\Pi + \mu)$, so $p = \bar{p} = \frac{1}{\sqrt{1+\rho}(1+\mu)}$.

Thus $p(1+\mu) = \frac{1}{\sqrt{1+\rho}}$. But then (13.6) $\Rightarrow \sqrt{\frac{a-q}{b}} = \frac{1}{p\sqrt{\bar{p}}(1+\mu)} = \frac{\sqrt{1+\rho}}{\sqrt{\bar{p}}}$; that is, $\frac{a-q}{b} = \frac{1+\rho}{\bar{p}}$. Hence $\frac{a-q}{\bar{p}q} = \frac{1+\rho}{\bar{p}}$. Rearranging, we have $q = \frac{a}{2+\rho} = \bar{q}$. Also,

$$p = \frac{\bar{b}}{q} = \frac{\frac{1+\rho}{\rho}m}{\frac{a}{2+\rho}} = \frac{(1+\rho)(2+\rho)m}{\rho a} = \bar{p}.$$

In the case where $m = 0$, the assumption that the cash-flow constraint is tight (and $b = d = \bar{b} = \bar{d}$) implies that either (a) $b = d = \bar{b} = \bar{d} = 0$ or (b) $\rho = 0$. We discard (a) because it implies an outcome of no trade (see the discussion regarding the Hahn paradox in Chapter 7). But with (b), we have a continuum of symmetric equilibria, each with $\rho = 0$, $q = \frac{a}{2}$, $b = d = \bar{b} = \bar{d} \in (0, \frac{M-2m}{2}]$, $g = 2d$, and $p = \frac{b}{q} = \frac{2b}{a}$. Note that the values for ρ and q represent limiting values from the $m \neq 0$ case, but $b = d = \bar{b} = \bar{d}$ now has a degree of freedom.

Finally, for the multipliers, we have

$$\Pi + \mu = \frac{1}{p\sqrt{1+\rho}} = \begin{cases} \frac{\rho a}{(1+\rho)^{3/2}(2+\rho)m}, & \text{if } m \neq 0 \\ \frac{a}{2b}, & \text{if } m = 0 \end{cases} \tag{13.18}$$

$$\lambda = \rho(\Pi + \mu) = \begin{cases} \frac{\rho^2 a}{(1+\rho)^{3/2}(2+\rho)m}, & \text{if } m \neq 0 \\ 0, & \text{if } m = 0. \end{cases} \tag{13.19}$$

We remark that the quantities above are valid so long as the multiplier μ is nonnegative. This gives a condition of

$$\begin{aligned} &\frac{\rho a}{(1+\rho)^{3/2}(2+\rho)m} \geq \Pi \Rightarrow \frac{m}{a} \leq \frac{\rho}{\Pi(1+\rho)^{3/2}(2+\rho)}, \text{ if } m > 0 \\ &b \leq \frac{a}{2\Pi}, \text{ if } m = 0. \end{aligned} \tag{13.20}$$

Note that the maximum value of $\frac{\rho}{(1+\rho)^{3/2}(2+\rho)}$ (on the interval $\rho \in [0, \infty)$) is about 0.12, which is much less than one half. Hence "Case 1" and "Case 2" do not cover all possibilities; that is, we must have at least one "intermediate value for m" case.

Case 3: Now suppose that neither Case 1 nor Case 2 holds. Hence exactly one of the constraints (λ) and (μ) holds tightly. But just as with the borrowers' problem in the money market model, it is impossible for (μ) to hold tightly but not (λ).[14] Hence the only case to consider here is for $\lambda > 0$ (so $m - b + d/(1+\rho) = 0$) and $\mu = 0$. Also, $\bar{\lambda} = \lambda > 0$ and $\bar{\mu} = 0$.

---

14 To repeat the argument from the money market model: (μ) tight and (λ) loose implies $d > 0$, which in turn implies Type 1 traders could improve by simultaneously raising b and lowering d.

First, note that (13.7) implies $\lambda = \Pi\rho$.

Next, we see that (13.5) is $\frac{1}{\sqrt{\bar{p}}}\sqrt{\frac{a-q}{b}} = \Pi + \lambda$ and (13.6) implies $\sqrt{\frac{a-q}{b}} = \frac{1}{\Pi p\sqrt{\bar{p}}}$, hence $\frac{1}{\Pi p\bar{p}} = \Pi + \lambda$. Using symmetry, we have $p = \bar{p} = \frac{1}{\sqrt{\Pi(\Pi+\lambda)}} = \frac{1}{\Pi\sqrt{1+\rho}}$.

Next, since $m + \frac{d}{1+\rho} - b = 0$ and $m + \frac{\bar{d}}{1+\rho} - \bar{b} = 0$ we have $b + \bar{b} = \frac{d+\bar{d}}{1+\rho} + 2m = g + 2m$. But now, since $\frac{\bar{b}}{q} = p = \bar{p} = \frac{b}{\bar{q}}$, we have $\frac{b+\bar{b}}{q+\bar{q}} = \frac{1}{\Pi\sqrt{1+\rho}}$, which is $q + \bar{q} = \Pi\sqrt{1+\rho}(b+\bar{b}) = \Pi\sqrt{1+\rho}(g+2m)$.

Next, we see that (13.5) implies $\frac{1}{\bar{p}}\frac{a-q}{b} = (\Pi + \lambda)^2 = \Pi^2(1+\rho)^2$, so $\frac{a-q}{b} = \Pi(1+\rho)^{3/2} = \frac{a-\bar{q}}{\bar{b}}$. This implies $\Pi(1+\rho)^{3/2} = \frac{2a-q-\bar{q}}{b+\bar{b}} = \frac{2a-\Pi\sqrt{1+\rho}(g+2m)}{g+2m} = \frac{2a}{g+2m} - \Pi\sqrt{1+\rho}$. Rearranging gives

$$g = g(\rho) = \frac{2a}{\Pi(1+\rho)^{3/2} + \Pi(1+\rho)^{1/2}} - 2m. \tag{13.21}$$

This implies

$$b = \bar{b} = \frac{g+2m}{2} = \frac{a}{\Pi(1+\rho)^{3/2} + \Pi(1+\rho)^{1/2}}. \tag{13.22}$$

Also,

$$q = \bar{q} = \frac{\Pi\sqrt{1+\rho}(g+2m)}{2} = \frac{a}{2+\rho}. \tag{13.23}$$

The banker will choose ρ so as to maximize $\rho g(\rho) = \frac{2a\rho}{\Pi(1+\rho)^{3/2}+\Pi(1+\rho)^{1/2}} - 2m\rho$. This can be done computationally. Two comments:

1. We remark that the maximization is valid only so long as M is large enough so that the ρ so obtained does not cause $g(\rho)$ to be more than $M - 2m$. This is certainly true if $M \geq \frac{a}{\Pi}$. Otherwise, $g(\rho)$ will stay at the bound of $M - 2m$ and ρ will satisfy $\frac{2a}{\Pi(1+\rho)^{3/2}+\Pi(1+\rho)^{1/2}} = M$. (The formulas for the other variables follow, using this "modified" value of ρ.)

2. Suppose $m \in (0, \frac{a}{2\Pi})$. If we are in Case 2 the bank gains positive optimal profits by choosing a positive ρ. And if we are in Case 3 there must exist a small positive ρ such that $\rho g(\rho) = \rho \left(\frac{2a}{\Pi(1+\rho)^{3/2}+\Pi(1+\rho)^{1/2}} - 2m \right) > 0$. This compares with $\rho g(\rho) = 0$ if $\rho = 0$. Hence again the bank's optimal strategy is to choose a positive ρ to gain positive profits. These conclusions are important in our analysis of Case 1.

13.6 APPENDIX B: THE VALUE OF $\rho(g)$

The inverse function of $g(\rho)$ when in Case 3 can be obtained as follows. We start with equation (13.21) from Appendix A:

$$g(\rho) = \frac{2a}{\Pi(1+\rho)^{\frac{1}{2}} + \Pi(1+\rho)^{\frac{3}{2}}} - 2m.$$

We substitute $x = \sqrt{1+\rho}$, giving

$$g = \frac{2a}{\Pi x + \Pi x^3} - 2m$$

or

$$\Pi(g+2m)x^3 + \Pi(g+2m)x - 2a = 0. \tag{13.24}$$

Now set $h = \Pi(g+2m)$. Solving (13.24) yields:

$$x = \sqrt{1+\rho} = \sqrt[3]{\left(\frac{a}{h} + \frac{1}{9}\frac{\sqrt{3}}{h}\sqrt{h^2 + 27a^2}\right)} - \frac{1}{3\sqrt[3]{\left(\frac{a}{h} + \frac{1}{9}\frac{\sqrt{3}}{h}\sqrt{h^2 + 27a^2}\right)}},$$

or

$$\rho = \left[\sqrt[3]{\left(\frac{a}{h} + \frac{1}{9}\frac{\sqrt{3}}{h}\sqrt{h^2 + 27a^2}\right)} - \frac{1}{3\sqrt[3]{\left(\frac{a}{h} + \frac{1}{9}\frac{\sqrt{3}}{h}\sqrt{h^2 + 27a^2}\right)}}\right]^2 - 1.$$

Substituting $\Pi(g+2m)$ back in for h gives an explicit expression for ρ as a function of g.

13.7 APPENDIX C: COMMODITY AND MONEY CONSUMING BANK

In the case where the bank consumes commodity in addition to money, we must be careful to specify exactly the timing of decisions, by traders and the bank, about how much commodity is put up for sale, and how much money is borrowed, lent, and/or bid for the commodity. In other words, we must specify an extensive form for the game. As we discussed in Section 6.3.1, our choice is to assume that the bank makes its decisions (b^*, $\bar{b}^*$, and g) first, and then the traders make their decisions afterward (regarding b^*, $\bar{b}^*$, and g as given parameters). We will then find a perfect Nash equilibrium for this game.

Mathematically, this implies that the bank must take into account the traders' "response functions" to its strategies when formulating its own decision problem—this makes the bank's first-order conditions extremely complicated. On the other hand, the traders' first-order conditions remain as before.

When we solve the game, we still can use the traders' first-order conditions as before, but we will not write down explicit first-order conditions for the bank. Rather, once we find the traders' response functions, we will substitute back directly into the bank's decision problem and solve.

Type 1 traders are endowed with a units of good 1 and m units of money. Type 2 traders are endowed with a units of good 2 and m units of money. The bank is endowed with $M - 2m$ units of money. The per-unit salvage value of money is assumed to be $\Pi = 1$.

TYPE I TRADERS

$$\max_{b,q,d} 2\sqrt{(a-q)\frac{b}{p}} + m + \frac{d}{1+\rho} - b + pq - d$$
$$\text{s.t. } m + \frac{d}{1+\rho} - b \geq 0 \qquad\qquad\qquad (\lambda)$$
$$m + \frac{d}{1+\rho} - b + pq - d \geq 0 \qquad\qquad (\mu)$$
$$b, d \geq 0, \ 0 \leq q \leq a$$

First-order conditions:

$$\frac{1}{\sqrt{p}}\sqrt{\frac{a-q}{b}} - 1 - \lambda - \mu = 0 \qquad\qquad\qquad\qquad (13.25)$$

$$\frac{-1}{\sqrt{p}}\sqrt{\frac{b}{a-q}} + p + \mu p = 0 \Rightarrow (1+\mu)p\sqrt{p} = \sqrt{\frac{b}{a-q}} \qquad (13.26)$$

$$\frac{1}{1+\rho} - 1 + \frac{\lambda}{1+\rho} + \frac{\mu}{1+\rho} - \mu = 0 \Rightarrow \lambda = \rho(1+\mu) \qquad (13.27)$$

$$m + \frac{d}{1+\rho} - b = 0 \text{ or } \lambda = 0 \qquad\qquad\qquad\qquad (13.28)$$

$$m + \frac{d}{1+\rho} - b + pq - d = 0 \text{ or } \mu = 0 \qquad\qquad\qquad (13.29)$$

TYPE 2 TRADERS

$$\max_{b,q,d} 2\sqrt{(a-\bar{q})\frac{\bar{b}}{p} + m + \frac{\bar{d}}{1+\rho}} - \bar{b} + \bar{p}\bar{q} - \bar{d}$$

$$\text{s.t. } m + \frac{\bar{d}}{1+\rho} - \bar{b} \geq 0 \qquad\qquad (\bar{\lambda})$$

$$m + \frac{\bar{d}}{1+\rho} - \bar{b} + \bar{p}\bar{q} - \bar{d} \geq 0 \qquad\qquad (\bar{\mu})$$

$$\bar{b}, \bar{d} \geq 0, \ 0 \leq \bar{q} \leq a$$

First-order conditions:

$$\frac{1}{\sqrt{p}}\sqrt{\frac{a-\bar{q}}{\bar{b}}} - 1 - \bar{\lambda} - \bar{\mu} = 0 \qquad\qquad (13.30)$$

$$\frac{-1}{\sqrt{p}}\sqrt{\frac{\bar{b}}{a-q}} + \bar{p} + \bar{\mu}\bar{p} = 0 \Rightarrow (1+\bar{\mu})\bar{p}\sqrt{p} = \sqrt{\frac{\bar{b}}{a-q}} \qquad\qquad (13.31)$$

$$\frac{1}{1+\rho} - 1 + \frac{\bar{\lambda}}{1+\rho} + \frac{\bar{\mu}}{1+\rho} - \bar{\mu} = 0 \Rightarrow \bar{\lambda} = \rho(1+\bar{\mu}) \qquad\qquad (13.32)$$

$$m + \frac{\bar{d}}{1+\rho} - \bar{b} = 0 \text{ or } \bar{\lambda} = 0 \qquad\qquad (13.33)$$

$$m + \frac{\bar{d}}{1+\rho} - \bar{b} + \bar{p}\bar{q} - \bar{d} = 0 \text{ or } \bar{\mu} = 0. \qquad\qquad (13.34)$$

Balancing conditions:

$$p = \frac{\bar{b}+b^*}{q}, \ \bar{p} = \frac{b+\bar{b}^*}{\bar{q}}, \ 1+\rho = \frac{d+\bar{d}}{g} \qquad\qquad (13.35)$$

BANKER'S PROBLEM

$$\max_{b^*,\bar{b}^*,g} 2\sqrt{\frac{b^*}{p}\cdot\frac{\bar{b}^*}{\bar{p}}} + M - 2m - b^* - \bar{b}^* + \rho \cdot g$$

$$\text{s.t. } M - 2m - g - b^* - \bar{b}^* \geq 0 \qquad\qquad (\lambda_B)$$

$$b^*, \bar{b}^*, g \geq 0.$$

We note here again that p, $\bar{p}$, and ρ are all indirectly functions of b^*, $\bar{b}^*$, and g (and so the banker's problem is nontrivial to solve). But as before, we may assume by symmetry that $p = \bar{p}$, $q = \bar{q}$, $b = \bar{b}$, $b^* = \bar{b}^*$, and $d = \bar{d}$.

Case 1: *m* large (*M* anything). In this case $\lambda = 0$ and $\mu = 0$ (and $\bar{\lambda} = \bar{\mu} = 0$). Hence (13.27) $\Rightarrow \rho = 0$. Also, we see from (13.26) that $\sqrt{\frac{a-q}{b}} = \frac{1}{p\sqrt{\bar{p}}}$. Plugging back into (13.25), we get

$$\frac{1}{\sqrt{\bar{p}}} \frac{1}{p\sqrt{\bar{p}}} - 1 = 0 \Rightarrow p\bar{p} = 1 \Rightarrow p = \bar{p} = 1.$$

But if $p = \bar{p} = 1$, (13.25) implies $\sqrt{\frac{a-q}{b}} = 1$, or

$$a - q = b. \qquad (13.36)$$

Also

$$p = \bar{p} = 1 \Rightarrow \bar{b} + b^* = q \text{ and } b + \bar{b}^* = \bar{q}. \qquad (13.37)$$

From these, we have $b = a - q = \bar{b}$ and $b^* = q - \bar{b} = 2q - a = \bar{b}^*$. Hence $q = \frac{a+b^*}{2} = \bar{q}$ and $b = \frac{a-b^*}{2} = b$. Substituting these, $\rho = 0$, and the balancing conditions for price (13.35) into the banker's problem simplifies it to

$$\max_{b^*, g} 2 \sqrt{\frac{b^*\left(\frac{a+b^*}{2}\right)}{\frac{a-b^*}{2} + b^*} \cdot \frac{b^*\left(\frac{a+b^*}{2}\right)}{\frac{a-b^*}{2} + b^*}} + M - 2m - 2b^*$$

s.t. $M - 2m - g - 2b^* \geq 0$ $\qquad (\lambda_B)$

$\qquad b^*, g \geq 0.$

This problem is vacuous, solving with any value of $b^* = \bar{b}^*$ which satisfies (λ_B), including zero. Thus, we cannot solve for any more of the variables— indeed, there are a continuum of symmetric solutions, each with $\rho = 0$, $p = \bar{p} = 1$, and satisfying (13.36) and (13.37). Hence, for any $q \in [\frac{a}{2}, a]$, we have $\bar{q} = q$, $b = \bar{b} = a - q$, and $b^* = \bar{b}^* = 2q - a$. For instance, both $\rho = 0$, $p = \bar{p} = 1$, $b = \bar{b} = q = \bar{q} = \frac{a}{2}$, $b^* = \bar{b}^* = 0$ and $\rho = 0$, $p = \bar{p} = 1$, $b = \bar{b} = \frac{a}{4}$, $q = \bar{q} = \frac{3a}{4}$, $b^* = \bar{b}^* = \frac{a}{2}$ are solutions. Comparing to our solution of Case 1 in Appendix B (the "*m* large" subcase of the "bank consumes only cash" case), we see that the presence of the commodity consuming bank gives a continuum of ways for the bidding process to yield an equilibrium price of 1.

Case 2: *m* and *M* both very small. Here $\lambda > 0$, $\mu > 0$ (and $\bar{\lambda} > 0$, $\bar{\mu} > 0$), and $\lambda_B > 0$.

We start by solving the Type 1 traders' problem. Specifically,

$$(13.27) \Rightarrow \lambda = \rho(1 + \mu),$$

and

$$(13.26) \Rightarrow \frac{1}{\sqrt{\bar{p}}} \sqrt{\frac{b}{a-q}} = p(1+\mu) \Rightarrow \sqrt{\frac{a-q}{b}} = \frac{1}{p\sqrt{\bar{p}}(1+\mu)}.$$

Hence,

$$(13.25) \Rightarrow \frac{1}{p\bar{p}(1+\mu)} = 1+\lambda+\mu$$

$$\Rightarrow p\bar{p} = \frac{1}{(1+\mu)(1+\lambda+\mu)}$$

$$\Rightarrow p = \bar{p} = \frac{1}{\sqrt{(1+\mu)(1+\lambda+\mu)}} = \frac{1}{\sqrt{(1+\mu)(1+\rho(1+\mu)+\mu)}}$$

$$= \frac{1}{(1+\mu)\sqrt{1+\rho}} = \frac{\rho}{\lambda\sqrt{1+\rho}}.$$

Next, $(13.28) \Rightarrow b = \frac{d}{1+\rho} + m = \frac{d}{(d+\bar{d})/g} + m = \frac{g}{2} + m$. Similarly, (13.33) $\Rightarrow \bar{b} = \frac{g}{2} + m$. Hence, $d = \bar{d} = (1+\rho)(b-m) = (1+\rho)\frac{g}{2}$. Next, $\bar{\lambda} > 0$ and $\bar{\mu} > 0$ together imply $\bar{p}\bar{q} = \bar{d}$, and

$$\bar{p}\bar{q} = \bar{d} \Rightarrow \frac{\rho}{\lambda\sqrt{1+\rho}}\bar{q} = (1+\rho)\frac{g}{2}$$

$$\Rightarrow q = \bar{q} = (1+\rho)\frac{g}{2} \cdot \frac{\lambda\sqrt{1+\rho}}{\rho} = \frac{\lambda}{2\rho}(1+\rho)^{3/2}g.$$

Then

$$(13.25) \Rightarrow \frac{1}{\sqrt{\bar{p}}}\sqrt{\frac{a-q}{b}} = 1+\lambda+\mu$$

$$\Rightarrow \frac{1}{\bar{p}}\left(\frac{a-q}{b}\right) = (1+\lambda+\mu)^2$$

$$\Rightarrow \frac{\lambda\sqrt{1+\rho}}{\rho}\left(\frac{a - \frac{\lambda}{2\rho}(1+\rho)^{3/2}g}{\frac{g}{2}+m}\right) = (1+\lambda+\mu)^2$$

$$\Rightarrow \frac{\lambda\sqrt{1+\rho}}{\rho}\left(\frac{2\rho a - \lambda(1+\rho)^{3/2}g}{\rho g + 2\rho m}\right) = (1+\rho)^2(1+\mu)^2$$

$$\Rightarrow \frac{2\lambda\rho\sqrt{1+\rho}a - \lambda^2(1+\rho)^2 g}{\rho^2 g + 2\rho^2 m} = (1+\rho)^2(1+\mu)^2$$

$$\Rightarrow \frac{2\rho^2(1+\mu)\sqrt{1+\rho}a - \rho^2(1+\mu)^2(1+\rho)^2g}{\rho^2g + 2\rho^2m} = (1+\rho)^2(1+\mu)^2$$

$$\Rightarrow \frac{2a - (1+\mu)(1+\rho)^{3/2}g}{g+2m} = (1+\rho)^{3/2}(1+\mu)$$

$$\Rightarrow \frac{2a}{g+2m} = (1+\rho)^{3/2}(1+\mu)\left(1 + \frac{g}{g+2m}\right)$$

$$\Rightarrow \frac{2a}{g+2m} = (1+\rho)^{3/2}(1+\mu)\left(\frac{2g+2m}{g+2m}\right)$$

$$\Rightarrow 2a = (1+\rho)^{3/2}(1+\mu)(2g+2m)$$

$$\Rightarrow a = (1+\rho)^{3/2}(1+\mu)(g+m)$$

$$\Rightarrow \frac{g+m}{a} = \frac{1}{(1+\rho)^{3/2}(1+\mu)} = \frac{1}{(1+\rho)(1+\mu)(1+\rho)^{1/2}} = \frac{\rho}{1+\rho}.$$

This finally implies:

$$p = \bar{p} = (1+\rho)\frac{g+m}{a}. \tag{13.38}$$

Next, since $\lambda_B > 0$ (the bank's constraint is tight), we have $M - 2m - g - b^* - \bar{b}^* = 0$, which implies

$$b^* = \bar{b}^* = \frac{M-g-2m}{2}. \tag{13.39}$$

Hence

$$p = \bar{p} = \frac{\bar{b}+b^*}{q} = \frac{\frac{g}{2}+m+\frac{M}{2}-\frac{g}{2}-m}{\frac{\lambda}{2\rho}(1+\rho)^{3/2}g}$$

$$= \frac{\rho M}{\lambda(1+\rho)^{3/2}g}.$$

At the same time, we had $p = \bar{p} = (1+\rho)\frac{g+m}{a}$, so

$$\frac{\rho M}{\lambda(1+\rho)^{3/2}g} = (1+\rho)\frac{g+m}{a}.$$

But then

$$\lambda = \rho(1+\mu) \Rightarrow \frac{\rho}{\lambda} = \frac{1}{1+\mu} \Rightarrow \frac{M}{(1+\mu)(1+\rho)^{3/2}g} = (1+\rho)\frac{g+m}{a}$$

$$\Rightarrow \frac{M}{(1+\rho)g}p = (1+\rho)\frac{g+m}{a} = p$$

$$\Rightarrow \frac{M}{(1+\rho)g} = 1 \Rightarrow 1+\rho = \frac{M}{g}.$$

So $\rho = \frac{M}{g} - 1$. We can now use this, (13.38), and (13.39) to rewrite the bank's problem

$$\max_{b^*, \bar{b}^*, g} 2\sqrt{\frac{b^*}{p} \cdot \frac{\bar{b}^*}{\bar{p}}} + M - 2m - b^* - \bar{b}^* + \rho \cdot g$$
$$\text{s.t. } M - 2m - g - b^* - \bar{b}^* \geq 0 \qquad (\lambda_B)$$
$$\bar{b}^*, b^*, g \geq 0$$

as

$$\max_{g} 2\sqrt{\left(\frac{M-g-2m}{2}\right)^2 \cdot \left(\frac{a}{(1+\rho)(g+m)}\right)^2}$$
$$+ M - 2m - 2\left(\frac{M-g-2m}{2}\right) + \left(\frac{M}{g} - 1\right) \cdot g$$

s.t. $g \geq 0$,

which simplifies to

$$\max_{g} \frac{ag(M-g-2m)}{M(g+m)} + M = W(g)$$
$$\text{s.t. } g \geq 0.$$

To find the optimal g for general values of a, m, and M, we need to find $W'(g)$ and set it equal to zero:

$$\frac{dW}{dg} = \frac{M(g+m)(aM - 2ag - 2am) - ag(M-g-2m)M}{M^2(g+m)^2}$$

$$= \frac{a(mM - 2mg - 2m^2 - g^2)}{M(g+m)^2}$$

This is equal to zero when $mM - 2mg - 2m^2 - g^2 = 0$, i.e., when $g^2 + 2mg + (2m^2 - Mm) = 0$. The quadratic formula gives

$$g = \frac{-2m + \sqrt{4m^2 - (8m^2 - 4Mm)}}{2}$$

$$= -m + \sqrt{Mm - m^2}.$$

The utility actually attained by the banker is

$$W(-m + \sqrt{Mm - m^2})$$

$$= \frac{a(-m + \sqrt{Mm - m^2})(M - (-m + \sqrt{Mm - m^2}) - 2m)}{M(-m + \sqrt{Mm - m^2} + m)} + M$$

(13.40)

$$= \frac{a(M\sqrt{Mm - m^2} - 2Mm + 2m^2)}{M\sqrt{Mm - m^2}} + M$$

$$= a - \frac{2a\sqrt{Mm - m^2}}{M} + M.$$

At this point, it is a simple matter to calculate values for all the other variables:

$$\rho = \frac{M}{g} - 1 = \frac{M}{-m + \sqrt{Mm - m^2}} - 1.$$

$$b = \frac{g}{2} + m = \frac{m + \sqrt{Mm - m^2}}{2} = \bar{b}.$$

$$d = (1 + \rho)\frac{g}{2} = \frac{M}{g}\frac{g}{2} = \frac{M}{2} = \bar{d}.$$

$$p = (1 + \rho)\frac{g + m}{a} = \frac{M}{g}\frac{g + m}{a} = \frac{M\sqrt{Mm - m^2}}{a(-m + \sqrt{Mm - m^2})} = \bar{p}.$$

$$q = \frac{d}{p} = \frac{M}{2}\frac{a(-m + \sqrt{Mm - m^2})}{M\sqrt{Mm - m^2}} = \frac{a(-m + \sqrt{Mm - m^2})}{2\sqrt{Mm - m^2}} = \bar{q}.$$

$$b^* = \frac{M - g - 2m}{2} = \frac{M - (-m + \sqrt{Mm - m^2}) - 2m}{2}$$

$$= \frac{M - m - \sqrt{Mm - m^2}}{2} = \bar{b}^*.$$

$$\lambda = \frac{\rho}{p\sqrt{1 + \rho}} = \frac{a(M + m - \sqrt{Mm - m^2})}{M\sqrt{Mm - m^2}}\sqrt{\frac{-m + \sqrt{Mm - m^2}}{M}} = \bar{\lambda}.$$

$$\mu = \frac{\lambda}{\rho} - 1 = \frac{1}{p\sqrt{1 + \rho}} - 1 = \frac{a(-m + \sqrt{Mm - m^2})^{3/2}}{M^{3/2}\sqrt{Mm - m^2}} - 1 = \bar{\mu}.$$

Keeping in mind that $0 \leq m \leq \frac{M}{2}$ by definition, it is clear that with one exception, all of the above expressions must be nonnegative. The lone exception is the expression for μ. Hence the formulas are valid so long as $(m \leq \frac{a}{2}$ and$)$ $\mu \geq 0$; that is,

$$\frac{a(-m + \sqrt{Mm - m^2})^{3/2}}{M^{3/2}\sqrt{Mm - m^2}} - 1 \geq 0.$$

which is

$$a(-m + \sqrt{Mm - m^2})^{3/2} \geq M^{3/2}\sqrt{Mm - m^2}. \tag{13.41}$$

As an example of parameter values which fit into Case 2, consider $a = 1$, $m = 0.01$, and $M = 0.1$ (so the bank's initial holding of money is 0.08). The formulas above yield the following equilibrium values: $g = 0.02$, $\rho = 4$, $b = \bar{b} = 0.02$, $d = \bar{d} = 0.05$, $p = \bar{p} = 0.15$, $q = \bar{q} = \frac{1}{3}$, $b^* = \bar{b}^* = 0.03$, $\lambda = \bar{\lambda} = \frac{16\sqrt{5}}{3}$, and $\mu = \bar{\mu} = \frac{4\sqrt{5}}{3} - 1$.

"Case 3": $\lambda > 0$, $\mu > 0$, $\bar{\lambda} > 0$, $\bar{\mu} > 0$ and $\lambda_B = 0$. This is a "case" in which the bank has a lot of initial money and the traders do not. The reader will notice that we have put the word "case" in quotations; the reason is that our analysis will shortly show that this case cannot occur.

Since this set of multipliers is the same on the traders' side, everything from the Case 2 analysis holds, up to equation (13.38). Hence, in particular,

$$b = \bar{b} = \frac{g}{2} + m$$

$$d = \bar{d} = (1 + \rho)\frac{g}{2}$$

$$d = pq$$

$$p = \bar{p} = (1 + \rho)\frac{g + m}{a}.$$

Hence

$$\rho = \frac{d + \bar{d}}{g} - 1 = \frac{2d}{g} - 1 = \frac{2pq}{g} - 1 = \frac{2(b + b^*)}{g} - 1 = \frac{2(\frac{g}{2} + m + b^*)}{g} - 1.$$

We can now write the bank's optimization problem

$$\max_{b^*, \bar{b}^*, g} 2\sqrt{\frac{b^*}{p} \cdot \frac{\bar{b}^*}{\bar{p}}} + M - 2m - b^* - \bar{b}^* + \rho \cdot g$$

$$\text{s.t. } M - 2m - g - b^* - \bar{b}^* \geq 0 \qquad (\lambda_B)$$

$$\bar{b}^*, b^*, g \geq 0$$

as

$$\max_{b^*,\bar{b}^*,g} 2\sqrt{\frac{b^*a}{(1+\rho)(g+m)}\cdot\frac{\bar{b}^*a}{(1+\rho)(g+m)}}+M-2m-b^*-\bar{b}^*+\rho\cdot g$$

s.t. $\bar{b}^*,b^*,g\geq 0$.

Using the symmetry assumption $\bar{b}^*=b^*$, this reduces to

$$\max_{b^*,g} 2\frac{b^*a}{(1+\rho)(g+m)}+M-2m-2b^*+\rho\cdot g$$

s.t. $b^*,g\geq 0$.

Substituting in our expression for ρ and simplifying, we have

$$\max_{b^*,g} 2\frac{b^*ag}{(g+m)(\frac{g}{2}+m+b^*)}+M=W(b^*,g)$$

s.t. $b^*,g\geq 0$.

Taking the derivative of the objective function with respect to b^*, we get

$$\frac{\partial W}{\partial b^*}=\frac{ag(g+m)(\frac{g}{2}+m+b^*)-b^*ag(g+m)}{(g+m)^2(\frac{g}{2}+m+b^*)^2}=\frac{\frac{ag^3}{2}+ag^2m+\frac{ag^2m}{2}+agm^2}{(g+m)^2(\frac{g}{2}+m+b^*)^2}.$$

This is positive everywhere, which implies that the banker should raise b^* as high as possible. But if the banker does this, this will cause the constraint (λ_B) to be tight. Hence it was impossible for $\lambda_B=0$ to begin with.

What has happened here? If we recall Case 2 of Appendix A (the case equivalent to this except that the bank consumes only cash), the bank in that model extracted all of the traders' $2m$ of money no matter what strategy it chose. Here again the traders' budget constraints are tight, so the bank must end up with all of the cash in the game no matter what it does. Hence, it might as well try to earn the highest possible utility from consumption of the commodity, via bidding as much as possible for the commodity. Hence b^* (and $\bar{b}^*$) are set as high as possible.

Case 4: $\lambda>0$, $\mu=0$, $\bar{\lambda}>0$, $\bar{\mu}=0$ and $\lambda_B=0$. We now move to the case where the bank has a lot of money and the traders have little, except the traders do end up with a positive amount of money at the end of the game.

Again we start by analyzing the traders' problems. This time (since $\mu=0$), (13.27) implies $\lambda=\rho$. And (13.26) gives $\frac{1}{\sqrt{p}}\sqrt{\frac{b}{a-q}}=p\Rightarrow\frac{1}{p\sqrt{p}}=\sqrt{\frac{a-q}{b}}=\sqrt{p}(1+\lambda)=\sqrt{p}(1+\rho)$, where the penultimate equality follows from (13.25). Hence, using symmetry, we have $p=\bar{p}=\frac{1}{\sqrt{1+\rho}}$.

Next, $(13.28) \Rightarrow b = \frac{d}{1+\rho} + m = \frac{d}{(d+\bar{d})/g} + m = \frac{g}{2} + m$. Similarly, (13.33)
$\Rightarrow \bar{b} = \frac{g}{2} + m$. In addition, $d = \bar{d} = (1+\rho)(b-m) = (1+\rho)\frac{g}{2}$.

Finally, $(13.25) \Rightarrow \frac{1}{\sqrt{\bar{p}}}\sqrt{\frac{a-q}{b}} = 1 + \lambda = 1 + \rho$. Squaring both sides and
rearranging gives $\frac{a-q}{b} = \bar{p}(1+\rho)^2 = (1+\rho)^{\frac{3}{2}}$. So $q = a - b(1+\rho)^{\frac{3}{2}}$.

Next we proceed to use these results to solve the bank's problem. Starting from

$$\max_{b^*, \bar{b}^*, g} 2\sqrt{\frac{b^*}{p} \cdot \frac{\bar{b}^*}{\bar{p}}} + M - 2m - b^* - \bar{b}^* + \rho \cdot g$$
$$\text{s.t. } M - 2m - g - b^* - \bar{b}^* \geq 0 \qquad (\lambda_B)$$
$$\bar{b}^*, b^*, g \geq 0$$

we substitute using symmetry $(\bar{b}^* = b^*)$ and the above expressions for p and $\bar{p}$ to get

$$\max_{b^*, g} 2b^*(\sqrt{1+\rho} - 1) + M - 2m + \rho \cdot g$$
$$\text{s.t. } b^*, g \geq 0.$$

The balancing constraint gives $b^* = pq - b = \frac{a-b(1+\rho)^{3/2}}{\sqrt{1+\rho}} - (\frac{g}{2} + m) = \frac{a-(\frac{g}{2}+m)(1+\rho)^{3/2}}{\sqrt{1+\rho}} - (\frac{g}{2} + m)$. So our optimization problem is now down to two variables, namely, ρ and g:

$$\max_{\rho, g} 2\left(\frac{a - (\frac{g}{2}+m)(1+\rho)^{3/2}}{\sqrt{1+\rho}} - (\frac{g}{2}+m)\right)(\sqrt{1+\rho} - 1)$$
$$+ M - 2m + \rho \cdot g$$
$$\text{s.t. } \rho, g \geq 0.$$

We denote the objective function by $W(\rho, g)$. Taking the derivative of this with respect to g, we get

$$\frac{\partial W}{\partial g} = \left(\sqrt{1+\rho} - 1\right)(-2 - \rho) + \rho.$$

We claim that this expression is negative for all nonnegative values of ρ (and g). To prove the claim, we show that; (1) $\frac{\partial W}{\partial g}(\rho = 0, g) = 0$ for all g; and (2) $\frac{\partial^2 W}{\partial g \partial \rho}(\rho, g) < 0$ for all (ρ, g). Now (1) is obvious. As for (2), we calculate the indicated second derivative and get $\frac{\partial^2 W}{\partial g \partial \rho} = (1 - \sqrt{1+\rho}) - \frac{2+\rho}{2\sqrt{1+\rho}} + 1$.

Here the first term is negative; hence (2) is proved if we can show that $\frac{2+\rho}{2\sqrt{1+\rho}}$ is always greater than 1. But this follows because (a) $\frac{2+\rho}{2\sqrt{1+\rho}}$ is equal to 1 when $\rho = 0$, and (b) $\frac{d}{d\rho}\left(\frac{2+\rho}{2\sqrt{1+\rho}}\right) = \frac{\rho}{4(1+\rho)\sqrt{1+\rho}}$, which is positive for all nonnegative ρ.

The above claim implies that the bank's problem will be optimized at some (ρ, g) where $g = 0$. Hence we can reduce the bank's problem to the following one-variable optimization:

$$\max_{\rho} 2\left(\frac{a - m(1+\rho)^{3/2}}{\sqrt{1+\rho}} - m\right)\left(\sqrt{1+\rho} - 1\right) + M - 2m \tag{13.42}$$

s.t. $\rho \geq 0$.

This can be solved by computational techniques. When the optimal ρ is found, together with $g = 0$ we can substitute back to find the values of all of the other variables.

Perhaps the reader will find it strange that the optimal value of g turns out to be zero. The reason is that by not lending money, the bank prevents the traders from getting their hands on much cash. This in turn prevents the traders from bidding much for the commodity. The upshot is that the bank can then buy more of the commodity for itself, at a cheaper price.

As an example of parameter values for this case, consider an example where $a = 1$, $m = 0.05$, and $M = 1$. Note that (13.41) is not satisfied, so we are not in Case 2. Using graphing software, we found that the optimization (13.42) is attained at approximately $\rho = 2.028$. With $\rho = 2.028$ and $g = 0$, we can work backward to get the other optimal variable values: $p = \bar{p} = \frac{1}{\sqrt{1+\rho}} = 0.575$, $b = \bar{b} = \frac{g}{2} + m = 0.05$, $d = \bar{d} = (1+\rho)\frac{g}{2} = 0$, $q = \bar{q} = a - b(1+\rho)^{3/2} = 0.737$, and $b^* = \bar{b}^* = pq - b = 0.374$. The bank consumes $\frac{b^*}{p} = \frac{\bar{b}^*}{\bar{p}} = 0.65$ of each good. Finally, we have $\lambda = \rho = 2.028$.

If m is lowered to 0.005, we obtain $\rho = 8.04$, $p = \bar{p} = 0.333$, $b = \bar{b} = 0.005$, $d = \bar{d} = 0$, $q = \bar{q} = 0.864$, and $b^* = \bar{b}^* = 0.283$. The bank consumes $\frac{b^*}{p} = \frac{\bar{b}^*}{\bar{p}} = 0.85$ of each good.

If m is lowered to 0.0005, we obtain $\rho = 26.45$, $p = \bar{p} = 0.191$, $b = \bar{b} = 0.0005$, $d = \bar{d} = 0$, $q = \bar{q} = 0.928$, and $b^* = \bar{b}^* = 0.177$. The bank consumes $\frac{b^*}{p} = \frac{\bar{b}^*}{\bar{p}} = 0.925$ of each good.

To summarize our conclusions from "Noncase" 3 and Case 4: If the bank is endowed with a lot of money and the traders little, it is in the bank's interest not to lend the traders anything!

Case 5: $\lambda > 0$, $\mu = 0$, $\bar{\lambda} > 0$, $\bar{\mu} = 0$ and $\lambda_B > 0$. Again we start by analyzing the traders' problems. Since the multipliers for the traders are unchanged from Case 4, we again have $\lambda = \rho$, $p = \bar{p} = \frac{1}{\sqrt{1+\rho}}$, $b = \bar{b} = \frac{g}{2} + m$, and $d = \bar{d} = (1+\rho)\frac{g}{2}$.

Next, since $\lambda_B > 0$, we have $M - 2m - g - b^* - \bar{b}^* = 0 \Rightarrow b^* = \bar{b}^* = \frac{M-g-2m}{2}$. Hence

$$p = \bar{p} = \frac{\bar{b} + b^*}{q} = \frac{\frac{g}{2} + m + \frac{M}{2} - \frac{g}{2} - m}{q} = \frac{M}{2q}.$$

And since $p = \bar{p} = \frac{1}{\sqrt{1+\rho}}$, we have $\frac{1}{\sqrt{1+\rho}} = \frac{M}{2q}$, or $q = \frac{M\sqrt{1+\rho}}{2}$.

Finally, (13.25) $\Rightarrow \frac{1}{\sqrt{\bar{p}}}\sqrt{\frac{a-q}{b}} = 1 + \lambda = 1 + \rho$. Squaring both sides and rearranging gives $\frac{a-q}{b} = \bar{p}(1+\rho)^2 = (1+\rho)^{3/2}$. Substituting in our known expressions for q and for b gives

$$\frac{a - \frac{M\sqrt{1+\rho}}{2}}{\frac{g}{2} + m} = (1+\rho)^{3/2} \Rightarrow 2a - M\sqrt{1+\rho} = (g+2m)(1+\rho)^{3/2}$$

$$\Rightarrow g = \frac{2a - M\sqrt{1+\rho}}{(1+\rho)^{3/2}} - 2m. \tag{13.43}$$

Note that this is an equation for g in terms of ρ, rather than the reverse. So to finish off the solution, all we need do is find the bank's optimal ρ. To do this, we rewrite the bank's problem, using ρ as the strategic variable instead of g. Start with the bank's problem

$$\max_{b^*, \bar{b}^*, g} 2\sqrt{\frac{b^*}{p} \cdot \frac{\bar{b}^*}{\bar{p}}} + M - 2m - b^* - \bar{b}^* + \rho \cdot g$$
$$\text{s.t. } M - 2m - g - b^* - \bar{b}^* \geq 0 \qquad\qquad (\lambda_B)$$
$$\bar{b}^*, b^*, g \geq 0$$

and substitute our known expressions for $b^* = \bar{b}^*$ and for $p = \bar{p}$. We get

$$\max_{\rho, g} 2\sqrt{1+\rho}\,\frac{M - g - 2m}{2} + M - 2m - (M - g - 2m) + \rho \cdot g$$
$$\text{s.t. } g = \frac{2a - M\sqrt{1+\rho}}{(1+\rho)^{3/2}} - 2m$$
$$\rho \geq 0,\ 0 \leq g \leq M - 2m.$$

Finally, substitute in for g:

$$\max_\rho \sqrt{1+\rho}\left[M - \left(\frac{2a-M\sqrt{1+\rho}}{(1+\rho)^{3/2}} - 2m\right) - 2m\right]$$
$$+ \left(\frac{2a - M\sqrt{1+\rho}}{(1+\rho)^{3/2}} - 2m\right) + \rho \cdot \left(\frac{2a - M\sqrt{1+\rho}}{(1+\rho)^{3/2}} - 2m\right)$$

s.t. $\rho \geq 0$

or

$$\max_\rho \sqrt{1+\rho}(M - 2m) + \left(\frac{2a - M\sqrt{1+\rho}}{(1+\rho)^{3/2}} - 2m\right)\left(1+\rho - \sqrt{1+\rho}\right)$$

s.t. $\rho \geq 0$.

This can be solved computationally. Once we have found ρ, we can go back and compute g from (13.43), and then all of the rest of the variables easily.

An example of parameter values that fit Case 5 would be $a = 1$, $m = 0.05$, and $M = 0.4$. Using graphing software, we find that the optimal ρ in the above is approximately 2.141. Substituting into (13.43), we get $g = 0.132$ (approximately). Then $p = \bar{p} = \frac{1}{\sqrt{1+\rho}} = 0.564$, $b = \bar{b} = \frac{g}{2} + m = 0.116$, $d = \bar{d} = (1 + \rho)\frac{g}{2} = 0.207$, $q = \bar{q} = \frac{M\sqrt{1+\rho}}{2} = 0.354$, and $b^* = \bar{b}^* = pq - b = 0.084$. Finally, we have $\lambda = \rho = 2.141$.

We remark that within Case 5 there is a wide range, qualitatively, of equilibrium behaviors for the bank. For instance, if the optimal ρ from above yields a g from (13.43) which is greater than $M - 2m$, the equilibrium solution will be to reset $g = M - 2m$, that is, to have the bank lend all of its money and use none in bidding for the commodity.[15] On the other hand, if we obtain a g from (13.43) which is negative, the equilibrium solution will have $g = 0$; that is, the bank lends nothing and uses all of its endowment in bidding for the commodity.

To demonstrate, consider the case in which $a = 1$, $m = 0.05$, and M is slowly lowered from 1. At $M = 1$, we are in Case 4 and the bank does not lend anything. When M reaches a value of about 0.85, we cross over from Case 4 to Case 5—but the bank still does not lend.[16] Finally, within Case 5, when M reaches a value of roughly 0.55, the equilibrium solution has the bank lending. As M decreases further, the bank lends more. Finally, at a value

---

15 Once we reset $g = M - 2m$, ρ must be reset so as to satisfy (13.43), and then the other variables can be calculated from these.

16 Remember, the distinction between Case 4 and Case 5 is not whether or not the bank *lends* money—but rather it is whether or not the bank *hoards* money.

of about $M = 0.31$, the bank lends all it has, and continues to do so all the way down to the lowest possible value $M = 0.1$.

13.8 APPENDIX D: OLIGOPOLISTIC BANKING

The traders' optimization problems here are identical to those in Appendix A. For ease in following the math, we reproduce them here.

The Type 1 traders face an optimization described by:

$$\max_{b,q,d} 2\sqrt{(a-q)\frac{b}{\bar{p}}} + \Pi\left(m + \frac{d}{1+\rho} - b + pq - d\right)$$

$$\text{s.t. } m + \tfrac{d}{1+\rho} - b \geq 0 \qquad\qquad (\lambda)\text{ (cash-flow constraint)} \qquad (13.44)$$

$$m + \tfrac{d}{1+\rho} - b + pq - d \geq 0 \qquad (\mu)\text{ (budget constraint)}$$

$$b, d \geq 0,\ 0 \leq q \leq a.$$

The first-order conditions wrt b, q, and d yield

$$\frac{1}{\sqrt{\bar{p}}}\sqrt{\frac{a-q}{b}} = \Pi + \lambda + \mu \qquad\qquad (13.45)$$

$$p\frac{1}{\sqrt{\bar{p}}}\sqrt{\frac{b}{a-q}} = \Pi p + \mu \qquad\qquad (13.46)$$

$$\frac{\Pi}{1+\rho} - \Pi + \frac{\lambda}{1+\rho} + \frac{\mu}{1+\rho} - \mu = 0 \qquad\qquad (13.47)$$

$$m + \frac{d}{1+\rho} - b = 0 \text{ or } \lambda = 0 \qquad\qquad (13.48)$$

$$m + \frac{d}{1+\rho} - b + pq - d = 0 \text{ or } \mu = 0. \qquad\qquad (13.49)$$

Similarly, the Type 2 traders face the optimization below:

$$\max_{\bar{b},\bar{q},\bar{d}} 2\sqrt{(a-\bar{q})\frac{\bar{b}}{p}} + \Pi\left(m + \frac{\bar{d}}{1+\rho} - \bar{b} + p\bar{q} - \bar{d}\right)$$

$$\text{s.t. } m + \tfrac{\bar{d}}{1+\rho} - \bar{b} \geq 0 \qquad\qquad (\bar{\lambda})\text{ (cash-flow constraint)} \qquad (13.50)$$

$$m + \tfrac{\bar{d}}{1+\rho} - \bar{b} + p\bar{q} - \bar{d} \geq 0 \qquad (\bar{\mu})\text{ (budget constraint)}$$

$$\bar{b}, \bar{d} \geq 0,\ 0 \leq \bar{q} \leq a.$$

The optimization conditions here are

$$\frac{1}{\sqrt{p}}\sqrt{\frac{a-\bar{q}}{\bar{b}}} = \Pi + \bar{\lambda} + \bar{\mu} \tag{13.51}$$

$$\frac{1}{\sqrt{p}}\sqrt{\frac{\bar{b}}{a-\bar{q}}} = \Pi\bar{p} + \bar{\mu}\bar{p} \tag{13.52}$$

$$\frac{\Pi}{1+\rho} - \Pi + \frac{\bar{\lambda}}{1+\rho} + \frac{\bar{\mu}}{1+\rho} - \bar{\mu} = 0 \tag{13.53}$$

$$m + \frac{\bar{d}}{1+\rho} - \bar{b} = 0 \text{ or } \bar{\lambda} = 0 \tag{13.54}$$

$$m + \frac{\bar{d}}{1+\rho} - \bar{b} + \bar{p}\bar{q} - \bar{d} = 0 \text{ or } \bar{\mu} = 0. \tag{13.55}$$

The difference between this model and the one in Appendix A is that here we have n bankers ($n \geq 2$) instead of one. Suppose Bank i ($i = 1, ..., n$) is endowed with B_i units of fiat. The optimization problem for this bank is:

$$\max_{g_i} B_i + \rho g_i$$
$$\text{s.t. } B_i - g_i \geq 0 \quad (\lambda_B) \tag{13.56}$$
$$g_i \geq 0.$$

Finally, the balance conditions are $p = \frac{\bar{b}}{q}$, $\bar{p} = \frac{b}{\bar{q}}$ and $1 + \rho = \frac{d+\bar{d}}{g_1+\cdots+g_n}$.

Case 1: m large. In this case both the traders' cash-flow and budget constraints are loose; that is, $\lambda = \bar{\lambda} = \mu = \bar{\mu} = 0$.

In this case the analysis follows that of Case 1 of Appendix A. First we note that Π can't be zero here, because otherwise traders could raise b and/or lower q in such a way as to increase their utility while maintaining feasibility. Hence we may assume here that $\Pi > 0$. Next, (13.45) implies $\sqrt{\frac{a-q}{b}} = \Pi\sqrt{p}$. Also, (13.46) implies $\sqrt{\frac{b}{a-q}} = \Pi p\sqrt{p}$. Hence $\Pi\sqrt{p} = \frac{1}{\Pi p\sqrt{p}}$, which (using symmetry) gives $p = \bar{p} = \frac{1}{\Pi}$.

Next, the balancing conditions give $\frac{1}{\Pi} = p = \frac{\bar{b}}{q} = \frac{b}{\bar{q}}$, so $q = \Pi b$. Since also $\sqrt{\frac{a-q}{b}} = \Pi\sqrt{\bar{p}} = \sqrt{\Pi}$, we have $\frac{a-q}{b} = \Pi$, or $q = a - \Pi b$. Hence we have $q = \Pi b$ and $q = a - \Pi b$, which together imply $q = \bar{q} = \frac{a}{2}$ and $b = \bar{b} = \frac{a}{2\Pi}$.

Also, condition (13.47) (with $\lambda = \mu = 0$) implies $\rho = 0$. This implies the banks each get profits of zero.

An argument in footnote 17, below, states that the mathematical condition for this case is $m \geq \frac{a}{2\Pi}$.[17]

None of the analysis above puts any restriction on d. Indeed, as long as $m \geq \frac{a}{2\Pi}$, we have a continuum here, with $d = \bar{d} \in [0, \frac{\sum_i B_i}{2}]$ and $g_1, ..., g_n$ satisfying $\sum_i g_i = 2d$ and $g_i \in [0, B_i]$ for all i.

Case 2: Very little money (m very small). Here both the traders' cash-flow and budget constraints are tight, that is, λ, $\bar{\lambda}$, μ, and $\bar{\mu} > 0$.

In this case the tight cash-flow and budget constraints together imply $pq = d$. Since the balancing condition (plus symmetry) implies $pq = b$, we have $b = d = \bar{b} = \bar{d}$. So then our tight cash-flow constraint can be written as

$$m + \frac{b}{1+\rho} - b = 0. \tag{13.57}$$

If $m \neq 0$, (13.57) implies $b = d = \bar{b} = \bar{d} = \frac{1+\rho}{\rho} m$. But then $g_1 + \cdots + g_n = \frac{d+\bar{d}}{1+\rho} = \frac{2\frac{1+\rho}{\rho} m}{1+\rho} = \frac{2m}{\rho}$. This then gives $\rho = \frac{2m}{g_1 + \cdots + g_n}$, so Bank i's problem (13.56) becomes

$$\max_{g_i} B_i + \frac{2mg_i}{g_1 + \cdots + g_n}$$
$$\text{s.t. } B_i - g_i \geq 0 \qquad (\lambda_B) \tag{13.58}$$
$$g_i \geq 0.$$

This is optimized (for any values of m and $\{g_k\}_{k \neq i}$) by setting $g_i = B_i$. So, in conclusion, each bank lends out all of its money and the interest rate becomes

---

17 We do this by proving that if $m < \frac{a}{2\Pi}$, there cannot be a symmetric perfect equilibrium in which $\rho = 0$. The proof is by contradiction—so suppose there was such a symmetric equilibrium, with $g_1 = g_2 = \cdots = g_n = \hat{g}$. Since $\rho = 0$, the banks are each getting a profit of zero from this equilibrium.

Now, if $\hat{g} = 0$, Bank 1 could change its strategy to $g_1 = g^*$, where g^* is the positive loan level associated with the positive ρ whose existence we argued for in list item 2 at the end of Appendix A, Case 3. In this case the traders will demand exactly the loans which will put the interest rate at that ρ, and so Bank 1's profits will be positive. This in turn implies $g_1 = g_2 = \cdots = g_n = 0$ is not an equilibrium.

Now suppose $\hat{g} > 0$. We have $1 + \rho = \frac{d+d}{n\hat{g}}$, with $\rho = 0$. Now Bank 1 can change its strategy by lowering its loans to $\hat{g} - \varepsilon$, where ε is an infinitesimal amount which would raise ρ to a small positive level at which the traders would demand loans. (Essentially, equation (13.21) gives the total amount g of loans demanded by traders as a function of ρ; if $m < \frac{a}{2\Pi}$ and if ρ is small enough, this will be positive) This again would make Bank 1's profits positive, and so again there is no equilibrium.

$\rho = \frac{2m}{B_1 + \cdots + B_n}$. One can then work backward, as in the analysis from Case 2 in Appendix A, to get the rest of the values: $b = d = \bar{b} = \bar{d} = \frac{1+\rho}{\rho} m$, $q = \bar{q} = \frac{a}{2+\rho}$, and $p = \bar{p} = \frac{(1+\rho)(2+\rho)m}{\rho a}$. The results are valid so long as $\frac{m}{a} \leq \frac{\rho}{\Pi(1+\rho)^{3/2}(2+\rho)}$ (again following the analysis from Appendix A, Case 2).

If $m = 0$, condition (13.57) implies that either (a) $b = d = \bar{b} = \bar{d} = 0$, or (b) $\rho = 0$. If (a) holds, there is no trade, so we disregard (a). If (b) holds, (13.47) implies that $\lambda = 0$. But then (13.45) implies $\sqrt{\frac{a-q}{b}} = \sqrt{\bar{p}}(\Pi + \mu)$ and (13.46) implies $\sqrt{\frac{b}{a-q}} = p\sqrt{\bar{p}}(\Pi + \mu)$. Substituting in for $\sqrt{\bar{p}}(\Pi + \mu)$, we get $\sqrt{\frac{b}{a-q}} = p\sqrt{\frac{a-q}{b}}$, which is $p = \frac{b}{a-q}$. But by symmetry and the balancing condition $p = \frac{b}{q}$; hence $\frac{b}{q} = \frac{b}{a-q}$ or $q = \frac{a}{2} = \bar{q}$. There is a degree of freedom regarding b, d, and p: any values work so long as: (a) $b = d = \bar{b} = \bar{d}$; (b) $p = \bar{p} = \frac{2b}{a}$; and (c) $g_1 + \cdots + g_n = d + \bar{d}$, with $g_i \in [0, B_i]$ for $i = 1, ..., n$.

Case 3: An intermediate amount of money. Here we assume that the traders' cash-flow constraints are tight ($\lambda, \bar{\lambda} > 0$) while their budget constraints are loose ($\mu, \bar{\mu} = 0$).

In this case let us define the quantity g as equal to $g_1 + \cdots + g_n$. We follow the analysis from Case 3 in Appendix A, obtaining

$$g = \frac{2a}{\Pi(1+\rho)^{3/2} + \Pi(1+\rho)^{1/2}} - 2m \tag{13.59}$$

$$b = \bar{b} = \frac{g + 2m}{2} = \frac{a}{\Pi(1+\rho)^{3/2} + \Pi(1+\rho)^{1/2}}. \tag{13.60}$$

$$q = \bar{q} = \frac{\Pi\sqrt{1+\rho}(g + 2m)}{2} = \frac{a}{2+\rho}. \tag{13.61}$$

(These equations are (13.21), (13.22), and (13.23), above.) Then $d = (1+\rho)(b - m) = \frac{(1+\rho)a}{\Pi(1+\rho)^{3/2}+\Pi(1+\rho)^{1/2}} - (1+\rho)m$. But the balance condition (plus symmetry) says $1 + \rho = \frac{2d}{g}$; hence $d = \frac{2ad/g}{\Pi(2d/g)^{3/2}+\Pi(2d/g)^{1/2}} - \frac{2md}{g}$, or $g = \frac{2a}{\Pi(2d/g)^{3/2}+\Pi(2d/g)^{1/2}} - 2m$. From this, we can derive d as a function of g, which we call $d(g)$. So then Bank i's problem (13.56) becomes:

$$\max_{g_i} B_i + \rho g_i = B_i + \left(\frac{2d(g)}{g} - 1\right)g_i$$
$$\text{s.t. } B_i - g_i \geq 0 \qquad (\lambda_B) \tag{13.62}$$
$$g_i \geq 0.$$

Let us suppose that the quantities $B_1, ..., B_n$ are all large, so that the conditions (λ_B) are all loose. Even so, the quantity g is itself dependent on g_i, so the first-order conditions for solving (13.62) become quite complicated:

$$2gg_id'(g) - 2g_id(g) + 2gd(g) = 0, \; i = 1, ..., n. \qquad (13.63)$$

Even allowing for symmetry $g_i = \frac{g}{n}$ $(i = 1, ..., n)$ does not make this easy, due to the complicated nature of the function $d(g)$. But presumably the optimal g_i's are interior to $[0, B_i]$, so the banks are lending out some, but not all, of their money. And if we can find the equilibrium d and g, and hence ρ, we can find b and q using (13.60)–(13.61).

Chapter 14 Competitive Banking I: Corporate Banking with a Central Bank

14.1 REDUCTIONISM OR EMERGENCE

Chapter 13 and several previous chapters have been exercises in reductionism. Our viewpoint is to try to fully analyze simple models which illustrate basic economic functions such as simple exchange, borrowing, and lending. Yet at the same time we value complexity and emergence. The basic economic models of the simplest markets and financial institutions do not reflect the new functions (such as reinsurance or credit enhancement) that arise, often unexpectedly, at a higher level of complexity. In his book on the evolution of individuality, the biologist Leo Buss (1987) states: "At the heart of my argument is the simple observation that the history of life is a history of the elaboration of new self-replicating entities by the self-replicating entities contained within them (or the incorporation of some self-replicating entities by others)" (p. viii). This statement concerning biological organisms can be applied to economic life and the relationship between a central bank and the commercial banks in an economy. But at this level of complexity simple general mathematical models are difficult to construct and analyze, although an example of an ad hoc model of a commercial bank in a partial equilibrium setting is provided by Tobin (1982a). Furthermore, there is a considerable literature on applied partial equilibrium theory and application to money and banking. See, for example, Diamond and Dybvig (1983), Diamond and Raghuram (2006), and Santomero (1984).

We utilize simplistic reductionism in keeping with the search for minimal mechanisms. As soon as one attempts to construct minimalist process models of a closed economy with a commercial bank and a central bank, one encounters grotesquely simplistic formulations. Nevertheless, these models are useful in answering several conventional, commonly asked questions about money and banking:

1. Can commercial banking be purely competitive?
2. What are the competitive variables under control of the individual banks?
3. Precisely what is meant by "bills only" commercial banking?
4. Where does uncertainty enter into any model of banking?
5. Why is the specification of default rules and bank failure laws critical to the specification of the simplest strategic models of the economy?
6. What are the necessary or sufficient conditions for the banking system to vary the money supply?
7. How can the money supply be changed?
8. What constitutes central bank reserves?
9. What constitutes commercial bank reserves?
10. What is the shortest time for which money can be borrowed?

The conventional wisdom, as ably exposited in the review article by Brunner and Meltzer (1990), is a macroeconomic point of view. As a source of advice to practitioners, it may have considerable value; but it is not sufficient to forge the links between the models discussed there and a microeconomic dynamic model that encompasses an approach that provides fully defined process models. By definition, any process model calls for an exercise in mathematical institutional economics, because the institutions and laws are required as carriers of process. Even the most trivial of microeconomic models with two player types engaged in simple exchange, when recast as a full process model, requires dozens of variables and parameters.

14.2 ON NATURAL PERSONS, LEGAL PERSONS, AND OWNERSHIP

In a modern organized society there are two types of "legal persons": (a) natural persons, and (b) corporate entities, such as for profit firms, universities, hospitals, government agencies, and so on. All legal persons who are not natural persons are ultimately owned in some form by natural persons.[1] Upon liquidation, their assets must be flowed through to their owners. This even includes governments, although the ongoing aspects of the nation-state make this essentially a fiction—the nation state rarely voluntarily "goes out of business"–it more often ends with war or revolution.

With the luxury of an experimental game with given initial and terminal conditions,[2] we can define a game where at the settlement day the resources of all legal persons who are not natural persons are turned over to the natural persons who are the ultimate owners.

Previously in this book, with the exception of references to corporate banks and a central bank, all of the agents are natural persons. In a modern economy, by value almost all transactions are between corporate entities and corporate entities, or corporate entities and natural persons. Beyond the individual acts of the natural person qua consumer, all other decisions are the acts of fiduciaries. This raises deep questions on how to attribute motivation to the fiduciary. We do not deal with the problems of agency here; instead, we call attention to this important critical problem in monetary theory, which is rarely considered even though the problems it raises are well known in the law. Although there are two types of legal persons in an economy, natural persons individually or collectively own all other legal persons. In well defining an economic model as a playable game, this poses a problem in the valuation of assets, including institutions, if anything is left over at the end of the game. In dynamic programming models this is recognized in the assignment of salvage value.

If one wishes to consider a finite time segment of a closed economy in the context of an ongoing process, the initial conditions encompass history

---

1 In actuality, an orderly liquidation of a society rarely if ever takes place; thus the liquidation of the central bank suggested is an accounting fiction that stresses ultimate ownership, not control, and lays stress on balancing the books.

2 The terminal conditions at their simplest may be a fixed set of prices for remaining resources, but they also could be books of instructions or algorithms based on the play of the game.

and all property rights. In order to describe the equations of motion, it is necessary to specify whether the motion depends on perception of the future. If behavior depends on the estimate of the state of the system in the period immediately after the last moves have been made, then the model builder must supply the terminal conditions for "the day of settlement" at the end of the game. This may be a simple set of disposal prices or a complex algorithm, depending on every play or path down the game tree. At this point one of the classical accounting problems appears: Do we evaluate corporations or other institutions at their liquidation values or at their ongoing business values? We do not pretend to solve this basic problem generally; but we do offer an approach consistent with rational expectations, perfect noncooperative equilibria in strategic market games, and the formulation of playable experimental games. Specifically, at the end of the game a set of prices for all physical resources is specified, all contracts are settled, and all institutions are unwound, with all of the assets of the corporate entities being assigned to their natural person owners. This includes the central bank, with the legal fiction that government is "owned by the people"; hence its assets should be distributed to all natural persons.

Financial arrangements and institutions are human creations. The rules of the game concerning fiat money and central bank reserves, although conforming with physical facts, are not uniquely determined by them. In particular, the special role of outside money and its relationship with fiat can be modeled by including the initial conditions of issue and the final deconstruction of all institutions at the end. These comments are exemplified in the models below.

14.3 MODELS OF COMPETITIVE BANKING

In order to model competitive lending, let alone banking, we require either an axiom of price-taking or the empirically implausible device of a continuum of bankers (as well as the usual continua of traders) in order to eliminate consideration of oligopolistic competition. All agents (except possibly the central bank, if it is in the model) take prices and the money interest rate as givens. In even casual empirical observation there is an oligopolistic component to banking; but as a benchmark we can consider the ideal of competitive behavior by minimal institutions that can make loans, accept deposits, and possibly create money.

Among the alternative modeling assumptions that we could reasonably consider are the following (asterisks indicate choices we have analyzed in this book):

Private bank goals: 1. maximize utility (for individually owned banks),* 2. maximize profits (for corporate banks),* 3. maximize managerial wealth (for corporate banks), 4. maximize corporate growth (for corporate banks), 5. accomplish other goals (such as: provide a variety of consumer services)

Private bank control variables: 1. bid for consumption of goods (for individually owned banks),* 2. specify rates of interest for loans and deposits, 3. specify the quantity of fiat offered for loan,* 4. set the quantity of gold offered for sale,* 5. set the quantity of credit offered*

The above examples do not include possibilities such as selling advisory services; acting as trustee; investing; providing foreign exchange services; and many other activities of a modern bank.

Private bank income disposal: 1. build reserves, 2. pay dividends,* 3. invest in growth, 4. other (such as managerial enrichment)

Trader goals: 1. maximize utility,* 2. other (such as: "good enough" or habitual trade)

Trader control variables: 1. offer goods,* 2. bid for goods,* 3. vote on bank management

Trader income disposal: 1. spend on consumption,* 2. save, 3. pay taxes, 4. other (such as: hoard, invest, or give away)

Central bank goals: 1. optimize money supply,* 2. maximize profit, 3. other (such as: aim to control inflation), 4. possibly consider model economies with no central bank*

Central bank control variables: 1. a rate of interest,* 2. the quantity of fiat,* 3. the quantity of gold,* 4. commercial bank reserve requirements,* 5. national debt operations

Central bank income disposal: 1. build reserves,* 2. pay to other parts of government, 3. other

Many of the items in each category are not mutually exclusive. Even ignoring the possibility of multiple choices, there are over 100,000 models we could construct. This does not include setting both the initial and terminal conditions; before one obtains a fully defined model, the initial holdings of the central bank, the corporate banks, and the traders must all be specified. This calls for the setting of many parameters. After that we also require a set of instructions specifying how to evaluate any terminal assets.

For many questions of interest a model of several periods is required. However, for the questions here we believe that a single-period model with initial conditions providing the link to the past, then active strategic behavior followed by a fully specified period of settlement, is sufficient.

Needless to say, with a multiplicity of possibilities to choose from, constructing and solving all of the possible models is well nigh impossible. Thus we have had to limit our modeling choices; and hence the asterisks in the list above. These choices bring down the number of models significantly, and of these we select five for our study of competitive banking. The first two, considered in this chapter, are of competitive corporate banks in the presence of a central bank, as presented in Table 14.1:

Table 14.1. Models of competitive corporate banking

	Corporate banks	Corporate banks (reserve system)
Type 1 traders	$(a, 0, m, m, \frac{1}{2})$	$(a, 0, m, \frac{1}{2}, 0, 0)$
Type 2 traders	$(0, a, m, m, \frac{1}{2})$	$(0, a, m, \frac{1}{2}, 0, 0)$
Gold merchants	$(0, 0, B, B, 0)$	No
Indiv owned banks	No	No
Corporate banks	$(0, 0, B, B, -1)$	$(0, 0, B, -1, B, 0)$
Central bank	Present	Present

For a full explanation of these initial endowment vectors, see the model descriptions in Sections 14.6 and 14.7. The term "present" for the central bank indicates that its presence is implicit in order to explain the behavior of banks or moneylenders in the model, but the central bank itself is not explicitly modeled.

The other three models of competitive banking are presented in Chapter 15. They are used to tell the story of demonetization.

14.3.1 Central Bank Goals

An important part of the mandate of a central bank is to provide its economy with an appropriately flexible money supply. It could do so using a large bureaucracy with many branches. Or it could utilize a system with many corporate commercial banks. Each bank's prime concern would be profit, not public service as interpreted by a bureaucratic system which may have an opaque incentive structure.

14.3.2 Central Bank and Corporate Banks: Disposal of Income

What happens to the money earned by the central bank? The central bank can create money, and (if the accountants will let it) should be able to destroy its profits—or at least sterilize them as reserves or surplus, as fiat is a fiction from the viewpoint of physical existence.[3] In general, the government can spend any income from the central bank on retiring debt, on payments to the bureaucracy, on other forms of public good production, on the purchase of public goods from private firms, or on subsidies to the private sector. Finally, if the government is a kleptocracy its top members will siphon off funds. In models as simple as those given here, limited to just one period and "a day of settlement," the problem of what the central bank does with earning (or losses) does not fully arise.

It is worth noting that the central bank, in theory, could control the variation in the money supply via the corporate bank with a zero net flow of money to or from the government. It could do this via the simple devices of paying no interest on the required reserves that the corporate banks must hold with the central bank, and by controlling the reserve ratio.

The corporate bank may divide its earnings between paying dividends to its stockholders, building reserves, or otherwise investing in the bank. This rules out self-dealing by management. In all instances clear definitions of what counts as money, how profit is measured, and how it is paid out are required if the conditions of conservation are to be understood.

14.3.3 Power

Generally, the central bank has the reputation and power of its society behind it (*pace* Andrew Jackson). Even the largest of corporate banks will at most be an oligopolist, benefiting from political connections but not as central in the political power structure as the central bank.

---

3 It is pure information, which nevertheless requires encoding and decoding devices to record and measure.

14.4 ON THE CREATION OF MONEY
AND THE VARYING OF ITS SUPPLY

Methods for the creation of money are highly institutional and often depend on initial conditions. Possibilities include:

- Print the money and pay the troops (i.e., purchase services for uncollectible government IOUs). The dollar presented for redemption will be replaced with another dollar.
- Adjust the money supply via open market operations, given the existence of government money in circulation and a national debt.
- Have one part of a government offer debt for sale, and another buy it with money it has printed. The money is then used for purchases or subsidies.
- Utilize gold coins as money and control minting. Vary the money supply by the purchase and sale of gold bullion together with the minting of coinage at a seigniorage charge, and store or melt coins into bullion.
- Utilize gold coins as money but permit private minting. The money supply is in the hands of the gold miners and the mints and exporters and importers.
- Have all individuals manufacture their own IOU notes that are universally accepted (with possible reputation discounts).
- Utilize a two-tier system with a central bank and commercial banks and a reserve ratio controlled by the central bank to enable the commercial banks to create bank credit that serves as a surrogate for fiat money.

Although the presence of the private banks is not a necessary condition for a central bank to efficiently vary the money supply, it is sufficient. Empirically, reserve ratio banking with private banks (as well as management of the national debt) has served to vary the supply over both space and time. The private banks can be regarded as economic sensors spread over the body economic. A comparison between the nationalized bank branches of the Soviet Union and the private banks of Western countries suggests that the bureaucratic and administrative costs of the centralized system may be lessened by decentralized delegation of many functions to private institutions.

14.5 A COMMENT ON BANKING COSTS

Often left out of high abstraction are the mundane costs of running the transaction mechanisms. In particular, a basic question in commercial banking concerns the variable cost of banking. What measures should be used? Is it costs per transaction, or possibly per large, small, and middling transaction, or should one use some other measure? Does the industry show unbounded increasing returns to scale, or are there serious limits that indicate that even with networks, computerized back offices, and less bricks-and-mortar expense, costs rise in a more or less conventional manner? We suspect that at some point marginal costs do rise.[4] In the models here, several of the practical aspects of costs are omitted; even with zero costs, strategies are bounded by the capacity constraints of reserve requirements.

14.6 COMPETITIVE CORPORATE BANKING
WITH A CENTRAL BANK AND FIAT MONEY

We consider a system of competitive corporate banks in the presence of a central bank. The corporate banks are themselves owned (through the holding of stock) by the traders. We remark that any economy in which such a system is embedded would be complex, and so would probably have developed a fiat money. Hence, the money in our model is fiat.

The use of a paper money requires a sophistication and availability of enforcement powers considerably larger than in a gold run economy. In particular, the fundamental physics of the price system changes with the introduction of paper. Gold is a physical commodity, and thus, given that a unit of measure has been specified, its quantity has physical meaning. Fiat money is a legal fiction such that even if the unit of measure is specified, the meaning of the amount of government money is a fiction—rules of the game must be specified to give it meaning. This involves a politico-economic process. Political and bureaucratic processes are intertwined with the economics in order to well define the quantity of fiat money. There are several institutional ways to achieve this goal. These are best understood if we adopt the possibly unimaginative but well-defined procedure of constructing an experimental game that could actually be played in a gaming laboratory. Two are noted immediately:

---

4 We further suspect that many of the functions of banking such as accounting, auditing, book keeping, as well as the computer services required for on-line accounts could all be subcontracted, obviating the increasing returns-to-scale arguments for large banks. For example, in the United States at this time, virtually all clearing for national and international trade takes place in two institutions: the Federal Reserve Bank and CHIPS, one public and the other private.

(1) a central bank dealing directly with the traders, and (2) a central bank dealing with corporate banks.

We have already discussed in Chapters 5–8 a central bank dealing directly with the traders. We now consider the second alternative.

THE CENTRAL BANK AND COMPETITIVE
CORPORATE BANKERS

We wish to examine a society using a central bank together with competitive corporate bankers, and show that this combination is able to provide a flexible money supply with minimal action from the central bank.

The minimal tasks of the central bank and legal system in a society that uses fiat money "good for all debts public and private" are to define the unit of account; to specify the amount of money to be issued; to ensure acceptability; and to specify the default rules concerning credit. All four of these tasks tend to be on different timescales. The specification of a unit of account may last for decades, if not centuries. The ensuring of acceptability involves a mixture of law, custom, and force requiring decades and possibly centuries to develop. The specification of default rules may last for many years without change; the adjustment of the money supply may take place many times a year. Through the device of bank credit that serves as a surrogate for fiat money, the flexibility of the monetary system can be manifested by the local perceptors, the local private banks.

Consider a sell-all economy with two types of goods and two continua of traders. The initial total endowments for the Type 1 traders are $(a, 0, m, \frac{1}{2}, 0)$ and for Type 2 are $(0, a, m, \frac{1}{2}, 0)$. Here, the first two components of the endowment vectors are the initial holdings of the first and second goods, the third entry is the initial holding of fiat, the fourth entry represents the condition that each trader type owns half the shares in a corporate bank mutual fund, and the last entry is the debt owed to the central bank.

The optimization for Type 1 traders is:

$$\max_{b_1, b_2, d} 2\sqrt{\frac{b_1}{p}\frac{b_2}{\bar{p}}} + \Pi\left(m + \frac{d}{1+\rho} - b_1 - b_2 + pa - d + \frac{D}{2}\right)$$

$$\text{s.t. } m + \frac{d}{1+\rho} - b_1 - b_2 \geq 0 \qquad (\lambda) \text{ (cash-flow constraint)} \qquad (14.1)$$

$$m + \frac{d}{1+\rho} - b_1 - b_2 + pa - d + \frac{D}{2} \geq 0 \quad (\mu) \text{ (budget constraint)}$$

$$b_1, b_2, d \geq 0.$$

where the decision variables b_1 and b_2 denote the total amounts bid for good 1 and good 2, respectively, while d is the loan amount to be repaid to the banks.[5] The symbol D is the aggregate share of the bank profits, half of which is paid to Type 1 individuals, based on the assumption that all traders hold the same portfolio, which consists of a mutual fund holding all bank shares. We note that the traders are permitted to use this amount to pay back their loans at settlement time.

There is a similar optimization problem for the Type 2 traders.

There are many ways to model corporate banks together with a central bank, and we begin with perhaps the simplest. The central bank is merely a strategically passive entity that licenses the corporate banks, sets a default parameter at μ^* (see Chapter 8), and supplies the corporate banks with an interest-free loan of B. It is as though the central bank and corporate banks have exchanged interest-free IOU notes. As, in theory, both the central bank and the corporate banks are institutions owned by natural persons, at one level of abstraction it should not make any difference if the central bank and corporate banks are merged as one, hence the device of having an interest-free exchange between IOU notes of the central bank (fiat) with the IOU notes of the corporate banks, or just amalgamating the institutions (see Section 14.2 for the discussion).

The corporate banks have as initial resources $(0, 0, B, -1, -B)$.[6] As we are looking only for symmetric equilibria, we omit modeling the mutual fund explicitly. This would involve adding another tier to the system.[7]

We next indulge in the modeling simplification that the corporate banks are run by profit maximizing agents who act as stewards of their stockholders, the traders. Thus they maximize monetary profits and flow them back to the owners. Hence, the bankers' problem is to maximize

$$z = \max_{g} \rho g$$
$$\text{s.t. } 0 \leq g \leq B.$$

---

5 We point out that the variables b_1, b_2, and d each represent aggregations of identical individual traders' strategies—see Chapters 3 and 5 for details.

6 We could add a little realism by reducing the measure of set of bankers by a factor of 15,000, and increasing the banks' holdings to $15,000B$. The computations would remain essentially the same. This contrasts with the model of the moneylenders as being more or less of the same size as the traders.

7 In order to do so, we would need to consider two types of shares: the individual corporate share, and the shares in the mutual fund. We note this to point out that this sweeps away the perception aspects of selection in a stock market and replaces the interface between the firms and their ultimate owners by an averaging device.

Note that the competitive banks individually are too small to influence the interest rate. Hence, they treat ρ as a constant. It is trivially easy to observe that if $\rho > 0$, then the optimal g is equal to B. In plain English, this means that with fully competitive banking without uncertainty or nonlinear costs, there can be no excess reserves.

Next, we note that each trader type's ultimate share of bank profits D is equal to $\frac{1}{2}z$. Hence, if $\rho > 0$, we will have that $D = \frac{\rho B}{2}$. On the other hand, if $\rho = 0$ we have $D = 0$, and the bankers' problem may not have a unique solution.

Finally, we have the market balance conditions

$$p = \frac{b_1 + \bar{b}_1}{a}, \bar{p} = \frac{b_2 + \bar{b}_2}{a}, \text{ and } 1 + \rho = \frac{d + \bar{d}}{g}.$$

The full solution to the model is in the Appendix. Briefly, we have:

Case 1: Enough money ($m \geq \frac{a}{\Pi} - \frac{B}{2}$):   In the first case, with enough money, we assume both the traders' cash-flow and budget constraints are loose ($\lambda = \bar{\lambda} = \mu = \bar{\mu} = 0$). The solutions are $p = \bar{p} = \frac{1}{\Pi}$, $b_1 = b_2 = \bar{b}_1 = \bar{b}_2 = \frac{a}{2\Pi}$, $\rho = 0$, and $d = \bar{d} \in [\frac{a}{\Pi} - m, \frac{B}{2}]$.

Case 2: Not enough money ($m \leq \frac{a}{\Pi} - \frac{B}{2}$):   In the only other case the traders' cash-flow constraints are tight but the budget constraints are loose. The solutions are $p = \bar{p} = \frac{B + 2m}{2a}$, $b_1 = b_2 = \bar{b}_1 = \bar{b}_2 = \frac{B}{4} + \frac{m}{2}$, $\rho = \frac{2a}{\Pi(B + 2m)} - 1$, and $d = \bar{d} = \frac{Ba}{\Pi(B + 2m)}$.

We note that the cycling of bank profits back to the traders implies that in a symmetric equilibrium, the traders always end up with the same amount of cash with which they started. Hence we have no case with the budget constraint tight, and no case in which the traders would strategically default if permitted (as in Chapter 8). At the day of settlement the central bank is liquidated, settles all contracts, and pays out all assets to the public. Its interchange with each corporate bank was nothing more than a swap between a better-known and lesser-known name and the corporate banks return the fiat to the central bank, who will then distribute it the ultimate owners. The fiat held originally by the owners could have been modeled the same way as for the corporate banks, but for this symmetric model at an equilibrium it makes no difference, as ultimately if they paid the fiat back to the central bank it would turn around and pay it back to them. This does not hold for the corporate banks.

14.7 RESERVE BANKING

We now introduce reserve ratio private banking, where the loans of the banks are no longer fiat money but instead are bank money or bank IOU notes that pass as perfect substitutes for fiat money in circulation (but not as reserves for the bank). Our purpose is not to establish the standard textbook story of the dynamic money multiplier, but to compare two logically well-defined strategic equilibrium models of competitive banking. The stress is on a strategic model, because in a straight competitive equilibrium model without exogenous uncertainty, the default (bankruptcy) conditions play no role. Here, even without exogenous uncertainty, they are required to prevent strategic default.

It might seem strange to use a single-period model (appropriately set up with initial and terminal conditions that enable it to be defined as a full process model), but nevertheless we can formally show the controlling role of the central bank in being able to vary the money and credit supplies.

14.7.1 The Model

There are many variants to even the simple monetary control system as described here. They depend in detail on the initial conditions.

ONE HAS TO START SOMEWHERE

Monetary history, like general history, has no clear beginning and no end; but the precise definition of a formal process model means that both must be supplied. A formal model with a money can have initial endowments being virtually anything, tracking a specific instance in history or not. In particular, in an economy utilizing fiat, the initial holdings of fiat by the public may or may not have an offsetting financial instrument written against it. Thus, some fiat may have government debt written against it and some may not. Furthermore, at the end of any finite game designed to model some part of the economy, one has to unwind all unsettled accounts; thus one must specify the expectation of the worth of all items left over. We can avoid these inconvenient features in two ways. First, one can ignore time, as was done in Debreu's (1959) masterful simplification. Second, one can study an infinite process invoking rational expectations as a way to avoid having to consider perceptions or expertise of any sort, and to avoid being explicit about terminal conditions.

THE ECONOMY WITH FIAT AND BANK MONEY

We assume almost the same initial endowments as in our previous model in the previous section: for the Type 1 traders $(a, 0, m, \frac{1}{2}, 0, 0)$ and for the Type

2 traders $(0, a, m, \frac{1}{2}, 0, 0)$. Here the first two entries are the initial holdings of the first and second goods, the third entry is the initial holding of fiat, the fourth entry represents the shares in a mutual fund holding all the corporate bank shares, and the fifth and sixth entries are holdings of bank money and trader individual IOU notes outstanding.

We could add a seventh component to the above endowment vectors, to signify that all traders have an equal ownership share in the government and hence the central bank. In the ultimate liquidation, the assets of the central bank are paid to its owners.

If (as is the case with the banking systems in the United States and most other countries) individual traders do not borrow directly from the central bank, and if the traders need to borrow (and do not grant one other credit), they will borrow from the corporate banks. Thus the optimization appears to be as before—with the b_j's and d's in terms of money—but a subtle change has taken place. The quantity of money no longer refers to "generic" fiat, but specifically to "heavy money" in the sense that it forms the bank reserves.

The initial conditions for the corporate banks are $(0, 0, B, -1, -B, 0)$. The first two terms indicate that they own none of the consumer goods, the third term indicates an initial ownership of B units of fiat, the fourth term indicates that all of their stock is issued, and the fifth term notes that they are required to pay the central bank B in fiat money at the end of the economy. The key parameter for the corporate banks is the reserve ratio k, whose magnitude is under the control of the central bank.

For the central bank, there two ways to model its initial holdings. First is to give it $(0, 0, R, 0, B, 0)$. This indicates that the central bank has no commodities. It does, however, have R units of fiat in reserve, but as has already been noted this may be not a physical amount, but a "permission to print." The fourth entry indicates that it does not own any stock in the corporate banks; the fifth entry indicates that the central bank is owed a long-term debt of B units of fiat money to be paid at final settlement when the institutions are unwound.

Another way arises if we start with the assumption that the ultimate owners of everything, including the assets of the central bank, are the natural persons. Hence we may regard the reserves B of the central bank as being owned indirectly by the traders, who will receive it when the banks are dissolved. Thus we could equally well write $(0, 0, R, 0, 0, 0)$ as the initial assets of the central bank. Under either of the schemes, at the day of final settlement the natural persons will end up with $2m + B + R$ of fiat money, either having been paid B from the corporate bank liquidation and R from the central bank liquidation or otherwise having received $B + R$ from the central bank in liquidation after it had received B from the liquidation of the corporate banks. Either way, the natural persons end up with all of the fiat money.[8]

The optimization for Type 1 traders is:

$$\max_{b_1,b_2,d} 2\sqrt{\frac{b_1}{p}\frac{b_2}{\bar{p}}} + \Pi\left(m + \frac{d}{1+\rho} - b_1 - b_2 + pa - d + D\right)$$

$$\text{s.t. } m + \frac{d}{1+\rho} - b_1 - b_2 \geq 0 \qquad (\lambda) \text{ (cash-flow constraint)} \qquad (14.2)$$

$$m + \frac{d}{1+\rho} - b_1 - b_2 + pa - d + D \geq 0 \quad (\mu) \text{ (budget constraint)}$$

$$b_1, b_2, d \geq 0,$$

where the notation is the same as that in Section 14.6. The first term in the objective function is the utility of consumption of the perishables, and the second the salvage value of the fiat. As before, D is the trader type's share of the mutual fund's flow of bank profits, based on the assumption that all traders hold the same portfolio, which consists of a mutual fund holding all bank shares.

There is a similar optimization for Type 2 traders.

The problem for the banks is to maximize ρg over all g such that $0 \leq g \leq kB$. As before, the balance conditions are

$$p = \frac{b_1 + \bar{b}_1}{a}, \ \bar{p} = \frac{b_2 + \bar{b}_2}{a}, \ 1 + \rho = \frac{d + \bar{d}}{g}, \text{ and } D = \frac{\rho g}{2}.$$

The central bank could use B and/or k as its strategic variables. The difference between the two depends on institutional cost, timing differences, political possibility, or political convenience. In either case, one may see that mathematically the only difference between this model and the

---

8 There is no problem with the Hahn paradox unraveling trade with the sell-all model. A somewhat different set of initial conditions can work for a buy-sell or bid-offer model. We classify the initially held $2m + B$ units of fiat as non-interest-bearing terminal debts to the central bank; thus at the end of the game, all issued fiat is canceled. There remains only the R, the unissued reserves of the central bank, but these are now of no operational meaning and no terminal worth; thus all terminal books balance.

one from Section 14.6 (and the Appendix) is that the bank's initial assets there of "B" have been replaced by "kB." Hence the model solutions are as follows:

Case 1: Enough money ($m \geq \frac{a}{\Pi} - \frac{kB}{2}$):   In the first case, with enough money, we assume both the traders' cash-flow and budget constraints are loose ($\lambda = \bar{\lambda} = \mu = \bar{\mu} = 0$). The solutions are $p = \bar{p} = \frac{1}{\Pi}$, $b_1 = b_2 = \bar{b}_1 = \bar{b}_2 = \frac{a}{2\Pi}$, $\rho = 0$, and $d = \bar{d} \in [\frac{a}{\Pi} - m, \frac{kB}{2}]$.

Case 2: Not enough money ($m \leq \frac{a}{\Pi} - \frac{kB}{2}$):   In the only other case, the traders' cash-flow constraints are tight but the budget constraints are loose. The solutions are $p = \bar{p} = \frac{kB + 2m}{2a}$, $b_1 = b_2 = \bar{b}_1 = \bar{b}_2 = \frac{kB}{4} + \frac{m}{2}$, $\rho = \frac{2a}{\Pi(kB + 2m)} - 1$, and $d = \bar{d} = \frac{kBa}{\Pi(kB + 2m)}$.

14.7.2 Real Bills, Uncertainty Perception, and Bill Brokers

There is a large literature in the history of commercial/corporate banking based on the idea that banks should lend only on "real bills." The underlying idea is that there is no chance of default and only short term transactions are being financed. In the words of Adam Smith (1776, 1937): "When a bank discounts to a merchant a real bill of exchange drawn by a real creditor on a real debtor; and which, as soon as it becomes due, is really paid by that debtor; it only advances to him a part of the value which he would otherwise be obliged to keep by him unemployed and in ready money for answering occasional demands"(p. 288).

Smith's real bill is an idealization that in essence does not exist, because it assumes no exogenous uncertainty about the future. Our work too has been devoted to models without exogenous uncertainty, but not because we believe in any way that economic and financial reality can be used for economic advice without taking into account uncertainty. Rather, our purpose is to take the first steps to demonstrate that a financial structure that at first glance seems to be a welter of ever-changing institutional details can nevertheless be somewhat codified and mathematized if one concentrates on understanding minimal mechanism and primary function.

For a masterful exposition of the role of the network of bill brokers evaluating bills of exchange and acting as an interface between the merchants and the banks, it is difficult to do better than to read chapter 11 of Bagehot's *Lombard Street* (1873).

14.8 FURTHER ITEMS OF IMPORTANCE IN BANKING

In this chapter we have attempted to set up an ideal control problem, limiting ourselves to extremely simple low-dimensional models. In actuality, we believe that the many different ways in which credit can be created, the many alternative assets available for the storage of wealth, and the key roles of both time lags and uncertainty are such that any applied macroeconomic model must be ad hoc and temporal. At best it needs a selection from a large group of temporally relevant variables and constant reestimation to be of applied value. This is not in conflict with the utilization of highly simplified models designed to explore the essential functions of a banking system.

Our models illustrate the simplest mechanism for varying the money supply. They do not illustrate the reasons for wanting to do so. A model with three time periods is sufficient to illustrate the need to finance a cyclical fluctuation.

Our models had competitive banks always loaned up with no excess reserves and zero profits. This was because no banking costs or uncertainty were present. Increasing costs would have been sufficient to yield profits, but banking costs have been empirically difficult to measure. Although cases have been made for increasing returns to scale over some ranges, it is probably true that they give out well before a monopoly is created. Furthermore, the tradeoff between increasing returns and oligopolistic behavior can provide a way to calculate the societally optimal number of competitors (see Powers, Shubik, and Yao, 1998, for such a calculation for insurance companies).

Modeling uncertainty with banking calls for a consideration of reserves. The definition of excess reserves requires the specification of the risk measurement criteria used to define the excess.

Our models have left out the explicit modeling of production, because many of the problems in production involve long-term lending and uncertainty. They are models of consumers seeking bridging loans or short-term consumption loans. They also approximate small businesses seeking circulating capital loans (as noted in the quotation from Adam Smith above). The stress is on transactions that approximate "real bills," that is, ideal loans that are presumed to involve no risk.

14.9 A RECONSIDERATION OF COMPETITIVE BANKING

One can make a case that commercial banking is special and can be naturally separated from investment banking and risky, long-term financing. Furthermore, it appears that it can be reasonably competitive in the context of government regulation, although less along the lines of price than in cost control.

The problem of whether there should be a separate commercial banking industry concentrating on the transactions aspects of money rather than the investment aspects is really a problem in comparative incentive systems and the efficiency, perceptivity, and flexibility of different forms of bureaucratic structure. Even the most conservative of consumer banks in actuality must have a problem of "matching book," where even minimal exogenous risk requires a matching of investment income with payments due (Shubik and Sobel, 1992).

In Section 14.1 some questions concerning banking were raised. We note briefly some answers:

- What are the competitive variables under control of the individual banks?
  Answer: Primarily costs and service.
- Precisely what is meant by "bills only" commercial banking?
  Answer: A totally riskless loan that in a friction-free world would permit unlimited zero reserve banking.
- Where does uncertainty enter into any model of banking?
  Answer: It creates the need for reserves against default, errors in judgment, and delays.
- Why is the specification of default rules and bank failure laws critical to the specification of the simplest strategic models of the economy?
  Answer: One cannot define the state space of feasible outcomes without rules to cover default.
- What are the necessary or sufficient conditions for the banking system to vary the money supply?
  Answer: The means of exchange must be defined, and the rules of issue for each of the agents must be specified. In actuality reputation, enforcement, and social acceptability cannot be disconnected from the framing of the models.
- What constitutes central bank reserves?
  Answer: Central bank reserves are more a matter of law and politics than physics. They are the rules of an artificial game with many variants.

- What constitutes commercial bank reserves?

  Answer: Commercial bank reserves are set by the central bank. All bank reserves are essentially formal rules for a societally constructed formal game.
- What is the role of expertise and evaluation in banking?

  Answer: It is critical and well summed up in the old banking adage devoted to assessment of Character, Competence, and Collateral.
- What is the shortest time for which money can be borrowed?

  Answer: We suspect that the clearance procedures of the U.S. Federal Reserve clearing system, which appear to charge debt and credit positions down to the minute, may be the shortest loan available. But, as technology changes so do transaction times and costs.

14.10 APPENDIX: A SELL-ALL MODEL WITH CORPORATE BANKING AND FIAT

Here the initial endowments for the two types of traders and for the banks are $(a, 0, m)$, $(0, a, m)$, and $(0, 0, B)$, respectively. The money is fiat. Bankers do not consume the perishable, and so act to only maximize their monetary profits. Finally, the amount of these profits (ρg in our notation) is divided equally between the two trader types and given back to them, in time for them to use it in paying off any loans. We denote the amount each trader type gets back as D, so we have $D = \frac{\rho g}{2}$.

The optimization for the Type 1 traders is

$$\max_{b_1, b_2, d} 2\sqrt{\frac{b_1}{p} \frac{b_2}{\bar{p}}} + \Pi\left(m + \frac{d}{1+\rho} - b_1 - b_2 + pa - d + D\right)$$

$$\text{s.t. } m + \frac{d}{1+\rho} - b_1 - b_2 \geq 0 \qquad \text{(cash-flow constraint)}$$

$$m + \frac{d}{1+\rho} - b_1 - b_2 + pa - d + D \geq 0 \qquad (\mu) \text{ (budget constraint)}$$

$$b_1, b_2, d \geq 0.$$

$$(14.3)$$

The first-order conditions wrt b_1, b_2, and d yield

$$\sqrt{\frac{b_2}{p\bar{p}b_1}} = \Pi + \lambda + \mu \qquad (14.4)$$

$$\sqrt{\frac{b_1}{p\bar{p}b_2}} = \Pi + \lambda + \mu \tag{14.5}$$

$$\frac{\Pi}{1+\rho} - \Pi + \frac{\lambda}{1+\rho} + \frac{\mu}{1+\rho} - \mu = 0 \tag{14.6}$$

$$m + \frac{d}{1+\rho} - b_1 - b_2 = 0 \text{ or } \lambda = 0 \tag{14.7}$$

$$m + \frac{d}{1+\rho} - b_1 - b_2 + pa - d + D = 0 \text{ or } \mu = 0. \tag{14.8}$$

Similarly, the Type 2 traders face the optimization below:

$$\max_{\bar{b}_1,\bar{b}_2,\bar{d}} 2\sqrt{\frac{\bar{b}_1 \bar{b}_2}{p \bar{p}}} + \Pi \left(m + \frac{\bar{d}}{1+\rho} - \bar{b}_1 - \bar{b}_2 + \bar{p}a - \bar{d} + D \right) \tag{14.9}$$

$$\text{s.t. } m + \frac{\bar{d}}{1+\rho} - \bar{b}_1 - \bar{b}_2 \geq 0 \qquad (\bar{\lambda}) \text{ (cash-flow constraint)} \tag{14.10}$$

$$m + \frac{\bar{d}}{1+\rho} - \bar{b}_1 - \bar{b}_2 + \bar{p}a - \bar{d} + D \geq 0 \qquad (\bar{\mu}) \text{ (budget constraint)} \tag{14.11}$$

$$\bar{b}_1, \bar{b}_2, \bar{d} \geq 0. \tag{14.12}$$

The optimization conditions here are

$$\sqrt{\frac{\bar{b}_2}{p\bar{p}\bar{b}_1}} = \Pi + \bar{\lambda} + \bar{\mu} \tag{14.13}$$

$$\sqrt{\frac{\bar{b}_1}{p\bar{p}\bar{b}_2}} = \Pi + \bar{\lambda} + \bar{\mu} \tag{14.14}$$

$$\frac{\Pi}{1+\rho} - \Pi + \frac{\bar{\lambda}}{1+\rho} + \frac{\bar{\mu}}{1+\rho} - \bar{\mu} = 0 \tag{14.15}$$

$$m + \frac{\bar{d}}{1+\rho} - \bar{b}_1 - \bar{b}_2 = 0 \text{ or } \bar{\lambda} = 0 \tag{14.16}$$

$$m + \frac{\bar{d}}{1+\rho} - \bar{b}_1 - \bar{b}_2 + \bar{p}a - \bar{d} + D = 0 \text{ or } \bar{\mu} = 0. \tag{14.17}$$

The bankers' decision problem is now

$$\max_{g} \rho g$$
$$\text{s.t. } B - g \geq 0 \quad (\lambda_B) \tag{14.18}$$
$$g \geq 0.$$

The optimization here is vastly simplified because: (a) the interest rate ρ is still treated as an exogenous parameter for the individual bankers on the continuum; and (b) the bankers do not consume the perishables. For positive ρ, the solution will obviously be to put $g = B$.

Finally, the balance conditions are $p = \frac{b_1 + \bar{b}_1}{a}$, $\bar{p} = \frac{b_2 + \bar{b}_2}{a}$, $1 + \rho = \frac{d + \bar{d}}{g}$, and $D = \frac{\rho g}{2}$.

We present the entire solution (for all possible ranges of m):

Case 1: Enough money ($m \geq \frac{a}{\Pi} - \frac{B}{2}$): In the first case, with enough money, we assume both the traders' cash-flow and budget constraints are loose ($\lambda = \bar{\lambda} = \mu = \bar{\mu} = 0$). Then (14.4) implies that $\sqrt{\frac{b_2}{p \bar{p} b_1}} = \Pi$, and so symmetry then gives $p = \bar{p} = \frac{1}{\Pi}$. Symmetry also implies that the price balance condition is $b_1 = b_2 = \bar{b}_1 = \bar{b}_2 = \frac{pa}{2}$; hence $b \equiv b_1 = b_2 = \bar{b}_1 = \bar{b}_2 = \frac{a}{2\Pi}$. Also, condition (14.6) implies $\rho = 0$ (because $\lambda = \mu = 0$ here).

All that remains is to determine d (and $\bar{d}$). There are two relevant constraints. First, because $g \in [0, B]$, $1 + \rho = \frac{d + \bar{d}}{g}$, $\rho = 0$, and $d = \bar{d}$, we have $0 \leq d = \bar{d} \leq \frac{B}{2}$. Second, the cash-flow constraint with $\rho = 0$ and $b = \frac{a}{2\Pi}$ gives $m + d - \frac{a}{\Pi} \geq 0$, which is $d \geq \frac{a}{\Pi} - m$. Hence, so long as $m \geq \frac{a}{\Pi} - \frac{B}{2}$ (and $m \geq 0$), we have a feasible range for d (and $\bar{d}$) of $[\frac{a}{\Pi} - m, \frac{B}{2}]$.

Case 2: Not enough money ($m \leq \frac{a}{\Pi} - \frac{B}{2}$): Our first inclination in this case is to try to set both the cash-flow and budget constraints tight ($\lambda, \bar{\lambda}, \mu, \bar{\mu} > 0$). However, the fact that all of the banks' monetary profits are cycled back to the traders means that in any symmetric solution the traders must end up with exactly the amount of cash they started with. Thus, in the general case where $m > 0$, it is impossible for the budget constraint to hold tightly—so we set λ and $\bar{\lambda}$ to be positive, but leave $\mu = \bar{\mu} = 0$. We also assume the interest rate ρ is positive, and so the optimal g is equal to B.

Since the cash-flow constraint holds tightly here, we have $d = (1 + \rho)(2b - m)$, where b is again the common value of $\bar{b}_1, \bar{b}_2, \bar{b}_1$, and $\bar{b}_2$. But the balance condition for the interest rate is $1 + \rho = \frac{d + \bar{d}}{g} = \frac{2d}{B}$, which gives $d = \frac{2d}{B}(2b - m)$, or $b = \frac{B}{4} + \frac{m}{2}$. Then the balance condition $p = \frac{2b}{a}$ gives

$p = \frac{B+2m}{2a} = \bar{p}$. Next, condition (14.4) gives $\sqrt{\frac{b_2}{p\bar{p}b_1}} = \Pi + \lambda$, which using symmetry is $p = \bar{p} = \frac{1}{\Pi + \lambda}$. But (14.6) (with $\mu = 0$) gives $\lambda = \Pi\rho$, so we have $p = \bar{p} = \frac{1}{\Pi + \Pi\rho} = \frac{1}{\Pi(1+\rho)}$. Setting our two expressions for p equal, we have $\frac{B+2m}{2a} = \frac{1}{\Pi(1+\rho)}$, which leaves $\rho = \frac{2a}{\Pi(B+2m)} - 1$. This is nonnegative because $m \le \frac{a}{\Pi} - \frac{B}{2}$.

Finally, we have $d = \frac{B(1+\rho)}{2} = \frac{Ba}{\Pi(B+2m)} = \bar{d}$, $D = \frac{\rho B}{2}$, and $\lambda = \Pi\rho$, where $\rho = \frac{2a}{\Pi(B+2m)} - 1$.

Chapter 15 Competitive Banking II:

Demonetization of Gold

15.1 MONEY AND TRANSACTIONS

In this chapter a series of simple examples is employed to show the relationship between gold and fiat money.[1] Specifically, we study the opening up of an economy to government control via the invention of symbolic money and the demonetization of gold. These acts call for the introduction of a central bank and a network of smaller banks that are either part of the central bank or are independent but subject to central rules regulation.

We consider three elementary one-period models of competitive money-lending. The first represents a simple two-perishable-good economy *before* a gold demonetization. It has gold as the money and no central bank, but it has a continuum of individuals who act as moneylenders. The second model considers the effects of a

---

1 This chapter is heavily based on Quint and Shubik (2011).

demonetization. The transaction use of gold is replaced by paper.[2] All holders of gold are given on a one-to-one basis paper money (but are allowed, in addition, to keep their gold). In the third model, when gold is demonetized the same amount of paper is issued as in the second model; but it is issued to a central bank instead of to the individuals. As the individuals own the central bank, there has been no change in ownership, just in control, which may or may not be justified in terms of expertise and professional role.

All three models are strategic market games in which there are markets for the two perishable goods; in addition, if it is demonetized, there is a market for gold as well.

Finally, we treat all markets as "buy-sell" rather than "sell-all." The one exception is at the end of our discussion of the first, "pre-demonetization" model, where we also compute a sell-all version in order to illustrate the considerable difference that a change in trading technology can make to the economic distribution.

The models we analyze in this chapter are outlined in Table 15.1. The entries in the vectors are the initial endowments of good 1, good 2, and gold, respectively. If there is a fourth and/or fifth entry, they represent the endowment of gold strip and of ownership shares in the central bank; see the text in Sections 15.3 and 15.5, respectively, for more explanation.

Our results show a gain in efficiency (in the case of "enough money") when a switch is made from a durable commodity money to a fiat money. This is due to players being able to enjoy both the full service value of gold and transactions value of money—something that cannot be done in the original model with gold money. When we further add in the central bank, there is a somewhat further efficiency gain in the case of "not enough money"; we close the chapter with a discussion of the usefulness of central banks.

Table 15.1.   Models for demonetization

	Gold money	Demonetized gold Private lenders	Demonetized gold Central bank lending
Type 1 traders	$(a, 0, m)$	$(a, 0, m, m)$	$(a, 0, m, 0, m)$
Type 2 traders	$(0, a, m)$	$(0, a, m, m)$	$(0, a, m, 0, m)$
Gold owners	$(0, 0, B)$	$(0, 0, B, B)$	$(0, 0, B, 0, B)$
Central bank	No	No	$(0, 0, 0, B + 2m, -(B + 2m))$

2 We use the term "paper" to stand for any form of symbolic money that has no intrinsic worth as a commodity.

15.2 MODEL 1: COMPETITIVE LENDING
WITH GOLD AS THE MONEY
15.2.1 Model 1a: Buy-Sell

Our first model has three player types: two types of traders, as well as moneylenders. For the traders, there is a continuum of each type. The traders trade in two perishable goods using a gold money, each with the same utility function $u(x, y, z) = 2\sqrt{xy} + z + \Pi\hat{z}$. Here x is the amount of the first good consumed, y is the amount of the second good consumed, z is the amount of gold services consumed, and $\hat{z}$ is the amount of gold owned at the end of the game.[3] Hence the first term is the utility derived from the consumption of perishables, the second is from the service value of gold, and the last is from the worth of gold at the end of the game (the parameter Π is the per-unit salvage value for gold).

Type 1 traders have a total initial endowment of a of good 1, none of good 2, and m units of the gold money; we write these endowments as $(a, 0, m)$. Type 2 traders have $(0, a, m)$.

We introduce a third agent type, a continuum of perfectly competitive moneylenders who start with an initial supply B of gold and no other commodities. They too have the same utility functions as the traders.

A strategy for the Type 1 traders is denoted by (b, q, d), where b is the total amount of money bid for good 2, summed across all Type 1 agents; q is the total amount of good 1 offered for sale, also summed across all Type 1 agents; and d is the total amount of loan to be paid back by the Type 1 traders to the moneylenders.

For further simplicity, we assume that borrowing is essentially instantaneous followed by trade. Thus, when the lenders lend gold, they lend it for the whole period, to be paid back at the "settlement time" at the end of the period.[4]

We assume that the measures of the set of traders of either type, as well as that of the set of lenders, are the same.[5]

---

3 For the purpose at hand (namely the study of the demonetization of gold and the introduction of fiat), utilizing a linear separable term for gold in the utility function presents no restriction. Meanwhile, there is a benefit in that it simplifies considerably the mathematics involved in the analysis.

4 See Chapter 6 for a detailed discussion of the distinction between consumption and transactions use of gold.

5 Realistically, the measures should be of the order of $10,000 : 1$ or more, depending upon the society. See Table 11.2.

The objective function for the Type 1 traders is:

$$\max_{b,q,d} 2\sqrt{(a-q)\frac{b}{\bar{p}}} + \left(m + \frac{d}{1+\rho} - b\right) + \Pi\left(m + \frac{d}{1+\rho} - b + pq - d\right).$$

$$(15.1)$$

Here the parameters p and $\bar{p}$ are the prices for the two goods, ρ is the interest rate on loans, and Π is the per-unit salvage value parameter for the gold money.[6] Thus, the first term above is the utility of consumption of the perishables, the second the utility from the service value of gold over the period, and the last term the salvage value of gold. We remark that a more precise model here would also include a default penalty term (see Chapter 8), but here we assume that default penalties are so great that the traders are essentially forbidden to go bankrupt.

The constraints on the optimization are:

$$m + \frac{d}{1+\rho} - b \geq 0 \qquad (\lambda) \text{ (cash-flow constraint)}$$
$$m + \frac{d}{1+\rho} - b + pq - d \geq 0 \quad (\mu) \text{ (budget constraint)} \qquad (15.2)$$
$$b, d \geq 0, \, 0 \leq q \leq a.$$

The constraints (λ) and (μ) are the usual cash-flow and budget constraints.

Similarly, the optimization problem for the Type 2 traders is

$$\max_{\bar{b},\bar{q},\bar{d}} 2\sqrt{(a-\bar{q})\frac{\bar{b}}{p}} + \left(m + \frac{\bar{d}}{1+\rho} - \bar{b}\right) + \Pi\left(m + \frac{\bar{d}}{1+\rho} - \bar{b} + \bar{p}\bar{q} - \bar{d}\right)$$

$$\text{s.t. } m + \frac{\bar{d}}{1+\rho} - \bar{b} \geq 0 \qquad (\bar{\lambda})$$
$$m + \frac{\bar{d}}{1+\rho} - \bar{b} + \bar{p}\bar{q} - \bar{d} \geq 0 \qquad (\bar{\mu})$$
$$\bar{b}, \bar{d} \geq 0, \, 0 \leq \bar{q} \leq a.$$

where the notation should be apparent.

The lenders in this model are private capitalists. They lend but do not accept deposits. Since they act both as consumers and as moneylenders, their

---

6 If the economy were stationary then we could imagine a discount rate β for which $\Pi = \frac{\beta}{1-\beta}$ and $1 + \rho = \frac{1}{\beta}$.

decision variables are b_1^* (the total amount bid by lenders for good 1), b_2^* (the total amount bid by lenders for good 2), and g (the total amount of gold lent to traders). Since there is a continuum of lenders, these variables represent aggregations of identical individual lenders' strategies, much as the traders' variables do.

The optimization for the lenders is:

$$
\max_{b_1^*, b_2^*, g} 2\sqrt{\frac{b_1^*}{p} \frac{b_2^*}{\bar{p}}} + \left(B - b_1^* - b_2^* - g\right) + \Pi \left(B - b_1^* - b_2^* + \rho g\right)
$$
$$
\text{s.t. } B - b_1^* - b_2^* - g \geq 0 \tag{15.3}
$$
$$
b_1^*, b_2^*, g \geq 0.
$$

Finally, the balance conditions for price are

$$
p = \frac{\bar{b} + b_1^*}{q} \tag{15.4}
$$
$$
\bar{p} = \frac{b + b_2^*}{\bar{q}}, \tag{15.5}
$$

while that for the interest rate is

$$
1 + \rho = \frac{d + \bar{d}}{g}. \tag{15.6}
$$

15.2.2 Results

In Appendix A, we solve the model for two cases. First, in Case 1, the traders begin with little gold but the lenders have a lot; that is, m is small and B is large. This gives tight cash-flow and budget constraints for the traders, but loose cash-flow constraints for the lenders. In Case 2, both m and B are small—and so all constraints for both traders and lenders are tight. The two cases above allow us to consider set values of m and Π (namely, $m = 0$ and $\Pi = 1$), while allowing B to range over an interval of values. The dividing line between Case 1 and Case 2 is where $B = \frac{a}{2}$.

In both cases, we shall see that the money interest rate is always at least 1. This reflects the marginal value of consumption of the services of gold, which is 1. When gold is in short supply, the interest rate increases from 1, reflecting the intensity of the shortage.

Finally, in both cases, we note that the consumption levels of the perishables is not Pareto efficient.[7]

Example 1:   If $B = 2a$, we are in Case 1 above. Our calculations yield $p = \bar{p} = \frac{1}{2}$, $\rho = 1$, $d = \bar{d} = \frac{a}{4}$, $b = \bar{b} = \frac{a}{8}$, $q = \bar{q} = \frac{a}{2}$, and the moneylenders lend $g = \frac{a}{4}$. Hence the consumption by each trader type is $\frac{a}{2}$ of "their own" perishable, and $\frac{a}{4}$ of the "other" perishable. The bids of the moneylenders are $b_1^* = b_2^* = \frac{a}{8}$, and so the consumption of the moneylenders is $\frac{a}{4}$ of each of the perishables. The final distribution of resources is $(\frac{a}{2}, \frac{a}{4}, 0)$, $(\frac{a}{4}, \frac{a}{2}, 0)$, and $(\frac{a}{4}, \frac{a}{4}, 2a)$ The utilities to the two trader types are given by $2\sqrt{\frac{a}{2}\frac{a}{4}} + 0 = \frac{\sqrt{2}a}{2}$, while that for the moneylenders is $2\sqrt{\frac{a}{4}\frac{a}{4}} + \frac{3a}{2} + \Pi(2a) = 4a$.

Example 2:   Suppose there were far less gold in the system: let us limit it to $B = a$. The solution will differ from Example 1 only in the payoff for the moneylenders that is now reduced to $2\sqrt{\frac{a}{4}\frac{a}{4}} + \frac{a}{2} + \Pi(a) = 2a$. We are still in Case 1.

Example 3:   Suppose there were still less gold in the system: let it be $B = \frac{a}{4}$. This now puts us into Case 2 from the analysis in Appendix A. Now we have $p = \bar{p} = \frac{1}{4}$, $\rho = 3$, $d = \bar{d} = \frac{a}{8}$, $b = \bar{b} = \frac{a}{32}$, $q = \bar{q} = \frac{a}{2}$, and the moneylenders lend $g = \frac{a}{16}$. Hence the consumption by each trader type is $\frac{a}{2}$ of "their own" perishable, and $\frac{a}{8}$ of the "other" perishable. The bids of the moneylenders are $b_1^* = b_2^* = \frac{3a}{32}$, and so the consumption of the moneylenders is $\frac{3a}{8}$ of each of the perishables. The final distribution of resources is $(\frac{a}{2}, \frac{a}{8}, 0)$, $(\frac{a}{8}, \frac{a}{2}, 0)$, and $(\frac{3a}{8}, \frac{3a}{8}, \frac{a}{4})$. The utilities to the two trader types are given by $2\sqrt{\frac{a}{2}\frac{a}{8}} + 0 = \frac{a}{2}$, while that for the moneylenders is $2\sqrt{\frac{3a}{8}\frac{3a}{8}} + 0 + \Pi(\frac{a}{4}) = a$. The interest rate $\rho = 3$ is above 1, to reflect the shadow price of the shortage of gold.

15.2.3 Model 1b: Sell-All

Here we consider a sell-all version of Model 1a. Now, when traders come to the perishable goods market, they must first sell off all of their endowments

---

7 In our models, consumption of perishables is Pareto efficient if and only if each of the three types of consumer (i.e., the two trader types and the lenders) consume equal amounts of good 1 and good 2.

and then buy back all they consume. Since they are selling and buying more, their need for money increases.

The notation for the model is similar to that of Model 1a, except for the traders' decision variables. For trader Type 1, they are b_1 (the total amount bid for perishable good 1, summed over all Type 1 traders), b_2 (the amount bid for perishable good 2, again summed over all Type 1 traders), and d (as in Model 1a, the total amount of loan to be paid back to the lenders). Note that we no longer have q as a strategic variable, because the amount of perishables put up for sale is no longer a decision.

The optimization for the Type 1 traders is

$$
\begin{aligned}
\max_{b_1, b_2, d} \ & 2\sqrt{\frac{b_1}{p} \frac{b_2}{\bar{p}}} + m + \frac{d}{1+\rho} - b_1 - b_2 + pa \\
& + \Pi\left(m + \frac{d}{1+\rho} - b_1 - b_2 + pa - d\right) \\
\text{s.t. } & m + \frac{d}{1+\rho} - b_1 - b_2 \geq 0 \qquad\qquad (\lambda) \text{ (cash-flow constraint)} \\
& m + \frac{d}{1+\rho} - b_1 - b_2 + pa - d \geq 0 \qquad (\mu) \text{ (budget constraint)} \\
& b_1, b_2, d \geq 0.
\end{aligned}
$$
(15.7)

There is a similar optimization for the Type 2 traders, with decision variables $\bar{b}_1$, $\bar{b}_2$, and $\bar{d}$. For the moneylenders, the optimization is precisely as before, namely:

$$
\begin{aligned}
\max_{b_1^*, b_2^*, g} \ & 2\sqrt{\frac{b_1^*}{p} \frac{b_2^*}{\bar{p}}} + (B - b_1^* - b_2^* - g) + \Pi\left(B - b_1^* - b_2^* + \rho g\right) \\
\text{s.t. } & B - b_1^* - b_2^* - g \geq 0 \\
& b_1^*, b_2^*, g \geq 0.
\end{aligned}
$$
(15.8)

Finally, we have the balance conditions $p = \frac{b_1 + \bar{b}_1 + b_1^*}{a}$, $\bar{p} = \frac{b_2 + \bar{b}_2 + b_2^*}{a}$, and $1 + \rho = \frac{d + \bar{d}}{g}$.

15.2.4 Results

In Appendix B, we solve the model for the special case where m is small. We again have two cases, depending upon whether constraint (λ^*) is tight—for high values of B (Case 1) it is not, while for low values of B (Case 2) it is.

The operational differences between Models 1a and 1b can be illustrated by comparing the same set of three examples, all with $\Pi = 1$ and $m = 0$. We note that with sell-all, the dividing line between Case 1 and Case 2 falls at a higher value of B, namely, $B = a$.

Also, note that in both cases the consumption of perishables is Pareto efficient. This contrasts with the buy-sell model, in which it was *never* efficient.

Example 1: Suppose $B = 2a$. Our calculations (in Case 1) yield $b_1 = b_2 = \bar{b}_1 = \bar{b}_2 = \frac{a}{8}$, $p = \bar{p} = \frac{1}{2}$, $\rho = 1$, $d = \bar{d} = \frac{a}{2}$, and the moneylenders lend $g = \frac{a}{2}$. Hence the consumption by each trader type is $\frac{a}{4}$ of both perishables. The bids of the moneylenders are $b_1^* = b_2^* = \frac{a}{4}$, and so the consumption of the moneylenders is $\frac{a}{2}$ of each of the commodities. The final distribution of resources is $(\frac{a}{4}, \frac{a}{4}, 0)$, $(\frac{a}{4}, \frac{a}{4}, 0)$, and $(\frac{a}{2}, \frac{a}{2}, 2a)$. The utilities to the two trader types are given by $2\sqrt{\frac{a}{4}\frac{a}{4}} + \frac{a}{2} = a$, while that for the moneylenders is $2\sqrt{\frac{a}{2}\frac{a}{2}} + a + \Pi(2a) = 4a$.

Example 2: Suppose there were far less gold in the system: let us limit it to $B = a$. Now we are at the dividing line between Case 1 and Case 2, so we can use either to compute the variable values. We obtain the same values as in Example 1, except the payoff for the moneylenders is now reduced to $2\sqrt{\frac{a}{2}\frac{a}{2}} + 0 + \Pi a = 2a$. In this example when $B = a$ there is precisely enough money to not constrain lending.

Example 3: Suppose there were still less gold in the system: let it be $B = \frac{a}{4}$. Now we are in the interior of Case 2. We obtain $b_1 = b_2 = \bar{b}_1 = \bar{b}_2 = \frac{a}{128}$, $p = \bar{p} = \frac{1}{8}$, $\rho = 7$, $d = \bar{d} = \frac{a}{8}$, $b_1^* = b_2^* = \frac{7a}{64}$, and the moneylenders lend $g = \frac{a}{32}$. The trader types consume $(\frac{a}{16}, \frac{a}{16}, 0)$ and $(\frac{a}{16}, \frac{a}{16}, 0)$, while the lenders consume $(\frac{7a}{8}, \frac{7a}{8}, \frac{a}{4})$.

Finally, we note the high value of ρ—this reflects the high shadow price of the shortage of gold.

15.2.5 A Comparison of Models 1a and 1b

We may glean several key properties of a commodity money from these models, and from other models appearing elsewhere.

1. The key idea associated with "enough money"[8] is that the price of the rental of gold money (ρ) should be exactly its consumption value (which is 1 here).

2. Although "enough money" is a well-defined concept, the precise mathematical conditions depend upon the institutional details of trade. The difference between the monetary requirements of the buy-sell and the sell-all models illustrates this.

3. Not only is the specific mechanism relevant, but so too is the speed of operation. If used in trade, the commodity money is unavailable for the whole period for consumption purposes. Quint and Shubik (2005a) examine the influence of time-in-trade in detail.

4. The above examples show that a commodity money's elasticity of demand (as a commodity) plays a role. This aspect of utilizing a commodity that does not enter the utility function in a separable form has been studied in detail by Dubey and Shapley (1994).

5. When a commodity money is borrowed, even in a stationary economy, the rate of interest is strictly higher than the money's consumption value. This introduces a wedge between buying and selling prices in the buy-sell model (or any model where the individual controls her offer). This wedge does not appear in the sell-all model.

15.2.6 An Aside on Enough Commodity Money

The selection of a commodity money depends upon physical properties, such as portability, cognizability, and durability. It also involves problems in the sensitivity of the elasticity of relative prices as its quantity changes. In our models, we assume the commodity money enters the utility function as a linear separable term. If we drop this assumption, new difficulties appear—consider the following example of a sell-all economy where we show that the commodity money can never be in sufficient supply to support competitive prices and distribution.

Suppose that initial holdings of three goods (by the three agent types) are $(3, 0, 0)$, $(0, 3, 0)$, and $(0, 0, 3)$, and all agents have the same utility function

---

8 By "enough money," we mean the case where there is enough money in the economy to finance efficient trade of the perishables. In Models 1a and 1b above, the "enough money" case is Case 1. See Chapter 3 for details.

$$U(x, y, m) = \frac{1}{3}(xy\dot{m})^{1/3} + \Pi m.$$

The first two goods are perishables, while the third good is a durable and has been selected as the money. The second term is the expected utility of the leftover durable, where Π is an exogenous parameter. For the example assume $\Pi = 1$.

It is easy to see that the general equilibrium solution calls for symmetric prices (p, p, p) and a distribution of $(1, 1, 1)$ of the commodities to each trader type. Since the transaction structure is sell-all, and the game with money is to achieve the competitive equilibrium outcome, each of the first two trader types would need to borrow $2p + 1$ units of the monetary commodity to buy the distribution $(1, 1, 1)$. But they have an income of only $3p$ each. Thus, if $p < 1$ the types do not have enough money to pay back their loans. On the other hand, if $p \geq 1$, the lenders do not have $2 * (2p + 1)$ in cash to lend.

Can this be cured by giving the moneylenders more money? We answer "no," by virtually the same argument. Suppose the lenders had some amount $m > 3$. We note that for an arbitrary m the competitive equilibrium prices and quantities become $(\frac{mp}{3}, \frac{mp}{3}, p)$ and $(1, 1, \frac{m}{3})$, respectively. The trader types each need $\frac{2mp}{3} + \frac{m}{3}$ in cash in order to buy the distribution $(1, 1, \frac{m}{3})$. They each have income mp. Hence if $p < 1$ the types do not have enough money to pay back their loans. And again if $p \geq 1$, the lenders do not have $2 * (\frac{2mp}{3} + \frac{m}{3})$ in cash to lend.

15.3 MODEL 2: TRADE WITH DEMONETIZED GOLD AND TRANSACTION STRIPS

We now analyze the model of the above (buy-sell) economy after gold has been demonetized. The physical asset gold is stripped of its monetary function. The old moneylenders become paper moneylenders/gold merchants. We use the term "strips" here to suggest that when a real asset A has more than one function, one might be able to modify the rules of the game to strip A of that function while creating object B, which takes it over. The legal modifications are many and subtle but the principle is relatively simple.

15.3.1 The Three Uses of Monetary Gold

A monetary gold has at least three uses: (1) a store of value (a property shared with all other durables), (2) a provider of consumption or production services (a property shared with all other durables), and (3) a provider of transaction services.[9] At any particular time, a monetary gold can provide only one of the last two services.

15.3.2 The Demonetization

A society that utilizes gold as money can switch to paper money, maintain full ownership claims of all agents, and provide transaction services to its members. It can accomplish this by stripping gold of its use in transactions and giving all owners of gold a paper (or other) symbolic claim to the gold, on a one-to-one basis. Thus against the B units of gold a piece of paper (a "gold certificate") inscribed with the legend "*This is one unit of transactions gold*" can be used instead of the gold itself to provide payment.

Of course, the gold owners still have the gold, which has value as a durable good (but not as a money). In an ideal world with no exogenous uncertainty and no opportunity for any individuals to print more transaction strips,[10] the gold is now freed up for use in production or consumption services, or to lease to others. And while the demonetization has stripped their gold of its use in market transactions, the owners are given two financial instruments that compensate for the loss. The first is the paper described above. The second is a call on gold that can be exercised at the time of settlement. For now we ignore the call feature, but we discuss it later, in Section 15.3.6.

In the new economy, the initial endowments now become $(a, 0, m, m)$ for the Type 1 traders, $(0, a, m, m)$ for the Type 2 traders, and $(0, 0, B, B)$ for the paper moneylenders/gold merchants (hereafter called "lender-merchants"). In each of these endowment vectors, the first two entries are the endowments of the two perishables, the third entry is that of gold (now without its monetary function), and the fourth entry is the amount of "strip" or separated asset issued against the gold to replace it for transactions services. This is in essence a 100 percent reserves system. The original Bank of Amsterdam appears to have paid in notes backed by its gold in this manner.

The specifics of how the paper is issued are a matter of the rules of the game, which depend upon the laws of the society. There are several ways in which this can happen. Perhaps the most obvious is by means of a warehouse receipt.

---

9 A fourth use is as a numeraire, and a fifth use is as scalar measure of value; but these are not particularly germane to this discussion.

10 Thereby violating the 1 : 1 relationship or the 100 percent reserves.

An individual depositing an amount of gold is presented with a warehouse paper receipt for that amount. But if this paper is nonnegotiable, it remains as two-party paper and cannot be utilized in transactions (because it cannot be transferred to a third party). But this restriction is a matter of the rules of the game—a legal system can recognize the legality of third-party utilization, at which point the warehouse receipts *can* be utilized as a money if they are universally accepted in payment.

15.3.3 Demonetized Gold, No Central Bank

We modify the previous buy-sell economy (Model 1a). The initial conditions have been specified above. There is now an extra market for gold, which is also buy-sell. Thus, the traders must specify both the amount of perishable they wish to put up for sale, as well as an amount of gold they wish to put up for sale. All trade must be intermediated with paper money backed by gold.

The objective function for the Type 1 traders is:

$$\max_{b,q,d,b_3,q_3} 2\sqrt{(a-q)\frac{b}{\bar{p}}} + \left(m + \frac{b_3}{p_3} - q_3\right)$$
$$+ \Pi_1\left(m + \frac{d}{1+\rho} - b_1 - b_3 + pq + p_3 q_3 - d\right) + \Pi_2\left(m + \frac{b_3}{p_3} - q_3\right).$$
$$(15.9)$$

Here the decision variables b and b_3 denote the total amounts bid for good 2 and gold, respectively; q and q_3 are the amounts of good 1 and gold put up for sale, respectively; and d is the amount of loan to be repaid to the lenders.[11] The p and $\bar{p}$ are the prices for the two goods, p_3 is the price of gold, ρ is the interest rate on loans, Π_1 is the per-unit salvage value parameter for the strips, and Π_2 is the per-unit salvage value for gold. Thus, the first term above is the utility of consumption of the perishables, the second term is the utility from the consumption value of the services of gold for the period, the third term is the salvage (terminal) value for leftover gold certificates, and the last term is the salvage value for the asset gold. Since they are modeled as nondepreciating durables, both gold and gold certificates will be left over at the period of final settlement.[12]

---

11 We point out that the variables b, q, d, b_3, and q_3 each represent aggregations of identical individual traders' strategies—see Section 3.1.2 for details.

12 As before, we note that a more precise model here covering all positions in the feasible payoff space would also include a default penalty term; and that here we assume that

The optimizations for the traders and the lender-merchants differ only because of their initial endowments. Technically, any individual holding gold could lend the strips she is given and thus could have a lending strategy; however, we have specified our initial conditions to be such that the traders would never lend and the lender-merchants would never borrow.

The constraints on the optimization for the Type 1 traders are:

$$m + \frac{d}{1+\rho} - b - b_3 \geq 0 \qquad (\lambda)$$
$$m + \frac{d}{1+\rho} - b - b_3 + pq + p_3q_3 - d \geq 0 \quad (\mu) \qquad (15.10)$$
$$b, b_3, d \geq 0, 0 \leq q_3 \leq m.$$

The constraints (λ) and (μ) are the cash-flow and budget constraints as in Model 1a.

The optimization problem for the Type 2 traders is similar.

The continuum of lender-merchants act both as consumers and as moneylenders. Their decision variables are b_1^*, b_2^* (the total amount they bid for goods 1 and 2), b_3^* (the total amount bid they bid for gold), q_3^* (the total amount of gold they put up for sale), and g (the total amount of gold strips lent to traders). Their optimization is:

$$\max_{b_1^*, b_2^*, b_G^*, q_G^*, g} 2\sqrt{\frac{b_1^*}{p}\frac{b_2^*}{\bar{p}}} + \left(B + \frac{b_3^*}{p_3} - q_3^*\right) + \Pi_1\left(B - b_1^* - b_2^* - b_3^* + p_3q_3^* + \rho g\right)$$
$$+ \Pi_2\left(B + \frac{b_3^*}{p_3} - q_3^*\right)$$
$$\text{s.t. } B - b_1^* - b_2^* - b_3^* - g \geq 0$$
$$b_1^*, b_2^*, b_3^*, g \geq 0, \ 0 \leq q_3^* \leq B.$$

Finally, the balance conditions for price are

$$p = \frac{\bar{b} + b_1^*}{q} \qquad (15.11)$$

$$\bar{p} = \frac{b + b_2^*}{\bar{q}} \qquad (15.12)$$

$$p_3 = \frac{b_3 + \bar{b}_3 + b_3^*}{q_3 + \bar{q}_3 + q_3^*} \qquad (15.13)$$

---

default penalties are so great that the traders are essentially forbidden to go bankrupt. See Chapter 8.

while that for the interest rate is

$$1 + \rho = \frac{d + \bar{d}}{g}. \tag{15.14}$$

We call the above "Model 2."

15.3.4 An Extra Constraint Concerning the Sale of Strips

In our formulation above, a conceptual problem emerges concerning the sale of strips. If a strip is backed by gold, then the moneylenders cannot be permitted to offer more strips than they have gold on hand—otherwise some of their lending would be unbacked by the 100 percent reserves of this system. This introduces the extra constraint

$$g \leq B - q_3^*.$$

This extra constraint is satisfied in all three examples below.[13]

15.3.5 Results

In Appendix B we solve the model, again for the case where m is small. With small m, we may assume the traders' cash-flow and budget constraints are both tight. In addition, we may assume that the traders do not sell gold ($q_3 = 0$) and the lender-merchants do not buy gold ($b_3^* = 0$).

There are again two cases, depending on the value of B. For higher values of B, we assume that the lender-merchants' cash-flow constraint is loose. In the second case, with lower values of B, we assume that this constraint is tight, and that the gold market is inactive.

We now set parameter values so as to most closely match the three examples calculated with Model 1a. To do this, we set $\Pi_1 = \Pi_2 = 1$, $m = 0$, and consider the same three values of B:

Example 1: If $B = 2a$, we are in Case 1 above. Our calculations yield a continuum of possible values for q, namely, the interval from $\frac{a}{2}$ to $\frac{2a}{3}$. For each such q, we have $p = \bar{p} = 1$, $\rho = 0$, $d = \bar{d} = q$, $b = \bar{b} = a - q$, and the lender-merchants lend $g = 2q$. Hence the consumption by each trader type is $(a - q, a - q)$ of the perishables. The bids of the lender-merchants

---

13 More generally, if there is a reserve requirement of k (expressed as a proportion), then the extra constraint would be $kg \leq B - q_3^*$. Since the three examples all satisfy this with $k = 1$, necessarily they all satisfy this with any lower values of k.

are $b_1^* = b_2^* = 2q - a$, and so they consume $2q - a$ of each of the perishables. In addition, we have $p_3 = 2$, $b_3 = \bar{b}_3 = 2q - a$, and $q_3^* = 2q - a$; hence the lender-merchants sell $2q - a$ units of gold ($q - \frac{a}{2}$ to each trader type). The final distribution of resources is $(a - q, a - q, q - \frac{a}{2}, 0)$, $(a - q, a - q, q - \frac{a}{2}, 0)$, and $(2q - a, 2q - a, 3a - 2q, 2a)$ for the two trader types and the merchant-lenders, respectively. For the traders, their final utility is $2\sqrt{(a-q)(a-q)} + q - \frac{a}{2} + \Pi_2(q - \frac{a}{2}) + 0 = a$, while for the merchant-lenders it is $2\sqrt{(2q-a)(2q-a)} + (3a - 2q) + \Pi_2(3a - 2q) + 2a = 6a$. These utilities do not depend upon the chosen value of q.

Note that the consumption of perishable is Pareto efficient; recall in the corresponding Example 1 of Model 1a it was not efficient. In fact, we can compare the final utilities to the agents in the two examples, as shown in Table 15.2.

Finally, notice here that for all values of q we have $g \leq B - q_3^*$, so the reserve requirement is indeed met.

Example 2: If $B = a$, we are on the border of Case 1 and Case 2. There is now only one equilibrium. Our calculations yield $p = \bar{p} = 1$, $\rho = 0$, $d = \bar{d} = \frac{a}{2}$, $b = \bar{b} = \frac{a}{2}$, $q = \bar{q} = \frac{a}{2}$, and the lender-merchants lend $g = a$. Hence the consumption by each trader type is $(\frac{a}{2}, \frac{a}{2})$ of the perishables. The bids of the lender-merchants are $b_1^* = b_2^* = 0$, and so they consume none of the perishables. In addition, we have $p_3 = 2$, $b_3 = \bar{b}_3 = 0$, and $q_3^* = 0$; hence the lender-merchants sell no gold to the traders. The final distribution of resources is $(\frac{a}{2}, \frac{a}{2}, 0, 0)$, $(\frac{a}{2}, \frac{a}{2}, 0, 0)$, and $(0, 0, a, a)$ for the two trader types and the merchant-lenders, respectively. Notice that here $g \leq B - q_3^*$, so the reserve requirement is indeed met.

Example 3: If $B = \frac{a}{4}$, we are in Case 2. Our calculations yield $p = \bar{p} = \frac{1}{4}$, $\rho = 3$, $d = \bar{d} = \frac{a}{8}$, $b = \bar{b} = \frac{a}{32}$, $q = \bar{q} = \frac{a}{2}$, and the lender-merchants lend $g = \frac{a}{16}$. Hence the consumption by each trader type is $\frac{a}{2}$ of their "own" perishable, and $\frac{a}{8}$ of the "other" perishable. The bids of the lender-merchants are

Table 15.2.

	Trader 1	Trader 2	Lender
Model 1a	$\frac{\sqrt{2}a}{2}$	$\frac{\sqrt{2}a}{2}$	$4a$
Model 2	a	a	$6a$

$b_1^* = b_2^* = \frac{3a}{32}$, and so they consume $\frac{3a}{8}$ of each of the perishables. The gold market is inactive; that is, the lender-merchants sell no gold to the traders. The final distribution of resources is $(\frac{a}{2}, \frac{a}{8}, 0, 0)$, $(\frac{a}{8}, \frac{a}{2}, 0, 0)$, and $(\frac{3a}{8}, \frac{3a}{8}, \frac{a}{4}, \frac{a}{4})$ for the two trader types and the merchant-lenders, respectively. This is not efficient.

15.3.6 The Worth of Strips at Settlement Day

At the day of settlement there is a modeling problem concerning end valuation of the gold strips. If this is viewed as an experimental game, then the only question to a player is how his or her leftover paper money is treated. If conversion to gold is not permitted, then all that matters is its salvage value. Alternatively, if ownership of the paper money includes a call on the gold, there is no reason to convert if the salvage value for the paper is the same as that for gold. Thus these games, without and with convertability, have a solution in common—namely, where there is no conversion. This appears to be double-counting, but it actually reflects that both the transactions and consumption values are being realized.

A different approach is to consider the infinite horizon version of the game. Here the strip need never be cashed; hence it has the full transactions value over all periods. At equilibrium, this transactions value is equal to the full-service value of the gold over all periods. (This is because at a stationary state equilibrium, there can be no advantageous arbitrage opportunities—it cannot pay for an individual with a strip to buy gold or vice versa.) This justifies our assumption (in the examples) of $\Pi_1 = \Pi_2$.

15.3.7 Fractional Reserves

> Drive for show, but putt for dough.
> —Old golf saying

We have provided a painstakingly precise set of process models within a grotesquely oversimplified economy in order to show how in the case of enough money, replacing gold by fully backed paper improves efficiency. Our second model has 100 percent backed gold reserves. The gold strips match the gold. The mathematics of this model does not justify fractional reserves; we conjecture, but do not prove, that the model can be modified to work for the infinite horizon with no uncertainty with any fractional reserve ratio. This problem is left for future work.

15.4 A DISCLAIMER ON UNCERTAINTY

In this book we do not model uncertainty. We note, with any exogenous uncertainty, that the meaning of "enough money" (and the ability to supply it) becomes difficult to define, and depends upon the default laws and the society's overall willingness to absorb risk.

15.5 MODEL 3: TRADE WITH CENTRAL BANK CONTROL OF THE STRIPS

A variation of Model 2 is offered where upon the demonetization of the gold the strips are *not* given out to the gold owners. Instead the society forms a central bank that lends the strips. The bank in turn is owned by holders of the gold, who receive shares in the bank but do not necessarily control it. The original holders of the gold, who were moneylenders in both Models 1 and 2, now are simply dealers in gold, and we call them "gold merchants."

15.5.1 The Negotiability of Bank Shares?

In this model, the gold and bank shares are packaged together. The individuals holding the gold hold the shares. Another possibility is that the shares are separately negotiable. This is a matter of choice in how a society constructs the rules of the game, either by law or by custom, or by both.

15.5.2 The Central Bank

In Model 3, all of the physical and ultimate ownership aspects of the economy for the natural persons are the same as in Model 2. However, there is a change in the number of agents and their strategic power. Instead of giving all agents with gold the strips, a new legal person is created: the central bank. The central bank is funded with all of the gold strips that have been created, but it is owned by those who have supplied the gold backing for the strips.

The initial holdings of the traders, the moneylenders, and the central bank in this economy are: Type 1 traders $(a, 0, m, 0, m)$; Type 2 traders $(0, a, m, 0, m)$; gold merchants $(0, 0, B, 0, B)$; and the central bank $(0, 0, 0, B + 2m, -(B + 2m))$, where components of these vectors represent: (1) the amount held of the first perishable good, (2) the amount held of the second perishable good, (3) the amount of gold held, (4) the amount of gold trading strips held, and (5) the shares held of the central bank.

As gold and central bank shares are traded together, we could easily simplify the notation for the endowments. However, it is perhaps more natural to leave gold and bank shares apart, to emphasize the two roles for gold here—as a commodity and as a backing for paper money.

The balance sheet of the central bank has two items, as indicated in Table 15.3:

Table 15.3.   Bank balance sheet

Assets	Liabilities
$B + 2m$ strips	
	$B + 2m$ shares
$B + 2m$	$B + 2m$

Next, we must specify how the central bank makes loans to the various agents. The simplest mechanism is as before, with lenders putting up gold notes and borrowing agents bidding for them; but here there is only one lender (the central bank). In order to fully close the model, we need to specify the motivation of the central bank. Is it profit maximizing (if so, it is a monopolist)? Is it a philanthropist concerned with the efficiency of the society? In this model we treat the bank as a strategic dummy, which offers G for loan no matter what.

Conceptually, there is complete freedom for the interest rate in this model, including the taking on of negative values. While logically possible, an outcome with a negative ρ can be ruled out as not occurring in an equilibrium state by using a simple arbitrage argument.

Model 3:   As in Models 1a and 2, we consider a buy-sell economy. The optimization problem for the Type 1 traders is almost as in Model 2:

$$\max_{b,q,d,b_3,q_3} 2\sqrt{(a-q)\frac{b}{p}} + \left(m + \frac{b_3}{p_3} - q_3\right)$$
$$+ \Pi_1\left(\frac{d}{1+\rho} - b - b_3 + pq - d + p_3 q_3 + D\right)$$
$$+ \Pi_2\left(m + \frac{b_3}{p_3} - q_3\right)$$

s.t. $\dfrac{d}{1+\rho} - b - b_3 \geq 0$ $\qquad\qquad$ (λ) (cash-flow constraint)

$$\frac{d}{1+\rho} - b - b_3 + pq - d + p_3 q_3 + D \geq 0 \quad (\mu) \text{ (budget constraint)}$$

$$b, b_3, d \geq 0, \ 0 \leq q \leq a, \ 0 \leq q_3 \leq m.$$

$$(15.15)$$

The only new notation here is the symbol "D," which stands for the Type 1 traders' share of the liquidation payout from the central bank. Also, note that there is no "m" in either the cash-flow constraint or the budget constraint. This is because there are now no gold certificates given to traders in recognition of their endowments of m units of gold.

The optimization for the second type of trader is similar:

$$\max_{\bar{b}, \bar{q}, \bar{d}, \bar{b}_3, \bar{q}_3} \ 2\sqrt{(a - \bar{q})\frac{\bar{b}}{p}} + \left(m + \frac{\bar{b}_3}{p_3} - \bar{q}_3\right)$$

$$+ \Pi_1 \left(\frac{\bar{d}}{1+\rho} - \bar{b} - \bar{b}_3 + \bar{p}\bar{q} - \bar{d} + p_3\bar{q}_3 + D\right) + \Pi_2 \left(m + \frac{\bar{b}_3}{p_3} - \bar{q}_3\right)$$

$$\text{s.t.} \ \frac{\bar{d}}{1+\rho} - \bar{b} - \bar{b}_3 \geq 0 \qquad\qquad (\lambda)$$

$$\frac{\bar{d}}{1+\rho} - \bar{b} - \bar{b}_3 + \bar{p}\bar{q} - \bar{d} + p_3\bar{q}_3 + D \geq 0 \qquad\qquad (\bar{\mu})$$

$$\bar{b}, \bar{b}_3, \bar{d} \geq 0, \ 0 \leq \bar{q} \leq a, \ 0 \leq \bar{q}_3 \leq m.$$

The former moneylenders have become gold merchants. Four of their decision variables are as before b_1^*, b_2^* (the total amount they bid for goods 1 and 2), b_3^* (the total amount they bid for gold), and q_3^* (amount of gold they put up for sale). They no longer have g (the total amount of gold strips lent to traders) as a strategic variable. This has been taken over by the central bank. Instead the merchants will bid d^* for their transactions loans. Their optimization is:

$$\max_{b_1^*, b_2^*, b_3^*, q_3^*, d^*} \ 2\sqrt{\frac{b_1^*}{p}\frac{b_2^*}{p}} + \left(B + \frac{b_3^*}{p_3} - q_3^*\right)$$

$$+ \Pi_1 \left(\frac{d^*}{1+\rho} - b_1^* - b_2^* - b_3^* - d^* + p_3 q_3^* + D^*\right)$$

$$+ \Pi_2 \left(B + \frac{b_3^*}{p_3} - q_3^*\right)$$

$$(15.16)$$

$$\text{s.t.} \ \frac{d^*}{1+\rho} - b_1^* - b_2^* - b_3^* \geq 0 \qquad\qquad (\lambda^*)$$

$$\frac{d^*}{1+\rho} - b_1^* - b_2^* - b_3^* - d^* + p_3 q_3^* + D^* \geq 0 \qquad\qquad (\mu^*)$$

$$b_1^*, b_2^*, b_3^*, d^* \geq 0, \ 0 \leq q_3^* \leq B.$$

Finally, the balance conditions for price are as before

$$p = \frac{\bar{b} + b_1^*}{q} \tag{15.17}$$

$$\bar{p} = \frac{b + b_2^*}{\bar{q}} \tag{15.18}$$

$$p_3 = \frac{b_3 + \bar{b}_3 + b_3^*}{q_3 + \bar{q}_3 + q_3^*}, \tag{15.19}$$

while that for the interest rate is

$$1 + \rho = \frac{d + \bar{d} + d^*}{g}. \tag{15.20}$$

15.5.3 Results

In Appendix D we solve the model for small values of m. As in Models 1 and 2, we have two cases, depending on whether G is "large" or "small." Qualitatively, the difference between Case 1 and Case 2 is whether the merchants' cash-flow and budget constraints both hold tightly, and whether the gold market shuts down.

We now set parameter values so as to most closely match the examples calculated with Models 1 and 2. So let us now set $\Pi_1 = \Pi_2 = 1$ and $m = 0$.

Example 1: If $G = 2a$ we are in Case 1. We obtain $p = \bar{p} = 1$, $\rho = 0$, $d = \bar{d} = \frac{2a}{3}$, $b = \bar{b} = \frac{a}{3}$, $q = \bar{q} = \frac{2a}{3}$. Hence, the consumption by each trader type is $(\frac{a}{3}, \frac{a}{3})$ of the perishables. The bids of the merchants are $b_1^* = b_2^* = \frac{a}{2}$, and so they too consume $\frac{a}{3}$ of each of the perishables. In addition, we have $p_3 = 2$, $b_3 = \bar{b}_3 = \frac{a}{3}$, and $q_3^* = \frac{a}{3}$; hence the merchants sell $\frac{a}{3}$ units of gold ($\frac{a}{6}$ to each trader type). The final distribution of resources is $(\frac{a}{3}, \frac{a}{3}, \frac{a}{6}, 0)$, $(\frac{a}{3}, \frac{a}{3}, \frac{a}{6}, 0)$, $(\frac{a}{3}, \frac{a}{3}, B - \frac{a}{3}, 0)$, and $(0, 0, 0, B)$ for the two trader types, the gold merchants, and the central bank, respectively. In addition, the central bank makes no profit; hence $D = D^* = 0$. For each trader type, its final utility is $2\sqrt{\frac{a}{3}\frac{a}{3}} + \frac{a}{6} + \Pi_2\frac{a}{6} + 0 = a$, while for the merchants it is $2\sqrt{\frac{a}{3}\frac{a}{3}} + B - \frac{a}{3} + \Pi_2(B - \frac{a}{3}) + 0 = 2B$.

The reader will note that these give the same (Pareto efficient) results as in Model 2.

Example 2: If we set $G = a$, we are on the boundary between Case 1 and Case 2. We obtain $p = \bar{p} = 1$, $\rho = 0$, $d = \bar{d} = \frac{a}{2}$, $b = \bar{b} = \frac{a}{2}$, and $q = \bar{q} = \frac{a}{2}$. Hence the consumption by each trader type is $(\frac{a}{2}, \frac{a}{2})$ of the perishables. The bids of the merchants are $b_1^* = b_2^* = 0$, and so they consume none of the perishables. In addition, we have $p_3 = 2$, $b_3 = \bar{b}_3 = 0$, and $q_3^* = 0$; hence the merchants sell no gold to the traders. The final distribution of resources is $(\frac{a}{2}, \frac{a}{2}, 0, 0)$, $(\frac{a}{2}, \frac{a}{2}, 0, 0)$, $(0, 0, B, 0)$, and $(0, 0, 0, B)$ for the two trader types, the gold merchants, and the central bank, respectively. Again, the central bank makes no profit; hence $D = D^* = 0$.

Example 3: If we set $G = \frac{a}{4}$, we are in Case 2. There are a continuum of equilibria, parametrized by ρ, which can take on any value between 0 and 3. For each such ρ, we have $p = \bar{p} = \frac{1}{4}$, $d = \bar{d} = \frac{a}{8}$, $b = \bar{b} = \frac{a}{8(1+\rho)}$, and $q = \bar{q} = \frac{a}{2}$. The consumption of perishables by the trader types is $(\frac{a}{2}, \frac{a}{2(1+\rho)})$ and $(\frac{a}{2(1+\rho)}, a)$. Again, no gold is traded. The merchants bid $\frac{a\rho}{8(1+\rho)}$ for each type of perishable, and end up consuming $\frac{a\rho}{2(1+\rho)}$ of each type of perishable. Consumption of the perishables is not efficient here. The "profit" for the central bank (ρG) is $\frac{a\rho}{4}$, all of which goes to the merchants.

The last two models fall under the rubric of Dubey, Mas-Colell, and Shubik (1980); they have noncooperative equilibria that give the competitive outcome if there is enough money. If there is not enough money, even in equilibrium the inequalities become binding. The definition of enough money, although mathematically well-defined, depends on institutional detail.

15.6 THE VALUE OF PAPER MONEY IN AN ECONOMY WITH ENOUGH GOLD

We say that an economy has "enough money" if there is enough money in the economy to finance efficient trade, even if it takes zero-interest loans to those with cash-flow constraints. Suppose gold is the money, and gold also has a linear utility as a commodity. If there is enough gold, the marginal *transactions* value of gold must equal its marginal *consumption* value. These both have to be equal to the money rate of interest.

Suppose instead that paper money is used. If we utilize it as both a means of exchange and a numeraire, then, as its amount is increased its marginal value as a store of value approaches zero as the price level inflates in proportion to its issue.[14]

---

14 More technically, in a strategic market game with borrowing, feasible bankruptcy penalties must be specified. This establishes a lower bound on price, as below some given

In the examples from Model 2, we selected parameters $\Pi_1 = \Pi_2 = 1$, so the marginal consumption value of gold is $1.$[15] Indeed, the value of the strips equals the marginal value of the services of gold, which equals 1.

When $B = a$ the discounted value of the strip equals that of the gold. When $B = 2a$ the discounted value to the lender is zero, but the sum of the discounted worth to the borrowers is still $2a$. It adds $\frac{a}{2}$ to each every period.

15.7 THE NEED FOR A CENTRAL BANK?

15.7.1 Results from Our Analysis

Let us summarize our results from the "enough money" (Example 1) cases above. First, in Model 1 (with gold as the money), we had inefficient consumption of the perishables. However, the demonetization of gold via the introduction of the strips permits one to "have one's cake and have the borrowers eat it." Both the consumption and transaction services of gold can be utilized simultaneously, and the consumption of perishable is efficient. In Model 3 we introduce a central bank (under the legal fiction that it is owned by the holders of the gold) which enables a government to control the money supply while limiting the amount of paper in circulation to at most a 1:1 ratio with gold. This third model is not only somewhat improbable, but appears to make a libertarian case that the central bank is unneeded—there is no change in efficiency as we move from Model 2 to Model 3.

Thus it seems that the central bank adds no value. But do not forget that our simple models assume a stationary economy, with perfect information flows, costless accounting, safekeeping, and many other transaction services. They have no exogenous uncertainty, but do have honest, error-free individuals in a society without public goods. Law and government are provided free of charge. At the very least, in the real world a central bank is useful in policing some of these functions.

In addition, our analysis shows the central bank *does* help increase efficiency in the case where there is not "enough money." For instance, in Example 3

---

price it will pay individuals to opt for strategic bankruptcy. Thus the no-bankruptcy equilibrium price is defined on the half open set $[p^*, \infty)$ if the amount of fiat grows in an unbounded manner and the marginal value of a unit of fiat approaches zero.

15 Interpreted in terms of an infinite-horizon model, this fits with a time discount of $\beta = \frac{1}{2}$ and the spot price of gold at $p_3 = 2$. Thus, if Π were reinterpreted as $\beta p_3 = \frac{1}{2}2 = 1$ we can connect to the steady state.

both Model 1 and Model 2 produce inefficient consumption of the perishable. But Model 3 gives a continuum of results, ranging from the Model 2 answer to an efficient result where $\rho = 0$.

15.7.2 Varying the Money Supply: Who Gets the Power?

Of course, our modern economy is not like our simple models here—we *do* have a public sector with a bureaucracy, politics, law, and uncertainty as facts of life. Hence, a valid question is whether we should have a central bank and paper money, or should we trust "the market" and the gold miners to take care of everything. It poses a Scylla and Charybdis choice. The choice is between an oligopolistic industry dependent on an arbitrary gold manufacturing technology with relatively little flexibility in increasing or decreasing the supply, and a monopolistist central bank that may be subject to considerable political pressure. The answer is essentially ad hoc; but sometimes the economy requires items such as an ability to vary the supply of money, a lender of last resort, a bank for the government, and a manager of the national debt. In this case, the central bank, though possibly not necessary, appears to be a sufficient institution that offers many if not all of these functions.

Possibly the most important question in the allocation of power to private or public institutions is who is in a position to vary the money supply in the economy (see Smith and Shubik, 2011). In considering a dynamic economy it is easy to construct models in which the causality runs in both directions. The availability of new products or processes may call for new money. Alternatively the availability of funding may call forth innovation. Our formal models above dealt with gold or paper as a means of payment where the paper was completely backed by gold. As soon as the rules are changed in a way that enables all legal persons to issue their own currency (see Sahi and Yao, 1989; Sorin, 1996) it is possible to design an abstract economy and a formal experimental game (see Angerer, Huber, Shubik, and Sunder, 2010) which achieves efficient trade using individual IOU notes as currency. The modeling requirements are so stringent that although logically feasible, the information, privacy, accounting, and enforcement conditions rule it out at this time.

The central bank as the creator of money appears to be the least bad of all current alternatives. But with this assignment of power goes public need for transparency and safeguards.

15.8 APPENDIX A: A BUY-SELL MODEL OF
COMPETITIVE MONEY-LENDING WITH GOLD

In this model there are the usual two continua of traders, plus a continuum of moneylenders. The trader types are endowed with $(a, 0, m)$ and $(0, a, m)$, respectively, while the lenders have $(0, 0, B)$. However, this time the money is gold. The gold can be used only for transactions or for jewelry (services) during the period, but not both. In the language of Chapter 6, the parameter values (k_1, k_2, k_3) are set equal to $(0, 0, 1)$.

The optimization for the Type 1 traders is

$$
\max_{b,q,d} 2\sqrt{(a-q)\tfrac{b}{p}} + \left(m + \tfrac{d}{1+\rho} - b\right) + \Pi\left(m + \tfrac{d}{1+\rho} - b + pq - d\right)
$$
$$
\text{s.t. } m + \tfrac{d}{1+\rho} - b \geq 0 \qquad\qquad (\lambda) \text{ (cash-flow constraint)}
$$
$$
\qquad m + \tfrac{d}{1+\rho} - b + pq - d \geq 0 \qquad (\mu) \text{ (budget constraint)} \qquad (15.21)
$$
$$
\qquad b, d \geq 0,\ 0 \leq q \leq a.
$$

The first-order conditions here are

$$
\frac{1}{\sqrt{p}}\sqrt{\frac{a-q}{b}} = 1 + \Pi + \lambda + \mu \qquad\qquad (15.22)
$$

$$
\frac{1}{\sqrt{p}}\sqrt{\frac{b}{a-q}} = (\mu + \Pi)p \qquad\qquad (15.23)
$$

$$
\lambda = (\mu + \Pi)\rho - 1 \qquad\qquad (15.24)
$$

$$
m + \frac{d}{1+\rho} - b = 0 \text{ or } \lambda = 0 \qquad\qquad (15.25)
$$

$$
m + \frac{d}{1+\rho} - b + pq - d = 0 \text{ or } \mu = 0. \qquad\qquad (15.26)
$$

Similarly, the optimization for the Type 2 traders is

$$
\max_{\bar{b},\bar{q},\bar{d}} 2\sqrt{(a-\bar{q})\tfrac{\bar{b}}{p}} + \left(m + \tfrac{\bar{d}}{1+\rho} - \bar{b}\right) + \Pi\left(m + \tfrac{\bar{d}}{1+\rho} - \bar{b} + \bar{p}\bar{q} - \bar{d}\right)
$$
$$
\text{s.t. } m + \tfrac{\bar{d}}{1+\rho} - \bar{b} \geq 0 \qquad\qquad (\bar{\lambda})
$$
$$
\qquad m + \tfrac{\bar{d}}{1+\rho} - \bar{b} + \bar{p}\bar{q} - \bar{d} \geq 0 \qquad (\bar{\mu})
$$
$$
\qquad \bar{b}, \bar{d} \geq 0,\ 0 \leq \bar{q} \leq a
$$

with first-order conditions

$$\frac{1}{\sqrt{p}}\sqrt{\frac{a-\bar{q}}{\bar{b}}} = 1 + \Pi + \bar{\lambda} + \bar{\mu} \tag{15.27}$$

$$\frac{1}{\sqrt{p}}\sqrt{\frac{\bar{b}}{a-\bar{q}}} = (\bar{\mu} + \Pi)\bar{p} \tag{15.28}$$

$$\bar{\lambda} = (\bar{\mu} + \Pi)\rho - 1 \tag{15.29}$$

$$m + \frac{\bar{d}}{1+\rho} - \bar{b} = 0 \text{ or } \bar{\lambda} = 0 \tag{15.30}$$

$$m + \frac{\bar{d}}{1+\rho} - \bar{b} + \bar{p}\bar{q} - \bar{d} = 0 \text{ or } \bar{\mu} = 0. \tag{15.31}$$

For the continuum of moneylenders, the optimization is

$$\max_{b_1^*, b_2^*, g} 2\sqrt{\frac{b_1^* \, b_2^*}{p \, \bar{p}}} + B - b_1^* - b_2^* - g + \Pi\left(B - b_1^* - b_2^* + \rho g\right)$$

$$\text{s.t. } B - b_1^* - b_2^* - g \geq 0 \qquad\qquad (\lambda^*) \tag{15.32}$$

$$b_1^*, b_2^*, g \geq 0.$$

Note here that the moneylenders have g as a decision variable, and not ρ. The reason is that individually, each lender can decide how much to lend—but each cannot individually influence the interest rate. The first-order conditions here are:

$$\sqrt{\frac{b_2^*}{p\bar{p}b_1^*}} = \Pi + \lambda^* + 1 \tag{15.33}$$

$$\sqrt{\frac{b_1^*}{p\bar{p}b_2^*}} = \Pi + \lambda^* + 1 \tag{15.34}$$

$$\Pi\rho - \lambda^* - 1 = 0 \tag{15.35}$$

$$B - b_1^* - b_2^* - g = 0 \text{ or } \lambda^* = 0. \tag{15.36}$$

Finally, we have the following balance conditions: $p = \frac{\bar{b}+b_1^*}{q}$, $\bar{p} = \frac{b+b_2^*}{\bar{q}}$, and $1+\rho = \frac{d+\bar{d}}{g}$.

Case 1:   We first analyze the case where the traders have little gold and the lenders have a lot. Thus the traders' constraints are all tight and the lenders' are loose; that is, $\lambda > 0$, $\mu > 0$, $\bar{\lambda} > 0$, $\bar{\mu} > 0$, and $\lambda^* = 0$. We also assume a symmetric solution; that is, $p = \bar{p}$, $b = \bar{b}$, $d = \bar{d}$, $q = \bar{q}$, and $b_1^* = b_2^*$.

Condition (15.35) gives $\rho = \frac{1}{\Pi}$. And (15.33) together with symmetry gives $\frac{1}{p} = \Pi + 1$, which is $p = \frac{1}{\Pi+1} = \bar{p}$.

Next, we find an expression for the multiplier μ. We begin with (15.23), which is $\sqrt{\frac{b}{a-q}} = (\mu + \Pi)p^{3/2}$, or $\sqrt{\frac{a-q}{b}} = \frac{1}{(\mu+\Pi)p^{3/2}}$. Substituting into (15.22), we have $\frac{1}{\sqrt{p}} \frac{1}{(\mu+\Pi)p^{3/2}} = 1 + \Pi + \lambda + \mu = 1 + \Pi + (\mu + \Pi)\rho - 1 + \mu = (1 + \rho)(\mu + \Pi)$. But $p = \frac{1}{\Pi+1}$; so we have $(\Pi + 1)^2 = (1 + \rho)(\mu + \Pi)^2$, which is $(\Pi + 1) = \sqrt{1+\rho}(\mu + \Pi) = \sqrt{1 + \frac{1}{\Pi}}(\mu + \Pi)$. Solving for μ yields $\mu = \sqrt{\Pi(1 + \Pi)} - \Pi$.

Next, we again start with (15.23), which is $\sqrt{\frac{b}{a-q}} = (\mu + \Pi)p^{3/2}$. Squaring both sides, we have $\frac{b}{a-q} = (\mu + \Pi)^2 p^3$. Now substitute in $p = \frac{1}{\Pi+1}$ and $\mu = \sqrt{\Pi(1 + \Pi)} - \Pi$. We end up with $b = (a - q)\frac{\Pi}{(1+\Pi)^2}$.

Next, since the traders' cash-flow and budget constraints are both tight, we know $d = pq = \frac{q}{1+\Pi}$. But the tight cash-flow constraint also means $d = (b - m)(1 + \rho) = (b - m)(1 + \frac{1}{\Pi}) = \left((a - q)\frac{\Pi}{(1+\Pi)^2} - m\right)(1 + \frac{1}{\Pi})$. Hence $\left((a - q)\frac{\Pi}{(1+\Pi)^2} - m\right)(1 + \frac{1}{\Pi}) = \frac{q}{1+\Pi}$. Solving for q yields

$$q = \frac{a}{2} - \frac{m(1 + \Pi)^2}{2\Pi} = \bar{q}. \tag{15.37}$$

At this point it becomes easy to solve for the other variables: $d = pq = \frac{q}{1+\Pi} = \frac{a}{2(1+\Pi)} - \frac{m(1+\Pi)}{2\Pi}$, $b = (a - q)\frac{\Pi}{(1+\Pi)^2} = \frac{a\Pi}{2(1+\Pi)^2} + \frac{m}{2}$, and $b_1^* = b_2^* = pq - b = d - b = \frac{a}{2(1+\Pi)^2} - \frac{m}{2\Pi} - m$. In addition, $g = \frac{2d}{1+\rho} = \frac{a\Pi}{(1+\Pi)^2} - m$. For the multipliers, we already found $\mu = \sqrt{\Pi(1 + \Pi)} - \Pi = \bar{\mu}$ and we are given $\lambda^* = 0$. Finally, we have $\lambda = \rho(\Pi + \mu) - 1 = \frac{1}{\Pi}(\Pi + \sqrt{\Pi(1 + \Pi)} - \Pi) - 1 = \sqrt{\frac{1+\Pi}{\Pi}} - 1$.

The results hold if $B - b_1^* - b_2^* - g \geq 0$, that is, if $B - \frac{a}{(1+\Pi)^2} + \frac{m}{\Pi} + 2m - \frac{a\Pi}{(1+\Pi)^2} + m \geq 0$. This yields a condition of $B \geq \frac{a}{1+\Pi} - \frac{m(1+\Pi)}{\Pi}$. In addition, we need the variables q, d, and $b_1^* = b_2^*$ to be nonnegative. This occurs if $m \leq \frac{\Pi a}{(1+\Pi)^2}$.

Case 2:   We analyze the case where B is smaller. Hence the traders' cash-flow and budget constraints are tight as before, but the lenders' cash-flow constraints are tight, that is, $\lambda > 0$, $\mu > 0$, and $\lambda^* > 0$. Again assume a symmetric solution, that is, $p = \bar{p}$, $b = \bar{b}$, $d = \bar{d}$, $q = \bar{q}$, and $b_1^* = b_2^*$.

First, (15.35) implies $\lambda^* = \Pi\rho - 1$. But also, from (15.33) and symmetry, we have $\lambda^* = \frac{1}{p} - \Pi - 1$. Hence $\Pi\rho = \frac{1}{p} - \Pi$, which is

$$p = \frac{1}{\Pi(1+\rho)} = \bar{p}. \tag{15.38}$$

Next, since the traders' cash-flow and budget constraints are tight, we have $d = pq$. But by the balance condition pq is equal to $\bar{b} + b_1^*$, and since the lenders' cash-flow constraints are tight, $b_1^* = b_2^* = \frac{B-g}{2}$. So we have $d = pq = \bar{b} + b_1^* = \bar{b} + \frac{B-g}{2} = \bar{b} + \frac{B - \frac{2d}{1+\rho}}{2} = \frac{B}{2} + \bar{b} - \frac{d}{1+\rho} = \frac{B}{2} + m$, where the fourth equality follows from the balance constraint, the fifth is just algebra, and the last follows from symmetry $b = \bar{b}$ and the tight traders' cash-flow constraint. So we have

$$d = \frac{B}{2} + m = \bar{d}. \tag{15.39}$$

At this point, we can obtain expressions for all of the variables in terms of ρ: $g = \frac{2d}{1+\rho} = \frac{B+2m}{1+\rho}$, $b = \frac{d}{1+\rho} + m = \frac{\frac{B}{2}+m}{1+\rho} + m = \bar{b}$, $b_1^* = b_2^* = \frac{1}{2}(B-g) = \frac{1}{2}(\frac{B+\rho B - B - 2m}{1+\rho}) = \frac{1}{2}(\frac{\rho B - 2m}{1+\rho})$. Recalling $p = \frac{1}{\Pi(1+\rho)}$, we also have $q = \bar{q} = \frac{d}{p} = \frac{\frac{B}{2}+m}{\frac{1}{\Pi(1+\rho)}} = \Pi(1+\rho)(\frac{B}{2}+m)$.

So now all that remains is to find an expression for ρ. To this end, we observe that (15.24) implies that

$$\lambda = \rho(\Pi + \mu) - 1. \tag{15.40}$$

Then

$$(15.22) \Rightarrow \frac{1}{\sqrt{\bar{p}}}\sqrt{\frac{a-q}{b}} = 1 + \Pi + \lambda + \mu \tag{15.41}$$

$$\Rightarrow \frac{1}{\bar{p}}\left(\frac{a-q}{b}\right) = (1 + \Pi + \lambda + \mu)^2 \tag{15.42}$$

$$\Rightarrow \frac{1}{\bar{p}}\left(\frac{a-q}{b}\right) = (1+\rho)^2(\Pi+\mu)^2 \text{ (using (15.40))} \tag{15.43}$$

$$\Rightarrow \frac{1}{\bar{p}}\left(\frac{a-q}{b}\right) = (1+\rho)^2 \frac{1}{\bar{p}^3}\left(\frac{b}{a-q}\right) \text{ (using (15.23))} \tag{15.44}$$

$$\Rightarrow \left(\frac{a-q}{b}\right)^2 = \frac{(1+\rho)^2}{\bar{p}^2} = \Pi^2(1+\rho)^4 \text{ (using 15.38)} \tag{15.45}$$

$$\Rightarrow \frac{a-q}{b} = \Pi(1+\rho)^2 \tag{15.46}$$

$$\Rightarrow \frac{a - \Pi(1+\rho)(\frac{B}{2}+m)}{\frac{\frac{B}{2}+m}{1+\rho}+m} = \Pi(1+\rho)^2 \tag{15.47}$$

$$\Rightarrow a - \Pi(1+\rho)\left(\frac{B}{2}+m\right) = \Pi(1+\rho)\left(\frac{B}{2}+m\right) + \Pi m(1+\rho)^2 \tag{15.48}$$

$$\Rightarrow \Pi m(1+\rho)^2 + 2\Pi(1+\rho)\left(\frac{B}{2}+m\right) - a = 0. \tag{15.49}$$

The above quadratic expression for $1+\rho$ solves in two cases: first, if $m=0$, we have $1+\rho = \frac{a}{\Pi(B+2m)}$. Otherwise, if $m>0$, we have

$$1+\rho = \frac{-\Pi(B+2m) + \sqrt{\Pi^2(B+2m)^2 + 4a\Pi m}}{2\Pi m}. \tag{15.50}$$

Finally, we may solve for the multipliers. First, we have $(15.23) \Rightarrow \mu = \frac{\frac{1}{\sqrt{\bar{p}}}\sqrt{\frac{b}{a-q}} - \Pi p}{p} = \frac{1}{p^{1.5}}\sqrt{\frac{1}{\Pi(1+\rho)^2}} - \Pi = \Pi^{1.5}(1+\rho)^{1.5}\sqrt{\frac{1}{\Pi(1+\rho)^2}} = \Pi\sqrt{1+\rho} - \Pi$, where the second equality follows from (15.46) and the third from (15.38). Also, $\lambda = \rho(\Pi+\mu) - 1 = \Pi\rho\sqrt{1+\rho} - 1$. Finally, condition (15.35) directly gives us $\lambda^* = \Pi\rho - 1$.

Note: In order for the above to be valid, we need ρ and all the multipliers to be nonnegative. This requires $\rho \geq \frac{1}{\Pi}$. In the case where $m=0$, this means $B+2m \leq \frac{a}{1+\Pi}$. In the case where $m>0$, the condition is not so easily stated but does hold whenever a is large compared to $B+2m$. We also need for b_1^* and b_1^* to be nonnegative, which means $\rho B \geq 2m$. Again, if $m=0$, this holds if $\rho \geq \frac{1}{\Pi}$, that is, if $B+2m \leq \frac{a}{1+\Pi}$. And again, if $m>0$ the condition is more complicated but holds if $a >> B+2m$.

15.9 APPENDIX B: A SELL-ALL MODEL OF COMPETITIVE MONEY-LENDING WITH GOLD

Both trader types are endowed with m units of gold money. The continuum of moneylenders is endowed with $B = M - 2m$ units of money (where $0 \leq$

$2m \leq M$). The lenders are utility maximizers, who (just like the traders) derive benefit from consumption of perishables, the service utility of the gold, and the salvage utility of the gold at the end of the game.

The notation we will use is the following. For the Type 1 traders, b_1 and b_2 denote the amount of gold bid in the market for good 1 and good 2, respectively. The amount they borrow from the banks is $\frac{d}{1+\rho}$ at interest rate ρ, so the amount they must pay back is d. For the Type 2 traders, the notation $\bar{b}_1$, $\bar{b}_2$, and $\bar{d}$ is defined similarly. The prices for the perishables are p and $\bar{p}$, while the salvage value for the gold is Π per unit. We assume that the service utility of the gold is one per unit-time,

The Type 1 traders face an optimization described by:

$$
\begin{aligned}
\max_{b_1,b_2,d} \; & 2\sqrt{\frac{b_1\,b_2}{p\,\bar{p}}} + m + \frac{d}{1+\rho} - b_1 - b_2 + pa \\
& + \Pi\left(m + \frac{d}{1+\rho} - b_1 - b_2 + pa - d\right)
\end{aligned}
\tag{a}
$$

$$
\text{s.t. } m + \frac{d}{1+\rho} - b_1 - b_2 \geq 0 \qquad (\lambda) \text{ (cash-flow constraint)} \tag{b}
$$

$$
m + \frac{d}{1+\rho} - b_1 - b_2 + pa - d \geq 0 \qquad (\mu) \text{ (budget constraint)} \tag{c}
$$

$$
b_1, b_2, d \geq 0. \tag{d}
$$

$$\tag{15.51}$$

The first-order conditions wrt b_1, b_2, and d yield

$$
\sqrt{\frac{b_2}{p\bar{p}b_1}} = 1 + \Pi + \lambda + \mu \tag{15.52}
$$

$$
\sqrt{\frac{b_1}{p\bar{p}b_2}} = 1 + \Pi + \lambda + \mu \tag{15.53}
$$

$$
\frac{1}{1+\rho} + \frac{\Pi}{1+\rho} - \Pi + \frac{\lambda}{1+\rho} + \frac{\mu}{1+\rho} - \mu = 0 \tag{15.54}
$$

$$
m + \frac{d}{1+\rho} - b_1 - b_2 = 0 \text{ or } \lambda = 0 \tag{15.55}
$$

$$
m + \frac{d}{1+\rho} - b_1 - b_2 + pa - d = 0 \text{ or } \mu = 0. \tag{15.56}
$$

We also point out that we require the feasibility conditions (15.51b)–(15.51d) for our solution.[16]

Similarly, the Type 2 traders face the optimization below:

$$\max_{\bar{b}_1, \bar{b}_2, \bar{d}} 2\sqrt{\frac{\bar{b}_1}{p}\frac{\bar{b}_2}{\bar{p}}} + m + \frac{\bar{d}}{1+\rho} - \bar{b}_1 - \bar{b}_2 + \bar{p}a$$

$$+ \Pi\left(m + \frac{\bar{d}}{1+\rho} - \bar{b}_1 - \bar{b}_2 + \bar{p}a - \bar{d}\right)$$

$$\text{s.t. } m + \frac{\bar{d}}{1+\rho} - \bar{b}_1 - \bar{b}_2 \geq 0 \qquad (\bar{\lambda}) \text{ (cash-flow constraint)} \qquad (15.57)$$

$$m + \frac{\bar{d}}{1+\rho} - \bar{b}_1 - \bar{b}_2 + \bar{p}a - \bar{d} \geq 0 \quad (\bar{\mu}) \text{ (budget constraint)}$$

$$\bar{b}_1, \bar{b}_2, \bar{d} \geq 0.$$

The first-order conditions here are

$$\sqrt{\frac{\bar{b}_2}{p\bar{p}\bar{b}_1}} = 1 + \Pi + \bar{\lambda} + \bar{\mu} \qquad (15.58)$$

$$\sqrt{\frac{\bar{b}_1}{p\bar{p}\bar{b}_2}} = 1 + \Pi + \bar{\lambda} + \bar{\mu} \qquad (15.59)$$

$$\frac{1}{1+\rho} + \frac{\Pi}{1+\rho} - \Pi + \frac{\bar{\lambda}}{1+\rho} + \frac{\bar{\mu}}{1+\rho} - \bar{\mu} = 0 \qquad (15.60)$$

$$m + \frac{\bar{d}}{1+\rho} - \bar{b}_1 - \bar{b}_2 = 0 \text{ or } \bar{\lambda} = 0 \qquad (15.61)$$

$$m + \frac{\bar{d}}{1+\rho} - \bar{b}_1 - \bar{b}_2 + \bar{p}a - \bar{d} = 0 \text{ or } \bar{\mu} = 0. \qquad (15.62)$$

The moneylender decision variables are b_1^* (the amount they collectively bid for good 1), b_2^* (the amount they collectively bid for good 2), and g (the

---

16 For the Type 2 traders' optimizations, and in Appendixes C and D below, we also have similar feasibility conditions, which we don't explicitly write down.

amount they offer for loan). Their optimization is expressed as:

$$\max_{b_1^*, b_2^*, g} 2\sqrt{\frac{b_1^*}{p} \frac{b_2^*}{\bar{p}}} + B - g - b_1^* - b_2^* + \Pi(B - g - b_1^* - b_2^* + (1+\rho)g)$$

$$\text{s.t. } B - g - b_1^* - b_2^* \geq 0 \qquad\qquad (\lambda^*)$$

$$b_1^*, b_2^*, g \geq 0. \qquad\qquad\qquad\qquad (15.63)$$

The first-order equations here are

$$\sqrt{\frac{b_2^*}{p\bar{p}b_1^*}} = \Pi + \lambda^* + 1 \qquad\qquad (15.64)$$

$$\sqrt{\frac{b_1^*}{p\bar{p}b_2^*}} = \Pi + \lambda^* + 1 \qquad\qquad (15.65)$$

$$\Pi\rho - \lambda^* - 1 = 0 \qquad\qquad\qquad (15.66)$$

$$B - b_1^* - b_2^* - g = 0 \text{ or } \lambda^* = 0. \qquad (15.67)$$

Finally, the balance conditions are $p = \frac{b_1 + \bar{b}_1 + b_1^*}{a}$, $\bar{p} = \frac{b_2 + \bar{b}_2 + b_2^*}{a}$, and $1 + \rho = \frac{d + \bar{d}}{g}$. We also remark that here the problems for Types 1 and 2 are isomorphic and so we may assume a symmetric solution where $b_1 = b_2 = \bar{b}_1 = \bar{b}_2 \equiv b$, $d = \bar{d}$, $b_1^* = b_2^* \equiv b^*$, and $p = \bar{p}$.

Case 1: m low and B high. There are several cases, but as before we first consider the case in which the traders have little money (*m* small) and the bankers have a lot of money (*B* large). In terms of our multipliers, we are assuming λ, $\bar{\lambda}$, μ, and $\bar{\mu}$ are positive, while $\lambda^* = 0$. The first observation is that condition (15.64) or (15.65), $\lambda^* = 0$, and symmetry together imply that $p = \bar{p} = \frac{1}{1+\Pi}$. Next, conditions ($\lambda$) and ($\mu$) holding tightly together imply that $pa = d$. Hence $d = \frac{a}{1+\Pi} = \bar{d}$. The cash-flow constraint holding tightly is $m + \frac{d}{1+\rho} - 2b = 0$, which gives $b = \frac{m + \frac{d}{1+\rho}}{2} = \frac{m(1+\rho)(1+\Pi)+a}{2(1+\rho)(1+\Pi)}$; but then condition (15.66) and $\lambda^* = 0$ together give $\rho = \frac{1}{\Pi}$, so $b = \frac{m(1+\frac{1}{\Pi})(1+\Pi)+a}{2(1+\frac{1}{\Pi})(1+\Pi)} = \frac{m(1+\Pi)^2+\Pi a}{2(1+\Pi)^2}$. So the traders consume $\frac{b}{p} = \frac{m(1+\Pi)^2+\Pi a}{2(1+\Pi)}$ of each good. Then, we can calculate b^* via the balance condition for price: $b^* = pa - 2b = \frac{a}{1+\Pi} - \frac{m(1+\Pi)^2+\Pi a}{(1+\Pi)^2} = \frac{a - m(1+\Pi)^2}{(1+\Pi)^2}$. So the lenders consume $\frac{b^*}{p} = \frac{a - m(1+\Pi)^2}{(1+\Pi)}$ of each good. They also lend an amount of $g = \frac{2d}{1+\rho} = \frac{2\Pi a}{(1+\Pi)^2}$.

Finally, for the multipliers, condition (15.52) with $p=\bar{p}=\frac{1}{1+\Pi}$ and $b_1=b_2$ gives $1+\Pi = 1+\Pi+\lambda+\mu$; since λ and μ are nonnegative, this gives $\lambda=\mu=0$.

We remark that the above results are valid only if: (a) the above expression for b^* is nonnegative, and if (b) the lenders' cash-flow constraints (λ^*) hold. These give the conditions: (a) $m\le \frac{a}{(1+\Pi)^2}$ and (b) $B\ge \frac{2\Pi a}{(1+\Pi)^2}+2\frac{a-m(1+\Pi)^2}{(1+\Pi)^2} = \frac{2a}{1+\Pi}-2m$, which is $B+2m\ge \frac{2a}{1+\Pi}$.

Case 2: m low and B low. Now we cover the case in which λ, $\bar{\lambda}$, μ, and $\bar{\mu}$ are again all positive, but $\lambda^* > 0$ also. We first note that condition (15.64) and symmetry together imply $\lambda^* = \frac{1}{p}-1-\Pi$; substituting this expression for λ^* back into (15.66) gives $\Pi\rho - (\frac{1}{p}-1-\Pi)-1=0$, which is

$$p = \frac{1}{\Pi(1+\rho)} = \bar{p}. \tag{15.68}$$

Next, we note from symmetry, the balance conditions, and the tight (λ^*) constraint that $d = \frac{(1+\rho)g}{2}$, $2b+b^*=pa$, and $b^*=\frac{B-g}{2}$. Hence, starting with the tight cash-flow constraint for the traders, we have $m+\frac{d}{1+\rho}-b-b= 0 \Rightarrow m+\frac{g}{2}-2b=0 \Rightarrow m+\frac{g}{2}-pa+b^*=0 \Rightarrow m+\frac{g}{2}-pa+\frac{B-g}{2}=0 \Rightarrow p= \frac{B+2m}{2a}=\bar{p}$. Not only does this give an expression for p, but this in combination with (15.68) gives $\frac{1}{\Pi(1+\rho)} = \frac{B+2m}{2a}$, or $\rho = \frac{2a}{\Pi(B+2m)}-1$.

It is now a simple exercise to calculate expressions for the other variables: $d = pa = \frac{B+2m}{2} = \bar{d}$, $g = \frac{2d}{1+\rho} = \frac{\Pi(B+2m)^2}{2a}$, $b = b_1 = b_2 = \frac{m+\frac{g}{2}}{2} = \frac{4am+\Pi(B+2m)^2}{8a} = \bar{b}_1 = \bar{b}_2$, $b^* = b_1^* = b_2^* = \frac{B-g}{2} = \frac{2aB-\Pi(B+2m)^2}{4a}$, $\lambda^* = \frac{1}{p}-1-\Pi = \frac{2a}{B+2m}-\Pi-1$, $\mu = \frac{1}{p}-1-\Pi-\lambda = \frac{1}{p}-1-\Pi-(\Pi+\mu)\rho+1 \Rightarrow \mu=0$, and $\lambda = \frac{2a}{B+2m}-\Pi-1$.

In order for these results to hold, we need $b^*\ge 0$, $\lambda^*\ge 0$, and $\lambda\ge 0$. These hold if $\Pi(B+2m)^2\le 2aB$ and $(1+\Pi)B\le 2a$. If $m=0$, all that is needed is $(1+\Pi)B\le 2a$.

15.10 APPENDIX C: DEMONETIZED GOLD, NO CENTRAL BANK, AND LENDERS ALSO ACT AS GOLD MERCHANTS

This model is similar to Appendix A, except now the gold has been demonetized. All holders of x units of gold are now endowed with x units of demonetized gold, plus x units of fiat ("gold strips"). Hence the Type 1 traders are now endowed with a units of good 1, plus m units of gold, plus m units of fiat. The Type 2 traders are endowed with a units of good 1, m units of gold, and m units of fiat. The lenders (now lender-merchants) are endowed with only B units of gold and B units of fiat.

We assume that the financial market (for fiat) operates first, over the time period $[0, k_1]$. This is followed by the goods markets for gold and for perishable, both of which operate over $[k_2, k_3]$ $(0 \leq k_1 \leq k_2 \leq k_3)$. However, while any money borrowed during the financial market is not obtained until the *end* of the market at time k_1, any gold or perishable bought during the second phase is credited at the *beginning* of that phase, at time k_2. This is an important assumption for the trade of gold, as the final owners of gold get to enjoy its service value over the period $[k_2, k_3]$. As in the previous model, we assume $k_1 = 0$, $k_2 = 0$, and $k_3 = 1$.

With the new market for demonetized gold, we have to define some new variables. First, for the traders, the amount they bid for gold is b_3. The amount of gold they put up for sale is q_3. For the lenders, the amount they bid for gold is denoted b_3^*, while the amount they put up for sale is q_3^*. The price of gold is given by p_3 and the parameters Π_1 and Π_2 are the per-unit salvage value of strips (fiat) and gold, respectively, at the end of the game.

The Type 1 traders attempt to solve

$$
\max_{b,q,d,b_3,q_3} 2\sqrt{(a-q)\frac{b}{\bar{p}} + \left(m + \frac{b_3}{p_3} - q_3\right)}
$$
$$
+ \Pi_1 \left(m + \frac{d}{1+\rho} - b - b_3 + pq - d + p_3 q_3\right)
$$
$$
+ \Pi_2 \left(m + \frac{b_3}{p_3} - q_3\right)
$$
$$
\text{s.t. } m + \frac{d}{1+\rho} - b - b_3 \geq 0 \qquad (\lambda) \text{ (cash-flow constraint)}
$$
$$
m + \frac{d}{1+\rho} - b - b_3 + pq - d + p_3 q_3 \geq 0 \qquad (\mu) \text{ (budget constraint)}
$$
$$
b, b_3, d \geq 0, \, 0 \leq q \leq a, \, 0 \leq q_3 \leq m.
$$

$$(15.69)$$

The first-order conditions here, wrt b, q, d, b_3, and q_3, are

$$
\frac{1}{\sqrt{\bar{p}}}\sqrt{\frac{a-q}{b}} = \Pi_1 + \lambda + \mu \tag{15.70}
$$

$$
\frac{1}{\sqrt{\bar{p}}}\sqrt{\frac{b}{a-q}} = (\mu + \Pi_1)p \tag{15.71}
$$

$$\lambda = (\mu + \Pi_1)\rho \tag{15.72}$$

$$\frac{1 + \Pi_2}{p_3} = \Pi_1 + \lambda + \mu \tag{15.73}$$

$$\Pi_1 p_3 - 1 - \Pi_2 + \mu p_3 = 0. \tag{15.74}$$

In addition, we have the complementarity constraints

$$m + \frac{d}{1 + \rho} - b - b_3 = 0 \text{ or } \lambda = 0, \tag{15.75}$$

$$m + \frac{d}{1 + \rho} - b - b_3 + pq - d + p_3 q_3 = 0 \text{ or } \mu = 0. \tag{15.76}$$

Similarly, the optimization for the Type 2 traders is

$$\max_{\bar{b},\bar{q},\bar{d},\bar{b}_3,\bar{q}_3} 2\sqrt{(a - \bar{q})\frac{\bar{b}}{p}} + \left(m + \frac{\bar{b}_3}{p_3} - \bar{q}_3\right)$$
$$+ \Pi_1\left(m + \frac{\bar{d}}{1 + \rho} - \bar{b} - \bar{b}_3 + \bar{p}\bar{q} - \bar{d} + p_3\bar{q}_3\right) + \Pi_2\left(m + \frac{\bar{b}_3}{p_3} - \bar{q}_3\right)$$

s.t. $m + \frac{\bar{d}}{1+\rho} - \bar{b} - \bar{b}_3 \geq 0$ ($\bar{\lambda}$)

      $m + \frac{\bar{d}}{1+\rho} - \bar{b} - \bar{b}_3 + \bar{p}\bar{q} - \bar{d} + p_3\bar{q}_3 \geq 0$ ($\bar{\mu}$)

      $\bar{b}, \bar{b}_3, \bar{d} \geq 0, \ 0 \leq \bar{q} \leq a, \ 0 \leq \bar{q}_3 \leq m,$

with first-order conditions

$$\frac{1}{\sqrt{p}}\sqrt{\frac{a - \bar{q}}{\bar{b}}} = \Pi_1 + \bar{\lambda} + \bar{\mu} \tag{15.77}$$

$$\frac{1}{\sqrt{p}}\sqrt{\frac{\bar{b}}{a - \bar{q}}} = (\bar{\mu} + \Pi_1)\bar{p} \tag{15.78}$$

$$\bar{\lambda} = (\bar{\mu} + \Pi_1)\rho \tag{15.79}$$

$$\frac{1 + \Pi_2}{p_3} = \Pi_1 + \bar{\lambda} + \bar{\mu} \tag{15.80}$$

$$\Pi_1 p_3 - 1 - \Pi_2 + \bar{\mu} p_3 = 0 \tag{15.81}$$

$$m + \frac{\bar{d}}{1 + \rho} - \bar{b} = 0 \text{ or } \bar{\lambda} = 0 \tag{15.82}$$

$$m + \frac{\bar{d}}{1 + \rho} - \bar{b} - \bar{b}_3 + \bar{p}\bar{q} - \bar{d} + p_3\bar{q}_3 = 0 \text{ or } \bar{\mu} = 0. \tag{15.83}$$

For the continuum of lender-merchants, the new decision variables are b_3^* (the amount the lenders bid for gold) and q_3^* (the amount of gold they put up for sale). Their optimization is

$$
\max_{b_1^*, b_2^*, b_3^*, q_3^*, g} 2\sqrt{\frac{b_1^*}{p}\frac{b_2^*}{\bar{p}}} + \left(B + \frac{b_3^*}{p_3} - q_3^*\right) + \Pi_1\left(B - b_1^* - b_2^* + \rho g + p_3 q_3^* - b_3^*\right)
$$
$$
+ \Pi_2\left(B + \frac{b_3^*}{p_3} - q_3^*\right)
$$

s.t. $B - b_1^* - b_2^* - b_3^* - g \geq 0 \qquad (\lambda^*)$

$b_1^*, b_2^*, b_3^*, g \geq 0, \ 0 \leq q_3^* \leq B.$

(15.84)

The first-order conditions here are:

$$
\sqrt{\frac{b_2^*}{p\bar{p}b_1^*}} = \Pi_1 + \lambda^* \tag{15.85}
$$

$$
\sqrt{\frac{b_1^*}{p\bar{p}b_2^*}} = \Pi_1 + \lambda^* \tag{15.86}
$$

$$
\Pi_1\rho - \lambda^* = 0 \tag{15.87}
$$

$$
-\Pi_1 + \frac{1+\Pi_2}{p_3} - \lambda^* = 0 \tag{15.88}
$$

$$
\Pi_1 p_3 - (1+\Pi_2) = 0 \tag{15.89}
$$

$$
B - b_1^* - b_2^* - b_3^* - g = 0 \text{ or } \lambda^* = 0. \tag{15.90}
$$

Finally, we have the balance conditions $p = \frac{\bar{b}+b_1^*}{q}$, $\bar{p} = \frac{b+b_2^*}{\bar{q}}$, $p_3 = \frac{b_3+\bar{b}_3+b_3^*}{q_3+\bar{q}_3+q_3^*}$, and $1 + \rho = \frac{d+\bar{d}}{g}$.

Case 1: We first consider the case where m is small and B is large, so we assume that the traders' cash-flow and budget constraints are both tight but that the lender-merchants' cash-flow constraint is loose ($\lambda^* = 0$). In addition, we assume m is much smaller than B, and so the lenders will be selling gold to the traders. Mathematically, this means $q_3 = \bar{q}_3 = 0$ and $b_3^* = 0$. However, by doing this we may no longer assume conditions (15.74), (15.81), and (15.88).

We also assume a symmetric solution; that is, $p = \bar{p}$, $q = \bar{q}$, $b = \bar{b}$, $d = \bar{d}$, and $b_1^* = b_2^*$.

Our analysis is as follows. First, condition (15.89) implies that $p_3 = \frac{1+\Pi_2}{\Pi_1}$. But then (15.73) is $\lambda + \mu = \frac{1+\Pi_2}{p_3} - \Pi_1 = \Pi_1 - \Pi_1 = 0$. Since λ and μ are both nonnegative, this implies $\lambda = \mu = 0 = \bar{\lambda} = \bar{\mu}$. But then (15.72) implies $\rho = 0$. And then (15.87) gives $\lambda^* = 0$. And then (15.85) gives $p = \frac{1}{\Pi_1} = \bar{p}$.

We can now get expressions for all of the other variables in terms of q. To begin, note that (15.70) along with $\lambda = \mu = 0$ gives $\sqrt{\frac{a-q}{b}} = \Pi_1\sqrt{\bar{p}}$; plugging in our previous expression for $\bar{p}$ gives $\sqrt{\frac{a-q}{b}} = \sqrt{\Pi_1}$, or $\frac{a-q}{b} = \Pi_1$. We can rewrite this as

$$b = \frac{a-q}{\Pi_1}. \tag{15.91}$$

Next, the Type 1 traders' cash-flow and budget constraints being tight together imply $pq - d + p_3q_3 = 0$; the assumption that $q_3 = 0$ further gives $d = pq = \frac{q}{\Pi_1}$. In addition, the balance condition for p gives $pq = d = \bar{b} + b_1^*$. Hence $b_1^* = d - \bar{b} = d - b = \frac{q}{\Pi_1} - \frac{a-q}{\Pi_1} = \frac{2q-a}{\Pi_1} = b_2^*$. Also, the balance condition for interest $1 + \rho = \frac{d+d}{g}$ yields $g = 2d$ (because of $\rho = 0$ and symmetry), so $g = \frac{2q}{\Pi_1}$. Furthermore, $b_3 = m + \frac{d}{1+\rho} - b = m + d - b = m + \frac{q}{\Pi_1} - \frac{a-q}{\Pi_1} = m + \frac{2q-a}{\Pi_1} = \bar{b}_3$. This in turn implies $q_3^* = \frac{b_3 + \bar{b}_3}{p_3} = \frac{2\left(m + \frac{2q-a}{\Pi_1}\right)\Pi_1}{1+\Pi_2} = \frac{2(\Pi_1 m + 2q - a)}{1+\Pi_2}$.

There is no way to pin down an exact value for q, so we have a continuum of solutions parametrized by q. However, we can find upper and lower bounds for q so that we end up with a "line segment" of solutions. First, since b_1^* and b_2^* are nonnegative, we must have $q \geq \frac{a}{2}$. But also the cash-flow constraint for the lenders must be satisfied, that is, $B - b_1^* - b_2^* - b_3^* - g \geq 0$. This reduces to $B - 2\left(\frac{2q-a}{\Pi_1}\right) - \frac{2q}{\Pi_1} \geq 0$, or $q \leq \frac{2a+\Pi_1 B}{6}$. In addition, we must have $q_3^* \leq B$, which is $\frac{2(\Pi_1 m + 2q - a)}{1+\Pi_2} \leq B$ or $q \leq \frac{(1+\Pi_2)B - 2\Pi_1 m + 2a}{4}$. So the range for q is $\frac{a}{2} \leq q \leq \min(\frac{2a+\Pi_1 B}{6}, \frac{(1+\Pi_2)B - 2\Pi_1 m + 2a}{4}, a)$. In order for this range to be nonempty we must have $\Pi_1 B \geq a$ and $(1+\Pi_2)B \geq 2\Pi_1 m$.

If one also requires a 100 percent reserve requirement for lending, that is, $B - q_3^* \geq g$, this gives the further condition $B \geq \frac{2(\Pi_1 m + 2q - a)}{1+\Pi_2} + \frac{2q}{\Pi_1}$. There will be at least one q to satisfy this (namely, $q = \frac{a}{2}$), so long as $B \geq \frac{2\Pi_1 m}{1+\Pi_2} + \frac{a}{\Pi_1}$.

Case 2: Now we consider the case where B is smaller (but still significantly larger than m). In this case, we assume that the gold market goes inactive—so in addition to $q_3 = \bar{q}_3 = 0$ and $b_3^* = 0$, we assume $b_3 = \bar{b}_3 = q_3^* = 0$. This means that we cannot use condition (15.73), (15.74), (15.80), (15.81), (15.88), or (15.89) in our analysis. In addition, we assume all trader and lender-merchant constraints are tight, including now the lender-merchants' cash-flow constraints.

We begin with the tight traders' cash-flow constraints: $m + \frac{d}{1+\rho} - b - b_3 = 0$. Assuming $b_3 = 0$, the balance condition $1 + \rho = \frac{2d}{g}$, and simplifying, this yields $m + \frac{g}{2} - b = 0$. But the tight lender-merchants' cash-flow constraints (plus symmetry $b_1^* = b_2^*$) imply $g = B - 2b_2^*$; hence we have $m + \frac{B}{2} - b_2^* - b = 0$. Next, the balance constraint for price implies $b + b_2^* = \bar{p}\bar{q} = pq$, and furthermore the tight cash-flow and budget constraints (plus assuming $q_3 = 0$) imply $pq = d$. So $m + \frac{B}{2} - b_2^* - b = 0$ implies $m + \frac{B}{2} - d = 0$, or

$$d = m + \frac{B}{2} = \bar{d}. \tag{15.92}$$

Next, (15.85) together with symmetry implies that $\frac{1}{p} = \Pi_1 + \lambda^* = \Pi_1 + \Pi_1\rho = \Pi_1(1 + \rho)$, where the second equality follows from (15.87). This is

$$1 + \rho = \frac{1}{\Pi_1 p}. \tag{15.93}$$

Next, substituting (15.92), (15.93), and $b_3 = 0$ into the tight traders' cash-flow constraint gives $m + \frac{m + \frac{B}{2}}{\frac{1}{\Pi_1 p}} - b = 0$, which is

$$b = m + \Pi_1 p(m + \frac{B}{2}) = \bar{b}. \tag{15.94}$$

Next, condition (15.70) is $\frac{1}{\sqrt{\bar{p}}}\sqrt{\frac{a-q}{b}} = \Pi_1 + \lambda + \mu$. Substituting in for λ using (15.72) gives $\frac{1}{\sqrt{\bar{p}}}\sqrt{\frac{a-q}{b}} = \Pi_1 + \mu + \rho(\Pi_1 + \mu) = (1 + \rho)(\Pi_1 + \mu)$. Now (15.71) implies $(\Pi_1 + \mu) = \frac{1}{p^{3/2}}\sqrt{\frac{b}{a-q}}$, so we have $\frac{1}{\sqrt{\bar{p}}}\sqrt{\frac{a-q}{b}} = (1 + \rho)\frac{1}{p^{3/2}}\sqrt{\frac{b}{a-q}}$, which is $p\left(\frac{a-q}{b}\right) = 1 + \rho$. Substituting in for $1 + \rho$ using (15.93) gives $p\left(\frac{a-q}{b}\right) = \frac{1}{\Pi_1 p}$, which is $b = \Pi_1 p^2(a - q)$. Now the traders' cash-flow and budget constraints being tight, together with the assumption $q_3 = 0$, imply $pq = d$; hence we can substitute $q = \frac{d}{p} = \frac{m + \frac{B}{2}}{p} = \frac{B + 2m}{2p}$ into the last equation for b, obtaining

$$b = \Pi_1 p^2 \left(a - \frac{B+2m}{2p} \right) = \bar{b}. \tag{15.95}$$

Equations (15.94) and (15.95) give two expressions for b; setting them equal to each other gives the following equation, which can be solved for p using computational methods:

$$m + \Pi_1 p \left(m + \frac{B}{2} \right) = \Pi_1 p^2 \left(a - \frac{B+2m}{2p} \right). \tag{15.96}$$

Once we know $p\ (=\bar{p})$, it is then a simple matter to compute q (and $\bar{q}$) via $q = \bar{q} = \frac{m+\frac{B}{2}}{p}$, $b = \bar{b}$ via (15.94) or (15.95), ρ via (15.93), g from $1 + \rho = \frac{2d}{g} = \frac{B+2m}{g}$, and $b_1^* = b_2^*$ from $g = B - 2b_2^*$. Consumption levels and final utilities can then be computed accordingly. Finally, for the multipliers, we may calculate λ^* from $\frac{1}{p} = \Pi_1 + \lambda^*$, μ from (15.71), and then λ from (15.72).

In the special case of $m=0$, equation (15.96) solves easily, with $p = \bar{p} = \frac{B}{a}$. We also get $q = \bar{q} = \frac{a}{2}$, $b = \bar{b} = \frac{\Pi_1 B^2}{2a}$, $\rho = \frac{a}{\Pi_1 B} - 1$, $g = \frac{\Pi_1 B^2}{a}$, and $b_1^* = b_2^* = \frac{B}{2}(1 - \frac{\Pi_1 B}{a})$. For the multipliers, $\lambda^* = \frac{a}{B} - \Pi_1$, $\mu = \sqrt{\Pi_1}(\sqrt{\frac{a}{B}} - \sqrt{\Pi_1}) = \bar{\mu}$, and $\lambda = \sqrt{\frac{a}{\Pi_1 B}}(\frac{a}{B} - \Pi_1)$. We note that in order for these quantities to be nonnegative, we need: $\Pi_1 B \le a$.

15.11 APPENDIX D: DEMONETIZED GOLD
WITH A CENTRAL BANK

Now we assume the demonetization of gold in the presence of a central bank. When the demonetization occurs, the holders of x units of gold are now endowed just with x units of demonetized gold. The accompanying x units of "gold strips" (fiat) go to the central bank. For the moneylenders of the previous models, this means that they are endowed with only (B units of) demonetized gold, making them "gold merchants."

The central bank is a strategic dummy, lending an amount G of fiat no matter what. It is essentially owned by the individuals of the society (the traders and the merchants). Thus, at the end of the game, its profits are divided up between the two types of trader and the merchants, in the ratio of m to m to B, reflecting the original ownership of the gold, which backs up the bank in the first place.

The Type 1 traders are endowed with m units of gold, 0 units of fiat, and a units of perishable good 1. Their optimization problem looks like this:

$$\max_{b,q,d,b_3,q_3} 2\sqrt{(a-q)\frac{b}{p} + \left(m + \frac{b_3}{p_3} - q_3\right)}$$
$$+ \Pi_1\left(\frac{d}{1+\rho} - b - b_3 + pq - d + p_3 q_3 + D\right)$$
$$+ \Pi_2\left(m + \frac{b_3}{p_3} - q_3\right)$$

$$\text{s.t.} \quad \frac{d}{1+\rho} - b - b_3 \geq 0 \qquad\qquad (\lambda) \text{ (cash-flow constraint)}$$
$$\frac{d}{1+\rho} - b - b_3 + pq - d + p_3 q_3 + D \geq 0 \quad (\mu) \text{ (budget constraint)}$$
$$b, b_3, d \geq 0, \, 0 \leq q \leq a, \, 0 \leq q_3 \leq m.$$

$$(15.97)$$

Here the new quantity "D" is the amount of fiat that comes back to the Type 1 traders, as a result of their ownership of $\frac{m}{B+2m}$ of the profits of the central bank. Also, note that here the cash-flow and budget constraints lack the quantity "m" on the left-hand side, reflecting that the traders now are assumed to begin with gold but no fiat as compensation for their gold's demonetization.

The first-order conditions in the above, with respect to b, q, d, b_3, and q_3 are

$$\frac{1}{\sqrt{p}}\sqrt{\frac{a-q}{b}} = \Pi_1 + \lambda + \mu \qquad\qquad (15.98)$$

$$\frac{1}{\sqrt{p}}\sqrt{\frac{b}{a-q}} = (\mu + \Pi_1)p \qquad\qquad (15.99)$$

$$\lambda = (\mu + \Pi_1)\rho \qquad\qquad (15.100)$$

$$\frac{1+\Pi_2}{p_3} = \Pi_1 + \lambda + \mu \qquad\qquad (15.101)$$

$$\Pi_1 p_3 - 1 - \Pi_2 + \mu p_3 = 0. \qquad\qquad (15.102)$$

In addition, we have the complementarity constraints

$$\frac{d}{1+\rho} - b - b_3 = 0 \text{ or } \lambda = 0 \qquad\qquad (15.103)$$

$$\frac{d}{1+\rho} - b - b_3 + pq - d + p_3 q_3 + D = 0 \text{ or } \mu = 0. \tag{15.104}$$

Similarly, the optimization for the Type 2 traders is

$$\max_{\bar{b},\bar{q},\bar{d},\bar{b}_3,\bar{q}_3} 2\sqrt{(a-\bar{q})\frac{\bar{b}}{p} + \left(m + \frac{\bar{b}_3}{p_3} - \bar{q}_3\right)}$$

$$+ \Pi_1\left(\frac{\bar{d}}{1+\rho} - \bar{b} - \bar{b}_3 + \bar{p}\bar{q} - \bar{d} + p_3\bar{q}_3 + D\right)$$

$$+ \Pi_2\left(m + \frac{\bar{b}_3}{p_3} - \bar{q}_3\right)$$

s.t. $\dfrac{\bar{d}}{1+\rho} - \bar{b} - \bar{b}_3 \geq 0$ $\qquad (\bar{\lambda})$

$\dfrac{\bar{d}}{1+\rho} - \bar{b} - \bar{b}_3 + \bar{p}\bar{q} - \bar{d} + p_3\bar{q}_3 + D \geq 0$ $\qquad (\bar{\mu})$

$\bar{b}, \bar{b}_3, \bar{d} \geq 0, \ 0 \leq \bar{q} \leq a, \ 0 \leq \bar{q}_3 \leq m,$

with first-order conditions

$$\frac{1}{\sqrt{p}}\sqrt{\frac{a-\bar{q}}{\bar{b}}} = \Pi_1 + \bar{\lambda} + \bar{\mu} \tag{15.105}$$

$$\frac{1}{\sqrt{p}}\sqrt{\frac{\bar{b}}{a-\bar{q}}} = (\bar{\mu} + \Pi_1)\bar{p} \tag{15.106}$$

$$\bar{\lambda} = (\bar{\mu} + \Pi_1)\rho \tag{15.107}$$

$$\frac{1+\Pi_2}{p_3} = \Pi_1 + \bar{\lambda} + \bar{\mu} \tag{15.108}$$

$$\Pi_1 p_3 - 1 - \Pi_2 + \bar{\mu}p_3 = 0 \tag{15.109}$$

$$m + \frac{\bar{d}}{1+\rho} - \bar{b} - \bar{b}_3 = 0 \text{ or } \bar{\lambda} = 0 \tag{15.110}$$

$$m + \frac{\bar{d}}{1+\rho} - \bar{b} - \bar{b}_3 + \bar{p}\bar{q} - \bar{d} + p_3\bar{q}_3 = 0 \text{ or } \bar{\mu} = 0. \tag{15.111}$$

The gold merchants begin with B units of gold; but like the traders, they begin with no fiat. They have been stripped of their former money-lending function. Instead, again like the traders, they have become money borrowers—the new variable d^* stands for the amount of loan (from the central bank) that they must repay. And as a result, they also now have a budget constraint, again just like the traders. Finally, they too have an owner-ship stake in the central bank, namely, $\frac{B}{B+2m}$ of its profits, which we denote by D^*. The merchants' optimization is as below:

$$
\begin{aligned}
\max_{b_1^*,b_2^*,b_3^*,q_3^*,d^*} \; & 2\sqrt{\frac{b_1^*}{p}\frac{b_2^*}{\bar{p}}} + \left(B + \frac{b_3^*}{p_3} - q_3^*\right) \\
& + \Pi_1\left(\frac{d^*}{1+\rho} - b_1^* - b_2^* - b_3^* - d^* + p_3 q_3^* + D^*\right) \\
& + \Pi_2\left(B + \frac{b_3^*}{p_3} - q_3^*\right)
\end{aligned}
\tag{15.112}
$$

s.t. $\dfrac{d^*}{1+\rho} - b_1^* - b_2^* - b_3^* \geq 0 \qquad\qquad (\lambda^*)$

$\dfrac{d^*}{1+\rho} - b_1^* - b_2^* - b_3^* - d^* + p_3 q_3^* + D^* \geq 0 \qquad (\mu^*)$

$b_1^*, b_2^*, b_3^*, d^* \geq 0, \; 0 \leq q_3^* \leq B.$

The first-order conditions here are:

$$
\sqrt{\frac{b_2^*}{p\bar{p}b_1^*}} = \Pi_1 + \lambda^* + \mu^*
\tag{15.113}
$$

$$
\sqrt{\frac{b_1^*}{p\bar{p}b_2^*}} = \Pi_1 + \lambda^* + \mu^*
\tag{15.114}
$$

$$
(\Pi_1 + \mu^*)\rho - \lambda^* = 0
\tag{15.115}
$$

$$
-\Pi_1 + \frac{1+\Pi_2}{p_3} - \lambda^* - \mu^* = 0
\tag{15.116}
$$

$$
\Pi_1 p_3 + \mu^* p_3 - (1 + \Pi_2) = 0
\tag{15.117}
$$

$$
\frac{d^*}{1+\rho} - b_1^* - b_2^* - b_3^* = 0 \text{ or } \lambda^* = 0
\tag{15.118}
$$

$$
\frac{d^*}{1+\rho} - b_1^* - b_2^* - b_3^* - d^* + p_3 q_3^* + D^* = 0 \text{ or } \mu^* = 0.
\tag{15.119}
$$

The central bank is endowed with only $B + 2m$ units of fiat. It is a strategic dummy—it always just lends a total of G units of fiat to the traders and merchants, where G is a given quantity with $0 \leq G \leq B + 2m$. Its profits are ρG, and so each trader type's share is $D = \frac{m}{B+2m}\rho G$, while the merchants' share is $D^* = \frac{B}{B+2m}\rho G$.

Next, we have the balance conditions: (a) $p = \frac{\bar{b}+b_1^*}{q}$, (b) $\bar{p} = \frac{b+b_2^*}{\bar{q}}$, (c) $p_3 = \frac{b_3+\bar{b}_3+b_3^*}{q_3+\bar{q}_3+q_3^*}$, and (d) $1 + \rho = \frac{d+\bar{d}+d^*}{G}$.

Finally, we make the same symmetry assumptions as usual: $p = \bar{p}$, $q = \bar{q}$, $b = \bar{b}$, $d = \bar{d}$, and $b_1^* = b_2^*$.

We will consider two cases. In both cases, m is relatively small compared to B and G. Since the traders are starting with much less gold than the merchants, we assume that the traders will not be selling gold to the merchants; that is, $q_3 = \bar{q}_3 = 0$ and $b_3^* = 0$. Also, since the traders and merchants both start with no fiat, we assume the cash-flow constraints are tight for both. In Case 1, the central bank lends out a relatively large amount of money (G large). Since B is large compared to m, we assume that when all of the money is recycled back to the merchants they will have loose budget constraints, so $\mu^* = 0$. In Case 2 (G small) there is a lot less money in the economy, so all constraints, for both traders and merchants, are tight.

Case 1: m small, G large. We first analyze the case in which the cash-flow constraints (for both types of traders and for merchants) are tight, and the budget constraints for the merchants are loose (so μ^* is equal to zero), $q_3 = \bar{q}_3 = 0$, and $b_3^* = 0$.

The analysis of this case goes as follows. First, $\mu^* = 0$ and equation (15.117) together imply that $p_3 = \frac{1+\Pi_2}{\Pi_1}$. Then (15.101) is $\frac{1+\Pi_2}{p_3} = \Pi_1 + \lambda + \mu$. But $p_3 = \frac{1+\Pi_2}{\Pi_1}$, so this reduces to $\lambda + \mu = 0$. Since the multipliers λ and μ are both constrained to be nonnegative, we have $\lambda = \mu = 0$. Similarly, $\bar{\lambda} = \bar{\mu} = 0$.

Next, $\lambda = 0$ and (15.100) together imply $\rho = 0$. But this in turn implies $D = D^* = 0$. Also, $\rho = 0$ together with (15.115) imply $\lambda^* = 0$. And then (15.113) plus symmetry imply $\frac{1}{p} = \Pi_1 + \lambda^* + \mu^* = \Pi_1$, so we have $p = \frac{1}{\Pi_1} = \bar{p}$. And then (15.98) (with $\lambda = \mu = 0$) gives $\sqrt{\frac{a-q}{b}} = \Pi_1 \sqrt{\bar{p}} = \sqrt{\Pi_1}$, which in turn gives

$$q = a - \Pi_1 b. \tag{15.120}$$

The next piece is to obtain an expression for b. This will be a somewhat long, tedious process. We begin by working with the budget constraint for the Type 1 traders: $\frac{d}{1+\rho} - b - b_3 + pq - d + p_3 q_3 + D \geq 0$. Substituting $\rho = 0$, $q_3 = 0$, and $D = 0$ yields $pq - b - b_3 \geq 0$. But by balancing condition (a) $pq - b = \bar{p}q - \bar{b} = b_1^*$, so we have

$$b_1^* - b_3 \geq 0. \tag{15.121}$$

But also, the budget constraint for the merchants is $\frac{d^*}{1+\rho} - b_1^* - b_2^* - b_3^* - d^* + p_3 q_3^* + D^* \geq 0$. Substituting $\rho = 0$, $b_3^* = 0$, and $D^* = 0$ yields

$p_3 q_3^* - b_1^* - b_2^* \geq 0$, which (by symmetry) is $p_3 q_3^* - 2b_1^* \geq 0$. But by balancing condition (c) (plus the assumptions $q_3 = \bar{q}_3 = b_3^* = 0$ and symmetry) we have $p_3 q_3^* = 2b_3$, and so $2b_3 - 2b_1^* \geq 0$. But this and (15.121) together imply

$$b_1^* = b_3. \tag{15.122}$$

Now look at the cash-flow constraint for the merchants. We assumed it was tight; that is, $\frac{d^*}{1+\rho} - b_1^* - b_2^* - b_3^* = 0$. Substituting in $\rho = 0$ and $b_3^* = 0$ and using symmetry gives $d^* - 2b_1^* = 0$, or $b_1^* = \frac{d^*}{2}$. But balancing condition (d) (with $\rho = 0$) gives $d^* = G - d - \bar{d} = G - 2d$; hence $b_1^* = \frac{G-2d}{2} = \frac{G}{2} - d = \frac{G}{2} - b - b_3 = \frac{G}{2} - b - b_1^*$. (In the previous chain of equalities, the penultimate equality follows from the tight Type 1 trader's cash-flow constraint (together with $\rho = 0$), while the last equality follows from (15.122).) Combining the "b_1^*" terms, we have $2b_1^* = \frac{G}{2} - b$, or

$$b_1^* = \frac{G}{4} - \frac{b}{2}. \tag{15.123}$$

Now we are finally in a position to obtain our expression for b. We start with balancing condition (a), which is $pq = b + b_1^*$. Substituting in our expressions $p = \frac{1}{\Pi_1}$, equation (15.120) for q, and (15.123) for b_1^*, we have $\frac{a - \Pi_1 b}{\Pi_1} = b + \frac{G}{4} - \frac{b}{2}$, which solves with $b = \frac{4a - \Pi_1 G}{6\Pi_1} = \bar{b}$.

The rest of the variables can now be easily obtained. First, using (15.123), we have $b_1^* = \frac{G}{4} - \frac{b}{2} = \frac{G}{4} - \frac{a}{3\Pi_1} + \frac{G}{12} = \frac{\Pi_1 G - a}{3\Pi_1} = b_2^*$. Because of (15.122), we also immediately have $b_3 = \frac{\Pi_1 G - a}{3\Pi_1} = \bar{b}_3$. Next, $q = a - \Pi_1 b = a - \Pi_1 \left(\frac{4a - \Pi_1 G}{6\Pi_1} \right) = \frac{2a + \Pi_1 G}{6} = \bar{q}$. Then $d^* = 2b_1^* = \frac{2(\Pi_1 G - a)}{3\Pi_1}$. And $d = \frac{G - d^*}{2} = \frac{\Pi_1 G + 2a}{6\Pi_1} = \bar{d}$. And finally $q_3^* = \frac{2b_3}{p_3} = \frac{2(\Pi_1 G - a)}{3(1 + \Pi_2)}$. For completeness, we also list all of the other values previously found: $p = \frac{1}{\Pi_1} = \bar{p}$, $p_3 = \frac{1 + \Pi_2}{\Pi_1}$, and $\rho = D = D^* = \lambda = \bar{\lambda} = \mu = \bar{\mu} = \lambda^* = \mu^* = 0$.

Last, we should state the values over which our calculations are valid. First, all of the calculated expressions for the variables above must be nonnegative; this requires $a \leq \Pi_1 G \leq 4a$. Second, the above value for q_3^* must be less than or equal to B, that is, $\frac{2(\Pi_1 G - a)}{3(1 + \Pi_2)} \leq B$.

Case 2: m small, G small. Now we consider what happens when $\Pi_1 G < a$. In this case we assume cash-flow and budget constraints for both traders and merchants are all tight; that is, the multipliers λ, $\bar{\lambda}$, μ, $\bar{\mu}$, λ^*, and μ^* are all positive. The values of q_3^*, b_3, and $\bar{b}_3$ from Case 1 (from the boundary case $\Pi_1 G = a$) lead us to assume the gold trade market shuts down; that is, in addition to our previous assumptions of $q_3 = \bar{q}_3 = 0$ and $b_3^* = 0$, we have $q_3^* = b_3 = \bar{b}_3 = 0$.

Our analysis begins with equation (15.98), namely $\frac{1}{\sqrt{\hat{p}}}\sqrt{\frac{a-q}{b}} = \Pi_1 + \lambda + \mu$. Substituting in for λ using (15.100) yields $\frac{1}{\sqrt{\hat{p}}}\sqrt{\frac{a-q}{b}} = (1+\rho)(\Pi_1 + \mu)$. But then substituting in for $\Pi_1 + \mu$ using (15.99) gives $\frac{1}{\sqrt{\hat{p}}}\sqrt{\frac{a-q}{b}} = (1 + \rho)\frac{1}{p\sqrt{\hat{p}}}\sqrt{\frac{b}{a-q}}$. Using symmetry $\bar{p} = p$ results in

$$p\left(\frac{a-q}{b}\right) = 1 + \rho. \tag{15.124}$$

Next, the balancing constraint for price is $b = pq - b_1^*$. But the tight (λ^*) constraint, together with $b_3^* = 0$ and symmetry $b_1^* = b_2^*$, yields $b_1^* = \frac{d^*}{2(1+\rho)}$; substituting this in the previous expression for b gives $b = pq - \frac{d^*}{2(1+\rho)}$. But the tight (λ) constraint implies $b = \frac{d}{1+\rho}$; setting the last two expressions for b equal gives $pq - \frac{d^*}{2(1+\rho)} = \frac{d}{1+\rho}$. This can be rearranged to read

$$q = \frac{d^* + 2d}{2p(1+\rho)}. \tag{15.125}$$

In addition, we may rewrite (15.124) as $\frac{p(a-q)}{1+\rho} = b = \frac{d}{1+\rho}$, so $d = ap - pq = ap - \frac{d^*+2d}{2(1+\rho)}$, which gives

$$ap = d + \frac{d^* + 2d}{2(1+\rho)}. \tag{15.126}$$

Next, the tight cash-flow and budget constraints for the merchants together imply that $-d^* + p_3 q_3^* + D^* = 0$. Now q_3^* is assumed to be zero, and D^* is equal to $\frac{B}{B+2m}\rho G$, so this reduces to $d^* = \frac{B}{B+2m}\rho G$. Next, the balance constraint for the interest rate implies that $d = \frac{(1+\rho)G - d^*}{2}$. Substituting in our previous expression for d^*, this simplifies to $d = \frac{(1+\rho)G - \frac{B}{B+2m}\rho G}{2} = \frac{G}{2} + \frac{m}{B+2m}\rho G$. Hence, $d^* + 2d = (1 + \rho)G$, and our previous expressions (15.126) and (15.125) for p and q reduce to $p = \frac{2d+G}{2a}$ and $q = \frac{G}{2p} = \frac{aG}{2d+G}$, respectively. In addition, substituting in $d = \frac{G}{2} + \frac{m}{B+2m}\rho G$ yields $p = \frac{1}{a}\left(G + \frac{m}{B+2m}\rho G\right) = \bar{p}$ and $q = \frac{a}{2}\left(\frac{B+2m}{B+2m+m\rho}\right) = \bar{q}$. We also have $b = \bar{b} = \frac{d}{1+\rho} = \frac{1}{1+\rho}\left(\frac{G}{2} + \frac{m}{B+2m}\rho G\right)$ and $b_1^* = b_2^* = \frac{d^*}{2(1+\rho)} = \frac{B}{B+2m}\frac{\rho G}{2(1+\rho)}$.

Note that we have a degree of freedom in our solutions here, as all of our variables are in terms of ρ.

Finally, we obtain expressions for the multipliers. First, from (15.99) we have $\mu = \frac{1}{p\sqrt{p}}\sqrt{\frac{b}{a-q}} - \Pi_1 = \left(\frac{2a}{2d+G}\right)^{\frac{3}{2}}\sqrt{\frac{d/(1+\rho)}{a-\frac{aG}{2d+G}}} = \frac{a}{2d+G}\frac{2}{\sqrt{1+\rho}} - \Pi_1 = \frac{a}{\sqrt{1+\rho}\left(G+\frac{m}{B+2m}\rho G\right)} - \Pi_1 = \bar{\mu}$. We also have $\lambda = (\mu + \Pi_1)\rho = \frac{a\rho}{\sqrt{1+\rho}\left(G+\frac{m}{B+2m}\rho G\right)} = \bar{\lambda}$. To find μ^* and λ^*, we need to solve the two equations in two unknowns given by (15.114) and (15.115). First, (15.115) gives us $\lambda^* = (\Pi_1 + \mu^*)\rho$. Substituting this expression for λ^* into (15.114) and using symmetry, we have $\frac{1}{p} = (1+\rho)(\Pi_1 + \mu^*)$, or $\mu^* = \frac{1}{(1+\rho)p} - \Pi_1 = \frac{a}{(1+\rho)\left(G+\frac{m}{B+2m}\rho G\right)} - \Pi_1$. Then $\lambda^* = (\Pi_1 + \mu^*)\rho = \frac{a\rho}{(1+\rho)\left(G+\frac{m}{B+2m}\rho G\right)}$.

In order for the results to be valid, ρ must be nonnegative, and the above expressions for the multipliers μ and μ^* must also be nonnegative. Looking closely at these, we see that there will be a range for ρ, with zero as the lower bound and the upper bound as the value of ρ for which $(1+\rho)\left(G+\frac{m}{B+2m}\rho G\right)$ is equal to $\frac{a}{\Pi_1}$. This range will be nonempty so long as $\Pi_1 G \leq a$.

Chapter 16 Multiperiod Models of Trade

16.1 INTRODUCTION

Although many monetary phenomena can be illustrated using one-period models, many of the features of a monetary economy are intrinsically dynamic. Hence, in this chapter the models are multiperiod. We illustrate the variation of the money supply and the financing by the transaction technology over time.

16.2 THE FLOAT AND THE "ANTI-FLOAT"

Transactions involve time, resources, and money. The role of time and other resources involved in the activity of exchange must be covered in a complete theory of exchange. One well-known issue caused by money and credit in transit is the "float." As defined by the New York Federal Reserve, float occurs when payment for checks is received before said checks are processed, thereby resulting in a brief period of time when (owing to time delays in the accounting) an extra asset is on hand.[1]

In our models, we are concerned with a dual problem to this, which one could call "anti-float." Traders wish to pay for goods with cash earned from selling their endowments—except they cannot do this because the earned cash comes in *after* the bill is due for the goods bought. Hence, there is a brief period of time when there is a *shortage* of cash asset. In the various dynamic models since the 1970s this has been often associated with a cash-in-advance condition. Clower suggested the importance of such a condition in 1967. Lucas (1978), Shubik and Whitt (1973), and many others have also utilized cash-in-advance, modeled as a one-period lag. The logic behind any process model of exchange utilizing some form of money or credit requires that a money or credit instrument is tied up during the exchange (Shapley and Shubik, 1977), because market prices are formed, not given. In actual economic life the length of the lag varies considerably. There are possible lags in the delivery of both money and goods. Here, for simplicity, we assume that the goods traded arrive in time to be utilized in the same period in which they are traded.[2]

---

1 Here is the actual definition given by the Federal Reserve:

> Float is money in the banking system that is counted twice, for a brief time, because of delays in processing checks. Float distorts the measurement of the money supply and complicates the implementation of monetary policy.
>
> Federal Reserve float is money that appears simultaneously in the Federal Reserve accounts of two depository institutions. These institutions include commercial banks, savings and loans, savings banks, and credit unions, but are widely referred to as banks. When check clearing is delayed, funds in the process of collection appear in the accounts of both the institutions that receive the checks for deposit and the institutions upon which the checks are drawn. Thus, float inflates, for a brief time, the amount of money in the banking system.
>
> Businesses and individuals deposit millions of checks at banks every day. When a bank receives a check for deposit, it provisionally credits the account of the check depositor and later collects the funds from the bank upon which the check is drawn. Rather than sort all the checks and send each one back to the bank it was drawn upon for settlement, depository institutions transfer many of their checks to Federal Reserve Banks for collection. In turn, Reserve Banks pay the depositing banks for the total amount of the checks, and then collect the funds from the banks on which the checks are drawn. The Federal Reserve processes about one-third of all checks in the United States. For 2000, this amounted to 17 billion checks, or roughly 68 million per business day.

2 In fact, lags in delivery of goods could be much larger.

A critical feature of a modern monetary system is that an intermediating device is inserted between the parties to almost all trades. This device is molded by custom and law and provides the loose control mechanism of the financial system over the physical economy.

16.3 SOME MODELING CONSIDERATIONS

The one-period trading models of the previous chapters are now generalized to multiperiod trade with a finite horizon. Care is required to be specific in the treatment of initial and terminal conditions.

16.3.1 The Proliferation of Models

Whenever process models involving more than a single move per person are considered, the proliferation of institutional structures becomes enormous. Following is a taxonomy of modeling options, together with a selection of specific models to analyze. The choices made in this book are marked with an asterisk, "*." We also indicate reasons for the choices in the following text.

The agents
Types: (1) traders,* (2) central bank,* (3) other banks.*
Numbers: traders $1, 2, n$, continuum;* central bank 0^*, $1;^*$ other banks $0,^* 1,^* n,^* \infty^*$.

Type of money
(1) commodity money (storable consumable) "barley,"* (2) commodity money (durable) "gold,"* (3) fiat money,* (4) credit.*

Time
(1) continuous, (2) discrete with fixed grid,* (3) event time.
If time is discrete, then is the grid size cardinal with second, minute, hour, day, week, month,* quarter, earth year,* or other time division considered?

Length of time
(1) 1 period,* (2) T periods,* (3) ∞ periods.*

Future discount
(1) no time discount,* (2) $0 < \beta < 1.^*$

Initial conditions
(1) current state only,* (2) one previous period of history, (3) several periods of history.

Life of agents

traders (1) ∞ (dynasty),* (2) overlapping generations, with life cycle indicated;* central bank ∞.*

Inheritance?

(1) yes,* (2) no.*

Taxation?

(1) taxation, (2) no taxation.*

Nature of goods

(1) perishables,* (2) durables, (3) storable consumables.

Terminal rules and salvage values

(1) "settlement day" valueless,* (2) "bite-the-tail,"*3 (3) general expectations.*

Solution dynamics

(1) stationary state,* (2) growth (3) cycle,* (4) random element.

Production

(1) yes, (2) no.*

With the thirteen categories noted, there are many thousands of different models that could be constructed. A problem that confronts economic model building, more as an art form than as a science, is knowing when an extra parameter, variable, or change in the structure of a functional form is critical to the answering of the questions posed. In our analysis only a few models have been selected and analyzed in order to illustrate some of the properties of money and monetary control.

16.3.2 Modeling More Than One Period

Our previous analysis of one-period models may be regarded as clearing away a conceptual underbrush concerning different monies, in order to be able to examine the ability of a central bank to control an exchange economy over time.

Our multiperiod models all use discrete time in regular intervals. The unit of time is not specified, but even casual empiricism indicates that the majority of payment lags lie within thirty days, with physical delivery and production lags sometimes possibly longer. In both microeconomic and macroeconomic

---

3 This is the requirement that terminal conditions equal initial conditions hence the phrase "bite the tail" for stationary state conditions.

affairs the tax year (often the same as the calendar year) is an important unit of time.

We consider models of an arbitrary length of T time periods, and comment on the limiting behavior of solutions as $T \to \infty$. The models in this chapter all have a time discount of β per period; one could posit a model with no time discount by setting $\beta = 1$, and considering a bounded flow.

The model of the central bank as a legal entity (rather than a natural person) gives the bank a life that lasts at least as long as the time range of the model. We model the lifetimes of agents as infinite in Section 16.4 (so-called *dynasty models*), but in Section 16.5 we assume that their lifetimes last only a set finite number of periods in *overlapping generations models*.

In our models, we consider only a perishable good for our goods market. This is in order to highlight the role of money. The analysis for a mix of perishables, storable consumables, and durables would be far more complicated. New strategic choice would be introduced, a cascade of new conditions would appear, and boundary solutions would proliferate. The actual constraints on the economy would involve the age profile of these assets. Again, we omit these features because many of the time aspects of money can be illustrated without having to introduce these extra difficulties.

A key consideration is how to handle the terminal conditions in a multistage model of finite length. There are at least two basic ways to do this. First, we can assign a zero value to fiat money left over at the end of the game, but permit any such money to be utilized during the $T + 1$st day to discharge any outstanding debts. Hence at the Final Settlement Day (or Day of Reckoning) the money can be of use. The second way involves expectations, and when combined with the analysis of the stationary state can be colloquially called the "bite-the-tail" approach. The idea here is that if there is no growth in the economy, the individuals are expected to end up with exactly their initial monetary resources. In terms of a playable game, a referee requires that at the end of the game each individual must return (to the referee) his or her initial holdings.

In general, we are concerned with noncooperative equilibrium solutions. The overall conditions to be examined include the stationary state, growth, and a cyclical economy. Production, growth, and cycle together with a random component provide the building blocks for the description of any economy; but the stationary state is still of value in illustrating many of the basic problems to be faced in the construction of any process model of the economy. Building the stationary exchange model first facilitates the extension to more complex process models.

16.4 MULTIPERIOD TRADE

16.4.1 Multiperiod Trade with No Loans

Our first multistage economy is one with a fiat money, but with no credit. The fiat has a salvage value at the terminal settlement period. This is examined under the simplest of stationary state conditions.

Suppose there is a (buy-sell) economy with our usual two trader types and two perishable goods. The economy now runs for T periods.

The Type 1 traders are endowed with m units of fiat money at the beginning of the game, as well as a units of good 1 at the beginning of each period. Similarly, the Type 2 traders begin with m units of money plus a units of good 2 at the beginning of each period.

All traders have the same utility function $\varphi(x, y) = 2\sqrt{xy}$ in all periods.

In the T-period economy, payments are made in money at time t $(t = 1, \ldots, T)$, but the payments are not available to be used by the recipient for purchase until time $t + 1$.

Let $q_t =$ the amount of good 1 offered for sale by Type 1 traders in period t where $t = 1, \ldots, T$.

Let $\bar{q}_t =$ the amount of good 2 offered for sale by Type 2 traders in period t where $t = 1, \ldots, T$.

Let $b_t =$ the amount of money bid for purchase of good 2 by Type 1 traders in period t.

Let $\bar{b}_t =$ the amount of money bid for purchase of good 1 by Type 2 traders in period t.

$m_t =$ the amount of money held by Type 1 traders at the start of period t.

$\bar{m}_t =$ the amount of money held by Type 2 traders at the start of period t.

$\beta =$ time discount factor per period.

$\Pi =$ the "spot"[4] salvage value of a unit of leftover fiat money.

The Type 1 individuals face an optimization of the form

$$\max_{b_t, q_t, m_t} \sum_{t=1}^{T} \beta^{t-1} \left(2\sqrt{(a - q_t)\frac{b_t}{\bar{p}_t}} \right) + \beta^T \Pi m_{T+1}$$

---

4 By "spot" salvage value, we mean the salvage value evaluated at the time in question (the end of the game). If the time in question is T time periods in the future, then the present value of the fiat is β^T times its spot value.

s.t. $m_t - b_t \geq 0$, $t = 1, \ldots, T$ (cash-flow constraints) (λ_t)

$\quad m_t = m_{t-1} + p_{t-1} q_{t-1} - b_{t-1}$, $t = 2, \ldots, T+1$ (accounting constraints)

$\quad m_1 = m$

$\quad b_t \geq 0$, $0 \leq q_t \leq a$

We append the extra linear term

$$\beta^T \Pi m_{T+1}$$

to the objective function to represent the value of excess fiat left over after the end of the game. In the constraints, note that we now have "accounting constraints," which keep track of how much money is held by the traders at the beginning of each period, as a function of their activities in the previous period. Finally, note that in the case where $T = 1$, we have a model which is equivalent to the "no-loan market" one-period game of Sections 7.1.4 and 7.3.[5]

There is a similar optimization problem for the Type 2 traders.

Prices are given by:

$$p_t = \frac{\bar{b}_t}{q_t} \text{ and } \bar{p}_t = \frac{b_t}{\bar{q}_t} \; t = 1, \ldots, T.$$

In this first model, there is just a fixed amount of money used as a means of exchange without any loan markets being present. The money finances the (anti)-float at no cost—but to prevent a backward induction that leads to no trade (the Hahn paradox), one requires a positive expectation of the future value of money.

Because there are no loans, it is impossible for traders to bid more money than they have. Hence, default conditions are not needed.

A distinct weakness of this model is that the expectations are presented as fixed and terminal. In fact they are adaptive and evolve over time. The shape of this adaptive process appears to depend on the length of time and the ad hoc aspects of the process under consideration. These call for a blend of institutional understanding together with the acceptance of a socio-psychological theory of game learning. At this time there is no generally accepted theory.

---

5 Note that the "Π" from the Chapter 7 models actually corresponds to "$\beta \Pi$" here. This is because here the Π represents the "spot" salvage value, rather than the present value of fiat one time period in the future.

The more modest goal here is to consider the extreme instance of "what if expectations are given?"

The complete model and its solution is given in Appendix A.

16.4.2 Multiperiod Trade with Loans, ρ Fixed

We modify the previous model by adding an outside bank. The bank is a strategic dummy whose objective is to maintain the interest rate at a given $\rho > 0$. This is one of the ways to avoid the Hahn paradox, and offers a societally economical way to finance the transactions. The traders receive an initial injection of fiat money which is eventually consumed by payments of interest to a government bank. The interest payments arise from the extra borrowing by the traders.

As soon as we introduce the possibility of lending, we need also to introduce default penalties to specify the rules of the game if any individual is unable to repay her loan.

Our model changes as follows. New variables are d_t and $\bar{d}_t$, the amount borrowed in period t by agents of Type 1 and 2, respectively. As before, the variables m_t and $\bar{m}_t$ represent the monetary holdings at the start of period t. However, if these go negative, the default penalty is assessed and they are reset to zero. Hence the optimization for the Type 1 traders becomes:

$$\max_{b_t, q_t, d_t, m_t} \sum_{t=1}^{T} \beta^{t-1} \left(2\sqrt{(a-q_t)\frac{b_t}{p_t}} + \mu^*[m_t]^- \right)$$
$$+ \beta^T (\mu^*[m_{T+1}]^- + \Pi[m_{T+1}]^+)$$

s.t. $[m_t]^+ + \dfrac{d_t}{1+\rho} - b_t \geq 0$ (cash-flow constraints) (λ_t)

$$m_t = [m_{t-1}]^+ + \frac{d_{t-1}}{1+\rho} - b_{t-1} + p_{t-1}q_{t-1} - d_{t-1}$$
(accounting constraints)

$m_1 = m$

$b_t, d_t \geq 0, 0 \leq q_t \leq a.$

We append the extra term for the settlement day $T+1$

$$\beta^T (\mu^*[m_{T+1}]^- + \Pi[m_{T+1}]^+)$$

to cover both bankruptcy and expected salvage value. The notation $[x]^+$ means $\max(x,0)$, while the notation $[x]^-$ means $\min(x,0)$.

A practical problem in multiperiod finance is the possibility of a Ponzi game, where at the start of a period when last period's loan is due, it is paid back by borrowing more. In the model presented above we have not permitted a Ponzi game, because at the start of any period an individual who is in debt cannot borrow again before she has either: (a) repaid the current debt, or (b) declared bankruptcy and paid the default penalty.

To change the model to allow a Ponzi game, one would simply: (a) remove the $\mu^*[m_t]^-$ terms (for periods $t = 1, \ldots, T$, but not for $t = T + 1$) from the objective function; and (b) replace the "$[m_{t-1}]^+$" and "$[m_t]^+$" terms in the constraints with "m_{t-1}" and "m_t," respectively. Note that the variables m_t would still be allowed to go negative.

In Appendix B we model a *non*-Ponzi game, in the special case where μ^* is very high. This specification for μ^* implies that the traders will never default, and so the variables m_t are nonnegative. This implies that the terms $[m_t]^-$ are all 0, and $[m_t]^+ = m_t$ for all t. The upshot is that the Type 1 traders' optimization problem reduces to

$$\max_{b_t, q_t, d_t, m_t} \sum_{t=1}^{T} \beta^{t-1} \left(2\sqrt{(a - q_t)\frac{b_t}{p_t}} \right) + \beta^T \Pi m_{T+1}$$

$$\text{s.t. } m_t + \frac{d_t}{1+\rho} - b_t \geq 0, \; t = 1, \ldots, T \text{ (cash-flow constraints) } (\lambda_t)$$

$$m_t = m_{t-1} + \frac{d_{t-1}}{1+\rho} - b_{t-1} + p_{t-1} q_{t-1} - d_{t-1}, \; t = 2, \ldots, T+1$$

$$\text{(accounting constraints)}$$

$$m_1 = m$$

$$b_t, d_t, m_t \geq 0, \; 0 \leq q_t \leq a.$$

Note the nonnegativity of the m_t's. The Type 2 traders have a similar problem.

Even with this simplification, there are still far too many cases to consider separately. In Appendix B, we consider two cases: one where m is large, and one where m is very small and $\Pi = 0$. In the first case we obtain our usual efficient consumption; in the second we get $q_t = \bar{q}_t = \frac{a}{2+\rho}$, plus geometrically changing bids and prices. Again, see Appendix B for details.

In Appendix C we present the sell-all version of this model, which illustrates considerable differences in cash flows as compared with buy-sell.

16.4.3 Multiperiod Trade with Loans, *g* Fixed

We reconsider the model above, where instead of utilizing the bank rate ρ as the control variable, the bank simply names the amount g to lend, where $0 \leq g \leq B$.

When the solutions are interior, the ρ and g are easily identifiable dual variables—using one will yield the other. However, if we have boundary- or capacity-constrained solutions the behavior is far more complex and requires many cases. We omit these calculations, remarking that they would resemble many of the detailed analyses done in some of our single-period models.

One more difference between this and the model with ρ fixed is that here, since it is endogenous, the interest rate can vary as $T \to \infty$.

16.4.4 Some Welfare Criteria

What conditions are desirable properties of a multiperiod monetary economy?

EFFICIENCY AND STATIONARITY

An important property is efficiency; but as soon as the interest rate is positive there is a wedge formed between buying and selling prices that destroys Pareto efficiency. If the money rate of interest is zero, a dynasty economy cannot be in a stationary state equilibrium—any small trader would be made better off by borrowing for consumption now. In an overlapping generations model an efficient stationary equilibrium is achieved with $\rho = 0$. But with $\rho = 0$ coordination is lost and the price of money alone does not serve as a decentralized rationing device.

For there to be a fixed price level in a dynasty economy, we must have $1 + \rho = \frac{1}{\beta}$, where β is the natural discount rate, which can be interpreted as an intergenerational welfare link.

CASH CONSUMPTION OR CONSTANT EXPECTATIONS

When we consider a multistage finite economy, we must specify the terminal conditions before any solution can be obtained. There are two ways to do so. One has the economy consume the initial amount of outside money if $\rho > 0$, while the other requires constant expectations that the marginal value of utility of money at salvage equals its marginal value during transactions. In the former the terminal amount of outside money is zero, and the system is never in a stationary state—although it approaches such a state as $T \to \infty$. In the latter the terminal amount of outside money equals the initial amount in the system, so the system is always in a stationary state (even if T is finite). It is as though the system is timeless.

DEFAULT AND TRUTH REVELATION

As soon as borrowing is a strategic option, one must specify not only default rules but also conditions concerning information and enforcement.

At repayment time, does the borrower have the opportunity to conceal assets, or are they known to the creditor without costly inspection? Is enforcement of contract costless? Here these problems are noted, but not analyzed. We observe, however, that this enforcement of contract is one of the basic tasks of a government bureaucracy (see Smith and Shubik, 2011).

COORDINATION AND SIGNALING?

One view of the financial system and the rules governing its operation is that it serves as a coordinating device to facilitate individual choice. The selection of default conditions implicitly selects among potentially multiple equilibria (see Qin and Shubik, 2012).

16.4.5 Other Models

The above model fits into the category of "a dynasty model with no production." This suggests three other possible models, or four in all: (1) overlapping generations without production; (2) overlapping generations with production; (3) a dynasty model without production; and (4) a dynasty model with production.

In the first (with a stationary population) the interperiod discount is 0 and the stationary money rate of interest will be $\rho = 0$; in the second the rate will be related to productive growth rate of the economy; in the third the interperiod real discount is β and the stationary interest rate satisfies $1 + \rho = \frac{1}{\beta}$. In the fourth there is a clash between the real discount and the growth rate. In an economy with a fixed money supply, no credit and a fixed velocity of transactions deflation can be achieved only by hoarding and inflation is bounded by the money supply.

In the next section we briefly investigate an overlapping generations model.

16.5 THE OVERLAPPING GENERATIONS MODEL

In the above models, we considered the financing of trade with an infinitely lived agent, who can be interpreted as a dynasty. Here we discuss the additional complexities introduced by an overlapping generations (OLG) model. As is well known, in dynasty models the time discount β plays a decisive role in interaction with the money rate of interest. The stationary state occurs when $1 + \rho = \frac{1}{\beta}$. A critical feature of the OLG model is that the β does not play a key role, as it no longer reflects a societal future discount. But it is reflected in each period of a stationary state as a standing wave. The stationary state simply calls for $\rho = 0$.

When we consider an OLG model with a finite expected life span for each individual, we are required to specify how intergenerational transfers are made. If it is feasible for individuals to die while in the possession of assets, we must specify the disposition of the assets. Edgeworth (1932) introduced a θ he called "the coefficient of concern," which described this intergenerational link in preferences.

Staying close to our previous models, we may consider a simple one-good, two-ages OLG model with $\theta = 0$ (no bequest motive). Cohorts are each endowed with goods but no money when they are young $(a, 0)$. Then, when they are old, they have only the money earned from selling the good when they were young. In both periods, their spot utility from consuming x is $2\sqrt{x}$, and there is an individual discount factor of β. It is straightforward to write the cohort's lifetime optimization problem as $\max_{0 \leq q \leq a} 2\sqrt{a - q} + 2\beta\sqrt{q}$, where q is the amount of good the young put up for sale. Solving this, we obtain a stationary equilibrium in which they consume $\frac{a}{1+\beta^2}$ when they are young (putting up $\frac{\beta^2 a}{1+\beta^2}$ for sale) and consume $\frac{\beta^2 a}{1+\beta^2}$ when they are old.

The above model exhibits only stationary behavior, with no need to vary the money supply. To construct an example in which this happens, we would need to introduce cyclical endowments, along the lines of the three-period cyclical dynasty models presented in Section 16.6.

COMMENTS ON GROWTH AND PRODUCTION

The study of production as evinced by Ramsey (1928), von Neumann (1945), and others (e.g., for example Kaneko, 1992) has shown that in a one- or higher-dimensional linear structure, the money rate of interest will equal the optimal growth rate. This is also reflected in the macroeconomic growth literature (Phelps, 2007). Thus in an economy with utility function homogeneous of order 1, with population growing at the same rate as production, the growth in the money supply will be the same as the physical linear growth. In other words, the real and monetary rates of interest are equal.

We do not consider production further here.[6] To do full justice to production would require the consideration of capital goods of different vintages and

---

6 For a discussion of this type of model with production and an interest rate, see Shubik (2011, chs. 3, 4).

production processes of different lengths. It is here that the details of financing proliferate.

16.6 VARYING THE MONEY SUPPLY: A MODEL WITH CYCLICAL ENDOWMENTS

In the previous sections we have focused on a stationary real economy. The analysis (see Appendixes B and C) demonstrates the three monetary phenomena of increasing, decreasing, and unchanging prices. But in order to exhibit nonmonotonic price variation (that is, a nonmonotonic or "varying" money supply), we need to add a new feature, namely, cyclical endowments of the perishable over time.

16.6.1 Choosing a Model

To model the variation of the money supply over time, we had originally intended to utilize our usual two-commodity, two-trader-type model. However, the essence of our investigation has already been provided by Bennie (2006), using a dynamic programming approach to a somewhat simpler sell-all model with one trader type and one commodity. Hence we summarize and comment on her results here.

16.6.2 A Cycle without Banking

Bennie (2006) considers an infinite horizon, cyclical sell-all dynasty economy, in which each cycle has a length of k periods. There is a set I of agents, assumed to lie on a continuum. Each agent $\alpha \in I$ has an initial monetary endowment m^α, an endowment d_t^α of some good in period t, as well as a spot utility function u which is constant over all time periods and all agents. Then, if agent α consumes x_t^α in period t, his valuation is $\sum_{t=1}^{\infty} \beta^{t-1} u(x_t^\alpha)$. The amounts of good available $a_t = \int d_t^\alpha$ is cyclical, that is, given by $a_1, a_2, \ldots a_k, a_1, a_2, \ldots$ in period $1, 2, \ldots, k, k+1, k+2, \ldots$.[7] Finally, define M as the total amount of money in the economy, that is, $M = m = \int m^\alpha$.

In each period, the players' strategies are to make bids b_t^α, from which prices are formed using the usual strategic market game mechanism. Consumption amounts and hence utility payoffs can then be determined.

---

7 Our endowments here are deterministic—hence, this can be regarded as a special case of Bennie's (2006) treatment, in which she assumes endowments are random variables.

Without loss of generality, we may assume that the maximum usage of money occurs during the last period of the cycle; that is,

$$a_k u'(a_k) = \max_{j \in \{1,2,\ldots,k\}} [a_j u'(a_j)].$$

(At this maximum the sum of all bids must equal the total money supply, as an equilibrium cannot exist with hoarding by all individuals in every period.) Then equilibrium strategies are given by: first, set $b_k^* = M$. "Working backward from k for each fixed value of $i \in \{1, 2, \ldots, k-1\}$, if

$$\frac{a_i u'(a_i)}{a_j u'(a_j)} \geq \beta^{j(i)-i} \text{ for all } j \in \{i+1, \ldots, k\}$$

define $b_i^* = M$. Otherwise, define

$$b_i^* = \frac{M}{\beta^{j(i)-i}} \cdot \frac{a_i u'(a_i)}{a_{j(i)} u'(a_{j(i)})},$$

where $j(i)$ is the first value in $\{i+1, \ldots, k\}$ such that $b_i^* = M$"(Bennie, 2006, p. 16).

A simple example is given with $k=3$ and $(a_1, a_2, a_3) = (1, 4, 9)$, $u(x) = 2\sqrt{x}$, $M = 9$, and $\beta = 0.8$. It is straightforward to check that the three bids are $(\frac{75}{16}, \frac{15}{2}, 9)$; thus the hoarding is $(\frac{69}{16}, \frac{3}{2}, 0)$ and spot prices are $(\frac{75}{16}, \frac{15}{8}, 1)$. These quantities cycle over and over.

The key element is the elasticity of wealth—hence if instead $u(x) = \log(x)$ there would be no hoarding, as the transactions demand for money would be constant regardless of endowments.

Finally, we note that in this model there is still no variation in the money supply because the same monies circulate among the traders. To get a variation in the money supply, we need to introduce banking into the model. We do this next.

16.6.3 A Cycle with Banking and an Exogenous Interest Rate

We now introduce a bank which charges an interest rate of ρ on loans and gives an interest rate of ρ on deposits.

When an outside bank is introduced, the market adjusts with borrowing during periods of high economic activity and depositing during periods of low activity—if expectations are sufficiently high, equilibrium spot prices are stationary. Hoarding is replaced by this borrowing and lending.

Mathematically, the traders' cash-flow constraints are tight. (The exception here is if $\rho = 0$, where hoarding cannot be distinguished from saving or depositing—the model requires considerable care to make sure it is well defined at that point.)

With a bank, the amount of money in the whole system (i.e., the money held by the traders plus the monetary resources of the central bank) is no longer necessarily fixed. It depends delicately on how the rules of bank operation are specified, in particular whether the bank can create money or is constrained to lending specific initial reserves.

If the bank is limited to existing reserves of, say B, then we are in the "fixed amount of money" case. The total money supply in the system is a constant $M = m + B$, but the supply in the goods markets can be variable, as money flows into and out of the bank.

On the other hand, if the bank is permitted to issue more money, then the amount in the overall system can vary. The amount of money held by the agents in period i is denoted by m_i, and M_i denotes the total amount of money in the system at that time. The definition of what constitutes reserves is more of a statement about the size of a strategy set of the bank than about physical quantities of gold or some other substance.

Bennie (2006, pp. 27–38) solved the cyclical model with banking generally to include the possibility of the creation of extra money and the existence of inflation or deflation. In order to do so, a variable γ_i (for $i \in \{1, 2, \ldots, k\}$) is defined:

$$\gamma_i = \frac{(1 + \rho)(1 - \beta^k)u'(a_i)}{\rho \sum_{j=0}^{k-1} u'(a_{i+j})a_{i+j}\beta^j}.$$

She then establishes that there is an equilibrium set of strategies where each agent bids $b_i = \gamma_i m_i$, where $m_{i+1} = \tau_i m_i$ and $\tau_i = 1 + \rho - \rho\gamma_i$. Here m_i is as defined above.[8] Prices are given by $p_i = \frac{b_i}{a_i} = \frac{\gamma_i m_i}{a_i}$. In general the system can be inflationary or deflationary, but the money supply and prices will be periodic if

$$\prod_{i=1}^{k} \tau_i = 1$$

---

8 Bennie's notation for our "m_i" is "M_i."

However, if $1 + \rho = \frac{1}{\beta}$, we have

$$\prod_{i=1}^{k} \tau_i = \prod_{i=1}^{k} (1 + \rho)\beta \frac{\gamma_i}{\gamma_{i+1}} \frac{u'(a_{i+1})a_{i+1}}{u'(a_i)a_i} = (1 + \rho)^k \beta^k = 1,$$

so indeed $1 + \rho = \frac{1}{\beta}$ implies periodicity.

Continuing our example from the previous section with $\beta = 0.8$, we again suppose the traders start with nine units of money, but now there is a bank (with a high amount of reserves) which charges an interest rate of $\rho = 0.25$ on loans. Hence we are in the $1 + \rho = \frac{1}{\beta}$ (periodic) case. We obtain $(\gamma_1, \gamma_2, \gamma_3) = (\frac{61}{113}, \frac{61}{63}, \frac{183}{127})$, $(\tau_1, \tau_2, \tau_3) = (\frac{126}{113}, \frac{127}{126}, \frac{113}{127})$, $(m_1, m_2, m_3) = (9, \frac{1134}{113}, \frac{1143}{113})$, $(b_1, b_2, b_3) = (\frac{549}{113}, \frac{1098}{113}, \frac{1647}{113})$, and $(p_1, p_2, p_3) = (\frac{549}{113}, \frac{549}{226}, \frac{183}{113})$. All of these quantities are cyclic, repeating with a period of 3.

16.6.4 The Role of the Default Rule

In the model of the previous section, by solving for the infinite horizon and ignoring default, some details were left out. The price level is determined by the parameters ρ, m, and β. However, if we include a default parameter μ^* this establishes a lower bound on the price level for an economy beyond which strategic bankruptcy will occur. As the price level drops, the marginal value of an extra unit of money increases. When the price level is low enough it will exceed μ^*, at which point strategic bankruptcy becomes attractive.

We note that there will be an interaction between the bankruptcy penalty and inflation. A rise in the interest rate increases inflation; hence if the penalty is not adjusted at the same speed as inflation it will influence strategic behavior as a function of length of the loan.

16.6.5 Cycles and Perfect Foresight

The assumption implicit in an economy with a cycle is that the agents know the cycle. But that is tantamount to indicating that they can gaze accurately into any finite future. For example, if the cycle were a billion years long the individuals would be expected to handle any arbitrary series with a billion terms. In economic fact, most individuals do have a well-defined concept of such cyclical influences as adjusting for the seasons or leap year or elections.

But even though an existence proof can hold for any finite cycle, practically speaking it would be unreasonable to imagine that even for a sixty-year cycle anyone would carry in memory a sixty-point series.[9]

16.7 COMMENTS ON UNCERTAINTY

Many of the basic problems in considering an adequate theory of money and financial institutions depend explicitly on some form of exogenous uncertainty in the economy. However, introducing uncertainty makes computation of even relatively simple examples difficult. One approach is via parallel dynamic programming with a continuum of agents (Karatzas, Shubik, and Sudderth, 1994; Lucas, 1978; Shubik and Whitt, 1973). We do not deal formally here with uncertainty; however, we make some observations.

There is a considerable difference between stochastic models with a representative agent and models with individual agents. In the latter the wealth distribution of the society appears—illustrating that the representative agent models can be highly misleading because they impose a symmetry on the model where no symmetry exists. Policies such as managing the national debt by taxation or increasing the issue (Barro, 1974), which appear neutral under representative agent models, are not neutral if the economy generates a skewed wealth distribution. The main reason for utilizing representative agent models is that generally, the individual agent models are highly intractable.

One encounters a purely mathematical intimation of the difficulties in controlling a monetary economy when one tries to mathematize a strategic market game model with exogenous uncertainty. With no uncertainty, there is a well-known intimate relationship between the Lagrangian multipliers in a general equilibrium model of exchange and the marginal utility of income. Even considering an exchange economy as a game with the option of strategic default, the bankruptcy penalties sufficient to prevent such default are coincidental with the Lagrangians, given the selection of a numeraire. If there are n individuals in the economy, Qin and Shubik (2012) showed, by the appropriate selection of numeraire and individual bankruptcy penalties, a

---

9 Even if one knew that the series repeated every sixty years, it is as though the individual faces a pseudo-random variable that repeats after sixty terms.

unique competitive equilibrium point may be selected; but this requires fixing $n + 1$ parameters, the numeraire, and n individual default penalties. In actuality, such fine-tuning does not exist in a society, although one can view individual legal processes as offering some hand-tailoring of the settlements. When exogenous uncertainty is introduced, say, with s possible states, the ideal selection of penalties to avoid strategic default would require $ns + 1$ parameters. Such fine-tuning is administratively and informationally out of the question. An alternative is to have just one Draconian penalty.

On further reflection, the introduction of exogenous uncertainty poses several new problems. With incomplete markets, the strength of a default penalty becomes a public good. A truly punitive penalty may cut off all borrowing, while no penalty may wipe out lending. An intermediate penalty will have some level of active bankruptcy. The exact level becomes a matter of public choice, depending on society's willingness to encourage risk-taking by its individual members (see Shubik, 1999a, chs. 11, 12).

A considerable source of risk-taking in a modern economy is in innovation. With innovation, the original status quo is destroyed; and if successful, the system proceeds to a more desirable level. If the invention fails, the environment must reallocate the residual resources. In bankruptcy proceedings physical resources do not disappear, rather they are reallocated. A society implicitly chooses the level of innovation it wishes to pay for by setting its bankruptcy and reorganization rules.

In contrast to the static spirit of general equilibrium theory, Schumpeter (1911, 1934) stressed innovation, dynamics, and what he termed as the "breaking of the circular flow of funds" in a money-using capitalist society. His highly attractive ideas have eluded mathematization using general equilibrium theory, because they call for a fully dynamic monetary model of the economy. In a formal process model of cost reduction, Shubik and Sudderth (2011) showed that even with a single random event the length of time required for a system to settle down to a new equilibrium, after an innovation has disturbed the initial conditions, is arbitrary. When there is a stream of random variables in the system, one may construct plausible models in which even though the system eventually attains an equilibrium it is impossible to predict where, because it is path-dependent (see Arthur 1994). These results suggest that the monetary control of a symbolic money utilizing economy with uncertainty is quite delicate. Comments on innovation and mutation are made in Chapter 17.

16.8 FINANCE, CONTROL, AND THE MATHEMATICS
OF BOUNDARY CONDITIONS

Many of the models of microeconomics and finance are based on competitive markets, usually solved with interior solutions. If utility (and production) functions can be reasonably well approximated by smooth functions, they are well suited for analyzing the equilibrium aspects of supply and demand. Little insight is provided about nonequilibrium behavior. Money and financial institutions have been designed (for the most part in an evolutionary way) to deal with the evaluation, control, and guidance of economic systems.

As soon as one is required to specify a fully dynamic model, one has to model institutions implicitly or explicitly, because one needs to specify the process and the carriers of process. Institutions are the carriers of process. In this book, we have modeled various forms of money and credit and the way they are utilized. Goods markets, the money market, and the central bank have been implicitly or explicitly modeled. In particular, to model economic process in a world that uses money, cash-flow conditions are critical. In attempting to obtain completely specified outcomes for all parameter values, we find that the cash-flow conditions often appear as inequalities, not equalities.

Economic problems that appear simple often break up into special cases depending on boundary conditions. It is easy to get lost in the wilderness of these cases or else pretend that all boundary conditions are satisfied. But we argue that boundary conditions are at the center of the control problem in economics and that money and financial institutions are the control mechanisms of the society.

Once one starts to consider many goods, many financial instruments, and many time periods simultaneously one becomes entangled with an astronomical number of special cases. Fortunately the single-period models with one or two markets and one or two financial instruments are sufficient to illustrate a considerable amount of the structure of boundary solutions and to illustrate the several zones that the solutions will display. In this chapter we have linked the one-period models with the multistage models, but we do not solve the multistage models for the many zones that exist.

A good practicing macroeconomist often views the actual economy as a selection from myriad could-be economies. He or she builds an ad hoc model and modifies his or her quantitative conclusions with qualitative concerns reflecting the context. He or she uses theory to aid thought.

Because of the computational complexity in examining boundary conditions, in this book we have attempted to understand the behavior of money and credit in a trivially simple economic exchange problem. We have laboriously calculated many variants in order to illustrate the amazing complexity and subtlety of a financially controlled economy. We have used a reductionist approach almost against itself in the sense that the level of complexity encountered is sufficient to raise questions concerning the reconciliation between static microeconomics such as general equilibrium theory and dynamic macroeconomics. Because it is so easy to overwhelm even simple micro models with more micro-micro detail in any attempt to construct multistage models, we conclude that the linking of macro- and microeconomic models must still take place via the filter of professionals evaluating the case at hand. Hence the roles of good bankers and central bankers and financiers are different from and complementary with the macroeconomic and microeconomic practitioners and theorists. The curse of dimensions, which lies in all of these problems, is ameliorated by the wisdom of specialists in selecting the appropriate simplifications in the models constructed to answer their questions.

16.9 APPENDIX A: MULTIPERIOD TRADE WITH FIAT MONEY, A SALVAGE VALUE, BUT NO BANK

This is our first model covering more than one time period—the time index t runs from 1 to T. We assume the Type 1 traders are endowed with a units of good 1 in each period, while the Type 2 traders have a units of good 2 in each period. All traders now make bids and put their own good up for sale in each time period. The notation m_t ($\bar{m}_t$) stands for the amount of cash on hand for the Type 1 (Type 2) traders at the beginning of period t. The discount factor is β.

The optimization problem for the Type 1 agents is:

$$\max_{b_t, q_t, m_t} \sum_{t=1}^{T} \beta^{t-1} \left(2\sqrt{(a - q_t)\frac{b_t}{p_t}} \right) + \beta^T \Pi m_{T+1}$$

s.t. $m_t - b_t \geq 0$, $t = 1, \ldots, T$ (cash-flow constraints) (λ_t)

$\quad m_t = m_{t-1} + p_{t-1}q_{t-1} - b_{t-1}$, $t = 2, \ldots, T+1$

$\qquad\qquad\qquad\qquad\qquad$ (accounting constraints)

$\quad m_1 = m$

$\quad b_t \geq 0$, $0 \leq q_t \leq a$.

We append the extra term $\beta^T \Pi m_{T+1}$ to the objective function to represent the value of excess fiat left over after the end of the game. In dynamic programming terms, the Π is a salvage value parameter. In economic terms it can be regarded as an expected value of money in the future. Finally, note that we do not need a nonnegativity constraint for the variables m_t because of the cash-flow constraints.

For the Type 2 agents, we have

$$\max_{\bar{b}_t, \bar{q}_t, \bar{m}_t} \sum_{t=1}^{T} \beta^{t-1} \left(2\sqrt{(a-\bar{q}_t)\frac{\bar{b}_t}{\bar{p}_t}} \right) + \beta^T \Pi \bar{m}_{T+1}$$

s.t. $\bar{m}_t - \bar{b}_t \geq 0,\ t=1,\ldots,T$ (cash-flow constraints) $(\bar{\lambda}_t)$

$\quad \bar{m}_t = \bar{m}_{t-1} + \bar{p}_{t-1}\bar{q}_{t-1} - \bar{b}_{t-1},\ t=2,\ldots,T+1$

$\qquad\qquad\qquad\qquad$ (accounting constraints)

$\bar{m}_1 = m$

$\bar{b}_t \geq 0,\ 0 \leq \bar{q}_t \leq a.$

By substitution (using the accounting constraints), we can rewrite the Type 1 agents' problem as:

$$\max_{b_t, q_t} \sum_{t=1}^{T} \beta^{t-1} \left(2\sqrt{(a-q_t)\frac{b_t}{\bar{p}_t}} \right) + \beta^T \Pi \left(m + \sum_{t=1}^{T} p_t q_t - \sum_{t=1}^{T} b_t \right)$$

s.t. $m + \sum_{k=1}^{t-1} p_k q_k - \sum_{k=1}^{t-1} b_k - b_t \geq 0,\ t=1,\ldots,T$ (cash-flow constraints) (λ_t)

$b_t \geq 0,\ 0 \leq q_t \leq a.$

The Lagrangian is:

$$L = \sum_{t=1}^{T} \beta^{t-1} \left(2\sqrt{(a-q_t)\frac{b_t}{\bar{p}_t}} \right) + \beta^T \Pi \left(m + \sum_{t=1}^{T} p_t q_t - \sum_{t=1}^{T} b_t \right)$$

$$+ \sum_{t=1}^{T} \lambda_t \left(m + \sum_{k=1}^{t-1} p_k q_k - \sum_{k=1}^{t} b_k \right).$$

The first-order conditions here are

$$\frac{\partial L}{\partial q_t} = -\beta^{t-1} \sqrt{\frac{b_t}{(a-q_t)\bar{p}_t}} + \beta^T \Pi p_t + p_t \left(\sum_{k=t+1}^{T} \lambda_k \right) = 0 \qquad (16.1)$$

and

$$\frac{\partial L}{\partial b_t} = \beta^{t-1} \sqrt{\frac{a - q_t}{b_t \bar{p}_t}} - \beta^T \Pi - \sum_{k=t}^{T} \lambda_k = 0. \tag{16.2}$$

Similarly, we can write the first-order conditions for the Type 2 agents as

$$-\beta^{t-1} \sqrt{\frac{\bar{b}_t}{(a - \bar{q}_t) p_t}} + \beta^T \Pi \bar{p}_t + \bar{p}_t \left(\sum_{k=t+1}^{T} \bar{\lambda}_k \right) = 0 \tag{16.3}$$

and

$$\beta^{t-1} \sqrt{\frac{a - \bar{q}_t}{\bar{b}_t p_t}} - \beta^T \Pi - \sum_{k=t}^{T} \bar{\lambda}_k = 0. \tag{16.4}$$

Finally, prices are formed by:

$$p_t = \frac{\bar{b}_t}{q_t} \text{ and } \bar{p}_t = \frac{b_t}{\bar{q}_t} \text{ for } t = 1, \dots, T. \tag{16.5}$$

Two further observations are important at this point. First, we will restrict our attention to solutions satisfying "symmetry," that is, where $\bar{p}_t = p_t$, $\bar{q}_t = q_t$, and $\bar{b}_t = b_t$. This symmetry, together with (16.5), implies that $p_t q_t = b_t$ in all periods t. But then the accounting constraints give $m_{T+1} = m_T = \cdots = m_1 = m$. In other words, symmetric solutions are also "stationary," in the sense that the players always begin each period with the same amount of money.

Case 1: m is large. In this case, the cash-flow constraints will all be loose; that is, we assume $\lambda_t = 0$ for all t. Thus (16.1) and (16.2) become

$$\beta^{t-1} \sqrt{\frac{b_t}{(a - q_t) \bar{p}_t}} = \beta^T \Pi p_t \tag{16.6}$$

and

$$\beta^{t-1} \sqrt{\frac{a - q_t}{b_t \bar{p}_t}} = \beta^T \Pi. \tag{16.7}$$

Then (16.6) and (16.7) together imply $\beta^{t-1} \sqrt{\frac{b_t}{(a-q_t)\bar{p}_t}} = \beta^{t-1} \sqrt{\frac{a-q_t}{b_t \bar{p}_t}} p_t$, which is $p_t = \frac{b_t}{a - q_t}$. Substituting back into (16.6) (and assuming symmetry $p_t = \bar{p}_t$) yields $\beta^T \Pi p_t = \beta^{t-1}$, which is

$$p_t = \bar{p}_t = \frac{1}{\Pi \beta^{T-t+1}}. \tag{16.8}$$

Next, using (16.6), symmetry, and the balancing constraint (16.5), we have $\beta^{t-1}\sqrt{\frac{b_t}{a\bar{p}_t-q_t\bar{p}_t}}=\beta^T\Pi p_t \Rightarrow \sqrt{\frac{b_t}{\frac{a}{\Pi\beta^{T-t+1}}-b_t}}=\beta^{T-t+1}\Pi p_t=1 \Rightarrow b_t=$ $\frac{a}{\Pi\beta^{T-t+1}}-b_t$, which in turn gives $b_t=\frac{a}{2\Pi\beta^{T-t+1}}=\bar{b}_t$. Finally, $q_t=\frac{\bar{b}_t}{\bar{p}_t}=\frac{a}{2}=$ $\bar{q}_t$. So, as in all of our previous one-period models, the "enough money" case yields the efficient consumption levels of $(\frac{a}{2},\frac{a}{2})$ for both types of players in each period.

Note that since $m_{T+1}=m_T=\cdots=m_1=m$, the cash-flow constraints hold if $m-b_t\geq 0$ for all t, which is precisely when $m\geq\frac{a}{2\Pi\beta^T}$. So this is the mathematical definition of "enough money."

Other Cases: Now suppose m was a little lower than $\frac{a}{2\Pi\beta^T}$. In this case, the solution from Case 1 satisfies all conditions except for the cash-flow constraint in period $t=1$. Hence, the correct values for the multipliers will have λ_1 positive, with $\lambda_2=\lambda_3=\cdots=\lambda_T=0$. The first-order conditions thus reduce to (16.6) and (16.7) in periods 2 through T, and so the solutions for b_t, q_t, and p_t (as well as $\bar{b}_t$, $\bar{q}_t$, and $\bar{p}_t$) in these periods are the same as in Case 1. However, in period 1, the conditions (16.1) and (16.2) reduce to

$$\sqrt{\frac{b_1}{(a-q_1)\bar{p}_1}}=\beta^T\Pi p_1 \tag{16.9}$$

and

$$\sqrt{\frac{a-q_1}{b_1\bar{p}_1}}=\beta^T\Pi+\lambda_1. \tag{16.10}$$

In addition, with $\lambda_1>0$, we have $b_1=m_1=m$.

To solve this system, we note that (16.9) and symmetry together imply $\frac{b_1}{(a-q_1)p_1}=\beta^{2T}\Pi^2p_1^2$, which in turn gives $\frac{m}{ap_1-m}=\beta^{2T}\Pi^2p_1^2$. Hence p_1 will be the solution to the cubic equation $a\beta^{2T}\Pi^2p_1^3-m\beta^{2T}\Pi^2p_1^2-m=0$. Once we have found p_1, we can get q_1 because $q_1=\frac{b_1}{p_1}=\frac{m}{p_1}$. Then we can calculate λ_1 from (16.10), if necessary.

As we continue to lower m, we expect that one by one, the multipliers $\lambda_2,\lambda_3,\ldots$, and λ_T turn positive. Thus, for any particular value of m, there exists a time index j for which $\lambda_1,\ldots,\lambda_j$ are positive, while $\lambda_{j+1},\ldots,\lambda_T$ are equal to zero. In periods $j+1,\ldots,T$, the first-order conditions will again reduce to (16.6) and (16.7), and so the solutions for b_t, q_t, and p_t (as well

$\bar{b}_t$, $\bar{q}_t$, and $\bar{p}_t$) in these periods will be the same as in Case 1. In period j, the first-order conditions are

$$\beta^{j-1} \sqrt{\frac{b_j}{(a - q_j)\bar{p}_j}} = \beta^T \Pi p_j \qquad (16.11)$$

and

$$\beta^{j-1} \sqrt{\frac{a - q_j}{b_j \bar{p}_j}} = \beta^T \Pi + \lambda_j. \qquad (16.12)$$

As in the analysis above (where $j = 1$), we use (16.11) to set up a cubic equation to solve for p_j (and $\bar{p}_j$), find q_j (and $\bar{q}_j$) via the condition $q_j = \bar{q}_j = \frac{m}{p_j}$, and then find λ_j ($= \bar{\lambda}_j$) using (16.12). But then, we can substitute this known value of λ_j in (16.1) (with $t = j - 1$) to generate another cubic equation, this time for p_{j-1}. This gives q_{j-1} via the condition $q_{j-1} = \frac{b_{j-1}}{p_{j-1}} = \frac{m}{p_{j-1}}$. And then we can get λ_{j-1} from (16.2) (with $t = j - 1$; again, we have to use the known value of λ_j). But then we can substitute our known values of λ_{j-1} and λ_j in (16.1) (with $t = j - 2$) to generate another cubic equation, this time for $p_{j-2}, \ldots$.

Continuing in this way, we can solve the entire model.

16.10 APPENDIX B: MULTIPERIOD TRADE WITH A BANK

We now add a bank to the model from Appendix A. The traders may borrow from the bank in each period, but they must pay back their loans at the beginning of the next period. Meanwhile, the bank will just be a strategic dummy whose single role is to offer the exact amount of money necessary to maintain the interest rate at some given ρ.

The optimization problem for the Type 1 traders is:

$$\max_{b_t, q_t, d_t, m_t} \sum_{t=1}^{T} \beta^{t-1} \left(2\sqrt{(a - q_t)\frac{b_t}{\bar{p}_t}} \right) + \beta^T \Pi m_{T+1}$$

s.t. $m_t + \dfrac{d_t}{1 + \rho} - b_t \geq 0$, $t = 1, \ldots, T$ (cash-flow constraints) (λ_t)

$\qquad m_t = m_{t-1} + \dfrac{d_{t-1}}{1 + \rho} - b_{t-1} + p_{t-1}q_{t-1} - d_{t-1}$, $t = 2, \ldots, T + 1$

$\qquad\qquad\qquad\qquad\qquad\qquad\qquad\qquad$ (accounting constraints)

$\quad m_1 = m$

$\quad b_t, d_t, m_t \geq 0$, $0 \leq q_t \leq a$

Here the new variables $\{d_t\}$ represent the amount the Type 1 traders need to pay back to the bank as a result of loans taken out in period t. Note also that satisfaction of the new cash-flow constraints no longer guarantees that the m_t's are nonnegative. Hence, we now must specifically put in the constraints $m_t \geq 0$ for $t = 2, \ldots, T$. These constraints, in fact, are what we've been calling the *budget constraints* in some of our other models.

As in Appendix A, we can use the accounting constraints to eliminate the variables $\{m_t\}$. But we must now write out the budget constraints in terms of the other variables:

$$\max_{b_t, q_t, d_t} \sum_{t=1}^{T} \beta^{t-1} \left(2\sqrt{(a - q_t)\frac{b_t}{p_t}} \right) + \beta^T \Pi \left(m + \sum_{t=1}^{T} p_t q_t - \sum_{t=1}^{T} b_t - \sum_{t=1}^{T} \frac{\rho d_t}{1+\rho} \right)$$

$$\text{s.t. } m + \sum_{k=1}^{t-1} p_k q_k - \sum_{k=1}^{t-1} b_k - \sum_{k=1}^{t-1} \frac{\rho d_k}{1+\rho} + \frac{d_t}{1+\rho} - b_t \geq 0, \ t = 1, \ldots, T$$

$$\text{(cash-flow constraints) } (\lambda_t)$$

$$m + \sum_{k=1}^{t} p_k q_k - \sum_{k=1}^{t} b_k - \sum_{k=1}^{t} \frac{\rho d_k}{1+\rho} \geq 0, \ t = 1, \ldots, T$$

$$\text{(budget constraints) } (\mu_t)$$

$$b_t, d_t \geq 0, \ 0 \leq q_t \leq a.$$

There is a similar problem for the Type 2 traders:

$$\max_{\bar{b}_t, \bar{q}_t, \bar{d}_t} \sum_{t=1}^{T} \beta^{t-1} \left(2\sqrt{(a - \bar{q}_t)\frac{\bar{b}_t}{\bar{p}_t}} \right) + \beta^T \Pi \left(m + \sum_{t=1}^{T} \bar{p}_t \bar{q}_t - \sum_{t=1}^{T} \bar{b}_t - \sum_{t=1}^{T} \frac{\rho \bar{d}_t}{1+\rho} \right)$$

$$\text{s.t. } m + \sum_{k=1}^{t-1} \bar{p}_k \bar{q}_k - \sum_{k=1}^{t-1} \bar{b}_k - \sum_{k=1}^{t-1} \frac{\rho \bar{d}_k}{1+\rho}$$

$$+ \frac{\bar{d}_t}{1+\rho} - \bar{b}_t \geq 0, \ t = 1, \ldots, T \text{ (cash-flow constraints) } (\bar{\lambda}_t)$$

$$m + \sum_{k=1}^{t} \bar{p}_k \bar{q}_k - \sum_{k=1}^{t} \bar{b}_k - \sum_{k=1}^{t} \frac{\rho \bar{d}_k}{1+\rho} \geq 0, \ t = 1, \ldots, T$$

$$\text{(budget constraints) } (\bar{\mu}_t)$$

$$\bar{b}_t, \bar{d}_t \geq 0, \ 0 \leq \bar{q}_t \leq a.$$

We also still have the balancing conditions for price formation

$$p_t = \frac{\bar{b}_t}{q_t} \text{ and } \bar{p}_t = \frac{b_t}{\bar{q}_t} \text{ for } t = 1, \ldots, T. \tag{16.13}$$

As stated above, the bank's task is to maintain the interest rate at ρ. It will be able to do this so long as its initial cash holdings B satisfy:

$$B + \sum_{k=1}^{t-1} \rho g_k(\rho) - g_t(\rho) \geq 0, \ t = 1, \ldots, T. \qquad (\lambda_{Bt}) \qquad (16.14)$$

The quantities $g_t(\rho)$ represent the amount that the bank needs to lend in order to maintain the interest rate ρ in period t. These function values are determined by the amounts that the traders wish to borrow at this interest rate, plus the balancing conditions $1 + \rho = \frac{d_t + \bar{d}_t}{g_t}$ for all t.

Case 1: m is large. In this case the multipliers λ_t, μ_t, $\bar{\lambda}_t$, and $\bar{\mu}_t$ are all equal to zero for all t. The first-order conditions for the Type 1 traders, with respect to q_t and b_t, reduce to (16.6) and (16.7). Hence we can follow the analysis from Case 1 of Appendix A, and get $p_t = \bar{p}_t = \frac{1}{\Pi \beta^{T-t+1}}$, $b_t = \bar{b}_t = \frac{a}{2\Pi \beta^{T-t+1}}$, and $q_t = \bar{q}_t = \frac{a}{2}$. With these values (since they satisfy the cash-flow constraints for the model with no bank), it is clear that no borrowing is needed; hence $d_t = \bar{d}_t = 0$ for all periods t. The bank lends nothing and earns nothing.

Other Cases: The reader will note in this model that there are T cash-flow constraints and T budget constraints, each of which may be loose or tight—thus, a full analysis of this model would be overly difficult and lengthy. However, there is one more case that we would like to present, because its solution gives us a nice look at how the interest rate (ρ) and discount factor (β) affect the markets in a case where the traders need to borrow.

Special Case: m is very small, so $\lambda_1, \lambda_2, \ldots, \lambda_T > 0$ (the cash-flow constraints are tight). Also, $\Pi = 0$; that is, the salvage value of money is zero. This in turn implies that the *last* budget constraints (μ_T) and ($\bar{\mu}_T$) are tight. However, the *other* budget constraints are loose ($\mu_1 = \mu_2 = \cdots = \mu_{T-1} = \bar{\mu}_1 = \bar{\mu}_2 = \cdots = \bar{\mu}_{T-1} = 0$).

Note that one could never hope to solve this model (with $\Pi = 0$) *without* the bank, due to the Hahn paradox (see Chapter 7).

The assumptions in this special case imply that we can rewrite the Type 1 traders' problem as

$$\max_{b_t,q_t,d_t} \sum_{t=1}^{T} \beta^{t-1}\left(2\sqrt{(a-q_t)\tfrac{b_t}{\bar{p}_t}}\right)$$

s.t. $m + \dfrac{d_1}{1+\rho} - b_1 = 0$ $\qquad (\lambda_1)$

$\quad p_1 q_1 - d_1 + \dfrac{d_2}{1+\rho} - b_2 = 0$ $\qquad (\lambda_2)$

$\quad p_2 q_2 - d_2 + \dfrac{d_3}{1+\rho} - b_3 = 0$ $\qquad (\lambda_3)$

$\qquad\qquad \vdots$

$\quad p_{T-1} q_{T-1} - d_{T-1} + \dfrac{d_T}{1+\rho} - b_T = 0$ $\quad (\lambda_T)$

$\quad p_1 q_1 - d_1 \geq 0$ $\qquad (\mu_1)$

$\qquad\qquad \vdots$

$\quad p_{T-1} q_{T-1} - d_{T-1} \geq 0$ $\qquad (\mu_{T-1})$

$\quad p_T q_T - d_T = 0$ $\qquad\qquad (\mu_T) \rightarrow (\lambda_{T+1})$

$\quad b_t, d_t \geq 0,\ 0 \leq q_t \leq a.$

The notation $(\mu_T) \rightarrow (\lambda_{T+1})$ here means that we are renaming constraint (μ_T) as (λ_{T+1}). This will help with the exposition as we go along. Also, our approach will be to ignore the constraints $(\mu_1),\ldots,(\mu_{T-1})$. However, this means that when we solve the model *without* these constraints, we will have to verify that our optimal solution for the traders actually satisfies these constraints.

The first-order conditions for the modified Type 1 traders problem (ignoring $(\mu_1),\ldots,(\mu_{T-1})$) are

$$-\beta^{t-1}\sqrt{\frac{b_t}{\bar{p}_t(a-q_t)}} + \lambda_{t+1}p_t = 0 \text{ for } t=1,\ldots,T \qquad (16.15)$$

$$\beta^{t-1}\sqrt{\frac{a-q_t}{b_t\bar{p}_t}} - \lambda_t = 0 \text{ for } t=1,\ldots,T \qquad (16.16)$$

$$\frac{\lambda_t}{1+\rho} - \lambda_{t+1} = 0 \text{ for } t=1,\ldots,T. \qquad (16.17)$$

First, formulas (16.16) and (16.17) together imply $\beta^{t-1}\sqrt{\frac{a-q_t}{b_t\bar{p}_t}} - \lambda_{t+1}(1+\rho) = 0$; whereupon substituting for λ_{t+1} using (16.15) gives $\beta^{t-1}\sqrt{\frac{a-q_t}{b_t\bar{p}_t}} = (1+\rho)\frac{\beta^{t-1}}{p_t}\sqrt{\frac{b_t}{\bar{p}_t(a-q_t)}}$. Rearranging gives $\frac{p_t(a-q_t)}{b_t} = 1+\rho$. The price formation balancing condition (16.13) plus symmetry tells us that $\frac{p_t}{b_t} = \frac{\bar{p}_t}{\bar{b}_t} = q_t$; so we have $\frac{a-q_t}{q_t} = 1+\rho$. This finally gives

$$q_t = \frac{a}{2+\rho} = \bar{q}_t \text{ for all } t. \qquad (16.18)$$

Next, (16.15) implies $\lambda_{t+1}p_t = \beta^{t-1}\sqrt{\frac{b_t}{p_t(a-q_t)}}$, but in the last paragraph we showed $\frac{p_t(a-q_t)}{b_t} = 1+\rho$; hence $\lambda_{t+1}p_t = \frac{\beta^{t-1}}{\sqrt{1+\rho}}$. Using (16.17) gives $\lambda_t p_t = \beta^{t-1}\sqrt{1+\rho}$, or

$$\lambda_t = \frac{\beta^{t-1}\sqrt{1+\rho}}{p_t}. \tag{16.19}$$

In particular, $\lambda_1 = \frac{\sqrt{1+\rho}}{p_1}$. And, since $\lambda_{t+1} = \frac{\lambda_t}{1+\rho}$, we have

$$\lambda_t = (1+\rho)^{1-t}\lambda_1 = (1+\rho)^{1-t}\frac{\sqrt{1+\rho}}{p_1} = \frac{(1+\rho)^{\frac{3}{2}-t}}{p_1}. \tag{16.20}$$

But now, using (16.19) and (16.20), we have $\frac{\beta^{t-1}\sqrt{1+\rho}}{p_t} = \frac{(1+\rho)^{\frac{3}{2}-t}}{p_1}$, which simplifies to

$$p_t = p_1[(1+\rho)\beta]^{t-1} = \bar{p}_t. \tag{16.21}$$

Hence, while the amounts that the traders put up for sale each period are constant $(q_t = \frac{a}{2+\rho} = \bar{q}_t$ each period), the prices either increase or decrease geometrically each period, depending upon whether the quantity $(1+\rho)\beta$ is larger or smaller than 1. The only case in which prices remain constant is when $(1+\rho)\beta$ is equal to 1. Since $b_t = \bar{b}_t = p_t q_t$, the bids will display the same behavior as the prices.

Our next task is to derive an expression for p_1. To do this, we add $(1+\rho)^T$ times constraint (λ_1), plus $(1+\rho)^{T-1}$ times constraint (λ_2), plus ... plus 1 times constraint (λ_{T+1}), to get

$$\sum_{t=1}^{T}(1+\rho)^{T-t}p_t q_t - \sum_{t=1}^{T}(1+\rho)^{T-t+1}b_t + (1+\rho)^T m = 0.$$

(Note that all of the "d's" canceled out.) Substituting in $q_t = \frac{a}{2+\rho}$ and $b_t = p_t q_t = p_t\frac{a}{2+\rho}$, we get

$$\frac{a}{2+\rho}\sum_{t=1}^{T}(1+\rho)^{T-t}p_t - \frac{a}{2+\rho}\sum_{t=1}^{T}(1+\rho)^{T-t+1}p_t + (1+\rho)^T m = 0,$$

which is

$$\frac{a\rho}{2+\rho}\sum_{t=1}^{T}(1+\rho)^{T-t}p_t = (1+\rho)^T m.$$

But now we substitute in for p_t using (16.21), and we have

$$\frac{a\rho}{2+\rho}\sum_{t=1}^{T}p_1(1+\rho)^{t-1}\beta^{t-1}(1+\rho)^{T-t}=(1+\rho)^T m$$

$$\Rightarrow \frac{a\rho}{2+\rho}p_1(1+\rho)^{T-1}\sum_{t=1}^{T}\beta^{t-1}=(1+\rho)^T m$$

$$\Rightarrow \frac{a\rho}{2+\rho}p_1\frac{1-\beta^T}{1-\beta}=(1+\rho)m.$$

This finally gives

$$p_1=\frac{m}{a}\frac{(1+\rho)(2+\rho)}{\rho}\frac{1-\beta}{1-\beta^T}=\bar{p}_1 \qquad (16.22)$$

$$p_t=\frac{m}{a}\frac{(1+\rho)^t(2+\rho)}{\rho}\frac{1-\beta}{1-\beta^T}\beta^{t-1}=\bar{p}_t, \text{ for } t=1,\ldots,T. \qquad (16.23)$$

We also have

$$b_t=p_t q_t=\frac{m(1+\rho)^t}{\rho}\frac{1-\beta}{1-\beta^T}\beta^{t-1}=\bar{b}_t, \text{ for } t=1,\ldots,T. \qquad (16.24)$$

Our next task is to derive a formula for d_t and $\bar{d}_t$. The first step is to add $(1+\rho)^T$ times constraint (λ_1), plus $(1+\rho)^{T-1}$ times constraint (λ_2), plus $\ldots$ plus $(1+\rho)^{T-t+1}$ times constraint (λ_t). This time all of the "d's" except d_t cancel out, and we get

$$(1+\rho)^{T-t}d_t+\sum_{k=1}^{t-1}(1+\rho)^{T-k}p_k q_k-\sum_{k=1}^{t}(1+\rho)^{T-k+1}b_k+(1+\rho)^T m=0.$$

This is

$$d_t=\sum_{k=1}^{t}(1+\rho)^{t-k+1}b_k-\sum_{k=1}^{t-1}(1+\rho)^{t-k}p_k q_k-(1+\rho)^t m.$$

Substituting in our expression for b_k from (16.21), and realizing that $p_k q_k=b_k$, we get

$$d_t = \sum_{k=1}^{t}(1+\rho)^{t-k+1}\frac{m(1+\rho)^k}{\rho}\frac{1-\beta}{1-\beta^T}\beta^{k-1}$$

$$-\sum_{k=1}^{t-1}(1+\rho)^{t-k}\frac{m(1+\rho)^k}{\rho}\frac{1-\beta}{1-\beta^T}\beta^{k-1}-(1+\rho)^t m$$

$$=(1+\rho)^{t+1}\frac{m}{\rho}\frac{1-\beta}{1-\beta^T}\sum_{k=1}^{t}\beta^{k-1}-(1+\rho)^t\frac{m}{\rho}\frac{1-\beta}{1-\beta^T}\sum_{k=1}^{t-1}\beta^{k-1}$$

$$-(1+\rho)^t m$$

$$=(1+\rho)^{t+1}\frac{m}{\rho}\frac{1-\beta}{1-\beta^T}\frac{1-\beta^t}{1-\beta}-(1+\rho)^t\frac{m}{\rho}\frac{1-\beta}{1-\beta^T}\frac{1-\beta^{t-1}}{1-\beta}-(1+\rho)^t m$$

$$=\frac{m(1+\rho)^t}{\rho(1-\beta^T)}(\rho-\beta^t-\rho\beta^t+\beta^{t-1})-m(1+\rho)^t=\bar{d}_t. \qquad (16.25)$$

Next we verify that the solutions for p_t, q_t, and d_t from (16.23), (16.18), and (16.25) do in fact satisfy the budget constraints $(\mu_1)-(\mu_{T-1})$. But $p_t q_t = b_t = \frac{m(1+\rho)^t}{\rho}\frac{1-\beta}{1-\beta^T}\beta^{t-1}$. This will be greater than or equal to d_t if

$$\frac{m(1+\rho)^t}{\rho}\frac{1-\beta}{1-\beta^T}\beta^{t-1} \geq \frac{m(1+\rho)^t}{\rho(1-\beta^T)}(\rho-\beta^t-\rho\beta^t+\beta^{t-1})-m(1+\rho)^t$$

which is

$$m(1+\rho)^t(1-\beta)\beta^{t-1}\geq m(1+\rho)^t(\rho-\beta^t-\rho\beta^t+\beta^{t-1})$$

$$-m\rho(1+\rho)^t(1-\beta^T), \text{ or}$$

$$(1-\beta)\beta^{t-1}\geq(\rho-\beta^t-\rho\beta^t+\beta^{t-1})-\rho(1-\beta^T), \text{ or}$$

$$(1-\beta)\beta^{t-1}\geq-\beta^t-\rho\beta^t+\beta^{t-1}+\rho\beta^T,$$

which is trivially always true.

However, we do need to remark that the results above are valid only so long as the above expression (16.25) for d_t (and for $\bar{d}_t$) turns out to be nonnegative. This will be the case if and only if $\rho-\beta^t-\rho\beta^t+\beta^{t-1}\geq\rho(1-\beta^T)$ for $t=1,\ldots T$, which is

$$\rho\beta^T-\beta^t-\rho\beta^t+\beta^{t-1}\geq 0, \text{ for } t=1,\ldots,T. \qquad (16.26)$$

An important case where (16.26) always holds is when $(1+\rho)\beta=1$; that is, we are in the "no inflation or deflation of prices" case (see above discussion). Now $(1+\rho)\beta=1$ implies $\rho=\frac{1-\beta}{\beta}$, so

$$p_t = p_1 = \frac{m}{a} \frac{(1+\rho)(2+\rho)}{\rho} \frac{1-\beta}{1-\beta^T} = \frac{m}{a} \frac{\beta(1+\rho)(2+\rho)}{1-\beta^T}$$

$$= \frac{m(2+\rho)}{a(1-\beta^T)} = \bar{p}_t,$$

$$q_t = \frac{a}{2+\rho} = \bar{q}_t,$$

$$b_t = p_t q_t = \frac{m}{1-\beta^T} = \bar{b}_t,$$

and

$$d_t = \frac{m(1+\rho)^t}{\rho(1-\beta^T)}\left(\rho - \beta^t - \rho\beta^t + \beta^{t-1}\right) - m(1+\rho)^t$$

$$= \frac{m\rho(1+\rho)^t - m\beta^t(1+\rho)^t - m\rho\beta^t(1+\rho)^t + m\beta^{t-1}(1+\rho)^t}{\rho(1-\beta^T)}$$

$$\quad - m(1+\rho)^t$$

$$= \frac{m\rho(1+\rho)^t - m - m\rho + m(1+\rho)}{\rho(1-\beta^T)} - m(1+\rho)^t$$

$$= \frac{m\rho(1+\rho)^t - m\rho(1-\beta^T)(1+\rho)^t}{\rho(1-\beta^T)} = \frac{m\beta^T(1+\rho)^t}{1-\beta^T} = \bar{d}_t.$$

Going back to the general case for ρ and β, all that remains is to remark that we can now quantify the minimal amount of initial cash B that the bank needs in order for the results above to be valid. (See the discussion surrounding inequalities (16.14).) Since $1 + \rho = \frac{d_t + \bar{d}_t}{g_t}$, we have $g_t(\rho) = \frac{d_t + \bar{d}_t}{1+\rho} = \frac{2\left(\frac{m(1+\rho)^t}{\rho(1-\beta^T)}(\rho - \beta^t - \rho\beta^t + \beta^{t-1}) - m(1+\rho)^t\right)}{1+\rho}$. We may then substitute this back into (16.14) to find the desired B.

16.11 APPENDIX C: A MULTIPERIOD SELL-ALL MARKET WITH A BANK

In this appendix we analyze a multiperiod model in which the market structure is sell-all. In particular, we consider the case analogous to that which we analyzed for buy-sell in Appendix B; that is, $\Pi = 0$ and m is so small that all of the cash-flow constraints are tight, the last budget constraint is tight, but the rest of the budget constraints are loose. The bank's role is again to maintain the interest rate at a constant ρ.

The Type 1 traders attempt to maximize

$$\max_{b_{1t},b_{2t},d_t,m_t} \sum_{t=1}^{T} 2\beta^{t-1}\sqrt{\frac{b_{1t}}{p_t}\frac{b_{2t}}{\bar{p}_t}} + \beta^T \Pi m_{T+1}$$

$$\text{s.t. } m_t + \frac{d_t}{1+\rho} - b_{1t} - b_{2t} \geq 0, \ t = 1, \dots, T$$

$$m_t = m_{t-1} + \frac{d_t}{1+\rho} - b_{1t} - b_{2t} + ap_{t-1} - d_{t-1}, \ t = 2, \dots, T+1$$

$$m_1 = m$$

$$b_{1t}, b_{2t}, d_t, m_t \geq 0.$$

Here the new notation is that b_{it} represents the amount bid by the Type 1 players for good i in period t. As in Appendix B, we can use the accounting constraints to eliminate the variables $\{m_t\}$; the result is:

$$\max_{b_{1t},b_{2t},d_t} \sum_{t=1}^{T} 2\beta^{t-1}\sqrt{\frac{b_{1t}}{p_t}\frac{b_{2t}}{\bar{p}_t}} + \beta^T \Pi$$

$$\left(m + \sum_{t=1}^{T} ap_t - \sum_{t=1}^{T} b_{1t} - \sum_{t=1}^{T} b_{2t} - \sum_{t=1}^{T} \frac{\rho d_t}{1+\rho} \right) \tag{a}$$

$$\text{s.t. } m + \sum_{k=1}^{t-1} ap_k - \sum_{k=1}^{t-1} b_{1k} - \sum_{k=1}^{t-1} b_{2k} - \sum_{k=1}^{t-1} \frac{\rho d_k}{1+\rho} + \frac{d_t}{1+\rho} - b_{1t} - b_{2t} \geq 0, \tag{b}$$

$$m + \sum_{k=1}^{t} ap_k - \sum_{k=1}^{t} b_{1k} - \sum_{k=1}^{t} b_{2k} - \sum_{k=1}^{t} \frac{\rho d_k}{1+\rho} \geq 0, \tag{c}$$

$$b_{1t}, b_{2t}, d_t \geq 0 \text{ for } t = 1, \dots, T. \tag{d}$$

$$\tag{16.27}$$

In this format constraints (16.27b) are the cash-flow constraints, and constraints (16.27c) are the budget constraints.

Similarly, the optimization problem for Type 2 traders is ($\bar{b}_{it}$ represents the amount Type 2 traders bid for good i in period t):

$$\max_{\bar{b}_{1t},\bar{b}_{2t},\bar{d}_t} \sum_{t=1}^{T} 2\beta^{t-1}\sqrt{\frac{b_{1t}}{p_t}\frac{b_{2t}}{\bar{p}_t}} + \beta^T \Pi$$

$$\left(m + \sum_{t=1}^{T} a\bar{p}_t - \sum_{t=1}^{T} \bar{b}_{1t} - \sum_{t=1}^{T} \bar{b}_{2t} - \sum_{t=1}^{T} \frac{\rho \bar{d}_t}{1+\rho} \right)$$

$$\text{s.t. } m + \sum_{k=1}^{t-1} a\bar{p}_k - \sum_{k=1}^{t-1} \bar{b}_{1k} - \sum_{k=1}^{t-1} \bar{b}_{2k} - \sum_{k=1}^{t-1} \frac{\rho \bar{d}_k}{1+\rho} + \frac{\bar{d}_t}{1+\rho} - \bar{b}_{1t} - \bar{b}_{2t} \geq 0,$$

$$m + \sum_{k=1}^{t} a\bar{p}_k - \sum_{k=1}^{t} \bar{b}_{1k} - \sum_{k=1}^{t} \bar{b}_{2k} - \sum_{k=1}^{t} \frac{\rho \bar{d}_k}{1+\rho} \geq 0,$$

$$\bar{b}_{1t}, \bar{b}_{2t}, \bar{d}_t \geq 0 \text{ for } t = 1, \dots, T.$$

Finally, we have the balance conditions

$$p_t = \frac{b_{1t} + \bar{b}_{1t}}{a} \text{ and } \bar{p}_t = \frac{b_{2t} + \bar{b}_{2t}}{a} \text{ for } t = 1, \ldots, T. \tag{16.28}$$

Let us now consider the Type 1 traders' problem. Since we assume that $\Pi = 0$, the cash-flow constraints are tight, and the last budget constraint is tight, we can reformulate (16.27a–d) as follows:

$$\max_{b_{1t}, b_{2t}, d_t} \sum_{t=1}^{T} 2\beta^{t-1} \sqrt{\frac{b_{1t}}{p^t} \frac{b_{2t}}{\bar{p}^t}}$$

$$\text{s.t. } m + \frac{d_1}{1+\rho} - b_{11} - b_{21} = 0, \qquad (\lambda_1)$$

$$ap_1 - d_1 + \frac{d_2}{1+\rho} - b_{12} - b_{22} = 0, \qquad (\lambda_2)$$

$$ap_2 - d_2 + \frac{d_3}{1+\rho} - b_{13} - b_{23} = 0, \qquad (\lambda_3)$$

$$\vdots$$

$$ap_{T-1} - d_{T-1} + \frac{d_T}{1+\rho} - b_{1T} - b_{2T} = 0, \quad (\lambda_T)$$

$$ap_1 - d_1 \geq 0, \qquad (\mu_1)$$

$$\vdots$$

$$ap_{T-1} - d_{T-1} \geq 0, \qquad (\mu_{T-1})$$

$$ap_T - d_T = 0. \qquad (\mu_T \rightarrow \lambda_{T+1})$$

We have $\lambda_1, \lambda_2, \ldots, \lambda_{T+1} > 0$. As in the analogous case from Appendix B, the budget constraints (μ_t) (except for the last one) are all loose—thus we ignore them for now but will verify that they are all satisfied when we obtain our equilibrium values.

Taking first-order conditions, we obtain

$$\frac{\partial L}{\partial b_{1t}} = \beta^{t-1} \sqrt{\frac{b_{2t}}{b_{1t} p_t \bar{p}_t}} - \lambda_t = 0, \, t = 1, \ldots, T \tag{16.29}$$

$$\frac{\partial L}{\partial b_{2t}} = \beta^{t-1} \sqrt{\frac{b_{1t}}{b_{2t} p_t \bar{p}_t}} - \lambda_t = 0, \, t = 1, \ldots, T \tag{16.30}$$

$$\frac{\partial L}{\partial d_t} = \frac{\lambda_t}{1+\rho} - \lambda_{t+1} = 0, \, t = 1, \ldots, T. \tag{16.31}$$

We get similar conditions (not written here) for the Type 2 traders. Also, as usual, we search for symmetric solutions, that is, where $b_{1t} = \bar{b}_{1t}$, $b_{2t} = \bar{b}_{2t}$, $d_t = \bar{d}_t$, and $p_t = \bar{p}_t$.

To begin our analysis, we note that (16.31) gives

$$\lambda_t = \lambda_{t+1}(1+\rho) \text{ for } t=1,\dots,T.$$

From (16.29) and (16.30) we have $b_{1t} = b_{2t}$; hence (16.29) gives $\lambda_t = \beta^{t-1}\sqrt{\frac{1}{p^t \bar{p}^t}}$. Symmetry then implies

$$\lambda_t = \frac{\beta^{t-1}}{p_t}. \tag{16.32}$$

From (16.31) and (16.32) we obtain

$$\frac{\beta^{t-1}}{p_t} = \frac{\beta^t(1+\rho)}{p_{t+1}} \Rightarrow p_{t+1} = \beta(1+\rho)p_t. \tag{16.33}$$

Since the balancing condition (16.28) and symmetry together imply that p_t is proportional to b_{1t} and to b_{2t}, we have $b_{1(t+1)} = \beta(1+\rho)b_{1t}$ and $b_{2(t+1)} = \beta(1+\rho)b_{2t}$. These plus (16.33) say that the bids and prices change geometrically over time, with ratio $\beta(1+\rho)$ each period. Hence

$$p_k = p_1\beta^{k-1}(1+\rho)^{k-1} \tag{16.34}$$

$$b_{1k} = b_{11}\beta^{k-1}(1+\rho)^{k-1} \tag{16.35}$$

$$b_{2k} = b_{21}\beta^{k-1}(1+\rho)^{k-1}. \tag{16.36}$$

To find p_1, b_{11}, and b_{21}, we add $(1+\rho)^T$ times constraint λ_1 above, plus $(1+\rho)^{T-1}$ times constraint λ_2, plus . . . , plus 1 times constraint λ_{T+1}. This gives[10]

$$(1+\rho)^T m - \sum_{k=1}^{T}(1+\rho)^{T+1-k}(b_{1k}+b_{2k}) + \sum_{k=1}^{T}(1+\rho)^{T-k}ap_k = 0$$

$$\Rightarrow (1+\rho)^T m - 2\sum_{k=1}^{T}(1+\rho)^{T+1-k}b_{1k} + \sum_{k=1}^{T}(1+\rho)^{T-k}2b_{1k} = 0$$

---

10 In the string of equalities below, we use $b_{1k} = b_{2k}$ for all k, (16.35)–(16.36), and also the price formation condition $p_k = (b_{1k} + \bar{b}_{1k})/a = 2b_{1k}/a$, so $ap_k = 2b_{1k}$.

$$\Rightarrow (1+\rho)^T m - 2 \sum_{k=1}^{T} (1+\rho)^{T+1-k} b_{11} \beta^{k-1} (1+\rho)^{k-1}$$

$$+ 2 \sum_{k=1}^{T} (1+\rho)^{T-k} \beta^{k-1} (1+\rho)^{k-1} b_{11} = 0$$

$$\Rightarrow (1+\rho)^T m - 2b_{11}(1+\rho)^T \sum_{k=1}^{T} \beta^{k-1} + 2b_{11}(1+\rho)^{T-1} \sum_{k=1}^{T} \beta^{k-1} = 0$$

$$\Rightarrow (1+\rho)^T m - 2b_{11}(1+\rho)^T \frac{1-\beta^T}{1-\beta} + 2b_{11}(1+\rho)^{T-1} \frac{1-\beta^T}{1-\beta} = 0$$

$$\Rightarrow (1+\rho)^T m = b_{11} \left(2(1+\rho)^T \frac{1-\beta^T}{1-\beta} - 2(1+\rho)^{T-1} \frac{1-\beta^T}{1-\beta} \right).$$

This gives

$$b_{11} = \frac{(1+\rho)^T m}{2(1+\rho)^T \frac{1-\beta^T}{1-\beta} - 2(1+\rho)^{T-1} \frac{1-\beta^T}{1-\beta}}$$

$$= \frac{(1+\rho)(1-\beta)}{2\rho(1-\beta^T)} m = b_{21}$$

$$p_1 = \frac{2b_1}{a} = \frac{(1+\rho)(1-\beta)m}{\rho(1-\beta^T)a} = \bar{p}_1.$$

Again, we remind the reader that

$$b_{1t} = (1+\rho)^{t-1} \beta^{t-1} b_{11}$$
$$p_t = (1+\rho)^{t-1} \beta^{t-1} p_1.$$

We now need to find d_t. Adding $(1+\rho)^T$ times constraint λ_1 above, plus $(1+\rho)^{T-1}$ times constraint λ_2, plus . . . , plus $(1+\rho)^{T-t+1}$ times constraint λ_t gives

$$(1+\rho)^T m - \sum_{k=1}^{t} (1+\rho)^{T+1-k} (b_{1k} + b_{2k}) + \sum_{k=1}^{t-1} a p_k (1+\rho)^{T-k}$$

$$+ (1+\rho)^{T-t} d_t = 0.$$

This implies

$$d_t = -(1+\rho)^t m + \sum_{k=1}^{t}(1+\rho)^{t+1-k}(b_{1k}+b_{2k}) - \sum_{k=1}^{t-1}2b_{1k}(1+\rho)^{t-k}$$

$$= \sum_{k=1}^{t}(1+\rho)^{t+1-k}2\frac{(1+\rho)(1-\beta)}{2\rho(1-\beta^T)}m(1+\rho)^{k-1}\beta^{k-1}$$

$$- \sum_{k=1}^{t-1}2(1+\rho)^{t-k}\frac{(1+\rho)(1-\beta)}{2\rho(1-\beta^T)}m(1+\rho)^{k-1}\beta^{k-1} - (1+\rho)^t m$$

$$= \sum_{k=1}^{t}(1+\rho)^{t+1}\frac{(1-\beta)}{\rho(1-\beta^T)}m\beta^{k-1} - \sum_{k=1}^{t-1}(1+\rho)^t\frac{(1-\beta)}{\rho(1-\beta^T)}m\beta^{k-1}$$

$$- (1+\rho)^t m$$

$$= \frac{(1+\rho)^{t+1}(1-\beta^t)m}{\rho(1-\beta^T)} - \frac{(1+\rho)^t(1-\beta^{t-1})m}{\rho(1-\beta^T)}$$

$$- (1+\rho)^t m$$

$$= \frac{m(1+\rho)^t}{\rho(1-\beta^T)}\left(\rho - \beta^t - \rho\beta^t + \beta^{t-1}\right) - m(1+\rho)^t = \bar{d}_t.$$

The reader will note that this is the exact same expression for d_t that we obtained in Appendix B.

Next, we have to verify that our solution satisfies the budget constraints $(\mu_1) - (\mu_{T-1})$; that is, that $ap_t \geq d_t$, where p_t and d_t are the equilibrium quantities found above. But $ap_t = 2b_{1t} = \frac{(1+\rho)^t(1-\beta)}{\rho(1-\beta^T)}m\beta^{t-1}$, and d_t is equal to the same expression as in Appendix B, so the verification follows from the argument directly following (16.25) in Appendix B. Finally, we should remark that, just as in Appendix B, our results are valid only if the above expression for d_t is nonnegative, that is, (16.26) holds.

Chapter 17 Pure Theory, Practice, and Context

17.1 A REMINDER FROM EDGEWORTH

In this book we have deconstructed a host of simple market and financial models. In a flip moment we had considered a subtitle of "Death by Lagrangian Multipliers," but our exercise is justified because it shows that the financial system is the control system for economic dynamics. The inequalities and boundary solutions on cash flows are indicators of the pressures from or on the control system.

A basic theme within the economics discipline is that there is often a substantial gap between applied economics and economic theory. In applications, it is virtually impossible to avoid the details that theory abstracts away. Applied economics requires both good operations research and social psychology, tempered with a historical understanding of context. One has to find, understand, and take into account the relevant details.

The challenges and the dangers of bridging the gap between theory and practice were eloquently noted in Edgeworth's inaugural address in 1891. He commented:

> It is worth while to consider why the path of applied economics is so slippery; and how it is possible to combine an enthusiastic admiration of theory with the coldest hesitation in practice. The explanation may be partially given in the words of a distinguished logician who has well and quaintly said, that if a malign spirit sought to annihilate to whole fabric of useful knowledge with the least effort and change, it would by no means be necessary that he should abrogate the laws of nature. The links of the chain of causation need not be corroded. Like effects shall still follow like causes; only like causes shall no longer occur in collocation. Every case is to be singular; every species, like the fabled Phoenix, to be unique. Now most of our practical problems have this character of singularity; every burning question is a Phoenix in the sense of being sui generis. (Edgeworth, 1891)

17.2 FROM STATICS TO DYNAMICS

In spite of the many successful applications of mathematics to equilibrium economics, the development of economics as a science has a considerable way to go. In particular, as is well known, there is no generally acceptable theory of dynamics. Yet the whole basis of macroeconomics requires economic dynamics.

In the broad sweep of the development of both pure and applied economics, techniques come and go and fashions change. It has been fashionable for microeconomic theorists to view macroeconomics as ad hoc and "unscientific," while macroeconomists return the compliment by branding such topics as general equilibrium (GE) theory as irrelevant.

We believe GE theory provided great and elegant insights into the potential role of price in providing optimal allocations under the appropriate conditions. But it did not completely solve the key problem of how coordination was to come about. That was relegated to the unspecified dynamics, and led to a clash between those who advocated competitive price formation and those who conceived of a centralized agency announcing prices. This clash could not be resolved by a mathematics that did not deal explicitly with price formation, although the debate on Marshallian versus Walrasian stability considering aggregated supply and demand functions could be regarded as an attempt to attack this problem.

Without getting down to models of individual optimizing behavior, the traditions in macroeconomics have been different. The attitude can better be expressed as economic engineering, where an ad hoc dynamic model is considered and the questions asked concern how well it fits current facts. Many approaches to macroeconomics have served to provide operational ad hoc advice. These practical concerns are not in opposition to the work of the microeconomic theorist, but are different from and, ideally, complementary with it.

17.3 GENERAL EQUILIBRIUM IS AN INCOMPLETE PARADIGM FOR DYNAMICS

An important question in microeconomic theory is: Does microeconomics have anything of value to say about the control and guidance of a free price forming enterprise economy? In order to be able to answer this question, which is naturally linked to macroeconomic concerns, the mechanism that forms price must be specified and the nature of the control must be considered. Many of the conceptual problems concerning the nature of money, the nature of substitutes for money, time lags in transactions, central banking reserves, and central bank goals can be sorted out at the level of the simple abstract well-defined models presented here.

The general equilibrium system offers neither process nor a picture of control. A primitive model that corrects these omissions is that of a strategic market game with a continuum of agents and one large atomic player, that is, a government of significant size in comparison with the individual small economic agents. This is the underlying model in many of the previous chapters.

Even a casual look at the last 5,000 years of history shows that society and the polity precede a developed economy. Furthermore, since at least the start of the Babylonian, Egyptian, and Chinese civilizations, it has been hard to find a ruling group that did not take somewhere between 10 percent and 60 percent of the income of city, empire, or other political entity being governed (Shubik, 2011, ch. 16). A bureaucracy has to be paid, and funding for defense is required. Without elementary laws, their enforcement, and rudimentary safety, an economy cannot thrive. As soon as a formal game is given with money, a large player with power to tax and control currency, and an adequate legal and enforcement system, the structure is rich enough for a government entity to provide coordination and control for the economy.

The control problems require that one specifies the instruments of control, the goals of the controller, and the goals of the controlled. It is easy to introduce ill-defined politically loaded questions such as "Does government control destroy free enterprise?" But upon a little reflection the concept of control is on a continuum, with the lower bound being "no control" (anarchy) and the upper bound being "total control" (a cenralized government that removes all economic choice from the individual small agents). Practically speaking, the government may be interested more in controlling the size of the individuals' strategy sets than in controlling their specific behavior. An immediate example is controlling the margin requirements in the purchase of stocks, not controlling which stocks are to be bought.

In the previous chapters our concern has been with the goals and motivations of the controlling entity. We have not introduced explicitly the political aspects of the vote or other mechanisms utilized by the governed to control their governors. This is taken here as a given.

17.4 THE PROBLEM WITH SOLUTIONS

Macroeconomists come in many political shadings; these differences are reflected in several approaches to macroeconomic theorizing. Popular macroeconomic policies, presented as though they have a sound basis in fundamental microeconomic theory, are overrated for the simple reason that there is no generally accepted theory of economic dynamics. Good applied macroeconomists such as Keynes, Tobin, and Friedman may have been perfectly capable of providing advice to those in power, but the scientific generality and validity of their views of the underlying dynamic are still matters of debate. This by no means detracts from their contributions—it merely indicates that there are some basic unanswered questions at the very underlying basis of economic theory and game theory.

The underlying approach adopted in this book is game-theoretic. A formal approach to economic dynamics requires games in extensive form. Unfortunately there are many suggested solution concepts for extensive form games, and this in turn implies there is no dominant accepted theory as to what constitutes a solution. Some proponents will push for an easy way out by proposing a "rational expectations" solution, and in the context of some economic problems a reasonable case may be made for rational expectations or the more precisely defined perfect noncooperative equilibrium analysis.

A solution to an *n*-person game in extensive form requires that three features of the strategic situation be well defined. They are: (1) the full description of the physical structure of the game; (2) the full description of the preferences and strategy sets of the individuals; and (3) a solution concept— most economists tend to prefer one that satisfies individual rationality and addresses the problems of conflict and coordination. Sociologists and psychologists tend to have a different viewpoint, with behavioral economists occupying a middle ground.

Any of the many theories of learning, signaling, and teaching may be considered (see, for example, Malaith and Samuelson, 2006). In spite of the search by Harsanyi and Selten (1988) to find a unique philosophically satisfactory noncooperative equilibrium point that would serve as the solution to all strategic problems, it appears that the notion of a satisfactory solution concept may be limited by context and environment. This is more congenial with an evolutionary view of an economy than with an equilibrium viewpoint.

17.5 A DYNAMIC MICROECONOMIC SOLUTION

As we have seen, the rational expectations solution to a dynamic model of an economy has a certain attraction, especially to those who see it as capturing the idea of highly independent individual strategic freedom. However, a high price is paid in terms of the explicit and often implicit assumptions made. In essence, the parallel dynamic programming approach takes a small step toward the study of equilibrium dynamics. But we learn little about the disequilibrium adjustment processes that are needed to lead an economy to equilibrium (if it exists). Below is a listing of the assumptions often made in such models, many of them similar to general equilibrium assumptions:

1. There is a continuum of small agents.
2. All agents are implicitly individually rational optimizers.
3. Government is a strategic dummy.
4. Context and history do not matter.
5. The infinite horizon unboundedness is overcome by the rational expectations assumption.

6. The mathematics of the models are often one-dimensional in commodities, plus another dimension for money. Extra dimensions are treated verbally by allegory.

7. The most significant lag is a cash-in-advance constraint, which has the important feature that it introduces cash-flow conditions explicitly.

8. The representative agent model is used to simplify the mathematics considerably.

In Chapter 16 we considered several multistage models, but without exogenous uncertainty present. As soon as one adds this feature to a multistage economic model, one is virtually driven to utilizing a dynamic programming or simulation approach.

We suggest that the parallel dynamic programming approach offers a natural extension to the study of multistage models when uncertainty is involved and boundary conditions are not critical.[1] In current usage, it has three potential applications:

1. The offering of macroeconomic advice challenging the ad hoc economic engineering approaches of macroeconomists such as Keynes and Tobin. The argument of Lucas (1980, 1996) and others is that these low-dimensional models are soundly based on microeconomic theory, unlike much of the work in macroeconomics. Unfortunately, most problems in macroeconomics deal with disequilibrium adjustments, and there is little development of formal multiperson dynamic programming that deals with the out-of-equilibrium adjustment. Thus their claim is moot.

2. Another use for the parallel dynamic programming approach is to investigate the control properties of models involving money and financial institutions in highly simplistic environments. For example, the work by Bewley (1980) illustrates the basic inventory aspects of money in a dynamic economy with uncertainty. Karatzas, Shubik, and Sudderth (1994) solve a dynamic programming model with uncertainty and independent agents utilizing fiat money acting in a market with loans and bankruptcy (Geanakoplos, Karatzas, Shubik, and Sudderth, 2000). These two models serve to warn us that in the presence of uncertainty, even completely symmetric agents do not necessarily behave symmetrically, as is forced on models utilizing representative agents. Furthermore, as soon as

---

1 Unfortunately, often they are critical.

loans and credit are introduced, bankruptcy appears as a logical necessity as well as an empirical fact.

3. The third use of these simple models is to produce playable games that can be utilized for experimentation. As yet, they have barely been tested to see if university students with an economics or business background actually approach behavior predicted by economic theory (see, e.g., Angerer, Huber, Shubik, and Sunder, 2010).

17.5.1 Why Experimental Games?

There are two important reasons for utilizing experimental games. The first is to gather experimental results concerning economic behavior in highly simplified and controlled economic environments. The second is that the construction and running of an experimental game guarantee that one has indeed modeled a fully playable game. It serves as a perfect complement to mathematical model building. Apparently minor details that can easily be missed in a formal mathematical model are often brought to the fore in the gaming laboratories. For example, players may ask naive questions such as, "Can I run the production process backward?" or, "In what order are we served?" exposing possibilities that the modeler would miss.

Perhaps most important, using experimental games forces one to become explicit about initial and terminal conditions. Experience from war gaming has shown that the initial conditions not only cannot be stated quantitatively, but also require a qualitative written or verbal description of context. Specifying terminal conditions raises questions concerning expectations and how to assign a salvage value for the assets remaining after the termination of a finite process that approximates an indefinitely long process. In particular, it is possible to specify terminal conditions consistent with rational expectations. Doing so allows us to test the economic behavior of individuals given long-term expectations as a datum.

17.5.2 Behavioral Economics?

The dichotomy between the individually rational economic actor and behavioral models of the individual is a false dichotomy. The rational economic actor model is merely one among several behavioral types. *Homo oeconomicus* provides an upper bound on personalityless abilities, while his companion, the random player, provides a lower bound. In between may be many types—for instance, in chess, where distinctions are made among beginners, amateur class players, experts, and grand masters.

One of the major challenges in formal game theory, psychology, and social psychology is to develop models of individuals with limited capacities. It is far easier to work with the extreme stereotypes, such as the player who can calculate everything, remembers everything, and has well-defined preferences over items; or the player who knows only the bounds of her strategy set and behaves randomly over the choices. In formal theory, the passions play no role.

A key contribution of the formal theory of games has been to point out that there is no natural unique extension of the concept of rational economic behavior of the individual beyond an extension to a two-person constant sum game, where a case can be made for a maxmin solution. Thus, solving a general multiperson game calls for both individual behavioral and societal assumptions. The literature on games with incomplete information (Horner and Lovo, 2009) and on games with learning and signaling (Malaith and Samuelson, 2006) indicates that those who contrast behavioral economic models with game-theoretic models do not understand that when a formal game model of a dynamic process is constructed, there is no universally acceptable extant game-theoretic solution. Formal game theory has not offered a unique way to solve the coordination problem that exists in a dynamic economy. The problem is primarily one not of mathematics but of the socio-physics of economic coordination.

17.5.3 Why Is There No General Economic Dynamics?

The political economy is a judging, hunting, evaluating, compromising, bargaining device. Adjustments often depend critically on time lags, and the control of time lags is one of the weapons broadly distributed through the society. In particular, in both the bureaucracy and the legal establishment, the control of timing is a potent force. Much of the world runs on doable deals and feasibility. Feasibility frequently depends on a time frame, and bureaucracies often destroy windows of opportunity. In finance, lawsuits are often brought not to win any litigation, but with the intention of delaying a takeover or a merger to the extent that the deal falls apart. In politics, a filibuster may be devoted to reading the works of Shakespeare into the record in order to force a potential bill to die on the vine.

These observations are not a counsel of despair. Rather, they are merely made to suggest that there is a large gap between a tractable theoretical model in economic dynamics and its application in the political economy.

The sources of the time lags at work on a system in disequilibrium must be specified, and many of them appear to be bureaucratic/political and not purely economic. Before the economist preaches about bribery and corruption, she needs to assess what it costs to get anything done in the context of the current institutions.

17.5.4 The Control Problem: Communication and Coordination

A society with a large government agent controlling a substantial part of its income has reasonably strong control if the rules of the polity and customs of the society prevent the other agents from introducing partially secured or unsecured credit instruments that serve as money substitutes. Otherwise these serve to provide both leverage and multiple points of partial control.

Especially in the presence of random events, leveraged credit instruments with multiple issuers can provide the conditions for considerable turbulence and swings in expectations. The control problem has involved and always will involve a socio-political tradeoff concerning constraints on individual and governmental choice. Control and coordination are not the same. Because it is the only universally known agent in the game, a government can send out signals to encourage the coordination of individual behavior instead of trying to restrict it. No other agents are in as strong a position to signal to the whole economy. In human affairs, an exogenous event such as a war or natural disaster can easily correlate or polarize the behavior of otherwise independent agents. Depending on context, such events may make it easier (for example, a war) or harder (a panic) for government control.

CONTROL AND INEQUALITIES

Throughout this work we have shown the critical role of the Lagrangian multipliers in guiding the system. We reiterate our position that financial control calls for the mathematics of inequalities and with it the attendant difficulties in fully analyzing the multitude of special cases created. In an infinite horizon stationary equilibrium model, the difference between monetary and nonmonetary systems superficially seems to vanish along with time and money. This phenomenon provides a straightforward, simple answer to the neutrality or nonneutrality of money. Suppose an economy has a monetary system. In equilibrium at an interior solution, money appears to be neutral; in disequilibrium it is always on some boundary and is never neutral. Mathematically this will show up as a shadow price on a constraint.

PERCEPTION, INFORMATION, AND EXPERTISE

The formal development of models with asymmetric information (Harsanyi, 1967–68), agency theory (Fama and Jensen, 1983), and incomplete contract theory (Aghion and Holden, 2011) indicates the basic understanding among economists and game theorists of the importance of asymmetric information and the need for contingency planning as information states change. But the appreciation of specialized expertise has been only lightly treated. In our formal work presented here, we too do not attempt to deal with the role of expertise. We are a long way from a satisfactory dynamics, but we believe that an important aspect of the financial system is to supply highly specialized experts who provide the economy with specialized sensors, and agencies to control and perform specialized functions.

17.6 PREDICTION AND CONTROL

In these chapters we have been concerned with different types of money and other financial instruments, and in the abilities of a central bank utilizing the quantity of money or rate of interest to control some aspects of the dynamics. We cannot overemphasize that control and prediction are by no means the same.

The ability of a government to accurately predict the specific dynamics of any economy is highly limited. It does not have information on time lags or on random events influencing motion. Much of the information needed lies with experts in specialized financial institutions—for example, fire insurance requires a different specialized body of knowledge from life insurance. In times of prosperity, the specialized services may function and implicitly coordinate without a needed role for government beyond setting broad bounds on behavior. Even though the legislators know relatively little about the technical details of the industry being regulated, and though the government bureaucrats may know a reasonable amount, they know less than those private industry bureaucrats who run many of the active private institutions. In times of recession, when the pressures of society lean heavily on the polity and the politicians are in a hurry to get things done, the importance of the difference between prediction and control is at its highest.

This work has been devoted to pure theory, but here we depart from theory briefly for one operational suggestion. In the United States the powers, governance, and bureaucratic structure of the Federal Reserve System has been reasonably successful. One of us has suggested (Shubik, 2011) that a similar institution should be in place in *every* country's economy, to continuously evaluate societally useful projects so that each political subdivision contains an inventory of assessed projects complete with an analysis of how they could be financed. Such an institution would also evaluate the nature of the work force needed, making recommendations for retraining. It is key to have such an institution bureaucratically institutionalized, so that the technical, financial, and bureaucratic expertise are both in place and co-opted into the system before economic prediction and coordination fail and considerable unemployment of human and other resources appears. Without such an institution, one should expect temporary, ill-considered political action without an appropriate bureaucratic, technical, and financial backup.

17.7 INNOVATION, MUTATION, AND BIOLOGY

Many of the interesting aspects of economic theory are still in a pre-mathematized state. In particular, despite Schumpeter's perceptive writing of around 100 years ago (Schumpeter, 1911, 1934), the innovation process and the potential breaking of the circular flow of capital have been better discussed in essay form rather than via a mathematical model. The discussion in the literature (e.g., Dosi et al., 1988; Nelson, 1996) stresses that the essence of innovation lies with disequilibrium and transient states.

The financial system, with its loans and laws of contract, together with the bankruptcy and default laws, provides the structure by which the body economic can mutate. The default laws help to control the level of mutation. If they are Draconian, no entrepreneur can risk to borrow. Self-financing may be feasible but is limited. On the other hand, if these laws are too lax, lenders may be unwilling to lend. In essence, the default and bankruptcy laws of a society are an important public good that controls the mutation rate of innovations within that society. They provide the means to "mop up" after a disequilibrium event such as a failure of an innovation. Credit may be destroyed, and organization and information may be destroyed, but money and physical resources remain and are redistributed by the system.

Failure of an innovation and failure of a mutation pose similar problems—disorganized or nonfunctional resources are left over and the system is required to distribute them for other uses.

17.8 WHY THE SUBTITLE: TOWARD A PURE THEORY OF MONEY?

The title of this book, *Barley, Gold, or Fiat*, is institutional; the subtitle, *Toward a Pure Theory of Money*, was selected to signal that we make no attempt to address burning operational questions of the day.[2] We further stress our belief in what some view as an oxymoron—the existence of a mathematical institutional economics. We suggest that formal stripped-down mathematical models are well worth studying, and that our approach stresses a need for a microeconomic anatomy and physiology of the most elementary of minimal institutions required to carry economic process. But even a casual attempt to count the number of variations in relevant models tells us that the gap between theory and application is considerable.

It is important to understand the need to develop pure theory that breaks out of the straightjacket of equilibrium theory and provides full process models. This enables us to investigate disequilibrium positions, even if we start by investigating equilibrium. Again, we emphasize that these basic models are complementary with, and not in contrast to, an institutional and verbal approach. With verbal treatments our understanding may be enlarged, but often at the cost of imprecision.

17.9 WHAT IS TO BE LEARNED?

In an economy controlled by a financial system, detail matters. The dynamics depends on many differentiated agents. Setting aside the aspects of different intelligence and basic abilities, noted above in Section 16.5, there are considerable professional differences in the relevant actors that cannot be ignored.

At the least we need to recognize the differentiated roles of the producers, the financiers, the bureaucrats, the politicians, and the lawyers, as well as the mass of citizens. An economy faces the basic problems of organization, coordination, and control. Prediction is probably of less import than the others.

How to coordinate markets is still an open question, which is not answered directly by the type of economic models we have discussed here. However, it is answered indirectly by the rules of the game. The rules are required to provide structure to channel competition. The coordination lies in the domain of political economy, and involves at least the politicians and the bureaucracy.

---

2 With one small exception in Section 17.6 above.

The cost of lack of coordination must be weighed against the cost of the bureaucracy, policing, and signaling.

A key point is that an economy that includes government as a strategic agent is a political economy. The granting of any form of taxation to pay for government, together with giving it control over the specification of weights and measures, the commercial code, contracts, and the specification of legal tender, sets up a control problem. But the control mechanisms are operationally different, depending upon the nature of the money to be used. A simple dimensional analysis shows that with fiat a fictitious asset has been created and its quantity, its issue, and the definition of reserves all depend on how the laws and "rules of the game" are written. The use of gold presents a far simpler and more constrained control problem.

Sometimes choice lies primarily with political and social choice, not with pure economics. The society that is not interested in a high level of innovation will tend to write harsh credit and default laws; the society promoting innovation will do the reverse.

The problem of expectations emerges in the analysis of any dynamic model of the economy. The invocation of rational expectations or perfect type-symmetric noncooperative equilibria is a device to look at some simple dynamic equilibrium processes, but it avoids the basic societal inductive problem of forming expectations. It also tells us next to nothing about disequilibrium dynamics.

17.10 A RECAPITULATION ON MONEY

17.10.1 The Roles of Money

We began with a listing of the three conventional textbook roles of money:

1. A means of payment.
2. A numeraire.
3. A store of value.

Actually, money has many other functions:

4. It serves as a means to distinguish agents. Banks and central banks have monetary strategic options not available to individuals.
5. It is an important information encoding device providing a many-to-one mapping to facilitate the construction of an imperfect but often useful scalar measure of economic worth.

6. It is a natural control device for governments. For example, over the past 2,500 years, the king or state usually has taken over control of weights and measures and control of issue.
7. It is used in the payment of taxation.
8. It alleviates some problems of indivisibility.
9. Together with credit and default laws, it provides the controls over innovation.
10. During much of history it has served as the sinews of war.

Much of the work on physical indivisibilities (Scarf, 1994) deals with goods represented in an appropriate space. However, there are also financial considerations that create a form of indivisibility in time. When a large investment is required for a capital good whose payback requires many periods, long-term borrowing becomes necessary to avoid default.

Another aspect of money is as a catalyst. Analogies are always tricky, yet the role of money in transactions appears analogous to the role of a catalyst in a chemical reaction. It enables an economic change to take place, but it emerges unchanged by the activity it has facilitated.

17.10.2 In (Mild) Praise of Gold and Physics

In the previous chapters, at a fairly basic and abstract level, we have considered several different models of money. In a different publication, following Jevons's (1875) lead, the specific physical properties of a money have also been discussed (Shubik 1999a). These include its portability, durability, cognizability, divisibility, and durability. The ingenuity of society is such that seemingly minor physical differences lead to new specialized markets and instruments such as paper written against 100 percent reserves in gold, or bank checks introduced to increase divisibility. Ricardo (1821, 1965) already recognized that gold was far from being a perfect monetary commodity, but in comparison with fiat the choice was between trusting gold and trusting politicians. Von Mises (1935) reiterated this viewpoint in two observations: "Dependence of the value of money on the production of gold does at least mean its independence of the politics of the hour" (p. 17), and "the gold standard is not free from shortcomings; ... but ... there is no other way of emancipating the system from the changing influences of party politics and government interference" (p. 20).

We do not fully agree with their pessimistic assessments, yet both Ricardo and Von Mises stress directly our thesis that a pure theory of money must be considered strategically and must include the government as a key atomic player in the game. The control of the government's strategies is a key problem in understanding the political economy of money. The basic attraction of gold to some, and to others the basic drawback of gold, is that it removes a considerable amount of the potential for financial maneuvre by the government.

It is an empirical question whether the rule of law, its enforcement, and/or the behavior of politicians have improved sufficiently in the last 300 years to make the governmental power presented by the use of fiat money a societal net positive. Although the evidence indicates that the flexibility of an abstract money was needed, how to control the powers of government and banks poses a stream of ongoing politico-economic problems whose resolution will remain in constant flux. The use of formal economic theory is to bolster the arguments concerning the virtues or failings of an ad hoc process.

From the viewpoint of physics, we reiterate that the use of gold as money is much easier and less mystical than fiat because one has ownership represented by a physically measurable commodity, not a virtual commodity whose quantity is difficult to define even if one knows how to describe the government's strategy set.

In the previous chapters, we have discussed both gold and fiat as money. We also attached goals to a central bank; but we did not discuss the nature of the political battle that exists when the House has the power of the purse.

17.11 DYNAMICS AND THE GAMES WITHIN THE GAME

The long-run conventions and habits of the society are the context of the politician. The maneuvers and bargains of the politicians are the context for the participants in the economy. In essence the actions of the economy are relatively short-run. The rules produced and enforced by the political and legal processes are accepted in the short run by the economic agents. Society acting on a longer time horizon modifies both the rule-making and enforcement.

The formal game-theoretic models presented here can be regarded only as spelling out the economic structure during a relatively short period of time. The basic market systems, money, and financial instruments are relatively few in structure; but the rules of the game such as accounting, bankruptcy/default laws, and margin requirements are modified on different timescales. Thus the one-period models considered in many of the chapters can be regarded as economic models with other considerations given; but the multiperiod models from Chapter 16 implicitly assume a frozen political and social environment over many periods that is rarely the case. Good applied macroeconomists appreciate this feature inasmuch as they understand that any long-term macroeconomic model must have its parameters reestimated every period to account for the forces of the polity and society on the economy.

17.12 FIDUCIARY CONTROL AND EXPERTISE

In our work we have changed from the paradigm of general equilibrium to that of a process-oriented strategic market game with government. We regard this as a necessary first step in producing a viable theory of money and financial institutions; but even without launching into socio-economics or bio-economics, a further change in paradigm is needed. This change is to develop the full import of fiduciary control, of expertise, and of the implications of the existence of many assets in a fiduciary-run society. This and the next section are devoted to these factors.

Even a casual look at a modern society reveals that the proportion of individuals who work for themselves with no other employees is not large. The predominant arrangement is of individuals associated with many formal and informal institutions. A good first-order approximation is that most of the major decisions of these institutions are made by a small body of fiduciaries. The description and motivation of fiduciary behavior are hardly captured by the conventional utility function.

There is yet another aspect to the existence of a fiduciary structure in a complex economy. The need for political, managerial, and technical skills calls for many of the higher positions in the organizations to have considerable expertise. The training and emergence of top surgeons or physicists is relatively clear, but the process that produces skilled politicians is less so. The location and training of human talent is mostly beyond the sole scope of pure economic theory, but one needs to recognize the role of expertise in understanding all institutions in general and financial institutions in particular.

17.13 PRODUCTION, ASSETS, AND SIDE PAYMENTS

We avoided the discussion of production in our formal models because this very real aspect of any organized economy was not needed to answer many of the standard problems of finance and exchange. Yet even the most casual empiricism indicates that any advanced economy has assets somewhere between five and fifteen times the value of gross domestic product (GDP) sloppily valued at somewhere near market prices. Put more simply, by almost any measure the ratio of assets to production is fairly large. Also, by value almost all of the economic decisions are being made by fiduciaries, most of whom are sufficiently endowed so that their style of living (*pace* conspicuous consumption) hardly depends on their fiduciary decisions. Finally, there are a small number of institutions compared with the number of natural persons (see Chapter 11). All this together suggests that for many economic and financial questions, a reasonable model is a game with quasi-transferable utility, with the players being the top fiduciary decision makers. Most of this activity involves the trading and retrading of assets among the fiduciaries. Nonlinearities appear on the boundaries or in bankruptcy.

The revolution in preference theory, beginning in the 1930s, laid much emphasis on an elegant development of consumer choice. However, one of its unintended consequences was that for many years, microeconomic thought was deflected from fiduciary decision-making.

17.14 CONCLUDING REMARKS

In God we trust!
All others pay cash.
—Old American folk saying

Outside money is "free trust" and is a (context-dependent) credit, information, and evaluation substitute.

Given the initial ownership claims, the sell-all model of exchange (where all individuals are required to send all assets to market) places a natural upper bound on the need for trust and evaluation. The buy-sell model (Dubey and Shubik, 1978) reflects the acceptance of immediate individual control over the established individual property rights, and hence is not as strategically limiting as the sell-all model. It more closely provides the context for the study of an individual ownership competitive price economy.

Perfect trust can be achieved in a Utopian world with completely accurate price and trade volume assessments, leading to the extension of perfect clearinghouse credits to all agents.

Depending upon the initial conditions, the required amount of money varies from zero to the value of all assets. The need for money as a surrogate for trust will be a function of the potential gains from trade and the nature of the trading process. This calls for an appropriate measurement of the potential gains from trade and a specific description of the trading process. There have been three suggested measures of the gains from trade (Debreu 1951; Dubey and Geanakoplos, 2003; Smith and Foley, 2008).[3]

As has been argued above, if transactions take time, a societal resource loss can be incurred by utilizing a commodity money. A way to avoid this loss is to replace a real commodity money with a societally constructed symbolic commodity money. But doing this requires that it be acceptable by a buyer in exchange.

As is noted in Section 7.1.3, there are many different institutionally meaningful minimal ways to avoid the Hahn paradox. One natural way out is a positive expected valuation for the future value of durable capital assets in the economy.

Custom, law, and modern society conspire to limit the power of the individual merchant-banker-king. Thus, although feasible, it is usually not just individual monopolistic power that supports the value of the currency. The goal of the individual banker may be to extract resources for herself, but this is best done when her credit is trusted. Translated mathematically, it is the tightness of the cash-flow constraints that indicates the worth of the transactions structure of the economy.

An alternative to the monopolistic banker is to introduce a central bank whose role is to promote efficient trade. The central bank can avoid the waste of natural resources by choosing a symbolic (fiat) money rather than a commodity money. But the choice of the symbolic money, as opposed to, say, gold, poses the question of trust in the central government and in the expectations of its performance.

The specific statement of Ricardo (1821) was: "Experience . . . shows that neither a state nor a bank ever have had the unrestricted power of issuing paper without abusing that power; in all states therefore, the issue of paper money ought to be under some check and control; and none seems so proper for that purpose as that of subjecting the issuers of paper money to the obligation of paying their notes either in gold coin or bullion" (p. 24).

Time, population, society, and technology have changed since Ricardo, but the essence of the monetary problem remains. The need for individual trust or

---

3 They all raise problems concerning the relationship between local and global measures.

for trust substitutes is central. The trust and the trust substitutes are generated in the context of the polity and society as a whole, not just the economy. The measurement of the economic value of trust requires a mathematical institutional economics which reflects the institutional richness of the society and its transactions structure. Yet this economics must also be amenable to a formal quantitative analysis, reflected in the structure of the constraints on the economic optimization.[4]

---

4 The mathematics of the general equilibrium system may be looked at as that of optimization subject to equalities. Monetary control and finance are more congenially considered in terms of optimization subject to several constraints, where the pressures on the constraints reflect the potential value of trust and the opportunity for control. Further investigation of trust calls for network analysis.

Bibliography

Aghion, P., and R. Holden. 2011. "Incomplete contracts and the theory of the firm: What have we learned over the past 25 years?" *Journal of Economic Perspectives* 25(2): 181–197.

Allais, M. 1947. *Economie et interet*. Paris: Imprimerie Nationale.

Angerer, M., J. Huber, M. Shubik, and S. Sunder. 2010. "An economy with personal currency: Theory and experimental evidence." *Annals of Finance* (2010) 6: 475–509.

Arthur, W. B. 1994. *Increasing Returns and Path Dependence in the Economy*. Ann Arbor: University of Michigan Press.

Asch, S. 1937. *A Tale of Three Cities*. London: Victor Gollancz Ltd.

Bagehot, W. [1873] 1962. *Lombard Street*. Reprint, with a new introduction by F. C. Genovese. Homewood, IL: Irwin.

Bailey, L. (2012). "An anlaysis of a strategic market game using gold as money and ornament," Masters Thesis, Department of Mathematics and Statistics, University of Nevada, Reno.

Bak, P., S. F. Norrelykke, and M. Shubik. 1999. "Dynamics of money." *Physical Review E* 60(3): 2528–2532.

Balasko, Y., and K. Shell. 1980. "The overlapping-generations model, I: The case of pure exchange without money." *Journal of Economic Theory* 23(3): 281–306.

Barro, R. J. 1974. "Are government bonds net wealth?" *Journal of Political Economy* 82(6): 1095–1117.

Baumol, W. J. 1952. The transactions demand for cash: An inventory-theoretic approach. *Quarterly Journal of Economics* 66(4): 545–556.

Bennie, B. A. 2006. "Strategic market games with cyclic production." Ph.D. Thesis, University of Minnesota.

Bewley, T. 1980. "The optimum quantity of money." In J. H. Kareken and N. Wallace, eds., *Models of Monetary Economies*. Minneapolis: Federal Reserve Bank of Minneapolis, pp. 169–210.

Brunner, K., and A. H. Meltzer. 1990. "Money supply." In M. Friedman and F. H. Hahn, eds., *Handbook of Monetary Economics*. Vol. 1. Amsterdam: North-Holland, 357–398.

Bryant, J., and N. Wallace. 1983. "A suggestion for further simplifying the theory of Money." RP 62, Federal Reserve Board of Minneapolis.

Buss, L. W. 1987. *The Evolution of Individuality*. Princeton: Princeton University Press.

Clower, R. 1967. "A reconsideration of the microfoundations of monetary theory." *Western Economic Journal* 6: 1–9.

Debreu, G. 1951. "The coefficient of resource utilization." *Econometrica* 19(3): 273–292.

Debreu, G. 1959. *Theory of Value*. New York: Wiley.

Diamond, D. W., and P. H. Dybvig. 1983. "Bank runs, deposit insurance, and liquidity." *Journal of Political Economy* 91(3): 401–429.

Diamond, D. W., and R. G. Raghuram. 2006. "Money in a theory of banking." *American Economic Review* 96(1): 30–53.

Dosi, G., C. Freeman, R. Nelson, G. Silverberg, and L. Soete. 1988. *Technical Change and Economic Theory*. London and New York: Pinter.

Dubey, P., and J. Geanakoplos. 1992. "The value of money in a finite-horizon economy: A role for banks." In P. Dasgupta, D. Gale, O. Hart, E. Maskin, eds., *Economic Analysis of Markets: Essays in Honor of Frank Hahn*. Cambridge: MIT Press, pp. 407–444.

Dubey, P., and J. Geanakoplos. 2003. "Inside and outside fiat money, gains to trade, and IS-LM," *Economic Theory* 21(2–3): 347–397.

Dubey, P., J. Geanakoplos, and M. Shubik. 1987. "Revelation of information in strategic market games: A critique of rational expectations." *Journal of Mathematical Economics* 16(2): 105–137.

Dubey, P., J. Geanakoplos, and M. Shubik. 2003. "Is gold an efficient store of value?" *Economic Theory* 21(4): 767–782.

Dubey, P., J. Geanakoplos, and M. Shubik. 2005. "Default and punishment in general equilibrium." *Econometrica* 73(1): 1–37.

Dubey, P., A. Mas-Colell, and M. Shubik. 1980. "Efficiency properties of strategic market games: An axiomatic approach." *Journal of Economic Theory* 22(2): 339–362.

Dubey, P., S. Sahi, and M. Shubik. 1993. "A repeated trade and the velocity of money." *Journal of Mathematical Economics* 22(2): 125–137.

Dubey, P., and L. S. Shapley. 1994. "Noncooperative general exchange with a continuum of traders: Two models." *Journal of Mathematical Economics* 23(3): 253–293.

Dubey, P., and M. Shubik, 1977. "A closed economic system with production and exchange modelled as a game of strategy." *Journal of Mathematical Economics* 4(1): 253–287.

Dubey, P., and M. Shubik. 1978. "The noncooperative equilibria of a closed trading economy with market supply and bidding strategies." *Journal of Economic Theory* 17(1): 1–20.

Edgeworth, F. Y. 1891. "An introductory lecture on political economy." *The Economic Journal* 1(4): 625–634.

Edgeworth, F. Y. 1932 [1881]. *Mathematical Psychics: An Essay on the Application of Mathematics to the Moral Sciences*, reprinted from original. London: Kegan Paul & Co.

Fama, Eugene, and Michael Jensen. 1983. "Agency Problems and Residual Claims." *Journal of Law and Economics* 26, 327–349.

Fisher, I. 1931. *The Purchasing Power of Money.* New York: Macmillan, 2nd edition.

Foley, D. 1970. "Economic equilibrium with costly marketing." *Journal of Economic Theory* 2: 276–291.

Friedman, M., 1969. *The Optimum Quantity of Money and Other Essays.* Chicago: Aldine.

Geanakoplos, J. I. Karatzas, M. Shubik, and W. Sudderth. 2000. "A strategic market game with active bankruptcy." *Journal of Mathematical Economics* 34(3): 359–396.

Grandmont, J. M. 1982. "Temporary general equilibrium." In K. J. Arrow and M. D. Intriligator, eds., *Handbook of Mathematical Economics*, Vol. II. Amsterdam: North Holland, 879–922.

Grandmont, J. M. 1983. *Money and Value.* Cambridge: Cambridge University Press.

Grandmont, J. M., and Y. Younes. 1972. "On the role of money and the existence of a monetary equilibrium." *Review of Economic Studies* 39: 355–372.

Gurley, J. G., and E. S. Shaw. 1960. *Money in a Theory of Finance.* Washington, DC: Brookings Institute.

Hahn, F. H. 1965. On some problems of proving the existence of an equilibrium in a monetary economy. In F. H. Hahn and F. Brechling, eds., *The Theory of Interest Rates.* New York: Macmillan, 126–135.

Hahn, F. H. 1971. "Equilibrium with transaction cost." *Econometrica,* 39(3): 417–439.

Harsanyi, J. C. 1967–68. "Games with incomplete information played by Bayesian players", *Management Science* 14, 159–182, 320–334, 486–502.

Harsanyi, J. C., and R. Selten. 1988. *A General Theory of Equilibrium Selection in Games.* Cambridge: MIT Press.

Hart, Oliver, and John Moore. 1988. "Incomplete Contracts and Renegotiation," *Econometrica* 56(4): 755–785.

Horner, J., and M. Lovo. 2009. "Belief-free equilibria in games with incomplete information." *Econometrica* 77: 453–487.

Huber, J., M. Shubik, and S. Sunder. 2007. "Three minimal market institutions with human and algorithmic agents: Theory and experimental evidence." Cowles Foundation Discussion Paper 1623R, Yale University (revised January 2010).

Huber, J., M. Shubik, and S. Sunder. 2008. "The value of fiat money with an outside bank: An experimental game." Cowles Foundation Discussion Paper 1675, Yale University (revised January 2010).

Hume, D. 1748. "Of interest." In *Essays, Moral, Political and Literary.* Part II, Essay IV. Washington, DC: Liberty Fund, Inc.

Hurwicz, L., 1980. "Explaining the existence and value of money: Comment." In J. H. Karaken and N. Wallace, eds., *Models of Monetary Economies*. Minneapolis: Federal Reserve Bank of Minneapolis.

Jevons, W. S. 1875. *Money and the Mechanism of Exchange*. London: Macmillan.

Kaneko, M. 1992. "A game theoretical description of the von Neumann growth economy." In B. Dutta, D. Mookherjee, T. Parthasarathy, T. E. Ragahaavan, D. Ray, S. Tijs, eds. *Game Theory and Economic Applications*. New York: Springer-Verlag, pp. 369–408.

Karatzas, I., M. Shubik, and W. Sudderth. 1994. "Construction of stationary Markov equilibria in a strategic market game." *Mathematics of Operations Research* 19(4): 975–1006.

Karatzas I., M. Shubik, and W. D. Sudderth. 2006. "Production, interest, and saving in deterministic economies with additive endowments." *Economic Theory* 29(3): 525–548.

Karatzas, I., M. Shubik, and W. Sudderth. 2008. "Financial control of a competitive economy without randomness." Cowles Foundation Discussion Paper 1681, Yale University.

Kiyotaki, N., and R. Wright. 1989. "On money as a medium of exchange." *Journal of Political Economy* 97(4): 927–954.

Koopmans, T. C. 1977. "Examples of production relations based on microdata." In G. C. Harcourt, ed. *The Microfoundations of Macroeconomics*. New York: Macmillan, 145–171.

Kurz M. 1974. "Equilibrium with transaction cost and money in a single market exchange economy." *Journal of Economic Theory* 7(4): 418–452.

Lucas, R. E. 1978. "Asset prices in an exchange economy." *Econometrica* 46(6): 1429–1445.

Lucas, R. E. 1980. "Equilibrium in a pure currency economy." *Economic Enquiry* 18(1): 203–220.

Lucas, R. E. 1996. "Nobel lecture: Monetary neutrality." *Journal of Political Economy* 104(4): 661–682.

Lucas, R. E., and N. L. Stokey. 1983. "Optimal fiscal and monetary policy in an economy without capital." *Journal of Monetary Economics* 12(1): 55–93.

Magill, M., and M. Quinzii. 1992. "Real effects of money in general equilibrium." *Journal of Mathematical Economics* 21(4): 302–342.

Malaith, G. J., and L. Samuelson. 2006. *Repeated Games and Reputations*. Oxford: Oxford University Press.

McCarthy, S., M. Shubik, and J. Yu. 2003. "Who refers to whom: A study of research references and the relationship between research reports and final publication." Cowles Foundation Discussion Paper 1396, Yale University.

Modigliani, F. 1944. "Liquidity, preference and the theory of interest and money." *Econometrica* 12(1): 45–88.

More, T. [1516] 1923. *More's Utopia*; translated into modern, translated into English by G. C. Richards: Oxford: B. Blackwell.

Nash, J. F. 1950. "The bargaining problem." *Econometrica* 18(2): 155–162.

Nelson, R. R. 1996. *The Sources of Economic Growth*. Cambridge: Harvard University Press.

Newcomb, S. 1886. *Principles of Political Economy*. New York: Harper & Brothers.

Ostroy, J. M., and R. M. Starr. 1974. "Money and the decentralization of exchange." *Econometrica* 42(6): 1093–1090.

Phelps, E. S. 2007. "Macroeconomics for a modern economy." *American Economic Review* 97(3): 543–561.

Powers, M., M. Shubik, and S. T. Yao. 1998. "Insurance market games: Scale effects and public policy." *Zeitschrift für Nationalökonomie* 67(2): 109–134.

Qin, C. Z., and M. Shubik. 2012. "Selecting a unique competitive equilibrium with default penalties," *Journal of Economics (Zeitschrift für Nationalökonomie)* 106(2), 119–132.

Quint, T., and M. Shubik. 2005a. "A consumable money: An elementary discussion of commodity money, fiat money and credit: Part 1." ICFAI *Journal of Monetary Economics* 3(1): 6–42.

Quint, T., and M. Shubik. 2005b. "Gold, fiat and credit. An elementary discussion of commodity money, fiat money, and credit: Part 2." ICFAI *Journal of Monetary Economics* 3(2): 6–50.

Quint, T., and M. Shubik. 2007. "Monopolistic and oligopolistic banking: An elementary discussion of commodity money, fiat money and credit: Part 3." ICFAI *Journal of Monetary Economics* 5(4): 6–67.

Quint, T., and M. Shubik. 2009. "Multistage models of monetary exchange: An elementary discussion of commodity money, fiat money, and credit, Part 4." ICFAI *Journal of Monetary Economics* 7 (1): 6–67.

Quint, T., and M. Shubik. 2011. "The demonetization of gold: Transactions and the change in control," Cowles Foundation Discussion Paper 1814, Cowles Foundation, Yale University (forthcoming, in *Annals of Finance*).

Ramsey, F. P. 1928. "A mathematical theory of saving." *Economic Journal* 38(151): 543–559.

Ricardo, D. [1821] 1965. The Principles of Political Economy and Taxation. 3rd ed. London: J. M. Dent.

Sahi, S., and Yao, S., 1989. "The noncooperative equilibria of a trading economy with complete markets and consistent prices." *Journal of Mathematical Economics* 18(4): 325–346.

Samuelson, P. A. 1947. *Foundations of Economic Analysis.* Cambridge: Harvard University Press.

Samuelson, P. A. 1958. "An exact consumption-loan model of interest with or without the social contrivance of money." *Journal of Political Economy* 66(6): 467–480.

Santomero, A. M. 1984. "Modeling the banking firm." *Journal of Money, Credit and Banking* 16(4): 576–602.

SAUS. See United States Department of Commerce, *Statistical Abstract of the United States.*

Scarf, H. S. 1994. "The allocation of resources in the presence of indivisibilities," *Journal of Economic Perspectives* 8(4): 111–128.

Scarf, H. S., with T. Hansen. 1973. *The Computation of Economic Equilibria.* New Haven: Yale University Press.

Schumpeter, J. A. 1911, 1934. *The Theory of Economic Development.* Cambridge: Harvard University Press. (1911 is original, in German).

Shapley, L. S. 1953. "A value for *n* person games." In H. Kuhn and A. W. Tucker, eds., *Annals of Mathematical Studies.* Princeton: Princeton University Press, pp. 307–317.

Shapley, L. S., and M. Shubik. 1977. "Trade using one commodity as a means of payment." *Journal of Political Economy* 85(5): 937–968.

Shubik, M. 1959. *Strategy and Market Structure.* New York: Wiley.

Shubik, M. 1970. "A theory of money and banking in a general equilibrium system." Institute for Advanced Study, Vienna RM 48, July.

Shubik, M. 1972. "A theory of money and financial institutions: Fiat money and noncooperative equilibrium in a closed economy." *International Journal of Game Theory* 1(4): 243–268.

Shubik, M. 1973. "Commodity money, oligopoly, credit, and bankruptcy in a general equilibrium model." *Western Economic Journal* 11(4), 24–38.

Shubik, M. 1976. "A noncooperative model of a closed trading economy with many traders and two bankers." *Zeitschrift für Nationalökonomie* 36(1–2): 49–60.

Shubik, M. 1980. "The capital stock modified competitive equilibrium." In J. H. Karaken and N. Wallace, eds. *Models of Monetary Economics.* Minneapolis: Federal Reserve Bank of Minneapolis.

Shubik, M. 1999a. *The Theory of Money and Financial Institutions,* Vol. 1. Cambridge: MIT Press.

Shubik, M. 1999b. *The Theory of Money and Financial Institutions,* Vol. 2. Cambridge: MIT Press.

Shubik M. 2003. "Money and the monetization of credit." In P. Mizen, ed., *Central Banking, Monetary Theory and Practice (Essays in Honor of Charles Goodhart).* Cheltenham, UK: Edward Elgar, pp. 262–286.

Shubik, M. 2011. *The Theory of Money and Financial Institutions,* Vol. 3. Cambridge: MIT Press.

Shubik, M., and E. Smith. 2005. "Fiat money and the natural scale of government." Cowles Foundation Discussion Paper 1509, Yale University.

Shubik, M., and E. Smith. 2007. Structure, clearinghouses and symmetry. *Economic Theory* 30(3): 587–597.

Shubik, M., and M. Sobel. 1992. "On matching book: A problem in banking and corporate finance." *Management Science* 38(6): 827–839.

Shubik, M., and W. Sudderth. 2011. "Cost Innovation: Schumpeter and Equilibrium. Part 1: Robinson Crusoe," CFDP 1786, Yale University.

Shubik, M., and W. Whitt. 1973. "Fiat money in an economy with one nondurable good and no credit (A noncooperative sequential game)." In A. Blaquiere, ed. *Topics in Differential Games.* Amsterdam: North Holland, 401–448.

Shubik, M., and C. Wilson. 1977. "The optimal bankruptcy rule in a trading economy using fiat money." *Zeitschrift für Nationalökonomie* 37(3/4): 333–354.

Shubik, M., and S. Yao. 1990. "The transactions cost of money (A strategic market game analysis)," *Mathematical Social Sciences* 20(2): 99–114.

Smith, A. 1937 [1776]. *The Wealth of Nations.* New York: Random House edition.

Smith, E., and D. K. Foley. 2008. "Classical thermodynamics and economic general equilibrium theory." *Journal of Economic Dynamics and Control* 32(1): 7–65.

Smith, E., and M. Shubik. 2003. "Strategic freedom, constraint and symmetry in one-period markets with cash and credit payment." *Economic Theory* 25(3): 513–551.

Smith, E., and M. Shubik. 2011. "Endogenizing the provision of money: Costs of commodity and fiat monies in relation to the value of trade, *Journal of Mathematical Economics* 47(4–5), 508–530.

Sorin, S. 1996. "Strategic market games with exchange rates." *Journal of Economic Theory* 68(2): 431–446.

Tobin, J., 1982a. "The commercial banking firm: A simple model." *Scandinavian Journal of Economics* 1984: 495–530.

Tobin, J. 1982b. "Money and finance in the macroeconomic process." *Journal of Money, Credit and Banking* 14(2): 171–204.

United States Department of Commerce. *Statistical Abstract of the United States*, 1999, 2001, 2003, 2006, 2008.

von Mises, L. 1935. *The Theory of Money and Credit* (translated from the German by H. E. Batson). New York: Harcourt Brace & Co.

von Neumann, J. 1945 [1937]. "A model of general economic equilibrium." *Review of Economic Studies* 13(1): 1–9.

von Neumann, J., and O. Morgenstern. 1944. *Theory of Games and Economic Behavior.* Princeton: Princeton University Press.

Vonnegut, K. Jr. 1965. *God Bless You, Mr. Rosewater (or Pearls before Swine).* New York: Dell Publishing Co.

Index

Wallace, N., 99
Walras, L., 4, 64, 306
Whitt, W., 270, 285
Wicksell, P., 64
Wilson, C., 29, 98, 117
Wright, R., 10

Yao, S., 77, 99, 218, 246
Younes, Y., 14, 63

Zhao, J., xv

SUBJECTS

An asterisk (*) indicates place(s) where a term is defined or best described.
If a section (chapter) number is underlined, it means that the term is a main idea throughout the whole section (chapter). The page numbers given are then for the whole section
(chapter).

Accounting constraints — 16.4.1
(p. 275)*, 16.4.2 (pp. 276–77), 16.9
(pp. 288–90), 16.10 (pp. 292–93)
Altruistic bank — 5.2.2 (p. 47), 5.3
(pp. 48–50), 5.4 (pp. 50–51), 5.8
(p. 62), 6.4 (pp. 77–81), 6.7
(pp. 87–93), 7.1.5 (pp. 102–5), 7.4
(pp. 110–14), 13.2.2 (pp. 170–71)
Anthropology — Preface (ix, x), 2 (p. 9),
3.1 (p. 17)
Anti-float — 16.2 (pp. 269–70)*
Asymmetric endowments — 4.1 (pp. 27–
33), 6.3.4 (pp. 71–76), 12.3
(pp. 157–58)
Asymmetric information — Preface (xiii),
17.5 (p. 314)

Balance condition for interest. See "Interest
rate, formation of"
Balance condition for price. See "Price,
formation of"
Bank of Amsterdam — 6.4.4 (p. 81),
15.3.2 (p. 234)
Bank reserves — Preface (xii), 5.3
(pp. 49–50), 5.4 (p. 50), 6.4 (p. 78),
6.4.4 (p. 81), 6.4.5 (p. 81), 7.1.5
(p. 103), 7.1.6 (p. 107), 7.2 (p. 108),
8.2.1 (p. 119, fn #5), 10.2 (p. 138),
11.3 (p. 150), 13.3 (p. 171), 13.3.3
(p. 174), 14.1 (p. 203), 14.2 (p. 205),
14.3 (p. 206), 14.3.2 (p. 208), 14.5

(p. 210), 14.6 (p. 213), 14.7
(pp. 214–16), 14.8 (p. 216), 14.9
(pp. 219–20), 15.3.2 (p. 234), 15.3.4
(pp. 237–38), 16.6.3 (pp. 283–84),
17.3 (p. 307), 17.9 (p. 317)
Bankruptcy. See "Default"
Bankruptcy constraint. See "Budget
constraint"
Bankruptcy penalty. See "Default penalty"
Barley — Preface (x), 3.1 (p. 17), 5.5
(pp. 51–52), 6.1 (p. 64), 10.4
(p. 140), 13.1 (p. 165), 16.2.1
(p. 271), 17.8 (p. 316). See also
"Storable consumable money"
Barter — 2 (p. 9), 6.1 (p. 64), 11.1
(p. 146)
Basic model — 1.8 (p. 6), 3 (pp. 16–26)*,
5.6 (p. 52), 6.3.1 (p. 65), 6.3.3
(p. 69), 7.1.1 (p. 96), 12.2 (pp. 154–
55), 13.1 (p. 165)
Beans, cans of. See "Storable consumable
money"
Bite-the-tail — 16.3.1 (p. 272, fn #3*),
16.3.2 (p. 273)*
Budget constraint (bankruptcy
constraint) – 4.1 (pp. 28*, 30–31,
34–37), 5.2.2 (p. 46), 5.7 (pp. 58–
59), 5.8 (p. 62), 6.3.2 (p. 68), 6.4.1
(p. 80), 6.7.2 (pp. 89–91), 7.1.3
(p. 99), 7.4 (pp. 111–13), 8.1
(p. 116), 8.2 (p. 118), 8.4.1